Religion and Family Life

Religion and Family Life

Special Issue Editor

Richard J. Petts

MDPI • Basel • Beijing • Wuhan • Barcelona • Belgrade

MDPI

Special Issue Editor
Richard J. Petts
Ball State University
USA

Editorial Office
MDPI
St. Alban-Anlage 66
4052 Basel, Switzerland

This is a reprint of articles from the Special Issue published online in the open access journal *Religions* (ISSN 2077-1444) from 2018 to 2019 (available at: https://www.mdpi.com/journal/religions/special_issues/familylife)

For citation purposes, cite each article independently as indicated on the article page online and as indicated below:

LastName, A.A.; LastName, B.B.; LastName, C.C. Article Title. *Journal Name* **Year**, *Article Number*, Page Range.

ISBN 978-3-03897-928-9 (Pbk)
ISBN 978-3-03897-929-6 (PDF)

Cover image courtesy of pexels.com user pixabay.

Contents

About the Special Issue Editor

Richard J. Petts is an Associate Professor of Sociology at Ball State University His research seeks to better understand and reduce family inequality, focusing on how various social institutions (e.g., religion) and policies (e.g., parental leave) may contribute to and/or help to reduce family inequality. His work has been cited by numerous media outlets including ABC News, Forbes, The Wall Street Journal, and Bloomberg News, and his research has been published in academic journals such as *American Sociological Review, Social Forces, Journal of Marriage and Family, Journal for the Scientific Study of Religion, and Sociology of Religion.*

religions

MDPI

Editorial

Introduction to the Special Issue of Religions—"Religion and Family Life"

Richard J. Petts

Department of Sociology, Ball State University, Muncie, IN 47306, USA; rjpetts@bsu.edu

Received: 3 April 2019; Accepted: 10 April 2019; Published: 13 April 2019

check for
updates

Family and religion are inherently intertwined social institutions. Religious institutions stress the importance of families, provide family advice and guidance, and even define appropriate family forms in some instances (Edgell 2006). Additionally, families often incorporate religion as a way of finding meaning in family relationships. Furthermore, in their daily lives, families serve as the primary source of religious socialization (Cornwall 1989; Smith and Denton 2005; Stolzenberg et al. 1995). However, despite this clear link, the breadth of research focusing on the intersection of religion and family life is not as extensive as one might expect given the broad societal importance of these two social institutions (Mahoney 2010).

The aim of this special issue is to increase and extend our understanding of the intersection between religion and family life. I believe that the articles included in this special issue fulfill this goal, and demonstrate the diversity of research in this area. These articles incorporate a range of methodological strategies (qualitative interviews, large-scale secondary survey data, cross-national studies, survey data that was independently collected); focus on both positive and negative consequences of various aspects of religion for families; take approaches that have national, international, and denomination-specific scopes; and emphasize various themes within the broad area of religion and family life.

I believe that the contributions in this special issue increase our understanding of the complex, diverse and important ways in which religion and family life are interconnected. My hope is that this body of research inspires future research to continue to advance our understanding of the various ways in which religion and spirituality may influence family life and family processes.

References

Cornwall, Marie. 1989. The Determinants of Religious Behavior: A Theoretical Model and Empirical Test. *Social Forces* 68: 572–92. [CrossRef]

Edgell, Penny. 2006. *Religion and Family in a Changing Society*. Princeton: Princeton University Press.

Mahoney, Annette. 2010. Religion in Families, 1999–2009: A Relational Spirituality Framework. *Journal of Marriage and Family* 72: 805–27. [CrossRef] [PubMed]

Smith, Christian, and Melinda Lundquist Denton. 2005. *Soul Searching: The Religious and Spiritual Lives of American Teenagers*. New York: Oxford University Press.

Stolzenberg, Ross M., Mary Blair-Loy, and Linda J. Waite. 1995. Religious Participation in Early Adulthood: Age and Family Life Cycle Effects on Church Membership. *American Sociological Review* 60: 84–103. [CrossRef]

Article

Beyond Religious Rigidities: Religious Firmness and Religious Flexibility as Complementary Loyalties in Faith Transmission

David C. Dollahite [1,*], Loren D. Marks [1], Kate P. Babcock [1], Betsy H. Barrow [1] and Andrew H. Rose [2]

[1]   School of Family Life, Brigham Young University, Provo, UT 84602, USA; loren_marks@byu.edu (L.D.M.); katepatterson7@gmail.com (K.P.B.); betsy001hughes@gmail.com (B.H.B.)
[2]   Department of Sociology, Anthropology, & Social Work, Texas Tech University, Box 41012, Lubbock, TX 79409-1012, USA; Andrew.Rose@ttu.edu
*   Correspondence: David_Dollahite@byu.edu

Received: 17 January 2019; Accepted: 10 February 2019; Published: 15 February 2019

Abstract: Research has found that intergenerational transmission of religiosity results in higher family functioning and improved family relationships. Yet the Pew Research Center found that 44% of Americans reported that they had left the religious affiliation of their childhood. And 78% of the expanding group of those who identify as religiously unaffiliated ("Nones") reported that they were raised in "highly religious families." We suggest that this may be, in part, associated with religious parents exercising excessive firmness with inadequate flexibility (rigidity). We used a multiphase, systematic, team-based process to code 8000+ pages of in-depth interviews from 198 Christian, Jewish, and Muslim families from 17 states in all 8 major religio-cultural regions of the United States. We framed firmness as mainly about loyalty to God and God's purposes, and flexibility as mainly about loyalty to family members and their needs and circumstances. The reported findings provided a range of examples illustrating (a) religious firmness, (b) religious flexibility, as well as (c) efforts to balance and combine firmness and flexibility. We discuss conceptual and practical implications of treating firmness and flexibility as complementary loyalties in intergenerational faith transmission.

Keywords: intergenerational transmission of religion; parenting; religious youth; parent-youth relationships

1. Introduction

Many religious parents desire to pass their own religious beliefs, practices, and commitments on to their children. Indeed, intergenerational transmission of religious belief is a well-established part of family studies (Bengtson et al. 2013; Spilman et al. 2013). Given the American penchant for change, including religious change, perhaps it is also not surprising that a 2009 study conducted by the Pew Research Center found that 44% of Americans reported that they had left the religious affiliation of their childhood (Pew Research Center 2009). But what may be surprising is that in a 2016 Pew Research Center survey, 78% of the expanding group of those who identify as religiously unaffiliated ("Nones") reported that they were raised in "highly religious families" (Pew Research Center 2016). In other words, nearly half of Americans do not retain the faith of their parents—and the great majority of those who have rejected institutional religion altogether were raised by parents who presumably highly valued religious identity and commitments.

Across a number of possible things parents hope their adult children continue to value (e.g., values, religion, politics, education, hobbies, traditions), each child likely will hold to some but not others. However, for parents who highly value their religious identity, it can be particularly painful to see children leave that religion behind or leave faith altogether (Bengtson et al. 2013). There are a number of possible reasons why people raised in highly religious homes and families would chose not to be formally religious themselves. Many of those reasons may have little or nothing to do with how parents acted toward their children in relation to religious things. However, one possible reason for intergenerational retreat from religion is that parents did not strike a healthy balance between devoted adherence to religious belief and practice (i.e., *religious firmness*) and willingness to adapt their religious devotion to the needs, challenges, and circumstances of family members (i.e., *religious flexibility*). In this study, we provide an in-depth exploration of the issues of firmness and flexibility in religious belief and practice among a racially and regionally diverse sample of religiously devoted families.

Despite some clear examples to the contrary, the empirical literature indicates that the effects of religion on marriage and family life are generally positive (Marks and Dollahite 2017; Walsh 2009). However, some processes around religious involvement have been found to be harmful to marriage and family relationships. Recent work details the realities that religion involves both help and harm in family life (Dollahite et al. 2018). One idea that has been repeatedly forwarded by social scientists is that rigidities in religious practice are problematic (Burr et al. 2012). What has not been adequately investigated are the processes that lead to rigidities at the nexus of religion and family relationships. Are there ways of being firm and consistent in religious matters that are positive for marriages and families? Are there ways of integrating firmness with flexibility in religious beliefs and practices that provide the greatest amount of good and the least amount of harm (Dollahite et al. 2018)?

Definition of Terms

Before moving to a review of the relevant literature, we briefly define five central terms.

Religious beliefs. Personal or family ideals, interpretations, and expectations based in religious ideology (e.g., doctrine, theology, scripture, tradition). Personal and family religious beliefs may or may not align with the "official" doctrines of a given faith community.

Religious practices. Personal or family religious rituals and traditions that involve some kind of patterned individual or family action (e.g., reading sacred texts, prayer, attending religious services). Personal or family religious practices may or may not align with the "official" practices (rituals, and traditions) taught or expected by a given faith community.

Religious firmness. Loyalty to God and devoted adherence to those things that are believed to represent or uphold God such as religious beliefs and practices.

Religious flexibility. Loyalty to family members that results in a principled or pragmatic willingness to adapt (at least to some extent) religious beliefs and practices to better meet perceived familial needs, challenges, and circumstances.

Integrating firmness and flexibility. A process that integrates firmness and flexibility in religious beliefs and practices in an attempt to honor *both* loyalty to God (and that which serves to represent or uphold God) *and* loyalty to family members (and that which meets their needs, challenges, and circumstances).

2. Review of the Literature

Herein, we review relevant literature touching on the issues of (a) intergenerational transmission of religion, (b) parenting style, and (c) family processes, particularly as they pertain to firmness and flexibility in religious beliefs and practices.

2.1. Intergenerational Transmission of Religion

A 20-year longitudinal study by Spilman et al. (2013) found that intergenerational transmission of religiosity was associated with higher quality of family relationships and family functioning. They concluded, "All in all, the results suggest that religiosity promotes competent family functioning across generations ... and was positively associated with observable attributes of family relationships" (772).

Many parents wonder how to best transmit their religious beliefs and values to their children and how to help their children have a desire to maintain these values through adolescence and into adulthood. Many studies have been conducted on how to effectively transmit religious values from parents to children (Bao et al. 1999; Myers 1996). Parental behavior has been identified as an important factor in transmitting values to adolescents (Bengtson et al. 2013; Flor and Knapp 2001; Kim-Spoon et al. 2012). Children often are observant of their parents' actions and values, including to what extent they are consistent—or firm—in their religious beliefs and practices. Dudley and Dudley (1986) found that conflict between parents or between parent and child can inhibit transmission of values, while intimacy in the home facilitated children internalizing values. Similarly, a recent landmark, three-decade, longitudinal study with more than 3,000 participants found that warmth and closeness between parent and child significantly predicted whether children continued in the parents' faith—a finding that held for both mother-child and father-child relations (Bengtson et al. 2013).

Across studies, it appears that when parents found a balance between emotional support and control with adolescents, they were more likely to be successful in transmitting their religious values. If parents were rigid in their approach to religion, their children were more likely to become disaffiliated with their parents' religion as adults (Hansen 1998).

Empirical work on family rituals has offered additional insight. Although family ritual typically benefits individuals and relationships (Chelladurai et al. 2018; Fiese et al. 2002; Marks and Dollahite 2012), additional empirical support for the danger of excessive religious rigidity is offered by a study that found that compulsory family worship was more detrimental than no family worship at all (Lee et al. 1997). It appears possible that a major cause of parent-parent and parent-child conflict over religious matters may stem from unhealthy levels of firmness (rigidity) and/or unwillingness to manifest appropriate kinds of flexibility in religious belief, practice, and ritual.

A study by Gane (2014) that examined parent to adolescent faith transmission found that (a) meaningful relationships with mentors within the adolescent's church and (b) parents openly sharing their faith with their children were both major contributors to transmitting faith to adolescents. Additional positive transmission influences identified in other studies include helping youth learn the stories of their religious heritage, encouraging youth to develop a personal relationship with God, providing opportunities for youth to engage with other members of the religious congregation, strengthening parent-child relationships, parental modeling of religious commitment, fostering connections between youth and religious leaders, and engaging in religious conversations with youth (Dollahite and Thatcher 2008; Smith and Denton 2005). One review has suggested that in adult-youth religious conversations, parental *listening* may be the most influential form of communication (Marks and Dollahite 2017). When asked what they consider the most important things for them to be in relation to their children, religious parents have identified being an example, authentic, and consistent to provide support, love, and help, and to teach religious values, traditions, and identity (Dollahite et al. 2019).

Laird et al. (2011) further noted that some types of religious commitment (God, faith tradition or denomination, scripture or sacred texts) were more important than others at different times, depending on the developmental stage of the adolescent or the family system. These shifts in relative influence can occur because of familial changes during an adolescent's life or because of the developmental processes of the adolescent. However, each of these commitment types seem to help transmit religious values to adolescents. Families apparently need to be flexible due to normative growth and change in family members and circumstances but also need to be responsive to non-normative changes and stressors (Walsh 2009). The issue of responsiveness is an important feature of parenting style, discussed next.

2.2. Parenting Styles

The type of parenting style that parents employ can be helpful or detrimental in transmitting faith to their children. Gane (2014) found that "affectionate independence is the optimal parenting style as it relates to Christian commitment and denominational loyalty" (p. 47). Also, excessively strict parental control has been found to be negatively related to church attendance in the adult years (Vermeer et al. 2012). On a related note, Ellison and Sherkat (1993) found that many Conservative Protestants had more of an authoritative style of parenting, where they valued obedience from their children but also valued their children's autonomy. Some Catholic participants tended to be closer to an authoritarian style of parenting and highly valued obedience but were less supportive of autonomy (although there was significant variation within denomination).

An authoritative parenting style has been shown to be the most likely way to encourage (lasting) religious participation and involvement in children. Children are also more likely to both adopt and maintain religious values similar to their parents if the parent-child relationship is warm and close (Bao et al. 1999; Bengtson et al. 2013). Children who reported distance from their parents were less likely to hold parent-similar religious values and beliefs (Kim-Spoon et al. 2012). When parents practiced warm, affirming, and respectful (authoritative) parenting, children were more likely to continue in their parents' religious traditions, practices, and beliefs. Recent qualitative work has similarly emphasized that parental belief-behavior congruence or "practicing what you preach" is also a profound and salient influence because children tend to believe what they see over what they are told (Marks and Dollahite 2017; see also Vermeer et al. 2012). Conversely, perceived belief-behavior incongruence and parental hypocrisy both tend to dispel ongoing faith involvement as children grow into emerging adulthood, although exceptions have been documented (Marks and Dollahite 2017). Longitudinal, mixed-methods research further indicates that parents who have inter-faith marriages, experience divorce, or practice ambivalent or mixed-message parenting are also significantly less likely to see their children continue in parents' religion (Bengtson et al. 2013).

Most major religions emphasize qualities of kindness, patience, other-orientation, peace-making, as well as striving to understand and serve others. Thus, it is possible that if children, teens, and young-adult children of religious parents perceive that their parents consistently placed loyalty to God and divine law unresponsively above loyalty to the real or perceived needs of family members (e.g., serving in the faith community to the level of familial neglect), children may be less likely to follow in the faith-based footsteps of their parents (Kim-Spoon et al. 2012).

In sum, studies indicate that it is important for parents to have a warm and consistent parenting style, and for them to be congruent in their modeling of faith in order for religious practice to be optimally transmitted to their children. Even so, these combined characteristics constitute only a marginal probability (about 56%), not a guarantee (Bengtson et al. 2013).

2.3. Family Processes

According to Olsen's Circumplex Model, balanced family systems usually function better than imbalanced family systems (Olson 2000). Using this model, Schrodt (2005) found that family expressiveness was positively associated with adaptability and cohesion within the family. When family members communicated with each other, they were more likely to adapt well to different situations, which can be helpful when it comes to religious beliefs, practices, and rituals (Colaner et al. 2014). However, a study among Orthodox Jews in Israel found that the Circumplex Model did not necessarily apply to them and their family functioning because these Orthodox Jews highly valued the familial transmission of religious behaviors and beliefs, which made a high degree of control adaptive and normative for their families. This noted exception may indicate variations in the ideal blend of firmness and flexibility across religio-cultural contexts (Pirutinsky and Kor 2013), a possibility that begs additional inquiry into how religious beliefs and practices are applied in family life across cultures (Dollahite and Marks 2018; Marks and Dollahite 2018).

Tamara Hareven, co-developer of life course theory with Glen Elder, frequently wrote about the importance of making allowances for the life course—acknowledging that what might be ideal and attainable at one stage of the life course may be burdensome and difficult at another stage. Although Hareven's work (Hareven and Trepagnier 2000) focused on macro-level and community-level cultural, historical, and economic forces (with religion being rarely mentioned), some narratives from our participants seem to capture and reflect life course patterns in religious practices that may call for such "allowances." Indeed, life course shifts such as marriages, births, children's schedules, teenagers, adult caregiving, health problems, and other factors may tend to promote or hinder certain religious practices depending on family circumstances and resources. Some degree of flexibility in religious practice may be beneficial, if not essential.

Finally, a substantial literature exists on the negative consequences of religious "rigidity." Little, if any, work has been done on the processes around and the potential benefits and problems associated with the idea of "religious firmness" (strong, consistent loyalty to God) in connection with religious parenting.

3. Method

3.1. Participants

The sample for this study included 198 families (476 individuals) from the Abrahamic faiths (Judaism, Christianity, Islam). The sample consisted of religiously and ethnically diverse couples and families from all eight major religio-cultural regions of the United States (Silk and Walsh 2008). This study purposely sampled religious persons and families in a two-stage selection process. First, clergy were contacted and asked to identify marriage-based families with children who were committed to and involved in their faith. Second, recommended families were contacted to determine willingness to participate. Among more difficult-to-access faiths (e.g., Islam, Orthodox Judaism), participant referral sampling was sometimes employed. In terms of affiliation, the sample includes a total of 148 Christian families (from more than 15 denominations), 30 Jewish families (including Hasidic, Modern Orthodox, Conservative, and Reformed), and 20 Muslim families (including Sunni and Shia). The final sample included 20+ denominations. More than half of the sample were from various religious minorities (Marks et al. 2018)

Given their level of attendance (most reported "at least weekly"), monetary contribution (Mean = 7% of income), hours spent in religious activities (Mean = 11 hours per week), and given that families were recommended by their religious leaders as being "strong in their faith" and "successful ... in their family relationships," we consider this sample of interviewed families to be exemplars (see Damon and Colby 2013). According to (Bronk et al. 2013), "the exemplar methodology is a sample selection technique that involves the intentional selection of individuals, groups, or entities that exemplify the construct of interest in a particularly intense or highly developed manner" (p. 2). They argue that exemplar research allows study of persons or groups at the "upper ends of development" as well as "not only what is but also what is possible with regard to the development of a particular characteristic" (p. 1). Our purpose in interviewing families that were religious exemplars was to discover how families that were committed to their faith drew from religious belief and practice in marriage and parenting.

Ethnic/Minority families comprised more than half (51%) of the overall sample of 198 families (N = 476 individuals). Sampled minorities included African American, Asian American, East Asian, Latino, Middle Eastern, Native American, and Pacific Islander families.

Geographically, participant families were from 17 states in all 8 major religio-cultural regions in the nation, including: the Mid Atlantic (6%; DE, MD, PA), Midwest (2.5%; OH, WI), Mountain West (3%; ID, UT), New England (16%; MA, CT), Northwest (12.5%; OR, WA), Pacific (12.5%; CA), the South/Gulf Coast (39.5%; FL, GA, LA), and Southern Crossroads regions (7.5%; KS, OK). Further, the families represented a wide range of socioeconomic and educational levels. In summary, the sample is characterized by: (a) religious diversity, (b) high levels of religious commitment, (c) rich racial and ethnic diversity, (d) geographic and regional diversity, and (e) a wide range of socioeconomic status.

Despite being a sample of religious and family exemplars, like all religious families, participants experienced a variety of relational and religious challenges (Dollahite et al. 2019).

3.2. Interviewing

Handel (1996) has indicated that family research is often based on a single individual representing the family, but he contends that this is not "family research" in the truest sense. Handel has stated, "No [single] member of any family is a sufficient source of information for that family" (346). In the present study, mothers, fathers, and children were interviewed in order to gather multiple perspectives on a variety of family relationships.

We wanted to explore both successes and challenges that religious families experience, therefore intensive interviewing was chosen as an appropriate method. We strived to address and check our biases in the interviewing processes as well. Each interview question was pretested to identify any potential problems. Each question was open-ended, and many had follow-up questions to clarify and add depth to the initial responses given.

Interviews were conducted as a couple. Babbie (2004) stated that joint interviewing "frequently brings out aspects of the topic that would not have been anticipated by the researcher and would not have emerged from interviews with individuals" (303). Seymour et al. (1995) argued that joint interviewing reveals different kinds of knowledge held by each person and produces more complete data as persons fill in each other's gaps and memory lapses.

Accordingly, interviewers encouraged wives and husbands to respond to each question and to comment on or add to the other's response. Interviews included much interchange, correcting, challenging, and adding to spouse's comments. Consistent with research involving couple interviews conducted by Holmberg et al. (2004), the wives corrected or added to comments made by their spouse more often than husbands. Interviews typically lasted about two hours. Questions focused on connections between religion, marriage, and family life. Core concepts emerged from systematic, team-based analyses of the data, as discussed next.

3.3. Coding Process

The initial ideas around firmness and flexibility emerged from repeated analyses of the transcripts. It became clear that religious families varied in how firmly or flexibly they approached their beliefs and practices. We then decided to intentionally and systematically explore the issues of firmness and flexibility. There were no specific questions about either firmness or flexibility on the questionnaire. These ideas emerged from inductive processes.

Coding occurred in three phases. First, we developed a codebook for the concepts of firmness and flexibility. To create the codebook, we followed formats described by MacQueen et al. (1998) and Bernard and Ryan (2010). Each pair of complement elements was developed in further detail based on our literature review and previous coding and analysis. In the first phase of coding (main coding phase), we trained eight advanced undergraduate coders, who coded interviews for all 198 families. We used NVIVO 10 and 11 software to assist with coding procedures and data management. Each student was paired with another student to review each other's codes and they discussed discrepancies as a check and balance system and to ensure inter-rater reliability (Marks 2015). Data analyses from all 198 families are included in Table 1 which summarizes the main concepts that were coded.

Table 1. Concepts: Firmness and Flexibility in Religious Practices and Religious Beliefs.

Themes	**Religious Firmness**	**Religious Flexibility**	**Integrated Firmness and Flexibility**
Religious Family Practices	Firmness in regular worship (e.g., attend worship services weekly)	Flexibility in regular worship (e.g., go to church some weeks if convenient, engage in weekly rituals when convenient)	Consistent and firm in worship or other rituals. Some flexibility depending on situation (e.g., modify ritual to fit your children's needs but still carry it out)
Religious Beliefs	Firmness in beliefs about church doctrine or practices	Flexible in beliefs and have unorthodox interpretations of many/some doctrines and practices	Know and seek to honor the religion's beliefs and practices but with adaptations that allow religion to work for them and their family

The accounts from Integrated Firmness and Flexibility, Flexibility, and then Firmness were reanalyzed to look for specific themes within these quotes. The accounts were reanalyzed until theoretical saturation was achieved. There were four to five main themes found throughout the accounts in each of the three categories [(1) Firmness, (2) Flexibility, (3) Integrated Firmness and Flexibility]. The two foci in this article include: (a) religious family practices and (b) religious beliefs. In Table 2, consistent with the aim of providing a data audit trail (Patton 2002), we present the number of coded excerpts for each of those categories.

Table 2. Frequencies and Percentages: Firmness and Flexibility in Religious Practices and Beliefs.

Themes	**Religious Firmness** 335	**Religious Flexibility** 121	**Integrated Firmness and Flexibility** 61
Religious Practices	101 (17.4)	62 (25.1)	29 (22.8)
Religious Beliefs	234 (40.2)	59 (23.9)	32 (25.2)

4. Results

The two themes we will address and illustrate in this section are: (1) Firmness and Flexibility in Religious Family Practices and (2) Firmness and Flexibility in Religious Beliefs. To facilitate links between the data and thematic concepts, we will italicize certain words or phrases in participant comments that capture the essence of the theme being illustrated. We will also present some data regarding parents' concern (or lack of concern) involving religious transmission.

4.1. Theme 1: Firmness and Flexibility in Religious Family Practices

There was a wide range of responses from the 476 participants as they discussed their approach to religious practices and rituals at the family level. Some reported more firmness (perhaps even rigidity) in their practices and rituals, while others conveyed a more relaxed approach. A few explained, often in a confessional style, that they had been so flexible with family ritual that some rituals had ceased altogether. There were many, however, who had seemed to find a healthy balance, often referencing both firmness and flexibility in the same comment regarding daily or weekly family religious practices. In connection with Theme 1 (Religious Family Practices), we will respectively discuss (a) religious firmness, (b) religious flexibility, and (c) integrating firmness and flexibility.

Firmness in Family Religious Practices: "[He] never missed a night." For many families, their sacred rituals were not optional and had reportedly become an important part of their family life and who they were. Kira[1], a Lutheran mother, shared how some family rituals were important to her; "I can't imagine *not* going to church on Sundays. And as ritual as that is, *I just can't imagine not [going]*." Claire, a Latter-day Saint mother, described how rituals have helped her family:

---

[1] All participants' names have been replaced with pseudonyms.

We [picked] a "family scripture" [verse]. ... We used it, and we read it together *every Monday night*, and it would kind of help the [kids], as they went into the teenage years, with all the challenges that were there, all the challenges that are out there for kids. [The family verse] had "watch" and "pray" in it, and it really helped strengthen our children and our family.

Faith, a Catholic mother, also shared how rituals have benefited her family:

We pray together as a family. Martin is so good about [praying] at bedtime. [He] has *never missed a night*, praying with the children, the boys in their room, because they're in the same room, and then the girls. I think for them it's routine. And for them, [those prayers mean] being a part of the family. I think that evens their day out. It's something they've learned to expect, and that Daddy's always going to be there, or Momma, to get that *constancy*, that *consistency* too.

Calvin, an African American, Baptist father, shared his stance on Sunday rituals when he said,

Yes, first of all, it's just going to church on Sundays. I mean, I think that's a practice that my family has and it's important. I think it's important for my kids. [Now] there are Sundays when they don't want to go, [but still] I said, "*We have to, you have to go to church.*" I mean, that's just a practice of this family.

Manuela, a Latina, Lutheran mother, shared her view on church attendance:

One thing we've tried to do, [we've taught our kids], "As long as you live under our roof, *you will go to church with us.*" If not every single week, then *absolutely, as much as possible*. [That is how] we grew up. There comes a time when you move out of the house or you're away from home, where you are going to stray, more than likely. You're not going to go to church, but our feeling is that if we have instilled it in them for 18 or 19 years, they may stray, but they're going to go back. ... They're going to [come] back ... [and when they do], it will be there. They'll know that it's important for their family, to do the same thing.

Charlotte, a Presbyterian mother, shared a similar story:

[One of the kids] made a comment a lot about, "How come we *have to* go to church? None of my other friends do. Why are we the only ones?" Which we're not. What do I say? "Because *that's what we do*. We're going to church and you'll be better off for it. *So, get out of bed [and] get in the car.*"

These accounts, especially the italicized portions, illustrate firmness in religious rituals and/or observance. Next we will discuss flexibility in connection with family-level religious practices.

Flexibility in Family Religious Practice: "It changes all the time." Many comments from participants emphasized the importance of flexibility in religiously-oriented family practices to them or their families. Some families were flexible with their religious practices and rituals because they (or at least one member of the family) valued other things more than religious observance. Martha, a Lutheran mother, said, "[My son], there's probably a couple of times that we dragged him to church and he wanted to do other things, or sports related things. But mostly *we let him do his sports instead of church.*" Abigail, a Reform Jewish mother, shared her family's flexibility with rituals:

And because we're tired on Friday night, we don't get to synagogue *as much as we want to*. And, because of other time commitments, there's just *never enough time* to do as much as maybe we should for the Jewish community.

Jim, a Caucasian, Latter-day Saint father, had seen their weekly ritual of Family Home Evening ebb and flow over the years and noted specific difficulties keeping the ritual firmly in place when children hit the teen years (a recurring struggle across faiths). He said,

[E]specially when kids were younger ... *we tried* to hold (family home evening) once a week
... [W]e would discuss Scriptures, principles, play a game or two, sing a few hymns, have a
[treat] ... I think we were pretty consistent when the kids were small, [but] we didn't do as
well as the kids got older ... [but] we were pretty consistent ... [but those were] *not quite as
rigidly structured* as the Sunday worship service.

The hallmark of more flexible families was that rituals did not always have to be done weekly
or daily, and the way in which the ritual was done reportedly changed over time. Brian, a Catholic
father, shared his family's experience with prayer when he said, "We have, as the family has grown,
we've sort of changed. ... [The] prayer that we used to say at night prayer, we don't say it *as often.*" For
Brian's family, changes in style and frequency had both occurred. Jamie, a Jehovah's Witness mother,
described her experience with being flexible in the amount of time she spent on religious involvement
outside the home. She explained,

I'm a strong believer in [being sensitive to] *circumstances...* [W]hen I was younger and I had ...
our babies, the time I could spend in the ministry was nothing like what I can do now. And I
feel that there are many families with *different circumstances.* So what we excel in now, maybe
ten years ago I didn't have that luxury to excel in.... So, *it changes all the time.*

Next, we will look at integrations of firmness and flexibility in religious family practices. Many
participants' families reportedly strived to find a balance between the two.

**Integrated Firmness and Flexibility in Religious Practices: "We usually read our scriptures
together [but] you don't need to ... do a certain thing [every time]."** Many families expressed a
balance between being firm in their approach to rituals, and also being flexible as changes arose.
They emphasized the importance of religion and rituals, while adapting them to work with their
family goals. Charlene, a Latter-day Saint mother, stated,

We *usually* [read our scriptures together] in the evening and we're either around the table or
in the family room or living room, *wherever we happen to be*, wherever most people happen
to be *at the moment.* And partly, we do that on purpose because we want them to feel like
anywhere you go, you can read scriptures. You *don't need to go and sit* at the table *or do a
certain thing* and when we read it, we have each person read however many verses we're
going to read. Right now, we went through reading a chapter at a time and I found that we
weren't really learning much, so *what we do now* is we [have each family member read] two
scripture [verses] each.

This family was consistent in their family practice of studying scriptures, but they were also
flexible as a family on how, when, and where the study was done.

Banafsha, an East Indian, Muslim mother, illustrated a similar point in connection with *salat*
(Islamic prayer five times daily):

We don't want to delay the prayer of anybody. *If they are studying, they can pray in their room*
and keep studying [and] not wait for the other ones because you see, we wash up before we
pray. So, that was a reason, *we didn't want to make it hard for anybody.* But I think that the good
thing was when you go to anybody's room, it's time for prayer, they either have already
prayed, or they are praying.

For Banafsha's family, prayer is non-negotiable, but where and (with some latitude) when the
prayer takes place is negotiable. Ariella, a Conservative Jewish mother, shared a similar experience
about her children's desire to perform their family sacred rituals. She said,

We do the same rituals for our holidays and all our Sabbath activities and you know, a lot
of times we have to nag them and pull them into things, but if we DON'T do something
or if something is missed or if we say, "We are not going to do Shabbat," [then] they say,

"What do you mean we're not doing it!?" [with animation] ... They'll get mad that we don't do it. *They're upset because it's not the way it usually is.* They get upset if we don't hallow [the Sabbath]. It's very interesting. Sometimes they act like we are annoying them by dragging them through the ritual but *if we don't have it there for them they get upset* by it.... The religion provides a lot of strength and comfort and structure.

As was the case in most of the Jewish families we interviewed (Marks et al. 2017), children in Ariella's family made it clear that some degree of consistency and predictability in religious rituals is important. Of course, when those children are older they may call on their parents to provide greater flexibility in timing and length of religious rituals if the rituals begin to compete with other valued activities in youth's lives.

Having examined firmness and flexibility in connection with religious family practices in Theme 1, we now turn our attention to firmness and flexibility in connection with religious beliefs in Theme 2.

4.2. Theme 2: Firmness and Flexibility in Religious Beliefs

Many of the participants we interviewed expressed firmness in the area of religious beliefs. That is, they were quite orthodox in how they approached the religious beliefs of their respective Abrahamic faith (and/or denomination). Many participants held at least some of their religious beliefs to be rooted in doctrines or practices that were divinely revealed and thus non-negotiable and not subject to significant personal or family adaptation. This has been called a "vertical" (divine) sense of morality and religion, as opposed to a "horizontal" (or socially constructed) view (Burr et al. 2012; Shichida et al. 2015). We explore this firmness of religious belief next.

Firmness in Religious Beliefs: "There is no discussion." Many participants, couples, and families were quite firm when it came to certain beliefs of their religion. They viewed following divinely revealed commandments as vital and departing from them was not an option. These families tended to look to their religion for guidance instead of secular texts or ideas.

Sabir, an East Indian Muslim father said, "If it is something that has already been prescribed religiously, *then there is no discussion.* Things like this, at least in our family, we tend to go back to the religion."

Mei, a Chinese Christian mother shared her beliefs on marriage that stem from the Bible when she said, "This is the principle; *we could not change the order.*"

Jerome, an African Methodist father, also shared a Bible-based belief:

And the law we follow, as the Bible says, is "Honor thy father and thy Mother." And I truly believe that. If you have sassy kids, don't bring them around me because *I'm not going to play....* You will treat my household as such. *We are not going to change.... You are going to abide by the rules* or you are not going to come in here.

Some families also expressed that every aspect of their life goes back to their religion and revolves around their religious beliefs. Elsu, a Native American, Christian father reported,

Our religious beliefs—*everything we chose;* who our kids were allowed to play with ... where they were allowed to go, what they were allowed to partake of, what churches they could go to, who they could affiliate with. *Every aspect of life was guided by our faith.*

Even though certain religious beliefs or practices may be difficult to follow, some individuals expressed their desire to follow them and honor God. Noor, a Muslim mother, said she was told by one man in her city,

"You know, for your own security, you probably should remove your *Hijab,* and the girls should remove their *Hijab* [veil, covering]." And I think that, gaining strength from my religious beliefs, I said, "No, I'm not going to." People have to realize I am Muslim.

Deshi and Jing, a Chinese Christian couple also shared their desire to honor God through action,

Deshi: One tenth offering is not a problem in our church. *We should do according to God's words.* Our faith is in God.

Jing: It is God's grace for me to find this job. The one-tenth money is the most meaningful because it is used for God's work.

Having outlined firmness in personal and familial religious beliefs, we now explore flexibility.
Flexibility in Religious Beliefs: "I don't agree ... so I ignore them." Although many participants, like those whose reports were featured in the previous section, focused on firmly grounded, even unalterable, beliefs, other participants described what they believed *personally* in relation to the official beliefs of their religious institutions. These individuals interpreted doctrine and teachings in varied and adaptive ways that reportedly fit better or made more sense to them and their families. Some spontaneously expressed, without any related questioning, that they did not have the same views as their religion and/or religious leaders on a few (or several) things. A number of participants and families were open to varying, less orthodox interpretations of their religion, and were flexible when it came to believing, partially believing, or thoroughly rejecting some doctrinal or theological or pragmatic elements of their faith. Some of these families seemed to select what they truly believed from their religion and then developed their own beliefs regarding certain issues.

Miriam, a Jewish mother, shared her view about certain Jewish perspectives on gender in worship:

I have a problem with gender roles [in] religion in general, *so I ignore them. I don't abide by them* or whatever. Like in Orthodox [Judaism], I'm often, not *offended*, but it's just that *I don't agree* with the idea of having women and men separated during ceremonies. Women are not allowed on the *bemah* [podium from which Torah is read] and you can't listen to a woman's solo voice and *I just don't believe in that part of it*.

Li-Fen, a Chinese Christian mother, shared her opinion on the doctrine of tithing:

We offer money at church. We all know how we should do, everyone should tithe. But this proportion *should be flexible rather than fixed* because the condition[s] of families are different. Those families which are in difficulties should *adjust*.

Li-Fens's argument for circumstantial flexibility resonates with Hareven and Trepagnier (2000) scholarly position that allowances should be made for the life course.

Erin, an Episcopalian mother, shared a view and approach to God images that presents a flexible non-orthodoxy that includes a "live and let live" approach to beliefs. Erin reported,

I certainly grew up saying God the Father [but now] there are lots of people at Grace [cathedral] who say "She" instead of "He," and to me those words *don't mean enough that I care*. I could see, I can see imagery of God as, you know, Father, Protector, Mother, Nurturer, Wind, Life. I don't need an attachment, *but I don't object to it*. So when somebody says [about] God, "He," *that doesn't bother me*.

A few participants, however, were not only less than fully reconciled to their faith's "institutional" beliefs, they were diametrically opposed to some beliefs and practices. One Orthodox Jewish father reported that, despite his connection to much of Jewish tradition, some aspects that he perceived as unnecessarily rigid were "anathema" to him. Elijah, another Jewish father, explained that in spite of his high level of both personal and synagogue-level involvement, "I profoundly disagree with institutional Judaism."

Additionally, many Muslim participants (both women and men, wives and husbands) expressed widely varying interpretations of *hijab* (the Islamic practice of covering) that reflected different levels of flexibility in both belief and practice. Indeed, the variations in our data were substantial enough to allow a recent article on the topic (Alghafli et al. 2017).

In connection with the theme of flexibility in religious beliefs, participants' views often differed from the traditional views held by their faith. As illustrated, these divergent patterns were evident in connection with gender roles, attitudes towards financial contribution, God images (including, but not limited to, gender), the degree of flexibility that should be permitted in ritual and practice, and how certain beliefs should be translated into practice (e.g., *hijab*). While these illustrations are a small sample of the 59 total reports related to "flexibility in beliefs," the preceding data indicate that even devotedly religious persons selected as "exemplars" by their own clergy often wrestle with at least some beliefs espoused by their traditions and actively incorporate some level of flexibility in their lived religious experience.

In summary, many of the exemplar (clergy-referred) families we interviewed were quite orthodox in belief and were devoted in their religious practices (i.e., orthopraxy). Many other families, however, were quite flexible in their beliefs, practices, and interpretations of their religion, and introduced moderate to major adaptations. Other families seemed to seek a balance between their beliefs and their faith's viewpoint—a type of negotiated hybrid. We now turn to reports from the data (N = 32) on families that strived to integrate religious firmness and religious flexibility.

Integrated Firmness and Flexibility in Beliefs: "[I] look to the religion and I look into the secular things." A body of empirical data indicates that sacred beliefs can be a beneficial (even profoundly meaningful) coping resource—particularly when these sacred beliefs are shared in couples and families (Marks and Dollahite 2017). For many highly religious families across the Abrahamic faiths, one frequently navigated issue is the extent to which non-religious materials and ideas should be integrated into how the family thinks about various matters, including family relationships themselves.

Yuusif, an East Indian, Muslim father, referenced this choice point when he said,

I do *primarily look to the religion*; however, I *look into the secular things to the extent* that if it's going to help me understand the situation we are up against [then I'll use it].... I look at [secular materials] to see how people think.

Tara, a Latter-day Saint mother, shared a similar view. Asked whether she would personally turn to sacred or secular sources in confronting a problem, she reported,

I would read *both*. I would give *more weight* to what was said *in the religious publication* but I would *read a lot everywhere*, hoping to find [useful information]. With the kids, for example, if there's a problem, I certainly will read the church [sources], but *I'll read other things as well*.

When individual participants and families were willing to look at different sources outside of religion to help them solve problems, they suggested it was beneficial to them as a whole. This integrated approach, however, raises the question of which source is primary versus secondary.

Iffah, an Arab American Muslim mother, discussed primacy when she explained,

Sometimes we even, we have *tradeoffs* between whether we want to have a religious view of something or have a cultural view of something. [However], for our family, the religious view is the view that we consider *first*. I would say it is the *priority*.

Vickie, an Episcopalian mother, shared her views on the Bible as a resource when she said,

Teaching Sunday school to the older kids, you don't have to take the Bible literally. The Bible ... guides us and we need to use it as such, but [we do] not [have] to live *literally* by it *only*, because with translations, things can get translated differently.

Wes, a Seventh-day Adventist father, also discussed interpretation and application of scripture:

In some places [in the Bible] it says, "*Above all things* you should do this." And I think some people would interpret that [as meaning 'Do this,] even at the cost of your family.' Like, 'You have to go here, even if your family will not go with you,' or '[Even] if this will cause major problems in your family [do it anyway].' I wouldn't think that God would want that to happen, *but to a certain extent*, depending upon your family, I would think [you need to be more flexible than that].

In this theme, we have seen some participants and their families exemplify both religious firmness (i.e., referencing sacred religious texts as their primary resource) while also demonstrating religious flexibility in being willing to move beyond sacred resources to also access potentially valuable secular resources.

5. Discussion

In this article, we have explored firmness and flexibility among a sample of highly religious exemplar parents. We used a multiphase, systematic, team-based process (see Marks 2015) to code more than 8000 double-spaced pages of in-depth interviews from 198 Christian, Jewish, and Muslim families from 17 states in all 8 major religio-cultural regions of the United States. We framed firmness as mainly about loyalty to God and God's purposes. We defined flexibility as mainly about loyalty to family members and their needs and circumstances. Findings provided examples illustrating (a) religious firmness, (b) religious flexibility, and (c) integration of religious firmness and religious flexibility.

Findings on religious family practices. Many religious parents were quite firm about attending religious services every week. Others were more flexible in their approach to religious attendance and other family religious practices. Flexibility was manifest in their approach to, the frequency of, and the location where religious rituals were practiced. Some families expressed an approach to religious practice that seemed to integrate firmness and flexibility. Often this involved some kind of negotiation with children regarding how to approach religious practices.

Findings on religious beliefs. Similarly, many participants were quite firm about their religious beliefs, indicating they held strictly to doctrines or theologies prescribed by their faith communities as they understood them. Others expressed some degree of flexibility toward their religious beliefs. This flexibility ranged from taking issue with some aspects of orthodox belief to outright rejection (or ignoring) of certain "official" or "traditional" doctrines they found problematic. Such beliefs tended to center on issues around gender, financial expectations, and the extent to which traditional practices are to be followed.

Findings on integrated firmness and flexibility. Others expressed ways that they were firm in their religious beliefs but made some religious allowances as well. A major theme here involved integrating reliance on religious resources (e.g., scriptures, doctrine, clergy) with secular resources (e.g., social science research, self-help books, professional counselors) in efforts to strengthen family relations and solve family problems. Even though flexibility in beliefs can be beneficial to an individual, flexibility could potentially be harmful to the family as a whole if there are conflicting beliefs about religious issues that are viewed as important and/or central.

The parental examples in this study suggest the potential effectiveness of parents integrating firmness and flexibility in daily and weekly family practices, as well as in religious beliefs. In order to instill religious beliefs and to make those beliefs and rituals meaningful, families reported that they thought it was important to be consistent in their rituals and beliefs, but to also leave room to modify or adapt rituals as circumstances changed. A conceptual slogan might be "sometimes bend but don't break." Families expressed that it was important to be flexible with religious practices, rituals, and beliefs when needed, yet firm enough to retain the vital, sacred elements.

Burr et al. (2012) suggested that on a variety of familial topics there seem to exist some principles and helpful practices that come from sacred sources—and other principles and helpful practices that originate or are developed through empirical and social research methods. If Burr and colleagues are correct in their assertion of unique and value-added strengths available in both sacred and social science domains—and they offer support for their position in several topical areas including coping, forgiveness, and prayer—then it may be that families that are willing to "firmly" seek insight from their faith's wisdom literature *and* "flexibly" seek understanding from high quality social science may be in a position of enviable strength.

5.1. Firmness and Flexibility as Complementary Loyalties

We have framed the processes of religious firmness and flexibility such that each process involves an important kind of loyalty. Thus, *religious firmness* may be conceptualized as cognitive and behavioral processes (religious beliefs and practices) centered in loyalty to God and that which serves to directly uphold or represent God (e.g., sacred texts, faith tradition, faith community, and divine commandments). Having clearly-defined and deeply-valued religious beliefs and practices suggests that the person and/or family feels a certain degree of sacred loyalty to God and those things believed to reflect or uphold God. This firmness is often manifest in (a) religious beliefs that (due to perceived divine origin) are non-negotiable and not subject to personal abrogation and (b) religious practices that are held sacred and inviolable and thus take precedence over other nonreligious or personal activities. Such practices are often maintained even in the face of personal and familial inconvenience or preferences.

Similarly, *religious flexibility* may be conceptualized as cognitive and behavioral processes centered in loyalty to family members (and other loved ones) by maintaining sensitivity to their needs, challenges, and circumstances. As we have observed, a "key challenge for [many] American churches in the 21st century will be to find a balance between supporting the standard of marriage-based families that are idealized [by most churches] … while addressing the pluralistic family realities that confront them" (Dollahite et al. 2004, p. 414). For faith communities and for families themselves, integration between these two complementary loyalties may be needed to optimize personal and family wellbeing in the context of acceptance of divine mandates and expectations.

Commenting on a draft of this study, a long-time colleague, Carol Le Blanc drew related connections between the challenges families face in finding healthy balance and integration between firmness and flexibility in relational and religious life with her work as an expert yogi and yoga instructor. She explained in personal communication with us that in yoga's "mountain pose" there is,

> a delicate balance of a firm, grounded base coupled with the flowing gentle movement of breath work together to steady the body and the mind. Too much firmness and we become like tin soldiers, easily brought down by the slightest knock or wind. Too much flexibility and we easily lose the pose or more likely, have difficulty finding the pose in the first place. If we hold too firmly to the goal of achieving a certain outcome, it will almost always elude us. Much like Nathaniel Hawthorne's *butterfly, which when pursued, is always just beyond your grasp, but which, if you will sit down quietly, may alight upon you.* Conversely, if we are too flexible we may allow ourselves to get carried away by distractions.

(Carol Le Blanc, personal communication, 02/14/2019)

We believe these observations may offer relevant insight to our focal topic. Consistent with research on authoritative parenting styles (that include high levels of both warmth and control), we suggest that parents who faithfully integrate religious firmness and religious flexibility may have the best chance to see their children continue in their faith. We think the findings of this study may imply that religious parents that effectively integrate these complementary loyalties to their God and their family members may be better able to be authoritative, balanced, functional, and healthy in how they attempt to pass their religious beliefs and practices on to the next generation.

Research has emphasized the importance of healthy relationships for successful transmission of religious identity and commitment (Bengtson et al. 2013). Given the inevitable conflicts that occur in religious families (Lambert and Dollahite 2006), it is crucial for religious parents who wish to maintain the kind of relationships that facilitate religious transmission to learn how to draw from religious beliefs and practices to bring relational reconciliation after conflict (Dollahite et al. n.d.).

In sum, we think that (a) religious firmness without religious flexibility may result in religious rigidity, (b) religious flexibility without religious firmness may result in religious haphazardness and loss of sacred beliefs and practices, while (c) religious firmness integrated with religious flexibility is more likely to result in a balanced, healthy style of religious parenting.

5.2. Limitations

This study is subject to the limitations of many qualitative research studies. However, for a qualitative study, the sample is unusually large (N = 476) and geographically diverse (i.e., national). Even so, the sample is neither random nor representative. Further, while the sample is ethnically and religiously diverse, only American families in the Abrahamic faiths were interviewed and the families selected were "exemplars," not average or median congregants. Therefore, findings from an exemplar sample may not be easily generalized to less religious families.

5.3. Future Research: Beyond Religious Rigidities

The social sciences have doggedly focused on the problems with religious rigidities for decades. It is time for scholars to become more flexible in how they think about and explore processes around firmness and flexibility in religious belief and practice. As a group, social scientists tend to be fairly irreligious and lean overwhelmingly to the political left (Duarte et al. 2014). Thus, it is not surprising that far more research has focused on the negative consequences of religious rigidities than on the potential benefits of religious firmness appropriately integrated with religious flexibility. We hope this study will be among the first of many to explore these important processes.

6. Conclusions

This study may suggest that religious parents who wish the fruits of their faith to be enjoyed by their children and grandchildren need to be firm enough in their faith that they plainly show their loyalty to God (and things that reflect or uphold God) by striving to clearly and consistently incorporate their religious beliefs and practices into family life across time and circumstance. Yet our findings also suggest that strongly religious parents could benefit their children by striving to be flexible enough in how those beliefs and practices are applied in families that they also show their loyalty to their family members by attending to their needs, challenges, and circumstances.

Author Contributions: Conceptualization, D.D. and L.M.; methodology, D.D. and L.M.; validation, D.D. and L.M.; formal analysis, D.D., L.M., and K.B.; D.D., K.B. and L.M.; resources, D.D. and L.M.; data curation, D.D. and L.M.; writing—original draft preparation, D.D., L.M., K.B., & B.B.; writing—review and editing, D.D., L.M., B. B., and A.R.; visualization, D.D., L.M., & A.R.; supervision, D.D. and L.M.; project administration, D.D. and L.M.; funding acquisition, D.D. and L.M.

Funding: This research received no external funding.

Acknowledgments: We appreciate funding for this project from the BYU Family Studies Center, BYU Religious Studies Center, and an Eliza R. Snow Grant to the first author as well as a grant to the second author from the LSU Council on Research. We are grateful to the following BYU students for help in coding the data: Hilary Dalton, Toshi Shichida, Kelsie Dean, Stephanie Seaborn, Beda Rose, Rebekah DeBoer, Heather Garbe Venera, JillAnne Jensen, Jordan Kohl, and Naomi Winters.

Conflicts of Interest: The authors declare no conflict of interest. The funders had no role in the design of the study; in the collection, analyses, or interpretation of data; in the writing of the manuscript, or in the decision to publish the results.

References

Alghafli, Zahra, Loren D. Marks, Trevan G. Hatch, and Andrew H. Rose. 2017. Veiling in Fear or in Faith? Meanings of the Hijab to Practicing Muslim Wives and Husbands in USA. *Marriage & Family Review* 53: 696–716.

Babbie, Earl R. 2004. *The Practice of Social Research*, 10th ed. Belmont: Wadsworth.

Bengtson, Vern L., Norella M. Putney, and Susan Harris. 2013. *Families and Faith: How Religion is Passed Down Across Generations.* New York: Oxford.

Bernard, Russel H., and Gery W. Ryan. 2010. *Analyzing Qualitative Data.* Los Angeles: Sage.

Bao, Wan-Ning, Les B. Whitbeck, and Danny R. Hoyt. 1999. Perceived Parental Acceptance as a Moderator of Religious Transmission among Adolescent Boys and Girls. *Journal of Marriage & Family* 61: 362–74.

Bronk, Kendall C., Pamela E. King, and Kyle M. Matsuba. 2013. An Introduction to Exemplar Research: A Definition, Rationale, and Conceptual Issues. In *Exemplar Methods and Research: Strategies for Investigation. New Directions for Child and Adolescent Development*. Edited by M. Kyle Matsuba, Pamela E. King and Kendall C. Bronk. San Francisco: Jossey-Bass, vol. 142, pp. 1–12.

Burr, Wesley R., Loren D. Marks, and Randal D. Day. 2012. *Sacred Matters: Religion and Spirituality in Families*. New York: Routledge/Taylor & Francis Group.

Chelladurai, Joe M., David C. Dollahite, and Loren D. Marks. 2018. 'The Family That Prays Together': Relational Processes Associated with Regular Family Prayer. *Journal of Family Psychology* 32: 849–59. [CrossRef] [PubMed]

Colaner, Colleen Warner, Jordan Soliz, and Leslie R. Nelson. 2014. Communicatively Managing Religious Identity Difference in Parent-Child Relationships: The Role of Accommodative and Nonaccommodative Communication. *Journal of Family Communication* 14: 310–27. [CrossRef]

Damon, William, and Anne Colby. 2013. Why a True Account of Human Development Requires Exemplar Research. In *Exemplar Methods and Research: Strategies for Investigation: New Directions for Child and Adolescent Development*. Edited by M. Kyle Matsuba, Pamela E. King and Kendall C. Bronk. Hoboken: John Wiley & Sons, Inc., vol. 142, pp. 13–25.

Dollahite, David C., and Loren D. Marks. 2018. Introduction to the Special Issue: Exploring Strengths in American Families of Faith. *Marriage & Family Review* 54: 617–34. [CrossRef]

Dollahite, David C., Loren D. Marks, and Betsy H. Barrow. n.d. Exploring Relational Reconciliation Processes in Christian, Jewish, and Muslim families. *Family Relations*. Forthcoming.

Dollahite, David C., Loren D. Marks, and Hilary Dalton. 2018. Why Religion Helps and Harms Families: A Conceptual Model of a System of Dualities at the Nexus of Faith and Family Life. *Journal of Family Theory & Review* 10: 219–41.

Dollahite, David C., Loren D. Marks, and Michael A. Goodman. 2004. Religiosity and Families: Relational and Spiritual Linkages in a Diverse and Dynamic Cultural Context. In *The Handbook of Contemporary Families: Considering the Past, Contemplating the Future*. Edited by Marilyn J. Coleman and Lawrence H. Ganong. Thousand Oaks: Sage, pp. 411–31.

Dollahite, David C., Loren D. Marks, and Kaity Pearl Young. 2019. Relational Struggles and Experiential Immediacy in Religious American Families. *Psychology of Religion and Spirituality* 11: 9–21. [CrossRef]

Dollahite, David C., and Jennifer Y. Thatcher. 2008. Talking about Religion: How Highly Religious Youth and Parents Discuss Their Faith. *Journal of Adolescent Research* 23: 611–41. [CrossRef]

Duarte, José L., Jarret T. Crawford, Charlotta Stern, Jonathan Haidt, Lee Jussim, and Philip E. Tetlock. 2014. Political Diversity Will Improve Social Psychological Science. *Behavioral and Brain Sciences* 38: 1–13. [CrossRef]

Dudley, Roger L., and Margaret G. Dudley. 1986. Transmission of Religious Values from Parents to Adolescents. *Review of Religious Research* 28: 3–15. [CrossRef]

Ellison, Christopher G., and Darren E. Sherkat. 1993. Obedience and Autonomy: Religion and Parental Values Reconsidered. *Journal for the Scientific Study of Religion* 32: 313–29. [CrossRef]

Fiese, Barbara H., Thomas J. Tomcho, Michael Douglas, Kimberly Josephs, Scott Poltrock, and Tim Baker. 2002. A Review of 50 Years of Research on Naturally Occurring Family Routines and Rituals: Cause for Celebration? *Journal of Family Psychology* 16: 381–90. [CrossRef] [PubMed]

Flor, Douglas L., and Nancy Flanagan Knapp. 2001. Transmission and Transaction: Predicting Adolescents' Internalization of Parental Religious Values. *Journal of Family Psychology* 15: 627–45. [CrossRef] [PubMed]

Gane, Barry. 2014. Adolescent Faith That Lasts. *Journal of Youth Ministry* 13: 42–61.

Handel, Gerald. 1996. Family Worlds and Qualitative Family Research: Emergence and Prospects of Whole-Family Methodology. *Marriage & Family Review* 24: 335–48.

Hansen, Cheri. 1998. Long-Term Effects of Religious Upbringing. *Mental Health, Religion & Culture* 1: 91–111.

Hareven, Tamara K., and Barbara Trepagnier. 2000. *Families, History and Social Change: Life Course & Cross-Cultural Perspectives*. New York: Routledge.

Holmberg, Diane, Terri L. Orbuch, and Joseph Veroff. 2004. *Thrice Told Tales: Married Couples Tell Their Stories*. Mahwah: Erlbaum.

Kim-Spoon, Jungmeen, Gregory S. Longo, and Michael E. McCullough. 2012. Parent-Adolescent Relationship Quality as a Moderator for the Influences of Parents' Religiousness on Adolescents' Religiousness and Adjustment. *Journal of Youth and Adolescence* 41: 1576–87. [CrossRef]

Laird, Robert D., Loren D. Marks, and Matthew D. Marrero. 2011. Religiosity, Self-Control, and Antisocial Behavior: Religiosity as a Promotive and Protective Factor. *Journal of Applied Developmental Psychology* 32: 78–85. [CrossRef]

Lambert, Nathaniel M., and David C. Dollahite. 2006. How Religiosity Helps Couples Prevent, Resolve, and Overcome Marital Conflict. *Family Relations: An Interdisciplinary Journal of Applied Family Studies* 55: 439–49. [CrossRef]

Lee, Jerry W., Gail T. Rice, and V. Bailey Gillespie. 1997. Family Worship Patterns and Their Correlation with Adolescent Behavior and Beliefs. *Journal for the Scientific Study of Religion* 36: 372–81. [CrossRef]

MacQueen, Kathleen M., Eleanor McLellan, Kelly Kay, and Bobby Milstein. 1998. Codebook Development for Team-Based Qualitative Analysis. *Cultural Anthropology Methods* 10: 31–36. [CrossRef]

Marks, Loren D. 2015. A Pragmatic, Step-by-Step Guide for Qualitative Methods: Capturing the Disaster and Long-Term Recovery Stories of Katrina and Rita. *Current Psychology: A Journal for Diverse Perspectives on Diverse Psychological Issues* 34: 494–505. [CrossRef]

Marks, Loren D., and David C. Dollahite. 2012. "Don't Forget Home": The Importance of Sacred Ritual in Families. In *Understanding Religious Rituals*. Edited by John P. Hoffman. New York: Routledge, pp. 186–203.

Marks, Loren D., and David C. Dollahite. 2017. *Religion and Families*. New York: Routledge.

Marks, Loren D., and David C. Dollahite. 2018. Surmounting the Empathy Wall: Deep Respect and Holy Envy in Qualitative Scholarship. *Marriage & Family Review* 54: 762–73. [CrossRef]

Marks, L. D., D. C. Dollahite, and K. P. Young. 2018. Struggles experienced by religious minority families in the United States. *Psychology of Religion and Spirituality*. [CrossRef]

Marks, Loren D., Trevan G. Hatch, and David C. Dollahite. 2017. Sacred Practices and Family Processes in a Jewish Context: Shabbat as the Weekly Family Ritual Par Excellence. *Family Process* 57: 448–61. [CrossRef] [PubMed]

Myers, Scott M. 1996. An Interactive Model of Religiosity Inheritance: The Importance of Family Context. *American Sociological Review* 61: 858–66. [CrossRef]

Olson, David H. 2000. Circumplex Model of Marital and Family Systems. *Journal of Family Therapy* 22: 144–67. [CrossRef]

Patton, Michael Q. 2002. *Qualitative Research & Evaluation Methods*, 3rd ed. Thousand Oaks: Sage.

Pew Research Center. 2009. *Faith in Flux*. Washington, DC: Pew Research Center, April, Available online: http://www.pewforum.org/2009/04/27/faith-in-flux/ (accessed on 13 February 2019).

Pew Research Center. 2016. *Why America's 'Nones' Left Religion Behind*. Washington, DC: Pew Research Center, August, Available online: http://www.pewresearch.org/fact-tank/2016/08/24/why-americas-nones-left-religion-behind/ (accessed on 13 February 2019).

Pirutinsky, Steven, and Ariel Kor. 2013. Relevance of the Circumplex Model to Family Functioning Among Orthodox Jews in Israel. *New School Psychology Bulletin* 10: 25–38.

Schrodt, Paul. 2005. Family Communication Schemata and the Circumplex Model of Family Functioning. *Western Journal of Communication* 69: 359–76. [CrossRef]

Shichida, Toshi, David C. Dollahite, and Jason S. Carroll. 2015. How the Perception of God as a Transcendent Moral Authority Influences Marital Connection among American Christians. *Journal of Psychology and Christianity* 34: 40–52.

Seymour, Julie, Gill Dix, and Tony Eardley. 1995. *Joint Accounts: Methodology and Practice in Research Interviews with Couples*. New York: Social Research Policy Unit.

Silk, Mark, and Andrew Walsh. 2008. *One Nation, Divisible: How Regional Religious Differences Shape American Politics*. Lanham: Rowman & Littlefield.

Smith, Christian, and Melina L. Denton. 2005. *Soul Searching: The Religious and Spiritual Lives of American Teenagers*. New York: Oxford.

Spilman, S. K., T. K. Neppl, M. B. Donnellan, T. J. Schofield, and R. D. Conger. 2013. Incorporating religiosity into a developmental model of positive family functioning across generations. *Developmental Psychology* 49: 762–74. [CrossRef] [PubMed]

Vermeer, Paul, Jacques Janssen, and Peer Scheepers. 2012. Authoritative Parenting and the Transmission of Religion in the Netherlands: A Panel Study. *International Journal for the Psychology of Religion* 22: 42–59. [CrossRef]

Walsh, Froma. 2009. *Spiritual Resources in Family Therapy*, 2nd ed. New York: Guilford.

religions

MDPI

Article

An Exploration of Family Factors Related to Emerging Adults' Religious Self-Identification

Anthony B. Walker

Department of Applied Health Sciences, Indiana State University, Terre Haute, IN 47809, USA;
Anthony.Walker@indstate.edu

Received: 4 February 2019; Accepted: 5 March 2019; Published: 8 March 2019

check for
updates

Abstract: Emerging or young adulthood is a time of identity exploration across a number of domains. Those domains include work, relationships, and beliefs and values. Specifically, emerging adults are tasked with differentiating religious beliefs and values from those of their parents. Much evidence suggests that emerging adults adopt the religious or non-religious ideals they were raised with. Family structure, parental divorce, parental marital quality and parental conflict have all been identified as factors related to degree of religiousness in emerging adulthood. It is less clear how those and other family factors may relate to types of religious identity. Using a subsample of wave 3 of the National Survey of Youth and Religion, researchers identified six types of religiousness in emerging adulthood. To our knowledge, family factors related to this typology have not been thoroughly investigated. Thus, the purpose of this qualitative study is to further explore and describe the family factors related to the six types of religiousness in emerging adulthood using a purposive sample of 49 college students from a large public university in the United States. Qualitative analyses describe themes related to five of the six types. Future directions are discussed.

Keywords: emerging adulthood; religiousness; religious identity; religious types; young adulthood; family; contexts; typology; practices; beliefs

1. Introduction

Emerging or young adulthood is a time of identity exploration across a number of domains (age 18–29; Arnett 2000, 2004). These domains are theorized to fall roughly into three categories: work, relationships and beliefs and values (Arnett 2000). Specifically, emerging adults are tasked with developing and differentiating religious beliefs and values that are personal to and independent from those of their parents (Erikson 1963). Emerging adults may settle on religious identities and values that largely mirror or are very different from that of their parents. Evidence suggests mirroring—or the intergenerational transmission of similar religious beliefs and values—as more normative than not. Indeed, Bengtson (2013) longitudinally demonstrated that emerging adults largely adopt the religious or non-religious beliefs and values of their parents. Arnett and Jensen, however, (Arnett and Jensen 2002) found virtually no relationship between parent and emerging adult offspring religious approaches. A number of family-related contexts and processes have been identified as potentially important to religiousness in emerging adulthood (Min et al. 2012; Myers 1996). For example, parental religious homogamy and marital quality is predictive of religious transmission (Myers 1996). Family structure, parental divorce, and parental conflict have all been identified as factors related to degree of religiousness in emerging adulthood (Denton 2012; Denton and Culver 2015; Ellison et al. 2011). It is less clear, however, how those and other family factors may relate to varying types of religious identities for emerging adults. Given that emerging adulthood is a developmental period qualitatively different from adolescence and adulthood, religious identities and types that spring from emerging adults themselves seems most appropriate (Arnett 2000). Quantitative and qualitative approaches have identified between four and six types of religious identities in emerging adults (Arnett and Jensen 2002; Denton 2012; Petts 2012; Smith and Snell 2009). Smith and Snell (2009) identified six types of religiousness or religious identities in emerging adulthood: Committed Traditionalists, Selective Adherents, Spiritually Open, Religiously Indifferent, Religiously Disconnected, and Irreligious. This typology was developed using a qualitative approach with a relatively large participant pool (*n* = 230) that is quasi-nationally representative (Smith and Snell 2009). Despite this unique and useful approach, only a brief summary of family related factors was initially provided. To our knowledge, family factors related to Smith and Snell's typology have not been thoroughly investigated. Thus, the purpose of this qualitative study is to further explore and describe the family factors related to the six types of religiousness in emerging adulthood using a purposive sample of 49 college students from a large public university in the southern United States.

1.1. Emerging Adulthood and Identity Exploration

Early and contemporary theorists alike delineated the time period between adolescence and adulthood—now early or emerging adulthood—as a time of marked identity exploration (Arnett 2000; Erikson 1963). One area important to this exploration is religious beliefs and world views (Arnett 2000; Erikson 1963). Successful resolution of the crisis of identity avoids role confusion and facilitates the resolution of future crises. In part, successful resolution of this crisis of identity is thought to include developing or adopting a set of values and beliefs that is personal, individual and separate from those held by parents (Erikson 1963). Applied to religious beliefs and values, the process of exploration and eventual resolution could conclude with adults that espouse religious identities that largely mirror those of their parents. It could also mean adults adopt identities that are very different from those which they were raised.

1.2. Intergenerational Transmission of Religious Values

Despite the theoretical need for differentiated religious beliefs and values, emerging adults largely report religious beliefs, values and identities that are similar to their parents. This intergenerational pattern is strongest when both parents frequently attend religious services together, adhere to the same religious denomination, and express that religion is high in importance (Smith and Snell 2009; Spilman et al. 2013). Furthermore, Denton (2012) found emerging adults with the highest level of religiosity across all measures had parents who were highly religious and engaged in religious practices. Interestingly, this intergenerational transmission of religious values is not limited to the highly religious. Longitudinal evidence also demonstrates parents that consistently demonstrate that religion is not valued tend towards emerging adult offspring who also strongly oppose a religious world view (Bengtson 2013; Denton 2012). For example, in a longitudinal analysis, 68% of young adults adopted the same religious tradition as their parents while 63% of non-affiliated parents had young adults who followed suit. The strong connection between parent and offspring religious and non-religious values is markedly consistent. Yet approximately one third of emerging adults settle on beliefs and values that are different. Furthermore, Arnett and Jensen, found the religious beliefs and values of emerging adults in their sample to be virtually unrelated to those of their parents (Arnett and Jensen 2002).

1.3. Family Contexts and Processes that Impact Religious Transmission

A number of family related contexts and processes impact the strength of the intergenerational transmission of religious values to emerging adults. Agreement between parents on religion is related to increased effectiveness in religious socialization. Longitudinal work suggests religious congruence—including denomination and practices—between parents as important to religious socialization (Bengtson 2013). For example, parental religious homogamy and marital quality is predictive of religious transmission (Myers 1996). Family structure also plays a part. Religious service attendance and importance of religion were found to be lower for youth raised in single-parent, cohabiting, or step-family contexts when compared with those from married two-parent families, in part due to challenges regarding religious socialization (Petts 2015). It may be that youth raised in a family structures congruent with the religious values they were socialized face fewer barriers in adopting and holding on to those beliefs and values (Petts 2009).

Marital quality, as indicated by a happy marriage and low levels of parental conflict, also plays a role in family religious socialization. For example, young adults with parents that were happily married and in relationships characterized as low-conflict reported few doubts and a positive outlook of God and their parents' religion (Ellison et al. 2011). Furthermore, young adults from homes where parents are unhappily married but conflict is low report greater levels of religious engagement compared to young adults from married, unhappy, high conflict homes (Ellison et al. 2011).

Parental divorce can also impact parental religious socialization outcomes for offspring. Parental divorce is specifically associated with identifying as spiritual but not religious for young adults (Zhai et al. 2007, 2008) and with being more skeptical of institutional religion and their parents own commitment to religion (Ellison et al. 2011). Family disruption, including divorce or parental break-up, was related to a decrease in both religious practice and the importance of religion for emerging adults who were highly religious as adolescents. However, adolescents who display average levels of religiousness appear turn towards religion after a family disruption (Denton 2012). Overall, parental conflict in conjunction with parental divorce, has been shown to be associated with low levels of religious engagement (Ellison et al. 2011). However, Denton and Culver (2015) demonstrate that the family disruption reduction in religiousness pattern may be accurate for whites, but it is less so for African American youth. It is unclear how divorce or disruption may impact other non-Whites.

Race and ethnicity may play a prominent role in religious transmission. In fact, religiousness has been identified as particularly salient within the lives of African Americans (Taylor and Chatters 2010). Furthermore, African American mothers and fathers differentially impact the religious beliefs and practices of daughters and sons (Halgunseth et al. 2016) and African American adolescents participate in religious services and other religious groups to a greater extent compared to other ethnic groups (Smith et al. 2002). Parent-child relationships within African American families have been characterized as largely positive, which may promote religious socialization intergenerationally (Gutierrez et al. 2014). Ecklund and Park (2007) suggest that Asian Americans and non-Christian religions are understudied groups and research also shows Asian American immigrant parents may rely on religion to strengthen parent-child relationships, increasing family unity and strengthening pro-social values across generations (Son et al. 2018). Asian American emerging adults in turn report that parents and other family members as influential to their own religious identities (Park and Ecklund 2007). For Hispanics religion and culture often deeply intertwine (Gallo et al. 2009) and religious identity may be particularly important to understanding this group (Westoff and Marshall 2010).

Finally, feeling close to one's parents is associated with a greater socialization influence for that offspring towards parental religion (Min et al. 2012). Communication and conversations between parents and youth is another potentially important source of religious socialization (Boyatzis et al. 2006; Dollahite and Thatcher 2008; Smith and Snell 2009).

Thus, family religious congruency, family structure, marital quality, divorce, race, ethnicity, feelings of closeness and having ongoing conversations around religion may all impact religious transmission. But what of religious identity?

1.4. Religious Identity Types in Emerging Adulthood

While most research on emerging adults and religiousness focuses on a specific measure that is usually some combination of religious service attendance and importance of religion, these minimal measures only tell part of the story. Religiousness is multidimensional and as such is likely to exhibit nuances that will be difficult to capture with only a few items. Indeed, there may be qualitative differences in religiousness specific to emerging adulthood that are masked by limited measurement.

Three typologies of religiousness or religious identity are of note. First, Denton (2012) utilizes a person-centered, latent-class approach combining eight items tapping various aspects of religiousness. The items address some expected areas such as importance of religion, prayer and religious service attendance. The items also address some unexpected areas, such as belief in and closeness to God, helping others, thinking on the meaning of life and exclusive attitudes towards religion. From these items five latent classes of religiousness from adolescence to early emerging adulthood are identified (for a detailed description see Denton 2012). Abiders are highest on all eight measures and are highly likely to have highly religious parents, come from a two parent family and have lived with them in the same house growing up. Atheists are lowest on all eight measures and have other family characteristics that are not unlike the rest of the population. Assenters are average. They believe in God and practice some forms of religious engagement. The typical Assenter identifies with a specific denomination or congregation, but is not overly active there. They come from stable families yet have parents who are average in their own religious practices and beliefs. Avoiders have social networks, friends and family, who are not religious. They exhibit fairly stable residential and family backgrounds. Adapters are largely average on a number of the eight items, with some notable distinctions. Adapters combine low levels of institutional involvement with high levels of personal religiosity. Adapters are more likely to be African American or Hispanic, have low family residential stability and to not live with both parents. A nationally representative sample with a multidimensional person-centered measure approach is a strength. While using eight items to tap into the multidimensionality of religiousness is a vast improvement over the historically popular yet conceptually limited frequency of religious service attendance and/or importance of religion items alone, it is entirely possible that a purely quantitative survey approach may have missed essential components due to items being selected a priori. A qualitative approach would not brook that limitation.

Second, Arnett and Jensen interviewed 140 emerging adults with an age range of 21–28 (2002). Six religious items from a survey were combined with two items that were presented during the interview schedule. The survey questions covered topics such as frequency and importance of religious service attendance, importance and certainty of religious beliefs, importance of religious faith to daily life and belief in God. The first interview question addressed religious family socialization, allowing participants to choose from high, moderate and low exposure to religion. Most indicated high exposure (64%), with only 13% moderate and 23% low. Low exposure was defined as parents rarely if ever taking children to church. In other ways parents conveyed that religion was simply unimportant. Moderate had family environments where parents were inconsistent in religious service attendance, religious socialization efforts, and communicated that religion was not important. High exposure was representative of parents who consistently took their children to religious services and gave high importance to religion. The second interview question invited participants to identify their religious or spiritual beliefs from one of four options: Agnostic/atheist (24%), Deist (29%), Liberal Christian (26%) or Conservative Christian (22%). The Agnostic/atheist response was defined as someone who is unsure about the possibility of knowing about God, one who is unsure about their own beliefs or one who rejects belief in religion all together. The Deist generally believes in God or endorses spirituality without an institutional sense. The Deist also may self-identify as Christian but only nominally, rejecting tradition specific teachings and including personalized beliefs from a variety of sources. The Liberal Christian also identifies with a specific denomination and largely accept much of the teachings of that tradition. However, some teachings are not adopted as truth and certain areas remain targets for open skepticism. Liberal Christians may think favorably on or reserve judgment against non-Christian faiths. Conservative Christians believe what is taught by their specific denominations or traditions. Some believe that Christianity is the only true faith. Approximately 77% of this sample may be thought of as Christian or having Christian leanings. The qualitative approach allows for conceptual complexity and for the participant to speak for themselves. One hundred and forty interviews is a significant sample size. However, the age range of the sample, combined with the sizeable proportion of participants that are married and have children, and fewer religious identification options compared to Denton (2012) all may indicate that this sample of emerging adults may be qualitatively farther along the path to adulthood than early emerging adults. An approach that combines the sampling strength of Denton with the openness of Arnett and Jensen's qualitative approach and high number of participants would be ideal.

Third, Smith and Snell's unique contribution to the religious typologies that may exist in emerging adulthood is bolstered by an unparalleled sampling strategy coupled with a substantial number of interviews. In the first stage of the sampling approach, participants were recruited as teens (ages 13–17) via national random digit dialing for a telephone survey in what is now known as the National Survey of Youth and Religion (Smith and Denton 2005). After participating in the telephone interview, a subsample of 267 youth were chosen to be interviewed face-to-face in part due to the diversity of responses to the survey questions and in part to reflect the nationally representative nature of the original sample across race, religion and region of residence. As part of Wave 2, 120 of the original participants were reinterviewed face-to-face approximately two years later. In Wave 3, 151 participants were selected from the pool of those who had been interviewed in Wave 1 and 67 participants who had never experienced a face-to-face interview combined to total 230 now early emerging adults (18–24 years old) while preserving the nationally representative nature of the original sample and striking a near equal ratio of males to females (Smith and Snell 2009). As to the religious denominations of the sample, 48% were Protestant, 15% Catholic, 6% Jewish, 6% Mormon, 11% not religious and the remaining 10% a combination of Christian and non-Christian approaches. The relatively high number of interviews allows for in-depth comparisons across groups and detailed description of the groups themselves. Smith and Snell applied a qualitative approach to face-to-face interviews (Smith and Snell 2009) and identified six types of religiousness or religious identities in emerging adulthood: Committed Traditionalists, Selective Adherents, Spiritually Open, Religiously Indifferent, Religiously Disconnected, and Irreligious. Smith and Snell suggest each group may be described by a single summary statement that captures each grouping's position in relation to religion in their lives. For example, "I am really committed," describes a Committed Traditionalist, while a Selective Adherent would more likely respond "I do some of what I can". Spiritually Open respondents suggest that "[T]here's probably something more out there", and "It just doesn't matter much," is the mantra of the Religiously Indifferent. "I really don't know what you are talking about," summarizes the Religiously Disconnected, while the Irreligious approach is captured by the phrase "Religion just makes no sense". Smith and Snell estimate that most emerging adults are either Selective Adherents (SAs; 30%) or Religiously Indifferent (RI; 25%). The next largest groups are thought to be Committed Traditionalists and Spiritually Open (CT; SO; 15% each respectively). Irreligious and Religiously Disconnected emerging adults represent the smallest proportions in the population at ten and five percent, respectively (I; RD). With respect to family related contexts and processes, the description of CTs is conspicuously silent. The SAs have a "fairly solid religious upbringing," and may have been raised in a religious faith (Smith and Snell, p. 167). SO's may have no religious background, or be a former believer. RIs can come from any religious tradition or be nonreligious all together. RDs have families and other social relationships that are wholly non-religious and come from non-religious backgrounds. Most IRs were raised in non-religious families or are no longer following the religious tradition in which they were raised.

Each typology of religious identity makes advances in categorizing and summarizing the somewhat discontinuous process of identity exploration and development in emerging adulthood. Each comes from emerging adults. Yet Smith and Snell's typology speaks little, if at all, to the family related contexts and processes that contributed to each type. Thus, the current project will attempt to replicate the six religious identities described by Smith and Snell (2009) using a purposive sample of college students from a large southern university. As part of the replication, special attention will be paid to the family context and processes that may be related to each type.

2. Methods

2.1. Sample

The sample included 49 university students from a large southern university. The average age of participants is almost 21 (M = 20.82, SD 1.34) with an age range of 19–24, indicating mostly upper classman. Most participants were female (41; 84%) and eight were male (16%). Most of the sample is white (40%), 22% Asian/Asian American, 14% African American, 12% Mexican/Mexican American, 8% Bi-racial, 2% Indian and 2% had missing data. Compared to national estimates of race and ethnicity for 18–24 year olds, the current sample underrepresents whites and Hispanics, closely represents African Americans, and over represents Asians and those who are Bi-racial (National Center for Education Statistics n.d.). The majority of the sample came from married two parent families (65%), with 16% from step-families, 12% from single-parent families and 2% each from cohabiting common law, divorced and not remarried and extended family backgrounds, respectively. Participants self-identified in the following denominations: Non-denominational (24%), Catholic/Roman Catholic (19%), Christian (16%), Baptist (12%), Agnostic (8%), Atheist (6%), Hindu (4%), Reformed Judaism (2%), Muslim (2%), Jehovah's Witness (2%), Higher Power (2%) and confused (2%). At the state level, adults in Texas report 77% Christian, including 1% Jehovah's Witnesses and other Christian, 1% Jewish and Muslim and less than 1% Hindu. Those that are religiously unaffiliated account for 18% of the adult population in Texas, with 2% Atheist and 3% Agnostic, respectively (PEW Research Center n.d.). Thus, at 73% the current sample slightly underrepresents adult Christians in the state of Texas while over representing non-Christians, atheists and agnostics.

2.2. Interviews

After receiving IRB approval, the qualitative data was acquired through semi-structured interviews with participants who were students at a large southern university. Participants were recruited through classroom visits using a stratified purposive sampling strategy with the intention of sampling those who have experienced change or struggle with respect to their religious identities since starting college (Palinkas et al. 2015). Potential participants were screened to insure they met the recruitment criteria. One-on-one interviews were conducted in a small conveniently located interview room on campus. Interviews lasted approximately one hour and were audio recorded. As part of the interview schedule, participants were asked a number of questions related to demographics and their family backgrounds. Key to this investigation, participants were read each of the summary statements indicated by Smith and Snell to capture and summarize each of the six religious types (Smith and Snell 2009; See Table 1). Participants were then invited to verbally select the summary statement that most closely aligned with their own approach to religion. Most self-identified within a specific type, while 10% of the current sample chose a self-identification that combined two conceptually proximal religious identities. Upon completion of the interview participants received $10. Interviews were then transcribed verbatim in preparation for analysis.

Table 1. Comparison of Frequency Distributions of Six Religious Types Across Independent Samples.

Religious Type	Summary Statement	Smith & Snell Estimated %[1]	Current Sample %
Committed Traditionalist	I am really committed.[2]	15	28
Committed Traditionalist/Selective Adherent	—	—	8[3]
Selective Adherent	I do some of what I can.	30	36
Spiritually Open	There's probably something more out there.	15	14
Spiritually Open/Religiously Indifferent	—	—	2

Table 1. *Cont.*

Religious Type	Summary Statement	Smith & Snell Estimated %[1]	Current Sample %
Religiously Indifferent	It just doesn't matter much.	25	8
Religiously Disconnected	I don't know what you're talking about.	5	0
Irreligious	Religion just makes no sense.	10	2

3. Data Analysis

Five content relevant questions in the interview schedule were identified for analysis. These questions tapped family contexts and processes as indicated by literature reviewed above. Participants were invited to describe the family structure they grew up in, conversations they had with their parents about religion growing up, conversations about religion right before coming to college, the degree of religious practices present in their homes and the degree of parental conflict in their homes. Demographics and interviews were initially reviewed to code each interview along the typology developed by (Smith and Snell 2009). Participants were placed in the religious identity type with which they self-identified (e.g., CT, SA, SO, RI, RD, I). Interviews that could not be coded due to missing data were removed, dropping the N from 52 to 49. Any relevant data associated with each question was gathered and collated from the 49 interviews into a single document. Data was then organized first by religious identity and then by content question, resulting in five pure groups with five content topic sub groups each, as responses to the conversations about religion growing up and conversations about religion before leaving for college question were combined. No participants self-identified as RD. For the smaller groups, (RI, I) content relevant data for all of the respondents were directly reported. For the larger groups (CT, SA and SO) data were then organized by question. All of the responses to one question were reviewed for patterns and themes. All names are pseudonyms (see Table 1 for a comparison of the frequency distribution of the six types across two independent samples).

4. Results

4.1. Committed Traditionalist

Approximately 46% of CTs indicated the degree of religious practices in their homes growing up was high. Only one suggested a medium amount of religious practices characterized their home and one was unsure. Surprisingly, over one third of CTs (38%) indicated that there was no religious practice present in their home growing up (see Table 2 for additional details).

---

[3] Smith and Snell suggest that some participants will not fit cleanly into a specific type 2009.
[2] Summary statements capturing each group cited from (Smith and Snell 2009, pp. 166–68).
[1] Population level estimates are based on the categorization of 230 participants while adjusting for oversampling specific religious traditions (Smith and Snell 2009, p. 334).

Table 2. Summary of Family Context, Process and Demographic Variables across Five Religious Identity Types.

Variables	Religious Identity Type				
	Committed Traditionalist	Selective Adherent	Spiritually Open	Religiously Indifferent	Irreligious
Religious practices in the home	46% high 8% medium 38% no practices 8% uncategorized	70% high 6% medium 24% occasional	29% high 14% medium 43% low	Extreme/High when young Occasional	High until parental divorce at age 8 then forced
Parental Conflict	77% little to no conflict 8% historically high now low 8% medium 8% high	50% little to no conflict 11% historically high now low 11% medium 6% high	43% little to no conflict 14% historically high but now low 14% medium 14% high	Minimal Passive aggressive Medium	high
Family Structure	57% nuclear 29% step family, 7% extended family or single mom	67% nuclear 17% single parent 5% divorced 5% cohabiting common law 5% multiple step-families	86% Nuclear 14% Step family	Nuclear	Multiple step-families
Religious Affiliation	Nondenominational, Christian or Baptist	44% Catholic 22% Nondenominational Christian 17% Baptist 6% Methodist 6% Hindu 6% Reformed Judaism	29% Agnostic 14% Atheist 14% Protestant 14% Baptist 14% Hindu 14% higher power	Atheist Agnostic Muslim	Agnostic
Race/Ethnicity	43% White 29% African American 14% Asian 7% Bi-racial 7% Latino	33% White 28% Latino/a 17% African American 11% Asian 6% Indian 6% Bi-racial	43% Asian 43% White 14% Latino/a	White Asian Hispanic	Latina

No overarching theme appeared that captured the essence of religious conversations growing up for CTs. A number of smaller themes did emerge from the data, however. One interesting theme is the idea of Unspoken Understanding. This pattern is that of CTs explaining that they had matured in their faiths to the point that their parents no longer have conversations with them regarding religion. CTs see themselves more as religious or spiritual equals than as parent and child. An illustrative example quote of this theme is as follows: "We had most of our conversations um about God and religion whenever I was like younger, um maybe. When was it? Middle school, maybe early high school. And then from there I like kind of developed my own sense of um like they didn't really talk to me about it anymore but, unless it came up in conversation, but it wasn't a concentrated really discussion if that makes sense. Whenever I was younger they were trying to like teach me about it. But as I grew older um, you know I kind of already had my sense of identity in term of my views and they've held pretty consistent so". This theme is in contrast to second theme, Radio Silence. Both themes share a lack of communication. However, where Unspoken Understanding is relying on a foundation that was built between the parent and child earlier in the relationship, Radio Silence represents how some parents have little to no communication at all with their children regarding religion. These emerging adults have been cut off from a potentially helpful resource in their task of deciding who they are. Instead they must rely on outside sources. A quote from a CT with the Radio Silence theme will illustrate:

"Not really uh I remember again going to Mass on Sundays, but outside of Mass there was never any uh conversations about religion or God or anything". Within CTs in this sample there seems to be a willingness to stand up for, own and defend one's religious beliefs, even if that means going against the beliefs of parents, or theme three: Spiritual Certainty. An example quote will illustrate:

"And then when [my parents] came here and had me I was sprinkled as a baby . . . but then I don't remember because I was a baby. And so that's Catholic. Uhm but then when I grew older I received my salvation and became baptized as a Baptist. So then I remember uhm a few years down the line looking into [laugh] those different denominations I was like wait like does that mean you know uhm is there, was there something that I did wrong with the technicality, because . . . can you, are you supposed to be baptized before you get saved, after you get saved, you know like . . . sprinkling versus you know baptism as being a symbol and things, and so when we were moving churches like they were trying to move back to the Catholic Church and I didn't want to. And so we had that conversation I guess about different denominations".

Approximately 77% of CTs come from family backgrounds with little to no conflict. Some have never seen their parents fight, while others have seen clear positive examples of how people can disagree and work through those disagreements to a resolution. For example:

"Right yeah it definitely has affected me. My parents have always expressed love for one another and um publically and like to us as children, to me. You know they got in disputes and stuff, misunderstandings, and you know get frustrated at times with one another but always um, it was never hostile or I never saw my parents yell at each other. Um or hit each other or anything like that. Um and when they would get into disputes they would kind of make it a point to make sure that they would reconcile things um I'm not sure always in front of us but they definitely did in front of us I think to show us like hey this is how it's done. You're never going to be in a relationship with a person where you won't uh it's not always going to be perfect and this is how you, you know this is how you cope with it. This is how you figure things out. This is how you apologize and stuff like that. That has affected me in my current relationships, and the girls that I've dated and um, and just really every kind of relationship I have so it's been good".

4.2. Selective Adherent

Five themes emerged from the data specific to the kinds of religious conversations that selective adherent emerging adults engaged in from childhood until the present with their parents. The first, most prevalent theme is called Keep the Faith. In these conversations, parents answered questions of faith to the best of their abilities and sought to encourage their offspring to live according to the religious values upon which they had been raised. Phrases like "stick to", "keep", or "stay in" are used with respect to the efforts parents hope their children will put forth regarding developing faith. An illustrative quote from this theme is as follows: "Conversations about religion growing up were minimal and more about the functions and rituals of the church".

"I mean, when I was little I really liked Sunday school and then, so we would talk about like things like that and I enjoyed like all the Noah's ark stories and stuff like that. They would kind of just like they always said like oh just like you have to keep the faith. Like pray and things will get better sort of a thing. We'd talk about that a lot even like up until now, it's like 'well just keep the faith, everything's going to work out, like there's a plan for you, kind of a thing.'"

A second, smaller theme—Just the Basics—takes a different approach to religious conversations. For this theme, discussions, if they occur, are largely to convey information about an upcoming religious event or ritual. Once the ritual is past the information and conversation is not revisited. An illustrative quote from this theme is as follows: "Conversations about religion growing up were minimal and more about the functions and rituals of the church".

Unspoken Understanding is the name of a third theme. The emerging adult selective adherents who fall into the Unspoken Understanding category expressed that their parents did not need to have on-going conversations with them about faith. Instead, these emerging adults have observed the religious examples set by their parents and have actively adopted what was being taught.

"Trying to think uhm ... To be honest I wasn't really a child—well I didn't ask a lot of questions about church, religion, none of that growing up. Uhm I just—I kind of just—I watched I was the ... like ... I'm the kind of person ... I observe everything. So it was like I didn't need to ask that many questions. I was always watching what was going on".

The fourth theme to emerge from analyses is Source of Wisdom. Under this theme, offspring go to and see their parents as a viable source to answer questions related to religion and life in general. Through conversation parents are able to show how religion can answer some of life's questions. A representative quote from this theme is as follows:

"[W]e had a lot of conversations about religion, like mostly like I would ask her about like other denominations and stuff or be like what does this mean with our religion? Um just like to clear things up or like I'd say um you know Jehovah's Witness like what do they do? Like or like what is different than what we do and then she would just clarify that kind of stuff. But yeah I mean, like everything that I know about my religion is pretty much because of [my mother]".

The fifth and final theme is Childhood Limited or Life Long, meaning that some conversations around religion began and ended in childhood, and parents or emerging adult children are no longer initiating nor receptive to religious conversations. An example of Childhood Limited religious conversation is as follows:

One SA emerging adult was struggling with the logical time order of God and dinosaurs. When asking her mom about the topic she replied 'Oh, God created the dinosaurs you know.' She learned not to ask questions for fear of offending her mom. She also began to fear admitting to herself she had questions.

On the other hand, some conversations that may have started in childhood maintain relevance into emerging adulthood and thus the channels of communication are kept open.

SA's indicated the degree of religious practices in their homes growing up varied from "100%" or "hardcore," to less than occasional. Going to church and praying, whether before meals, bed-time or in general, were the most frequent religious practices mentioned by SAs (76% and 47%). For some church attendance meant weekly, including Shabbat. For others it was less frequent, with emphasis on attending during holidays, such as Christmas or Easter. Other special occasions include the Virgin of Guadalupe's birthday, Rosh Hashanah, Yom-Kippur, Hanukkah and other special occasions. A small group of SAs perceived attending sporadically or only on special occasions as being less than fully invested. Another small group of SAs reported parental attitudes that were clearly anti-institutional. For example, one mother of an SA indicated "you don't have to go to church to feel connected to God". Another father of an SA stated that one does not need to go to church or read the Bible to know one's faith and beliefs. Catholic and former Catholic SAs clearly articulated the educational process and pathway they walked. For example, one Catholic SA indicated she would attend church with her parents every Sunday, attend classes for Catholic Children's Education every week during the school year and had completed the sacraments, baptism, first communion, reconciliation and confirmation. Interestingly, she would go on her own even if her parents would not make it to services. Less common practices included reading from or taking a class or Bible seminar, Vacation Bible School, and learning holy music. For SAs, it seems as though there is a wide range of commitment levels and exposure to things religious.

When it comes to parental conflict growing up, half of SAs report little to no conflict. Two report high historic conflict but concurrent levels are down to lower levels. Two report an average or normal amount of parental conflict and one reports high levels due to both parents working in a family business. On the whole, SAs seem to be members of families that are largely able to keep conflict out of the picture. Approximately 15% of SAs perceive the level of parental conflict in their home growing up to be of average or moderate levels. The remaining 8% have parents who are perceived to be high in conflict

4.3. Spiritually Open

Of the seven who selected spiritually open, all but one come from a nuclear family. This identity includes two agnostics, one atheist, a Protestant, a Baptist, a Hindu and one who follows a high power. Three of seven SO emerging adults characterized the level of religious practices in their homes growing up as low to fairly low. For example, one emerging adult from this family environment endorsed the following rating: "Probably about a one [on] a scale of ten". A fourth SO emerging adult reported the degree of religious practices in her home as "fairly strong," especially around holidays and special occasions, which typically took the form of religious service attendance. Two endorsed the idea that religious practices were very present growing up. A culturally Jewish emerging adult described how her mother simultaneously promoted Judaism while allowing space to explore and engage with other worldviews. Her mother made sure they went to temple, Sunday school, completing bot mitzvah, doing confirmation. "You are doing these things," she would tell them. They celebrated the Jewish holidays, Shabbat every Friday but they were more family and culturally focused events rather than religious. Despite her mom's strong push towards Judaism, she also gave her children space to choose what activities they would like to do even in the community with other faiths. It was ok and encouraged to be part of the non-Jewish culture. Both parents encouraged her to find what worked for her while creating a foundation in Judaism. The family even celebrated Christmas due to her fathers' relatives being Christian. Thus, there appears to be a wide variety of religious engagement throughout the home for emerging adults with an SO identity.

For many emerging adults who self-identify as spiritually open, conversations about religion with parents growing up seemed to lack depth. Intentionally or otherwise, this lack of depth discouraged open and honest dialogue about religion and potentially divergent views being explored by emerging adults in their youth. Some emerging adults did not feel comfortable discussing their doubts. A few emerging adults were able speak openly about their beliefs with parents growing up, with diverging results. One female emerging adult has developed what she terms more "liberal" values than her mother. They disagree on topics such as the morality of homosexuality and waiting for marriage to have sex, which her mother promotes but did not practice herself. "[W]e clash a lot with it". This clash includes being forced to attend midnight Mass against her will. Yet, she went anyway to please her mother. For this participant "[R]eligion is not super strong or specific religion isn't—organized religion isn't strong in my beliefs". In contrast to the clash of the previous example, efforts by parents to reach out and have deep conversations sometimes are well received. As a teen Fran was feeling a bit rebellious and hid under her bed to avoid going to religious services one day. Her father was able to coax her out and engage in a meaningful conversation in the car on the way there. "'You know Fran, like it's okay to not believe in something' and I must have been like in my early teens, like maybe like maybe even a little bit before that I want to say I was like 10 or 11. Um and that was just kind of like, it was kind of the seed, you know what I mean? He planted the seed of like, not that you don't have to believe anything but that there's a lot of things to believe in. and so you know you have to choose what's right for you basically."

In four of seven SO households, there was little to no observable parental conflict. As one participant put it "[T]hings were pretty calm at my house". In the other homes parental conflict ranged from historically high to currently low thanks to separate sleeping quarters, above average due to the strain of working a small business together and divorced parents who do not get along.

In sum, SO's come from nuclear families, a wide variety of denominations but possibly more atheists and agnostics than SAs and CTs. Conversations about religion growing up were largely limited and shallow and parental conflict is not the norm.

4.4. Religiously Indifferent

Three participants elected the religiously indifferent identity. One is atheist, one agnostic and one is Muslim. Two are Asian and one Hispanic. All come from nuclear families. Henry, a Muslim, was born on the west coast of the United States but spent most of his childhood in Saudi Arabia. When asked about the presence of religious practices in his home growing up he responded "[I]t was extreme". He would go on to describe Saudi Arabia as the most Muslim country in the world. He would attend Mosque once a week and pray five times a day and attend what he termed "religion school," once a week. Conflict was minimal. When it came to religion, he just did what he was told. Conversations about religion focused on whether Henry would continue to practice his religion while away at college. He is, he tells them, but not as much. Henry says yes out of fear of disappointing his family, but he shares "truthfully it wasn't like on my priority list or anything". Laura, a self-identified agnostic, comes from a "really, really Catholic" home. Religious practices included praying before each meal, an emphasized prayer before bed, church on Sundays and Bible study throughout elementary, junior high and high school. She describes conflict in her home as more passive aggressive and making "horrible remarks" than anything. Laura connects her parent's approach to conflict to the Catholic teaching of never getting a divorce. High levels of overt conflict could lead to divorce. So instead her parents resolved conflicts in a passive aggressive manner. She also pointed out the potential danger of being involved in the church and having "Tia Rosa," the lady that is always there doing things, find out you are getting a divorce. When it came to conversations about religion, Laura would go to Bible study despite fears of being rejected by "another set of kids". She didn't want to go but instead she kept quiet and "kind of just went through the motions". Her father encouraged Laura to find a church while she was away at college. She said she would, but has not. Than self-identifies as Atheist. His father is Christian and his mother is a traditional Buddhist after the Vietnamese tradition. It is unclear whether Than's father was Christian before his side of the family immigrated, but during the process their family became close with a host family in a Southern state where the host father was a pastor. His Dad's family went to church every Sunday in that Southern state. Than indicated that even though he didn't see his father as the most devout Christian, they still went to church a lot every time he visited that side of the family. Growing up attending church was not mandatory for Than. The family did attend for big holidays like Easter. He would occasionally go to Mass just to see what his Catholic friends were doing. The building of a Buddhist temple in his hometown sparked a greater interested in that religion. Than watched his mother attend, donate money and join that faith community. There was a language barrier, as the worship services were in Vietnamese. Nonetheless, he would listen to the Buddhist monks as they led the prayer session from their knees. He reflects on how his attendance at temple has changed "I used to go a lot more when I was younger because it was cool and there was food and you were around like the other young kids and stuff. It was kind of like a family kind of thing". Now he attends temple on special occasions like Chinese New Year and to celebrate the Lunar year with the August moon festival. When prompted to discuss religious practices within his home, Than describes an altar with incense in a pot of dry rice surrounded by pictures of his Dad's parents and grandparents. The intent, he says, is to "pay homage to your ancestors". You do so through placing their favorite food and drink next to their pictures, praying and sharing your thoughts with them. When asked about parental conflict, he relays that his parents have always fought but that they do not share public displays of affection. Contrasting this with a stereotypical American couple who Than feels will kiss and hug, his parents' relationship never sat quite right in his mind. Two years prior to our interview Than's father explained that he is choosing to stay married to Than's mother so that Than and his brother can "prosper economically". Conversations about religion growing up went differently depending on who he was speaking with. As a 13-year old he would tell his mother he didn't believe in God. She did not engage him in conversation, leading Than to feel dismissed. His father made space for Than to express his disbelief in God but suggested that "it's always good to believe in something". He felt a desire to logically discuss religion with his parents but did not feel capable of fully bringing that discussion to fruition. Than shares in the interview that he grew up logically, scientific and taking an empirical view of things. Interestingly, Than does feel as though something he can't quite describe—something spiritual—is missing from his life. He is trying to eat right, exercise, do yoga and meditate to find it.

4.5. Religiously Disconnected

No participants self-identified as religiously disconnected. This finding is likely due to two major reasons. First, if the Religiously Disconnected truly make up only 5% of the emerging adult population they will be difficult to find. Second, the sampling strategy targeted people who had at least some concept of God. By the nature of this sampling approach, potential RDs who may have otherwise joined the study were excluded.

4.6. Irreligious

There was only one participant who self-identified as Irreligious, about 8% below what Smith and Snell predicted 2009. This participant, Fiona, identifies as Agnostic, which is in line with the Irreligious identity. She was raised Catholic by an atheist mother and a Catholic father who she describes, along with his side of the family, as "very Catholic". Up until age 8 there was a high degree of religious practices in the home. After her parents divorced those dropped off sharply. Her mother still dropped her off for Catechism class three times a week for twelve years. In response to the question about level of conflict between parents growing up Fiona states "(laugh). As worse as possibly could be [sic]. They are very happily divorced, so . . . they hate each other. They hated each other when I was little. Still hate each other". When the same question is applied to her mothers' on and off husbands she says "[M]y mom likes to get married for fun so she's like working on husband four right now. They all suck. My mom just has horrible taste in men. Like, none of them lasted long, [she] should never have gotten married". Conversations about religion in the home growing up were minimal beyond her mother pushing Fiona to go to church. Attending church was not particularly meaningful for Fiona, as all of the meetings were in Spanish, and she only spoke English. Given Fiona's family background, it is not a surprise she is now Irreligious as an emerging adult.

5. Discussion and Limitations

The purpose of this qualitative study was to explore and describe the family factors related to the six types of religiousness in emerging adulthood initially identified by Smith and Snell (2009) using a purposive sample of 49 college students from a large public university in the United States. A comparison of frequencies across samples and taking into account the different sampling methods the current sample distribution across types appears at least somewhat similar to the distribution theorized by previously (Smith and Snell 2009). The largest discrepancy in distributions is found within the CT category; a difference of 13% in favor of the current sample. Given the sampling strategy, with a focus on variability, it is counterintuitive to have CTs make up such a large proportion of the sample. The inflated CT proportion may be an artifact of an order effect. The CT summary statement was read first of all the options. However, if an order effect was at work we would expect the CT religious identity to be the largest group. Instead, SAs, the second available option, are the largest group. Furthermore, respondents were read all of the summary statements before respondents shared the statement that most closely aligns with their approach the religion. It may also be that some participants felt social pressure to choose a socially desirable response. While it may be impossible to know to what degree this occurred, if at all, the interviewers actively sought to emphasize the value neutral position of the interview procedure throughout the interview, attempting to allay such concerns. The high levels of CTs in the sample may also be related to the significant degree of racial and ethnic diversity and oversampling of females in the current sample. Approximately 40% of Smith and Snell's sample can be characterized as non-White and 50% male, while the current sample is 84% female and 60% non-White (Smith and Snell 2009, p. 319). As females and non-Whites tend towards greater levels of religiousness, these demographic differences by sample appear to be a plausible explanation of the CT discrepancy across samples (Denton and Culver 2015; PEW Research Center 2016). High levels of CTs and SAs may also be related to region of the country, as residents of Southern and Midwestern states consistently report higher levels of religiousness compared to residents from other regions in the United States (Lipka and Wormald 2016). Interestingly, 38% of CTs in the current sample reported no religious practices in the home growing up. This is somewhat similar to the high personal religion and low institutional religion of Adapters described by Denton 2012. The differences across RI, RD and IR are likely a combination of sampling strategy, availability in the population and willingness to declare an identity that may not be viewed socially acceptable. Family factors such as parental conflict, religious practices in the home and religious conversations were described for each religious identity, and themes emerged for those identities with sufficient data. CTs are Spiritually Certain and may have either an Unspoken Understanding of faith or alternately are on the receiving end of Radio Silence. SAs have the next lowest levels of parental conflict. They can experience quite a varying degree of religious practices as well as a wide variety in types of practices. Themes that emerged among SA religious discussions with parents included efforts of parents to exhort their offspring to Keep the Faith, as well as parents being seen as keepers of valuable religious knowledge as Sources of Wisdom. Unspoken Understanding, or the recognition of spiritually mature SAs, was found here as well. Just Basics captured parents sharing little, if any information about religious rituals and beliefs with their offspring. The timing and duration of religious discussions was described in the Childhood Limited or Lifetime theme. SOs came from family backgrounds with the third lowest parental conflict levels. Most came from families where the degree of religious practices was low or when higher were encouraged to find their own truth. Furthermore, religious conversations with parents of SOs lacked depth on the parent's side. The RI emerging adults in this sample all come from religious backgrounds but are now less invested and active in religion than their parents would like them to be. The Irreligious emerging adult has a forced Catholic background with high levels of parental conflict, divorce and parental religious heterogamy. When comparing religious practices in the home across religious identity types a few findings are of note. First, and in line with previous research, the religious identity types that entirely or partially endorse religion (i.e., CT and SA) reported the highest levels of religious practice (Myers 1996). Spiritually Open was largely characterized by low levels, while RI and I report high levels but only in childhood and often against their will. Parental conflict across the typology was also as expected and in line with previous research (Ellison et al. 2011), such that as endorsement of religion or spirituality increases, the level of parental conflict decreases across SO, SA and CT emerging adults and is high for Irreligious emerging adults. The patterns on family structure run largely counter to expectations, with SO and RI emerging adults growing up largely in nuclear families and only 57% of CT emerging adults being raised in a nuclear family. Nearly 30% of CTs report growing up in step families, which may account for the low levels of religious practices for that group as well. In line with Smith and Snell (2009), most CTs in this study were nondenominational or Christian, while SAs are largely Catholic. Also in line with previous research (2009), the SO category represented the largest concentration of Atheists, Agnostics and a variety of Christian and non-Christian religions whereas RI and I are largely Agnostic or Atheist. Catholics made up 44% of SAs. African Americans in this study were found in greatest proportions in the CT designation. This finding is in line with research suggesting that religion is highly important in the lives of African Americans (Taylor and Chatters 2010). SOs on the whole were almost exclusively Asian and White. It may be that culturally, Asian Americans may be predisposed towards the SO religious identity. SAs were mostly White and Latino, likely connected with the large Catholic presence identified earlier. The diversity of religious identities in conjunction with the racial and ethnic diversity is a strength. This study is not without limitations. First, the sample is largely of female emerging adults in college, recruited from a single university. A greater male presences may have rounded out the RI and I religious identities, providing substantial depth to the descriptions of each category. Second, these identities, including RD, may have been better represented with multi-site data collection across less religious regions of the country. Third, emerging adults not in college were not included in the sample. As non-attendance of college may impact religious and spiritual development, their exclusion likely biased the sample in favor of more religiously oriented identities. Though additionally limited due to the purposive sample, geographic restriction and small sample size, this study forwards descriptions of family related factors for five of the six types of religious identity specific to emerging adults.

6. Future Directions

Alternative sampling methods may yield frequency distributions by religious identity type that are more comparable to those set forth by (Smith and Snell 2009). Also, the current research design allowed for co-types (e.g., CT/SA), an area that is yet untouched. Another potentially fruitful future direction could be to explore how one's closeness to God fluctuates over time within and between each religious type. Another area of investigation may be delving into the CTs that reported no religious practices in the home growing up, as understanding this group may lead to a greater understanding of resiliency. The potential cultural connection between SO and Asian Americans may be particularly illuminating as well. Qualitative data analysis is of high utility, especially when attempting to address multidimensional constructs such as religiousness and identity. This study largely replicated the religious identity types in emerging adulthood initially identified by Smith and Snell (2009) and described the connection to and role of religious practices, religious discussions, parental conflict, race, ethnicity and family structure for five of the six types, expanding the understanding family contexts and processes for this innovative typology.

Funding: This research received no external funding.

Acknowledgments: I would like to thank the Editor, an anonymous reviewer, and Pamela Payne for their constructive and helpful comments on earlier drafts of this paper. I would also like to thank research assistants Emily Taylor and Kacey Titzer for their organizational contributions to this project.

Conflicts of Interest: The author declares no conflict of interest.

References

Arnett, Jeffrey. 2004. *Emerging Adulthood: The Winding Road from the Late Teens through the Twenties*. New York: Oxford University Press.

Arnett, Jeffrey Jensen. 2000. Emerging adulthood: A theory of development from the late teens through the twenties. *American Psychologist* 55: 469–80. [CrossRef] [PubMed]

Arnett, Jeffrey Jensen, and Lene Arnett Jensen. 2002. A congregation of one: Individualized religious beliefs among emerging adults. *Journal of Adolescent Research* 17: 451–67. [CrossRef]

Bengtson, Vern L. 2013. *Families and Faith: How Religion Is Passed down across Generations*. New York: Oxford University.

Boyatzis, Chris J., David C. Dollahite, and Loren D. Marks. 2006. The family as a context for religious and spiritual development in children and youth. In *The Handbook of Spiritual Development in Childhood and Adolescence*. Edited by E. C. Roehlkepartain, P. Ebstyne King, L. Wagener and P. L. Benson. Thousand Oaks: Sage, pp. 297–309.

Denton, Melinda Lundquist. 2012. Family structure, family disruption, and profiles of adolescent religiosity. *Journal for the Scientific Study of Religion* 51: 42–64. [CrossRef] [PubMed]

Denton, Melinda Lundquist, and Julian Culver. 2015. Family disruption and racial variation in adolescent and emerging adult religiosity. *Sociology of Religion* 76: 222–39. [CrossRef]

Dollahite, David C., and Jennifer Y. Thatcher. 2008. Talking about religion: How highly religious youth and parents discuss their faith. *Journal of Adolescent Research* 23: 611–41. [CrossRef]

Ecklund, Elaine H., and Jerry Z. Park. 2007. Religious diversity and community volunteerism among Asian Americans. *Journal for the Scientific Study of Religion* 46: 233–44. [CrossRef]

Ellison, Christopher G., Anthony B. Walker, Norval D. Glenn, and Elizabeth Marquardt. 2011. The effects of parental marital discord and divorce on the spiritual lives of young adults. *Social Science Research* 40: 538–51. [CrossRef]

Erikson, Erik H. 1963. *Childhood and Society*, 2nd ed. New York: Norton.

Gallo, Linda C., Frank Penedo, Karla Espinosa de los Monteros, and William Arguelles. 2009. Resiliency in the face of disadvantage: Do Hispanic cultural characteristics protect health outcomes? *Journal of Personality* 77: 1707–46. [CrossRef] [PubMed]

Gutierrez, Ian A., Lucas J Goodwin, and Jacqueline S. Mattis. 2014. Religious socialization in African American families: The relative influence of parents, grandparents, and siblings. *Journal of Family Psychology* 28: 779–89. [CrossRef] [PubMed]

Halgunseth, Linda C., Alexander C. Jensen, Kari-Lyn Sakuma, and Susan M. McHale. 2016. The role of mothers' and fathers' religiosity in African American adolescents' religious beliefs and practices. *Cultural Diversity and Ethnic Minority Psychology* 22: 386–94. [CrossRef] [PubMed]

Min, Joohong, Merril D. Silverstein, and Jessica P. Lendon. 2012. Intergenerational transmission of values over the family life course. *Advances in Life Course Research* 17: 112–20. [CrossRef]

Myers, Scott M. 1996. An interactive model of religiosity inheritance: The importance of family context. *American Sociological Review* 61: 858–66. [CrossRef]

National Center for Education Statistics. n.d. Status and Trends in the Education of Racial and Ethnic Groups. Available online: https://nces.ed.gov/programs/raceindicators/indicator_raa.asp (accessed on 21 February 2019).

Palinkas, Lawrence. A., Sarah M. Horwitz, Carla A. Green, Jennifer P. Wisdom, Naihua Duan, and Kimberly Hoagwood. 2015. Purposeful sampling for qualitative data collection and analysis in mixed method implementation research. *Administration and Policy in Mental Health* 42: 533–44. [CrossRef] [PubMed]

Park, Jerry Z., and Elaine Howard Ecklund. 2007. Negotiating continuity: Family and religious socialization for second-generation Asian Americans. *The Sociological Quarterly* 48: 93–118. [CrossRef]

Lipka, Michael, and Benjamin Wormald. 2016. How Religious Is Your State? Pew Research Center. Available online: http://www.pewresearch.org/fact-tank/2016/02/29/how-religious-is-your-state/?state=alabama (accessed on 1 March 2019).

PEW Research Center. n.d. Religious Landscape Study: Adults in Texas. Available online: http://www.pewforum.org/religious-landscape-study/state/texas/ (accessed on 1 March 2019).

PEW Research Center. 2016. The Gender Gap in Religion around the World: Women Are Generally More Religious than Men, Particularly among Christians. Available online: http://www.pewforum.org/2016/03/22/the-gender-gap-in-religion-around-the-world/ (accessed on 1 March 2019).

Petts, Richard J. 2015. Parental religiosity and youth religiosity: Variations by family structure. *Sociology of Religion* 76: 95–120. [CrossRef]

Petts, Richard J. 2012. Single mother's religious participation and early childhood behavior. *Journal of Marriage and Family* 74: 251–68. [CrossRef]

Petts, Richard J. 2009. Trajectories of religious participation from adolescence to young adulthood. *Journal for the Scientific Study of Religion* 48: 552–71. [CrossRef]

Smith, Christian, Melinda Lundquist Denton, Robert Faris, and Mark Regnerus. 2002. Mapping American adolescent religious participation. *Journal for the Scientific Study of Religion* 41: 597–612. [CrossRef]

Smith, Christian, and Melinda Lundquist Denton. 2005. *Soul Searching*. New York: Oxford University Press.

Smith, Christian, and Patricia Snell. 2009. *Souls in Transition: The Religious and Spiritual Lives of Emerging Adults*. New York: Oxford University Press.

Son, Daye, Braquel R. Egginton, Yaxin Lu, Amy L. Ai, Loren D. Marks, and David C. Dollahite. 2018. New Christians in a new land: Faith journeys of Asian American immigrant families. *Marriage & Family Review* 54: 648–61. [CrossRef]

Spilman, Sarah K., Tricia K. Neppl, M. Brent Donnellan, Thomas J. Schofield, and Rand D. Conger. 2013. Incorporating religiosity into a developmental model of positive family functioning across generations. *Developmental Psychology* 49: 762–74. [CrossRef]

Taylor, Robert Joseph, and Linda M. Chatters. 2010. Importance of religion and spirituality in the lives of African Americans, Caribbean Blacks, and Non-Hispanic Whites. *Journal of Negro Education* 79: 280–94.

Westoff, Charles F., and Emily A. Marshall. 2010. Hispanic fertility, religion and religiousness in the U.S. *Population Research and Policy Review* 29: 441–52. [CrossRef] [PubMed]

Zhai, Jiexia Elisa, Christopher G. Ellison, Norval D. Glenn, and Elizabeth Marquardt. 2007. Parental Divorce and Religious Involvement among Young Adults. *Sociology of Religion* 68: 125–44. [CrossRef]

Zhai, Jiexia Elisa, Christopher G. Ellison, Charles E. Stokes, and Norval D. Glenn. 2008. Spiritual, but Not Religious: The Impact of Parental Divorce on the Religious and Spiritual Identities of Young Adults in the United States. *Review of Religious Research* 49: 379–94.

religions

MDPI

Article

Religious Heterogamy and the Intergenerational Transmission of Religion: A Cross-National Analysis

Brian L. McPhail

Department of Sociology, Purdue University, 700 W. State Street, West Lafayette, IN 47907, USA;
bmcphail@purdue.edu

Received: 15 January 2019; Accepted: 11 February 2019; Published: 14 February 2019

check for
updates

Abstract: This study examines the effect of religious heterogamy on the transmission of religion from one generation to the next. Using data from 37 countries in the 2008 Religion III Module of the International Social Survey Programme (ISSP), I conduct a cross-national analysis of the relationship between parents' religious heterogamy and their adult childrens' religious lives. By estimating fixed effects regression models, I adjust for national-level confounders to examine patterns of association between having interreligious parents during childhood and level of adult religiosity as measured by self-rated religiousness, belief in God, and frequencies of religious attendance and prayer. The results indicate that having religiously heterogamous parents or parents with dissimilar religious attendance patterns are both associated with lower overall religiosity in respondents. Parents' religious attendance, however, mediates the relationship when each parent has a different religion. Having one unaffiliated parent is associated with lower religiosity regardless of parents' levels of religious attendance. The negative impact of parents' religious heterogamy on religious inheritance is independent of national-level factors and has implications for anticipating changes in the religious landscapes of societies characterized by religious diversity and growing numbers of interreligious marriages.

Keywords: religious heterogamy; parents; socialization; international; religiosity; religious affiliation; religious attendance

1. Introduction

For several decades, researchers have documented the profound and persistent influence of parents on the religious identities, beliefs, and behaviors of their children (Glass et al. 1986; Myers 1996; Sherkat 1998; Smith and Denton 2009; Bengtson 2013). Relatively little research, however, has examined the impact of religious heterogamy[1] on the religious development of children, and fewer still have explored the phenomenon of religious inheritance in other societies. This study extends the study of religious socialization[2] beyond the United States to conduct a cross-national investigation of the effect of religious heterogamy on the intergenerational transmission of religion. How does having interreligious parents during childhood impact an individual's later religiosity?

Prior studies in the U.S. have consistently found that parents who do not share the same religion produce less religious children than parents who do (Hoge and Petrillo 1978; Nelsen 1990; Myers 1996; Bengtson 2013). The primary question of this study is whether this effect holds across a variety of societal

---

[1] I use the terms religious heterogamy, religious intermarriage, and interreligious marriage interchangeably to refer to marriage in which spouses do not identify with the same religion.

[2] I use the terms religious socialization, religious inheritance, and the intergenerational transmission of religion interchangeably to refer to the phenomenon of children learning or adopting religious identities, beliefs, orientations, values, and/or practices from their parents.

contexts. The answer is not inconsequential. Religiously heterogamous marriages represent a nontrivial proportion of the married populations in many nations (see Figure 1). Furthermore, interreligious marriages have been growing, not only in the United States (Glenn 1982; McCutcheon 1988; Kalmijn 1991; Lehrer 1998; Rosenfeld 2008; Putnam and Campbell 2010; Pew Research Center 2016) but also around the world (see Figure 2) (O'Leary 2001; Voas 2003). If having religiously heterogamous parents is associated with lower levels of religiosity than having religiously homogamous parents, there are important implications for anticipating and understanding changes in the religious landscapes of societies characterized by religious diversity. Because a major factor in the growth or decline of religion in a society is the effectiveness of one generation to reproduce religion in the next generation (Voas 2003; Bisin et al. 2004; Bengtson et al. 2009; Bengtson 2013), there is a need to better understand the impact of having interreligious parents on the future religiosities of children from these families.

This study extends previous research on religious heterogamy by using cross-national data from the International Social Survey Programme (ISSP) to examine the effect of interreligious marriages on the transmission of religion from one generation to the next. I contrast having religiously heterogamous parents with having religiously homogamous parents to examine patterns of association with levels of adult religiosity as measured by self-rated religiousness, belief in God, and frequencies of religious attendance and prayer. Analyses suggest that the impact of parents' religious heterogamy on religious inheritance is independent of societal-level contextual factors. This finding contributes to the larger research project of examining family factors related to generational differences in religiosity, particularly in religiously diverse societies with rising levels of religious intermarriage.

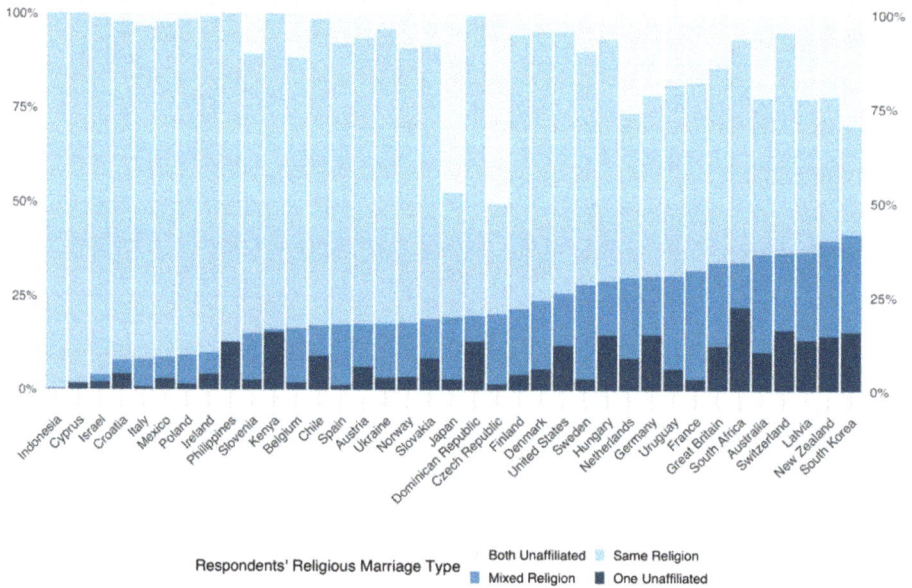

Figure 1. Percent religious heterogamy by country, ISSP 2008.

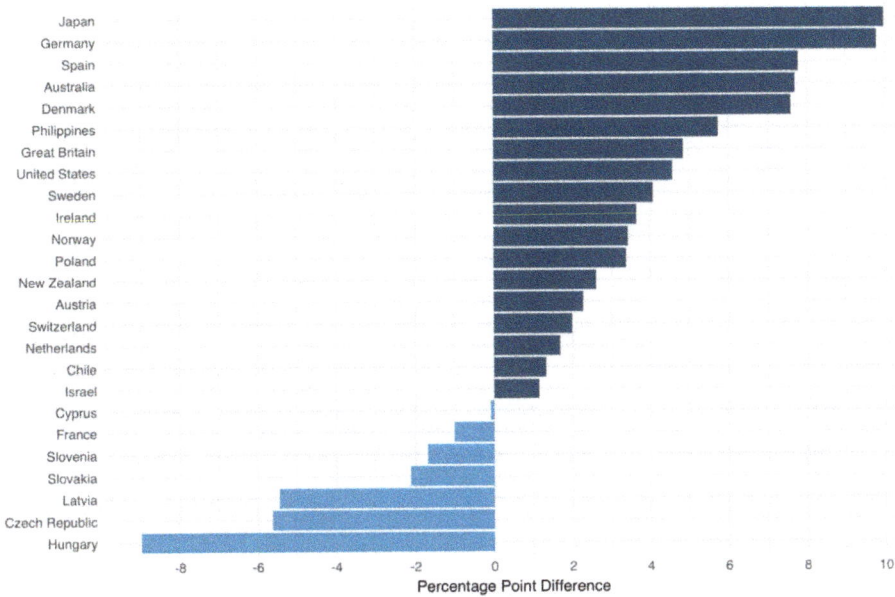

Figure 2. Percentage point change in religious heterogamy by country, ISSP 1998–2008.

2. Conceptual Framework

2.1. The Intergenerational Transmission of Religion

Parents are the most important social influence that shapes the religious lives of their children, both during adolescence and adulthood (Myers 1996; Regnerus et al. 2004; Smith and Denton 2009; Denton and Culver 2015). Other factors such as aging and life course events (i.e., marriage and parenthood), friend networks, spouse's religiosity, and recent religious experiences are also key determinants of adult religiosity (Roof and Hoge 1980; Willits and Crider 1989; Chaves 1991; Hoge et al. 1994; Wilson and Sherkat 1994; Stolzenberg et al. 1995; Regnerus et al. 2004), but parental religiosity remains the strongest predictor overall. To explain the mechanisms by which religious beliefs, values, and behaviors are transmitted, reinforced, and reproduced across generations, several major theoretical explanations exist in the literature on religious socialization: (1) Parents model religion that their children imitate, (2) parents channel their children into religious institutions, environments, and social networks where religion is reinforced, and (3) positive affective relationships between parents and children facilitate religious inheritance.

The first explanation, which stems from social learning theory, theorizes that human beings learn religious behavior primarily through modeling: children observe and imitate the behavior of others (i.e., parents) in their social context (Bandura and Walters 1977). Therefore, parents who practice religion more often or who emphasize religion in the home produce children who are more religious (Hunsberger and Brown 1984; Willits and Crider 1989; Myers 1996; Bengtson et al. 2009; Smith and Denton 2009).

The second explanation, the channeling hypothesis, claims that parents indirectly socialize their children into religion by "channeling" them into social institutions and environments where religious values are reinforced (Himmelfarb 1980). Taking children to religious services or venues, sending children to religious schools, and introducing children to peer networks are all ways that parents "channel" them into social situations where they learn religion. Several studies suggest that peer networks and religious communities have a greater influence on the religious development of individuals than previously acknowledged (Cornwall 1989; Erickson 1992; Martin et al. 2003; Regnerus et al. 2004).

The third explanation argues that the degree of parental affection and the quality of family relationships moderate the influence of parental religiosity on the religiosity of children. The greater the affection and the stronger the social bonds in the family, the more effective parents are at transmitting religion (Bengtson et al. 2002). The quality of the relationship between parents and children (Hoge and Petrillo 1978; Clark and Worthington 1990; Myers 1996; Sherkat 1998; Bengtson et al. 2002; Smith and Denton 2009; Bengtson 2013; Denton and Culver 2015) and between the parents themselves (Myers 1996; Lawton and Bures 2001; Regnerus et al. 2004; Copen and Silverstein 2007; Zhai et al. 2007) strongly predict the future religiosity of children.

Although most research on religious socialization has focused on factors within the family context, a few notable studies evidence the significant influence of the societal context on the transmission of religion across generations. Kelley and Graaf (1997) found that a nation's religious environment significantly impacts the effectiveness of parents' religious socialization of their children: Family religiosity more strongly influences an individual's religious life in more secular nations than in more religious nations. A follow-up study also demonstrated that national contexts with high levels of income inequality allow religion to be more easily transmitted from parents to children; however, former socialist nations increase socialization costs while nations with high economic development do not significantly impact religious socialization efforts (Müller et al. 2014).

2.2. Religious Heterogamy

Heterogamy commonly refers to marriage in which partners differ on some attribute (e.g., race, education). Religious heterogamy, then, implies marriage in which spouses do not identify with the same religion. This can take several forms. Spouses can either each identify with a different religion or one spouse can identify with a religion while the other does not. Some U.S.-based studies have even explored denominational heterogamy in which partners are identified as belonging to two different Protestant denominations (Curtis and Ellison 2002; Petts and Knoester 2007; Bengtson 2013). For the purposes of this international study, however, I operationalize religious heterogamy as any observation in which a respondent and his/her spouse do not identify with the same of 11 broad religion categories of the ISSP (ISSP Research Group 2012). Alternative to examining spousal differences in religious affiliation, some researchers have explored other forms of religious dissimilarity in which partners differ in other aspects of their religious lives such as religious beliefs, participation, or practices (Call and Heaton 1997; Ellison and Sherkat 1999; Curtis and Ellison 2002; Wilcox and Wolfinger 2008; Vaaler et al. 2009; Mahoney 2010).

Although religious homogamy is still predominant in most societies, religious heterogamy is increasingly common. Figure 1 illustrates the percentage of married respondents in religiously heterogamous marriages from each country in the 2008 ISSP dataset. Countries are rank ordered by the percentage of respondents that do not share the same religious affiliation with their partners, either because each partner has a different religious affiliation or because one partner is religiously unaffiliated. Of the 37 countries included, 29 have greater than 10 percent religious heterogamy and 14 have greater than 25 percent religious heterogamy. Furthermore, the phenomenon of religious heterogamy is growing, not only in the United States (Glenn 1982; McCutcheon 1988; Kalmijn 1991; Lehrer 1998; Sherkat 2004; Rosenfeld 2008; Putnam and Campbell 2010; Pew Research Center 2016) but also around the world (O'Leary 2001; Voas 2003). Figure 2 shows that among the 25 countries included in both the 1998 and 2008 ISSP Religion modules, more than half had a greater than 2.5 percentage point increase in religious heterogamy over that 10-year period.[3]

---

[3] The decreases in religious heterogamy in the Czech Republic, Latvia, Slovakia, and France since 1998 is associated with increases in the percentage of respondents reporting that both they and their spouses are both religiously unaffiliated.

2.3. Religious Heterogamy and the Intergenerational Transmission of Religion

Early studies of denominational heterogamy in the U.S. found that individuals with parents who did not belong to the same religious denomination were less religious overall than individuals with parents who did (Anders 1955; Putney and Middleton 1961; Havens 1964; Hoge and Petrillo 1978). More recent studies confirm these earlier findings, showing that having religiously heterogamous parents is negatively associated with religiosity compared to having religiously homogamous parents (Nelsen 1990; Myers 1996; Bengtson 2013). Furthermore, compared to having parents who identify with two separate religions, having one parent who is religiously unaffiliated is related to even lower levels of religiousness (Nelsen 1990).

Several possible explanations can account for the relationship between parental religious heterogamy and weaker religious socialization outcomes. First, religious heterogamy is associated with lower levels of overall religiosity (Williams and Lawler 2002; Pew Research Center 2016) and less frequent religious practice among marriage partners themselves (Petersen 1986; Petts and Knoester 2007; Pew Research Center 2016). Additionally, religious intermarriage is associated with greater likelihood of eventual religious disaffiliation by one or more partners (Sherkat 1991; Voas 2003), less emphasis on religion in the home (Williams and Lawler 2002; Pew Research Center 2016), and less frequent prayer or reading of scripture with children (Pew Research Center 2016). If interreligious parents are less religious themselves, then social learning theory predicts corresponding lower levels of religiosity among their children.

Second, religiously heterogamous parents are less likely to "channel" their children into religious environments where they can learn religion. Interreligious parents report participating in fewer religious activities with their children (e.g., attending worship services) than religiously homogamous parents (Petts and Knoester 2007; Pew Research Center 2016). Recent survey evidence also indicates that they are less likely to send children to religious education activities or to a religious school (Pew Research Center 2016).

Third, interreligious couples are more likely to experience interpersonal conflict or marital instability (Myers 1996; Call and Heaton 1997; Curtis and Ellison 2002; Petts and Knoester 2007; Wright et al. 2017). These disrupt the affective bonds of the family that are believed to facilitate effective religious socialization (Bengtson et al. 2002; Bengtson 2013). Parents with greater marital happiness and marital stability produce children with higher levels of religiosity (Myers 1996; Copen and Silverstein 2007; Zhai et al. 2007). Religious heterogamy (Glenn 1982; Heaton 1984) and dissimilarity in religious attendance patterns (Heaton and Pratt 1990), however, are associated with decreased happiness and satisfaction in marriage. In addition, interreligious marriages and couples with other significant differences in religious participation or theological beliefs are more likely to experience higher levels of marital conflict (Chinitz and Brown 2001; Curtis and Ellison 2002; Petts and Knoester 2007) and are more likely to end in divorce (Heaton and Pratt 1990; Lehrer and Chiswick 1993; Kalmijn et al. 2005).

3. Hypotheses

The conceptual framework and prior research lead to the following hypotheses.

Hypothesis 1. *Having parents who each have a different religious affiliation will be negatively associated with respondent religiosity compared to having parents who share the same religious affiliation.*

Hypothesis 2. *Having one religiously unaffiliated parent will be negatively associated with respondent religiosity compared to having parents who share the same religious affiliation.*

Hypothesis 3. *Having one religiously unaffiliated parent will be negatively associated with respondent religiosity compared to having parents who each have a different religious affiliation.*

Hypothesis 4. *Having parents who attended religious services at different frequency levels will be negatively associated with respondent religiosity compared to having parents who attended religious services at the same frequency level.*

Hypothesis 5. *The relationship between parental religious heterogamy and respondent religiosity will be partially mediated by parental religious attendance.*

4. Data and Methods

4.1. Sample

The data in this analysis come from the 2008 Religion III Module of the International Social Survey Programme (ISSP). Each year, the ISSP, which is a consortium of survey agencies in member countries, prepare a module of questions that are fielded either as an individual survey or alongside a regular national survey. For the 2008 ISSP Religion III Module, a total of 59,986 respondents ages 18 years and older[4] in 40 member nations were interviewed about their religious affiliations, beliefs, practices, traditions, and attitudes. This module was also administered in four non-ISSP member countries (Indonesia, Kenya, Sri Lanka, and Tanzania) and is published as a separate dataset. To increase the representation of non-Western societies in the analysis, the data from these four countries (N = 6697) were appended for these analyses. The sampling strategies (simple random and multi-stage stratified) and mode of data collection (face-to-face interviews, self-completed mail surveys, and phone interviews) varied by nation. For additional information on the ISSP and the 2008 Religion III Module, including sampling procedures, modes of data collection, and response rates, see ISSP Research Group (2012).

Information on key variables was not available for some respondents, because some questions were not included on the survey fielded in Portugal (urbanity), Venezuela (marital status and parents' religious attendance), Turkey (marital status), Taiwan (children in the household), and Sri Lanka (respondent's religious attendance). Additionally, more than 40 percent of respondents in Tanzania and Russia did not provide responses for parents' religious attendance. Because there is no information or not enough information on these key variables, all observations from these 7 countries were excluded from the analyses. After dropping these countries, approximately 3 percent of respondents had no mother and/or no father present in the home as a child; therefore, these were excluded as well. About 11 percent of respondents either did not know or refused to answer the survey question about the religious attendance of at least one of their parents. After the list-wise deletion of these cases with missing responses, my final analysis sample size was 41,941 from 37 nations.

4.2. Respondent Religiosity

The dependent variable in this analysis is a measure of the overall religiosity of the respondents, which I operationalize using a standardized scale comprised of four ISSP survey items: self-identification as religious, belief in God, and the frequencies of religious attendance and prayer (Schwadel 2015). In the ISSP self-identification as religious is measured using a 7-point index ranging from "extremely nonreligious" to "extremely religious." Belief in God is measured using a 6-point index ranging from "I don't believe in God" to "I know God really exists and I have no doubts about it." The frequencies of religious service attendance and prayer are both measured using a 9-point index ranging from "never" to "several times a week." To obtain a measure of overall religiosity, I standardized each of these variables by converting the values to z-scores, then summed them and

---

[4] Five nations included respondents younger than 18: Finland (15), South Africa (16), Japan (16), Russia (16), and Sweden (17).

standardized the total so that the overall religiosity scale has a mean of 0 and a standard deviation of 1. Cronbach's alpha for this scale is 0.86.

4.3. Parental Religious Heterogamy and Religious Attendance

In this analysis, the focal independent variables are a measure of parents' religious marriage type when respondents were children and a measure of similarity in parents' religious attendance. The first uses the religious affiliation combination of the respondents' fathers and mothers to categorize their religious marriage type. The ISSP asks respondents to indicate the religious preference of both their fathers and mothers when the respondents were children and then recodes these preferences into 11 categories: "None," "Roman Catholic," "Protestant," "Christian Orthodox," "Jewish," "Islam," "Buddhism," "Hinduism," "Other Christian Religions," "Other Eastern Religions," and "Other Religions." Using these 11 religious affiliation categories for respondents' fathers and mothers, I construct a new nominal variable in which the marriages of respondents' parents are compared and categorized into four categories: "Same Religion," "Mixed Religion," "One Unaffiliated," and "Both Unaffiliated." The "Same Religion" category is the reference group. Parents who have two different religious affiliations (Mixed Religion) and parents in which one is religiously unaffiliated are both a form of parental religious heterogamy and are analyzed as separate categories in the models that follow.

The second measure, parents' religious attendance, compares the religious practice of the respondents' two parents. Although the frequency of religious attendance is not an ideal cross-cultural measure of religious practice, it is the only measure of parents' religious practice in the 2008 ISSP Religion III Module. The ISSP asks respondents to indicate the frequency of their fathers' and mothers' religious attendance when the respondents were children. These items were measured using a 7-point index ranging from "Never" to "Several times a week." I recoded the religious attendance of both the respondents' fathers and mothers into three categories: "High" (at least once per month), "Low" (less than once per month), and "Never" (less than once per year). Then I created a new nominal variable with six religious attendance combinations of the respondents' parents: "High-High," "High-Low," "High-Never," "Low-Low," "Low-Never," and "Never-Never." For example, the category "High-Low" indicates that a respondent had one parent who attended at least once per month and one parent who attended less than once per month. The "High-High" category is the reference group.

4.4. Sociodemographic Control Variables

To control for other factors that might have a confounding influence on the association between the religiosity of the respondents and their parents, I include the following indicator variables: gender (woman = 1), university degree (university degree = 1), marital status (married = 1), and the presence of at least one child in the household (children in household = 1)[5]. The models also include indicator variables that control for urban and suburban locations with town/rural as the reference category. Age is a continuous measure ranging from 15–89 years. All respondents 89 years old or older were recoded into the 89 years old category because the U.S. survey pooled older respondents in this way. To account for non-linearities in the effect of age on religiosity, the models also include an age-squared term.

4.5. Analytic Strategy

To examine the associations between parental religious heterogamy and respondent religiosity, I test my hypotheses using fixed effects regression models. Because the aim of this study is to examine the effect of an individual-level characteristic (parental religious heterogamy) on an individual-level outcome (respondent religiosity), a fixed effects approach allows me to estimate this effect, while

---

[5] The respondent may not necessarily be the parent of the child/children in the household.

simultaneously controlling for all observed and unobserved country-level characteristics that might confound the relationship between parental religious heterogamy and respondent religiosity. Prior studies show that the economic, political, and social characteristics of a society impact processes of religious socialization (Kelley and Graaf 1997; Müller et al. 2014). Using fixed effects models, I can adjust for these and other national-level differences—such as political climate, social norms, or levels of religious tolerance—that may bias the estimates. In these analyses, I first estimate separate fixed effects models with controls for parents' religious marriage type (religious affiliation) and parents' religious attendance. Then, I estimate a model that includes both the parents' religious marriage type and parents' religious attendance to test whether parental attendance mediates the relationship between parents' religious marriage type and respondent religiosity.

5. Results

Descriptive statistics of all variables are shown in Table 1. About 83 percent of the final analysis sample (N = 41,941 individual respondents in 37 countries) had parents who shared the same religious affiliation, 4 percent had parents with two different affiliations, 6 percent had one unaffiliated parent, and 7 percent had two unaffiliated parents. About 22 percent of the sample reported having parents who attended religious services at different frequencies (High-Low, High-Never, Low-Never), while 45 percent reported having parents who both attended at least once per month (High-High). The final analysis sample is 55 percent women, 56 percent married, and 43 percent urban or suburban residents. Forty-two percent live in a household with children, 16 percent have a university degree, and the average age of respondents is about 46 years old.

Table 1. Descriptive statistics.

Variables	Mean/Prop.	SD	Min.	Max.
Dependent Variable				
Overall Religiosity Score	0.00	1.00	−2.00	1.58
Independent Variables				
Parents' Religious Marriage Type				
Same Religion *	0.83		0	1
Mixed Religion	0.04		0	1
One Unaffiliated	0.06		0	1
Both Unaffiliated	0.07		0	1
Parents' Religious Attendance				
Never-Never	0.17		0	1
Low-Never	0.07		0	1
Low-Low	0.16		0	1
High-Never	0.06		0	1
High-Low	0.09		0	1
High-High *	0.45		0	1
Sociodemographic Controls				
Age	45.96	17.07	15.00	89.00
University Degree	0.16		0	1
Woman	0.55		0	1
Married	0.56		0	1
Has Children in Household	0.42		0	1
Location				
Urban	0.30		0	1
Suburban	0.13		0	1
Town/Rural *	0.58		0	1

N = 41,941 in 37 countries; * Used as reference category.

Table 2 presents the results of the fixed effects regression models of respondent religiosity, adjusting for both individual-level control variables and all potential observed and unobserved national-level confounders. Consistent with Hypotheses 1 and 2, Model 1 indicates that respondents with religiously heterogamous parents during childhood score significantly lower on the overall religiosity scale than respondents with religiously homogamous parents. Individuals with mixed religion parents ($b = -0.104$) and one unaffiliated parent ($b = -0.404$) are less religious than individuals with parents who had the same religious affiliation (both $p < 0.001$). Model 1 also suggests that having one unaffiliated parent is associated with significantly lower levels of religiosity than having mixed religion parents. Supporting Hypothesis 3, supplementary analyses (not shown) confirm this pattern ($p < 0.001$). Figure 3, which presents predicted values on the religiosity scale for individuals with each parental marriage type, illustrates these relationships. Respondents with mixed religion parents have average levels of religiosity, while respondents with one unaffiliated parent have significantly below- z levels of religiosity.

Table 2. Results from fixed effects regression models predicting respondent religiosity.

Variable	1		2		3	
	b	**SE**	*b*	**SE**	*b*	**SE**
Parents' Religious Marriage Type						
Mixed Religion	−0.104 ***	(0.019)			0.028	(0.018)
One Unaffiliated	−0.404 ***	(0.016)			−0.125 ***	(0.016)
Both Unaffiliated	−0.817 ***	(0.016)			−0.329 ***	(0.017)
Parents' Religious Attendance						
Never-Never			−1.063 ***	(0.011)	−0.961 ***	(0.012)
Low-Never			−0.756 ***	(0.015)	−0.728 ***	(0.016)
Low-Low			−0.531 ***	(0.011)	−0.525 ***	(0.011)
High-Never			−0.460 ***	(0.016)	−0.429 ***	(0.017)
High-Low			−0.250 ***	(0.013)	−0.250 ***	(0.013)
Sociodemographic Controls						
Age	−0.006 ***	(0.001)	−0.005 ***	(0.001)	−0.005 ***	(0.001)
Age^2	0.000 ***	(0.000)	0.000 ***	(0.000)	0.000 ***	(0.000)
University Degree	−0.045 ***	(0.011)	−0.067 ***	(0.010)	−0.063 ***	(0.010)
Woman	0.280 ***	(0.008)	0.285 ***	(0.007)	0.283 ***	(0.007)
Married	0.113 ***	(0.009)	0.097 ***	(0.008)	0.096 ***	(0.008)
Children in Household	0.065 ***	(0.009)	0.064 ***	(0.008)	0.064 ***	(0.008)
Urban	−0.099 ***	(0.009)	−0.075 ***	(0.009)	−0.073 ***	(0.009)
Suburban	−0.065 ***	(0.012)	−0.051 ***	(0.011)	−0.046 ***	(0.011)
Constant	−0.210 ***	(0.029)	0.076 **	(0.028)	0.098 ***	(0.028)
R^2	0.142		0.255		0.262	

$N = 41,941$; ** $p < 0.01$, *** $p < 0.001$.

Model 2 shows that dissimilarity in parents' attendance patterns also has a significant negative effect on respondent religiosity, adjusting for individual-level factors and all observed and unobserved national-level confounders. Respondents whose parents had High-Low ($b = -0.250$), High-Never ($b = -0.460$), and Low-Never ($b = -0.756$) attendance patterns are significantly less religious overall than respondents whose two parents both attended religious services at least once a month (High-High; all $p < 0.001$). Supplementary analyses (not shown) confirm that respondents whose parents had a Low-Never attendance pattern are significantly less religious than respondents whose parents had a Low-Low attendance pattern ($p < 0.001$). Respondents, however, with only one parent who attended once per month (High-Low, High-Never) are more religious overall than respondents whose parents both attended but less than once per month (Low-Low; both $p < 0.001$). Figure 4 shows the predicted values of respondent religiosity for each pattern of parents' religious attendance. Consistent with Hypothesis 4, having only one parent who attends at least once a month is associated with lower respondent religiosity than having two parents who attend at least once a month, and having only one parent who attends more than once per year is associated with lower respondent religiosity than having two parents who attend more than once per year.

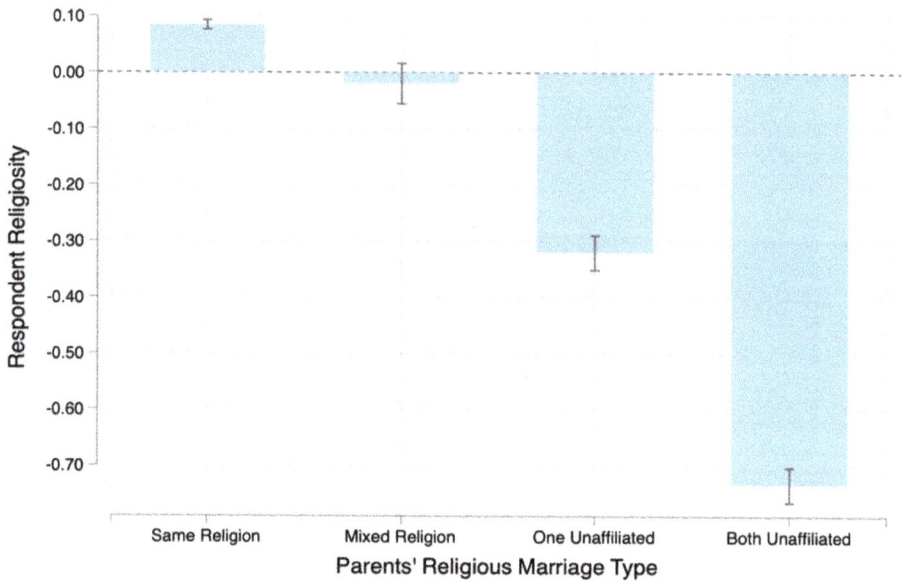

Figure 3. Predicted values of respondent religiosity by parents' religious affiliation combination. Values less than 0 indicate below-average respondent religiosity.

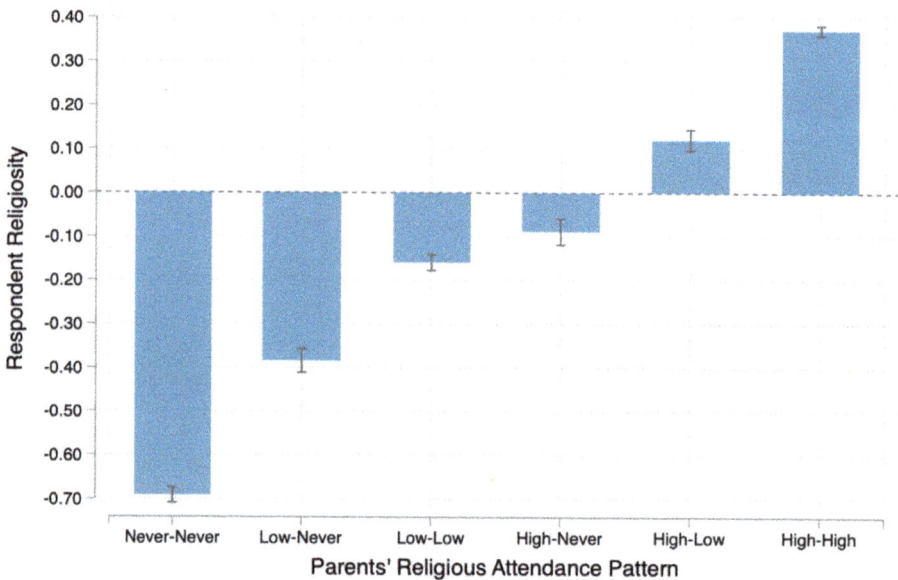

Figure 4. Predicted values of respondent religiosity by parents' religious attendance pattern. Values less than 0 indicate below-average respondent religiosity.

Results assessing whether parents' religious attendance patterns mediate the effect of parents' religious affiliation on the overall religiosity of the respondents are presented in Model 3. Separate tests for mediation indicate support for Hypothesis 5, confirming that parents' religious attendance fully mediates the negative effect of having parents with two different religious affiliations on respondent religiosity and partially mediates the negative effect of having one unaffiliated parent on respondent religiosity (both $p < 0.001$). Figure 5 illustrates that after accounting for parents' religious attendance levels there is no statistical difference in the religiosity levels of respondents with same religion parents and mixed religion parents. Both are associated with above-average levels of religiosity. Having parents with two different religious affiliations is only indirectly associated with lower levels of religiosity as this association is attributable to lower levels of religious attendance among parents who have two different religions. However, as Figure 5 also shows, having one unaffiliated parent is still associated with lower levels of religiosity even when adjusting for parents' levels of religious attendance. Parental religious attendance only partially accounts for the difference in religiosity between respondents with parents of the same religion and respondents with one unaffiliated parent.

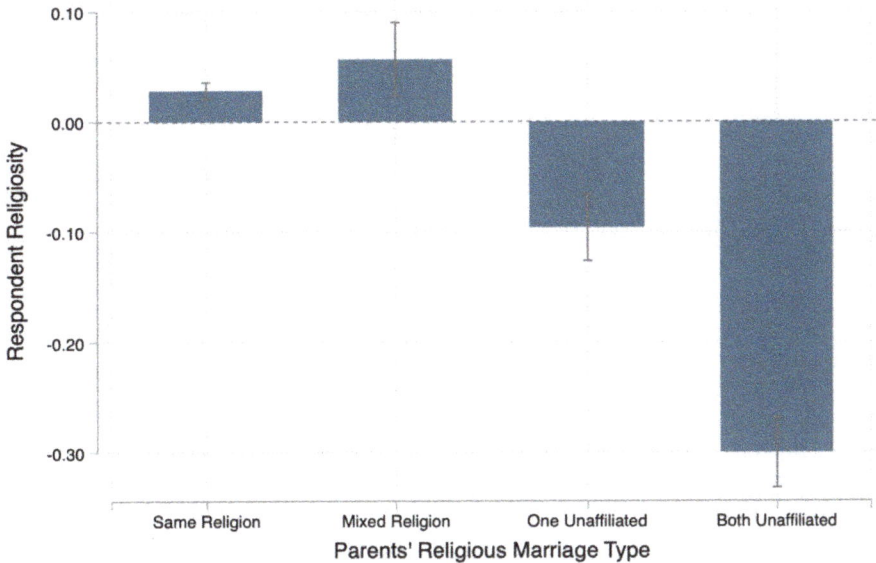

Figure 5. Predicted values of respondent religiosity by parents' religious affiliation combination adjusted for parents' religious attendance. Values less than 0 indicate below-average respondent religiosity.

6. Discussion and Conclusions

Using cross-national data from the 2008 ISSP Religion III Module, this study examined the effect of religious heterogamy on the intergenerational transmission of religion. Results confirm prior research (Hoge and Petrillo 1978; Nelsen 1990; Myers 1996; Bengtson 2013) but extend our understanding of religious socialization processes by demonstrating that the negative association between having interreligious parents during childhood and levels of religiosity in adulthood is independent of national-level factors. Using fixed effects regression models, which adjust for country-level contextual factors, these analyses provide evidence that having parents who do not share the same religious affiliation is associated with lower overall religiosity in individuals across a variety of social contexts (Kelley and Graaf 1997; Müller et al. 2014). Prior studies on the association between parental religious heterogamy and personal religiosity have been limited to predominantly Christian societies in the West. The present study has demonstrated that the negative association found in previous research is not an exclusively Western phenomenon but is independent of societal context. These analyses find a clear pattern that cannot be accounted for by contextual differences (i.e., social, economic, political, cultural) between respondents. Individuals with parents who identify with two different religions are less religious as adults than individuals with parents who identify with the same religion, and individuals with one unaffiliated parent are less religious than individuals with parents who identify with two different religions. Consistent with the religious socialization literature, this finding highlights the strength of the influence that parents have on the later religiosity of their children. Two parents who share the same religion are more effective at transmitting religion to their children than parents who have different religions.

This study has also demonstrated that parents' religious attendance mediates the relationship between parental religious heterogamy and lower levels of adult religiosity. In agreement with prior studies on the religiosity of interreligious couples (Petersen 1986; Williams and Lawler 2002; Petts and Knoester 2007; Pew Research Center 2016) and the importance of parents' religious activity on religious inheritance (Hunsberger and Brown 1984; Willits and Crider 1989; Myers 1996; Bengtson et al. 2009; Smith and Denton 2009; Bengtson 2013; Petts 2015), the results from this study indicate that individuals whose parents identify with two different religions are less religious because their parents attend religious services less frequently. Religious attendance also partially accounts for lower religiosity among individuals who had one unaffiliated parent during childhood. This finding supports the explanation of social learning theory that children learn religion by imitating the behavior modeled by their parents (Bandura and Walters 1977). Because interreligious parents participate in religion less frequently, they model religion less intensely for their children.

This study also has important implications for anticipating and understanding changes in the religious landscapes of societies characterized by religious diversity and increasing levels of religious heterogamy. Researchers have identified the effectiveness of one generation to reproduce religion in the next generation as a major factor in the growth or decline of religion in a society (Voas 2003; Bisin et al. 2004; Bengtson et al. 2009; Bengtson 2013). Numerous social factors such as parents' religiosity, parents' education, quality of family relationships, family structures, the role of grandparents, and participation in religious communities affect the reproduction of religion across generations (Myers 1996; Bengtson 2013). As this study demonstrates, parental religious heterogamy and dissimilarity in religious participation are additional factors that significantly impact the transmission of religion from parents to children. As the number of interreligious marriages changes in a given society, we can anticipate generational changes in the overall religious characteristics of that society. As we try to better understand the determinants and trends of religiosity in society, more attention should be paid to the role of families and the social factors that influence religious inheritance.

Several important limitations to this study warrant mention. First, these analyses were constrained to using self-identification as religious, belief in God, and the frequencies of religious attendance and prayer to measure religiosity. Because these conventional measures may not adequately capture the religiosities of individuals in non-Abrahamic faiths, non-Western contexts, or interreligious families (Traphagan 2005; Arweck and Nesbitt 2010; Seamon 2012; Tanaka 2010; Chao and Yang 2018), improved measures are needed for future studies of religiously diverse populations. For interreligious families in particular, what is interpreted as "less" religious on these conventional religiosity measures might be better understood as "differently" religious. Field studies exploring the complexities of religious life in religious intermarriages have argued that the terms *religious transformation* and *multiculturalism* more accurately characterize these families, who are believed to be representative of broader changes in the religious environments of religiously diverse societies (Arweck and Nesbitt 2010; Seamon 2012).

Second, societies that are not predominantly Christian and societies from Asia, Africa, and South America are underrepresented in the ISSP data set. Although the findings here suggest that religious heterogamy impacts religious socialization in similar ways across societies, more research is needed to better understand processes of religious inheritance in regions outside of Europe and North America and in regions where Christianity is not the dominant religion. Data for additional countries would provide stronger support for the findings presented here.

Third, the ISSP 2008 dataset includes little information about respondents' parents or about other characteristics of the respondents' families. Religious socialization literature proposes numerous family characteristics that affect the transmission of religion from parents to children (Myers 1996; Bengtson 2013).

For example, prior findings show that parents' marital stability significantly weakens the transmission of religion to children (Zhai et al. 2007; Ellison et al. 2011; Uecker and Ellison 2012) and that religiously heterogamous marriages are less stable than religiously homogamous marriages (Heaton and Pratt 1990; Lehrer and Chiswick 1993; Call and Heaton 1997; Kalmijn et al. 2005; Wright et al. 2017). Information about parents' marital status and other family characteristics was not available in the 2008 ISSP dataset but should be included in future studies as important confounders.

Despite these limitations, the current study contributes to our understanding of the relationship between religious heterogamy and the intergenerational transmission of religion. Although previous research has demonstrated the negative association between having interreligious parents and an individual's religiosity, this study is the first to examine whether this relationship is independent of national-level social, political, or economic factors and, therefore, generalizable across societies. The findings presented here not only indicate that religiously heterogamous parents produce weaker religious socialization outcomes than religiously homogamous parents but also that this relationship exists across nations and is independent of contextual factors. Evidence also suggests that lower levels of parental religious attendance fully account for this difference when each parent identifies with a different religion. Future research should further explore the mechanisms (i.e., modeling, channeling, affective bonds) of parents' religious influence on their children, how these mechanisms are impacted by religious heterogamy, and how these relationships might differ across societies and religious groups.

Funding: This research received no external funding.

Conflicts of Interest: The author declares no conflict of interest.

References

Anders, Sarah F. 1955. Religious Behavior of Church Families. *Marriage and Family Living* 17: 54–57. [CrossRef]

Arweck, Elisabeth, and Eleanor Nesbitt. 2010. Plurality at Close Quarters: Mixed-Faith Families in the UK. *Journal of Religion in Europe* 3: 155–82. [CrossRef]

Bandura, Albert, and Richard H. Walters. 1977. *Social Learning Theory*. Upper Saddle River: Prentice-Hall.

Bengtson, Vern L. 2013. *Families and Faith: How Religion Is Passed down across Generations*. Oxford: Oxford University Press.

Bengtson, Vern L., Timothy J. Biblarz, and Robert E. L. Roberts. 2002. *How Families Still Matter: A Longitudinal Study of Youth in Two Generations*. Cambridge: Cambridge University Press.

Bengtson, Vern L., Casey E. Copen, Norella M. Putney, and Merril Silverstein. 2009. A Longitudinal Study of the Intergenerational Transmission of Religion. *International Sociology* 24: 325–45. [CrossRef]

Bisin, Alberto, Giorgio Topa, and Thierry Verdier. 2004. Religious Intermarriage and Socialization in the United States. *Journal of Political Economy* 112: 615–64. [CrossRef]

Call, Vaughn R. A., and Tim B. Heaton. 1997. Religious Influence on Marital Stability. *Journal for the Scientific Study of Religion* 36: 382–92. [CrossRef]

Chao, L. Luke, and Fenggang Yang. 2018. Measuring Religiosity in a Religiously Diverse Society: The China Case. *Social Science Research* 74: 187–95. [CrossRef] [PubMed]

Chaves, Mark. 1991. Family Structure and Protestant Church Attendance: The Sociological Basis of Cohort and Age Effects. *Journal for the Scientific Study of Religion* 30: 501–14. [CrossRef]

Chinitz, Joshua G., and Robert A. Brown. 2001. Religious Homogamy, Marital Conflict, and Stability in Same-Faith and Interfaith Jewish Marriages. *Journal for the Scientific Study of Religion* 40: 723–33. [CrossRef]

Clark, Cynthia A., and Everett L. Worthington. 1990. *Family Variables Affecting the Transmission of Religious Values from Parents to Adolescents: A Review*. Lanham: University Press of America.

Copen, Casey, and Merril Silverstein. 2007. Transmission of Religious Beliefs Across Generations: Do Grandparents Matter? *Journal of Comparative Family Studies* 38: 497–510.

Cornwall, Marie. 1989. The Determinants of Religious Behavior: A Theoretical Model and Empirical Test. *Social Forces* 68: 572–92. [CrossRef]

Curtis, Kristen Taylor, and Christopher G. Ellison. 2002. Religious Heterogamy and Marital Conflict: Findings from the National Survey of Families and Households. *Journal of Family Issues* 23: 551–76. [CrossRef]

Denton, Melinda Lundquist, and Julian Culver. 2015. Family Disruption and Racial Variation in Adolescent and Emerging Adult Religiosity. *Sociology of Religion; Washington* 76: 222–39. [CrossRef]

Ellison, Christopher G., and Darren E. Sherkat. 1999. Identifying the Semi-Involuntary Institution: A Clarification. *Social Forces* 78: 793–802. [CrossRef]

Ellison, Christopher G., Anthony B. Walker, Norval D. Glenn, and Elizabeth Marquardt. 2011. The Effects of Parental Marital Discord and Divorce on the Religious and Spiritual Lives of Young Adults. *Social Science Research* 40: 538–51. [CrossRef]

Erickson, Joseph A. 1992. Adolescent Religious Development and Commitment: A Structural Equation Model of the Role of Family, Peer Group, and Educational Influences. *Journal for the Scientific Study of Religion* 31: 131–52. [CrossRef]

Glass, Jennifer, Vern L. Bengtson, and Charlotte Chorn Dunham. 1986. Attitude Similarity in Three-Generation Families: Socialization, Status Inheritance, or Reciprocal Influence? *American Sociological Review* 51: 685–98. [CrossRef]

Glenn, Norval D. 1982. Interreligious Marriage in the United States: Patterns and Recent Trends. *Journal of Marriage and Family* 44: 555–66. [CrossRef]

Havens, Joseph. 1964. A Study of Religious Conflict in College Students. *The Journal of Social Psychology* 64: 77–87. [CrossRef] [PubMed]

Heaton, Tim B. 1984. Religious Homogamy and Marital Satisfaction Reconsidered. *Journal of Marriage and the Family* 46: 729–33. [CrossRef]

Heaton, Tim B., and Edith L. Pratt. 1990. The Effects of Religious Homogamy on Marital Satisfaction and Stability. *Journal of Family Issues* 11: 191–207. [CrossRef]

Himmelfarb, Harold S. 1980. The Study of American Jewish Identification: How It Is Defined, Measured, Obtained, Sustained and Lost. *Journal for the Scientific Study of Religion* 19: 48–60. [CrossRef]

Hoge, Dean R., and Gregory H. Petrillo. 1978. Determinants of Church Participation and Attitudes Among High School Youth. *Journal for the Scientific Study of Religion* 17: 359–79. [CrossRef]

Hoge, Dean R., Benton Johnson, and Donald A. Luidens. 1994. *Vanishing Boundaries: The Religion of Mainline Protestant Baby Boomers.* Louisville: Westminster/John Knox Press.

Hunsberger, Bruce, and Laurence B. Brown. 1984. Religious Socialization, Apostasy, and the Impact of Family Background. *Journal for the Scientific Study of Religion* 23: 239–51. [CrossRef]

ISSP Research Group. 2012. *International Social Survey Programme 2008: Religion III (ISSP 2008).* ZA4950 No. Data File Version 2.2.0. Cologne: GESIS Data Archive.

Kalmijn, Matthijs. 1991. Shifting Boundaries: Trends in Religious and Educational Homogamy. *American Sociological Review* 56: 786–800. [CrossRef]

Kalmijn, Matthijs, Paul M. De Graaf, and Jacques P. G. Janssen. 2005. Intermarriage and the Risk of Divorce in The Netherlands: The Effects of Differences in Religion and in Nationality, 197494. *Population Studies* 59: 71–85. [CrossRef] [PubMed]

Kelley, Jonathan, and Nan Dirk De Graaf. 1997. National Context, Parental Socialization, and Religious Belief: Results from 15 Nations. *American Sociological Review* 62: 639–59. [CrossRef]

Lawton, Leora E., and Regina Bures. 2001. Parental Divorce and the "Switching" of Religious Identity. *Journal for the Scientific Study of Religion* 40: 99–111. [CrossRef]

Lehrer, Evelyn L. 1998. Religious Intermarriage in the United States: Determinants and Trends. *Social Science Research* 27: 245–63. [CrossRef]

Lehrer, Evelyn L., and Carmel U. Chiswick. 1993. Religion as a Determinant of Marital Stability. *Demography* 30: 385–404. [CrossRef]

Mahoney, Annette. 2010. Religion in Families, 1999–2009: A Relational Spirituality Framework. *Journal of Marriage and Family* 72: 805–27. [CrossRef]

Martin, Todd F., James M. White, and Daniel Perlman. 2003. Religious Socialization: A Test of the Channeling Hypothesis of Parental Influence on Adolescent Faith Maturity. *Journal of Adolescent Research* 18: 169–87. [CrossRef]

McCutcheon, Allan L. 1988. Denominations and Religious Intermarriage: Trends Among White Americans in the Twentieth Century. *Review of Religious Research* 29: 213–27. [CrossRef]

Müller, Tim S., Nan Dirk De Graaf, and Peter Schmidt. 2014. Which Societies Provide a Strong Religious Socialization Context? Explanations Beyond the Effects of National Religiosity. *Journal for the Scientific Study of Religion* 53: 739–59. [CrossRef]

Myers, Scott M. 1996. An Interactive Model of Religiosity Inheritance: The Importance of Family Context. *American Sociological Review* 61: 858–66. [CrossRef]

Nelsen, Hart M. 1990. The Religious Identification of Children of Interfaith Marriages. *Review of Religious Research* 32: 122–34. [CrossRef]

O'Leary, Richard. 2001. Modernization and Religious Intermarriage in the Republic of Ireland. *The British Journal of Sociology* 52: 647–65. [CrossRef]

Petersen, Larry R. 1986. Interfaith Marriage and Religious Commitment Among Catholics. *Journal of Marriage and Family* 48: 725–35. [CrossRef]

Petts, Richard J. 2015. Parental Religiosity and Youth Religiosity: Variations by Family Structure. *Sociology of Religion* 76: 95–120. [CrossRef]

Petts, Richard J., and Chris Knoester. 2007. Parents' Religious Heterogamy and Children's Well-Being. *Journal for the Scientific Study of Religion* 46: 373–89. [CrossRef]

Pew Research Center. 2016. *One-in-Five U.S. Adults Were Raised in Interfaith Homes*. Washington: Pew Research Center.

Putnam, Robert D., and David E. Campbell. 2010. *American Grace: How Religion Divides and Unites US*. New York: Simon and Schuster.

Putney, Snell, and Russell Middleton. 1961. Rebellion, Conformity, and Parental Religious Ideologies. *Sociometry* 24: 125–35. [CrossRef]

Regnerus, Mark D., Christian Smith, and Brad Smith. 2004. Social Context in the Development of Adolescent Religiosity. *Applied Developmental Science* 8: 27–38. [CrossRef]

Roof, Wade Clark, and Dean R. Hoge. 1980. Church Involvement in America: Social Factors Affecting Membership and Participation. *Review of Religious Research* 21: 405–26. [CrossRef]

Rosenfeld, Michael J. 2008. Racial, Educational and Religious Endogamy in the United States: A Comparative Historical Perspective. *Social Forces* 87: 1–31. [CrossRef]

Schwadel, Philip. 2015. Explaining Cross-National Variation in the Effect of Higher Education on Religiosity. *Journal for the Scientific Study of Religion* 54: 402–18. [CrossRef]

Seamon, Erika B. 2012. *Interfaith Marriage in America: The Transformation of Religion and Christianity*. New York: Palgrave Macmillan.

Sherkat, Darren E. 1991. Leaving the Faith: Testing Theories of Religious Switching Using Survival Models. *Social Science Research* 20: 171–87. [CrossRef]

Sherkat, Darren E. 1998. Counterculture or Continuity? Competing Influences on Baby Boomers' Religious Orientations and Participation. *Social Forces* 76: 1087–14. [CrossRef]

Sherkat, Darren E. 2004. Religious Intermarriage in the United States: Trends, Patterns, and Predictors. *Social Science Research* 33: 606–25. [CrossRef]

Smith, Christian, and Melinda Lundquist Denton. 2009. *Soul Searching: The Religious and Spiritual Lives of American Teenagers*. New York: Oxford University Press.

Stolzenberg, Ross M., Mary Blair-Loy, and Linda J. Waite. 1995. Religious Participation in Early Adulthood: Age and Family Life Cycle Effects on Church Membership. *American Sociological Review* 60: 84–103. [CrossRef]

Tanaka, Kimiko. 2010. Limitations for Measuring Religion in a Different Cultural Context: The Case of Japan. *The Social Science Journal* 47: 845–52. [CrossRef] [PubMed]

Traphagan, John W. 2005. Multidimensional Measurement of Religiousness/Spirituality for Use in Health Research in Cross-Cultural Perspective. *Research on Aging* 27: 387–419. [CrossRef]

Uecker, Jeremy E., and Christopher G. Ellison. 2012. Parental Divorce, Parental Religious Characteristics, and Religious Outcomes in Adulthood. *Journal for the Scientific Study of Religion* 51: 777–94. [CrossRef] [PubMed]

Vaaler, Margaret L., Christopher G. Ellison, and Daniel A. Powers. 2009. Religious Influences on the Risk of Marital Dissolution. *Journal of Marriage and Family* 71: 917–34. [CrossRef]

Voas, David. 2003. Intermarriage and the Demography of Secularization. *The British Journal of Sociology* 54: 83–108. [CrossRef] [PubMed]

Wilcox, W. Bradford, and Nicholas H. Wolfinger. 2008. Living and Loving 'Decent': Religion and Relationship Quality Among Urban Parents. *Social Science Research* 37: 828–43. [CrossRef] [PubMed]

Williams, Lee M., and Michael G. Lawler. 2002. Religious Heterogamy and Religiosity: A Comparison of Interchurch and Same-Church Individuals. *Journal for the Scientific Study of Religion* 40: 465–78. [CrossRef]

Willits, Fern K., and Donald M. Crider. 1989. Church Attendance and Traditional Religious Beliefs in Adolescence and Young Adulthood: A Panel Study. *Review of Religious Research* 31: 68–81. [CrossRef]

Wilson, John, and Darren E. Sherkat. 1994. Returning to the Fold. *Journal for the Scientific Study of Religion* 33: 148–61. [CrossRef]

Wright, David M., Michael Rosato, and Dermot O'Reilly. 2017. Influence of Heterogamy by Religion on Risk of Marital Dissolution: A Cohort Study of 20,000 Couples. *European Journal of Population* 33: 87–107. [CrossRef]

Zhai, Jiexia Elisa, Christopher G. Ellison, Norval D. Glenn, and Elizabeth Marquardt. 2007. Parental Divorce and Religious Involvement Among Young Adults. *Sociology of Religion* 68: 125–44. [CrossRef]

religions

MDPI

Article

Religious Heterogamy, Marital Quality, and Paternal Engagement

Young-Il Kim * and Isaak Swan

Department of History, Sociology, and Politics, George Fox University, Newberg, OR 97132, USA; iswan15@georgefox.edu
* Correspondence: ykim@georgefox.edu

Received: 15 January 2019; Accepted: 8 February 2019; Published: 10 February 2019

check for updates

Abstract: Using data from a nationally representative sample of married fathers of school-aged children, we examined the association between religious heterogamy of parents and fathers' involvement in children's lives. We further examined whether that association is mediated by marital quality and father–child religious discord. Results showed that greater religious heterogamy is associated with less interaction and more relational distance between fathers and children. Results also suggested that fathers' reports of marital happiness play an important role in mediating the association between religious heterogamy and paternal engagement. We concluded that religious fathers are more involved in their children's lives insofar as their wives are equally religious and they are in happy marriages.

Keywords: religious heterogamy; paternal engagement; marital happiness; religious discord

1. Introduction

The last half-century has seen a substantial increase in the percentage of Americans taking an egalitarian view of the role that fathers should play in the lives of their children (Ishizuka 2018). Nevertheless, the shift in cultural norms of paternal parenting is not consistently reflected in the actual behavior of fathers (LaRossa 1988), and some fathers appear to meet these cultural expectations better than others. A large body of research has shown, for example, that religious fathers tend to be more involved in children's lives than nonreligious fathers.

Despite a large amount of evidence supporting the positive relationship between religion and paternal engagement, research is often conducted without due consideration to the mothers' religiosity or the role that they play in fathers' parenting. This oversight is surprising in light of the fact that fathers' parenting is correlated with mothers' parenting, and vice versa. In this study, we took into account the religiosity of mothers as well as fathers and addressed the following question: Does religious heterogamy of parents discourage fathers' involvement in children's lives? If so, why? Using data from a representative sample of heterosexual married men of school-aged children in the US, this study examined the association between religious heterogamy and paternal engagement. We also attempted to explain why religious heterogamy—especially in couples where the husbands are more religious than the wives—discourages paternal engagement. To the best of our knowledge, this is the first study to focus on the effects of religious heterogamy on paternal engagement.

2. Theoretical Background

2.1. Religion and Paternal Engagement

Over the past two decades, numerous researchers have investigated associations between religion and paternal engagement. Earlier studies of this topic focused on the role that religious culture plays in paternal engagement. Bartkowski and Xu (2000) and Wilcox (2002) found that conservative Protestants were more likely to be affectionate in their interactions with and supervision of their children and to spend more one-on-one time with them. However, beginning with King (2003), later studies found little denominational differences (DeMaris et al. 2011; King 2010; Petts 2007; Wildeman 2008), and traditional measures of religiosity, such as religious affiliation and attendance, have been criticized for their inability to measure the extent that religion affects everyday life and relationships, including those of a father with his children (DeMaris et al. 2011; King 2003; Mahoney et al. 2003).

To fill this gap in the literature, religious salience was introduced as an additional measure. While attendance and affiliation are publicly oriented indicators gauging immersion in religious culture, religious salience captures a private aspect of religion, namely, how important religion is to an individual's daily life (DeMaris et al. 2011; King 2003; King 2010). Religious salience, thus, provided a more direct measure of the association between religion and father–child relationships by narrowing measurements of religion to the private, family sphere, where the relationships between a father and his children have their primary place. The results showed that measures of religious salience were positively associated with paternal involvement. That is, fathers who rated the importance of religion in their life and their overall religiosity as high were more likely to enjoy a good relationship quality with their children and to put greater effort into the relationship than those who gave lower ratings (King 2003). Additionally, the father's religious salience was positively associated with his adult children's reports of paternal involvement during the child's teenage years and with high ratings of current relationship quality between the father and the child (King 2010). Although some other measures of religiosity have been employed to understand paternal involvement, the three noted here have received the most attention.

2.2. Research on Religious Homogamy/Heterogamy

One important aspect of religion that has remained understudied with respect to paternal engagement is religious homogamy—the extent to which husbands and wives share religious beliefs and practices. Beginning in the 1920s and continuing to the present day, there has been a steady increase in interfaith marriages (Kalmijn 1991; Lofquist et al. 2012). This trend provokes the question of whether couples benefit from religiously homogamous marriages.

A large body of research has documented influences of religious homogamy on marriage and family outcomes. First, religious homogamy has been shown to support the stability of marriages and relationships. Using data from the National Survey of Families and Households (NSFH), Call and Heaton (1997) found that differences in religious attendance within couples predicted higher rates of divorce. More recently, another NSFH study reported that the effects of denominational affiliation homogamy were dependent on religious attendance, meaning that same-faith couples only experienced higher relationship stability when they also frequently attended religious services together (Vaaler et al. 2009). Cohabiting couples also appear to benefit from religious homogamy. Using data from the Fragile Families and Child Wellbeing Study (FFCWS), Petts (2016) found that denominational homogamy increased the stability of cohabiting unions. These findings suggest that marital and relationship stability are greatly influenced by religious homogamy.

Second, religious homogamy influences other family outcomes, such as relationship satisfaction and marital adjustment, which indicates a couple's ability to adapt relationally to each other and contributes to positive marital health and well-being. Two studies, which used nonrepresentative samples from select US states, found positive results for religious homogamy for couples in their first marriage. Schramm et al. (2012) found that when husbands and wives both reported high levels of religiousness and shared a religious denomination, they reported better marital adjustment. Likewise, remarried couples with the same level of religiousness and similar beliefs experienced increased marital adjustment and suffered fewer negative effects from their past divorces. Olson et al. (2015) also found that religious homogamy was positively correlated with marital satisfaction.

Lastly, religiously heterogamous marriages are associated with negative outcomes for child well-being. Using measures of religious affiliation, school-aged children with religiously dissimilar parents have been found to be twice as likely to use alcohol and three times as likely to use marijuana than children with same-faith parents (Petts and Knoester 2007). Using measures of religious salience, children younger than school age of low-income, urban parents have been found to experience a negative correlation between parental religious heterogamy and positive behaviors (Petts 2011). Additionally, the frequency of parental arguments over religion is negatively associated with child development in homes of kindergarten-aged children (Bartkowski et al. 2008). Taken together, these studies show that children can benefit behaviorally from religious similarity between their parents.

2.3. Religious Heterogamy and Paternal Engagement

Although much research has been done on religious heterogamy and relationship outcomes, virtually none has been done in relation to paternal engagement. There are a few studies, however, that provided some insight into the role that religious heterogamy plays in family outcomes. Using data from Waves I and II of the NSFH, Petts and Knoester (2007) included parental engagement as a moderating variable between religious heterogamy and child well-being. Their measure did not differentiate between the time spent by the mother versus the father with the children; thus, the mean score of the couple was used to measure overall engagement. The authors hypothesized that parental involvement would moderate the negative effects of marital conflict and low religious participation on child well-being, dispelling any potentially harmful effects of religious heterogamy. The results showed that, while parental involvement was associated with positive child well-being, it had no moderating effect on marital conflict or religious participation. In a later study, Petts (2011) found comparable results in a sample from the FFCWS: Parental involvement found a place as a family structure variable, but no hypothesis or subsequent results noted any link among religious homogamy, parental involvement, and child well-being. DeMaris et al. (2011) examined both religious homogamy and fathers' child care. It was hypothesized that similar spousal levels of theistic sanctification and spiritual investment would increase the amount of fathers' child-care work. However, greater religiosity, by any measure, was found to negatively affect paternal involvement, and no further explanation was provided on the relationship between religious homogamy and paternal involvement. As a result, little has been established about the association between religious heterogamy and paternal involvement. Despite this dearth of evidence, it is plausible to predict that religious heterogamy would discourage paternal engagement in children's lives for the reasons we describe in the next section.

3. Explaining the Association between Religious Heterogamy and Paternal Engagement

3.1. Marital Quality

We examined marital quality as a mediating variable that may account for the effect of religious heterogamy on paternal involvement. It is plausible that religious dissimilarity between spouses would lead to a negative impact on marital quality, which in turn would lead fathers to be less involved in children's lives. It is well established that religious homogamy is positively associated with marital quality (Myers 2006) and marital stability (Waite and Lehrer 2003; Lehrer and Chiswick 1993). This implies that religious heterogamy will reduce marital quality. The impact of this factor would be particularly consequential for couples in which the husband is more religious than his spouse. Research indicates that couples in which fathers attend religious services more often than their wives have a higher likelihood of divorce than those couples with more equal levels of attendance (Vaaler et al. 2009). Another study found that children whose fathers attended religious services more than their mothers were more likely to be sad and lonely as a result of the frequency of arguments between their parents than children whose parents attended church at similar rates (Bartkowski et al. 2008). This leads to a significant disadvantage for paternal engagement, which is promoted by marital quality, as men with better relationships with their wives experience stronger pulls from their wives toward the family and into the parenting role (Furstenberg and Cherlin 1991; King 2003). Fathers with low-quality marriages may not be pulled as strongly into a paternal role. Of course, it is also possible that men with good-quality marriages are already expending their energy in family life and are already more likely to be involved with their children. For these reasons, we hypothesized that the negative association between religious heterogamy and paternal engagement can be explained by marital quality.

3.2. Father–Child Religious Discord

A second theoretical explanation for the relationship between religious heterogamy and paternal involvement centers on religious transmission, which tends to be more successful in families where the parents share religious beliefs and practices. When couples belong to different faiths or have different levels of religiosity, their children cannot easily acquire a shared set of beliefs (Pearce and Axinn 1998; Rossi and Rossi 1990). In such a case, children often identify with their mother's religion more strongly than their father's (Bengtson et al. 2013, p. 116). Thus, religious dissimilarity between fathers and children may occur in these religiously heterogamous families. This religious dissimilarity can be a source of intergenerational tension, indicating value divergence and weakening father–child ties (King et al. 2013; Sechrist et al. 2011). It stands to reason that the weakening of father–child ties would also depress paternal involvement. Thus, when a father is more religious than his wife, his children will be less likely to share his beliefs, which may lead to increased father–child relational distance and decreased paternal involvement. This reasoning leads to the following hypothesis: The negative association between religious heterogamy and paternal engagement is explained by father–child religious discord.

4. Methods

4.1. Data and Sample

To test the aforementioned hypotheses, we used data from the Culture of American Families Survey, a nationally representative web-based survey of American parents of at least one child aged 5–18 living in the household. A survey research firm, Knowledge Networks, administered the survey to a random sample of 2904 respondents who were selected from their survey panel between 30 September 2011 and 18 January 2012. The sampling was based on a comprehensive, address-based sampling frame provided by the United States Postal Service. Respondents without Internet access were offered a laptop and Internet connection to complete the survey (Bowman 2012).

Of the 2904 respondents, 2075 (71%) were female respondents and 829 (29%) were male respondents. Of the 829 male respondents, 710 (86%) were married. There were 36 cohabiting fathers (4%), but they were excluded from the analysis because the item on marital happiness, a key mediating variable, was asked only to married respondents. Missing data were less than 5% for all variables in the analyses; thus, cases with missing values ($n = 35$) were deleted listwise for all analyses, yielding an analytic sample of 675 married fathers.

4.2. Dependent Variables

Paternal engagement was measured using two items, each of which taps the quantity of father–child interaction and quality of father–child relationship, respectively. First, respondents were asked " . . . on a typical school day, about how much time do you spend interacting with your children?" (1 = *none* to 7 = *more than 3 hours*; $M = 5.50$, $SD = 1.25$). Respondents were also asked, "How would you generally describe your relationship to your children?" Responses ranged from 1 = *very close* to 7 = *very distant*. We reverse-coded this item so that higher numbers indicate greater closeness between fathers and children ($M = 5.93$, $SD = 1.05$).

4.3. Independent Variables

Our key independent variable was religious heterogamy. Respondents were asked, "Would you describe yourself as more religious, less religious, or as having about the same level of religious interest as your spouse/partner?" The response categories were "much less religious than my spouse/partner," "somewhat less religious than my spouse/partner," "about the same level of religious interest," "somewhat more religious than my spouse/partner," "much more religious than my spouse/partner." We collapsed these five categories into three, creating dummy variables for husbands who reported they were more religious than their wives (17%) and those husbands whose wives were more religious (29%). The reference category was those husbands reporting the same level of religious interest as their wives (54%).

4.4. Mediating Variables

Marital happiness. We measured marital happiness using a single item: "Taking all things together, how happy has your marriage been for you?" A 4-point response scale ranged from 1 (very happy) to 4 (not at all happy). We reverse-coded this item so that higher scores indicate a greater marital happiness ($M = 3.44$, $SD = 0.64$).

Religious discord. Parent–child religious discord was measured based on the respondent's agreement with the following item: "My children share my views of faith and religion." Respondents answered using a 7-point scale, ranging from $1 = completely disagree$ to $7 = completely agree$. We reverse-coded this item with higher scores indicating a high level of religious discord ($M = 2.69$, $SD = 1.47$).

4.5. Control Variables

We employed other measures as control variables that were known to be associated with father engagement in previous studies: religious service attendance ($0 = never$ to $7 = daily$; $M = 3.33$, $SD = 1.84$), importance of religion ($1 = not at all important$ to $5 = the most important thing in my life$; $M = 3.18$, $SD = 1.31$), and religious affiliation (Mainline Protestant [22%], Catholic [24%], Jewish [3%], Other [10%], nonaffiliated [13%], evangelical Protestant [27%] as being a reference category). Fathers' parenting role is a single item tapping fathers' attitudes toward the importance of fathers in childrearing. Respondents were asked about their agreement with the statement: "The mother's role in raising children is more important than the father's." Responses were originally coded from $1 = completely disagree$ to $7 = completely agree$. We reverse-coded this item so that higher scores indicate a disagreement with the statement ($M = 5.13$, $SD = 1.71$).

Finally, we included other control variables as follows: age ($M = 44.64$, $SD = 8.07$), race/ethnicity (black/Hispanic/other/non-Hispanic white [reference category]; 79% were white), education ($1 = less than high school$, $5 = graduate school$; $M = 3.65$, $SD = 1.03$), household income ($1 = less than \$5000$, $19 = \$175,000 or more$; $M = 13.83$, $SD = 3.46$), employed (77%), having a son (76%), children are all biological (79%), children do not divide their time between the respondent's home and another residence (89%), number of children in the household ($M = 2.23$, $SD = 1.07$), and social support ($1 = very independent$, $4 = very well supported$; $M = 2.57$, $SD = 1.02$).

4.6. Analytic Approach

We used ordinary least squares (OLS) regression analyses to test our hypotheses. Because our dependent variables are measured ordinally, we first ran ordinal regression models. A likelihood ratio test, however, revealed that the proportional odds assumption does not hold for all multivariate models (Long and Freese 2006). As a next step, we used Stata's *gologit2* and estimated generalized ordered logit models that relax the parallel lines assumption (Williams 2006), which yielded similar results (results available upon request). Because the results from OLS regression are easier to interpret, we treated ordinal variables as continuous variables and used OLS regression models.

The models are organized into three nested regression models for each dependent variable. Models 1 and 4 are baseline models that include religious homogamy variables as well as control variables. In Models 2 and 5, our first mediating variable, marital quality, is added to the baseline models. Models 3 and 6 exclude marital quality and include another mediating variable, religious discord. All regression analyses were weighted to adjust for different probabilities of selection and nonresponse bias. In order to account for the complex sampling designs, all tests of significance were computed using *svy* commands in Stata.

5. Results

5.1. Descriptive Statistics

Table A1 (See Appendix A) presents descriptive statistics for all variables included in our models. Respondents, on average, spent about an hour interacting with their children on a typical school day and reported a close relationship with their children. On average, respondents reported a happy marriage. When it comes to sharing religious views with their children, respondents reported that their children share their views on faith and religion slightly. Respondents, on average, reported that they receive a good amount of parental support from their wives.

5.2. Multivariate Analyses

Table A2 reports OLS regression standardized beta coefficients predicting two types of paternal engagement: father-child interaction and father–child closeness. Model 1 indicates that fathers who reported being more religious than their wives spent less time interacting with their children, compared to those fathers whose wives had about the same level of religious interest. There was no difference in levels of paternal engagement between fathers whose wives were more religious and those whose wives had the same level of religious interest. In Model 2, we introduced our first mediating variable, marital happiness, which was positively associated with father–child interaction. More importantly, when we added marital happiness to the model, the difference in father–child interaction between religiously heterogamous and homogamous fathers became nonsignificant. This means that fathers who were more religious than their wives spent less time with children because of the poor quality of their relationship with their wives. We conducted Sobel (1982) test to determine whether the indirect effect of religious heterogamy on father–child interaction via marital quality is statistically significant. The results showed that these indirect paths are significant ($p < 0.01$), accounting for 22 percent of the total heterogamy effect on father–child interaction. Model 3 indicates that religious discord between fathers and children is negatively associated with fathers' interaction with their children. The addition of religious discord rendered the difference in father–child interaction between religiously heterogamous and homogamous fathers marginally significant ($p < 0.10$).

When looking at the quality of the father–child relationship, we found similar results. Model 4 indicates that fathers in religiously heterogamous marriages reported less closeness with their children. Model 5 shows that part of the reason is that, as shown in Model 2, they were less happy in their marriage. The Sobel test shows that this mediation model is significant ($p < 0.01$), with 30 percent of the total heterogamy effect on father–child closeness being explained by marital quality. Interestingly, marital happiness is more significantly associated with father–child closeness than father–child interaction. Contrary to the hypothesis, however, Model 6 provides no indication that religious discord mediates the association between religious heterogamy and father–child closeness.

In addition to the main findings, there are other findings that are worth mentioning. Fathers who are well supported by a network of friends and family tend to be more involved in children's lives (Models 1–3). Social support, however, is not associated with father–child closeness. Religious salience is significantly associated with father–child closeness, but not father–child interaction (Models 4–6). Father role attitudes tend to be positively associated with both measures of paternal engagement.

6. Discussion and Conclusions

Using a nationally representative sample of married fathers of school-aged children, we examined the association between religious heterogamy and paternal engagement. We further sought to examine what might account for such an association. Our multivariate regression analysis produced three significant findings.

First, previous findings of a positive association between fathers' subjective religiousness and their relationship with their children were confirmed. We found that fathers who believe that religion is important in their lives reported more relational closeness, which is consistent with the findings of previous work such as King (2003). Religious salience, however, was not associated with the amount of time spent with the children. This suggests that a father's subjective religiousness is more predictive of the emotional aspects of the father–child relationship than the actual amount of time the father spends with his children. As was found by King (2003), religious attendance, a public aspect of religiosity, was not associated with the quantity or quality of paternal engagement. As for religious affiliation, there was little difference in paternal engagement between fathers who were evangelical Protestants and those of other religious denominations. The only significant difference found was that Jewish fathers spend less time with their children than evangelical Protestant fathers. Because of the small sample size ($n = 19$), however, this cannot be considered definitive, so we simply concur with King (2003), who found only a limited influence of religious affiliation on paternal involvement.

In addition to the findings of previous studies, we provide new findings on the association between religious heterogamy and paternal engagement. Our results showed that fathers who were more religious than their wives reported less interaction and lower quality relationships with their children than fathers of equal religiosity with their wives. These findings are important because previous study of religion and paternal involvement has paid little attention to the role that wives play in paternal engagement. To be sure, our study is not the first to recognize that marital quality is important for paternal involvement (e.g., Booth and Amato 1994). To the best of our knowledge, however, no evidence has been found of the mediating role of marital quality on the relationship between religious heterogamy and paternal engagement. Our results showed that fathers' reports of marital happiness were positively associated with the amount and quality of paternal involvement, and marital happiness fully accounted for that association. This means that those fathers who were more religious than their wives tended to report less happy marriages than fathers whose wives were equally religious. This, in turn, fully explains why they were less involved in their children's lives and felt less close to their children. These findings are consistent with the belief that if a marriage weakens, the father's paternal role also attenuates (King 2003, p. 385).

Another mediating factor that we found to be marginally significantly related to paternal engagement was father–child religious discord. Our results showed that religious discord between fathers and children was negatively associated with both measures of paternal engagement ($p < 0.05$ for father–child interaction and $p < 0.01$ for father–child closeness). With the inclusion of religious discord in the model, the association between religious heterogamy and father–child interaction was moderately attenuated, which lent some support to our hypothesis. These results suggest that fathers who are more religious than their wives have less interaction with their children, in part because they and their children have different views on religion and faith. The negative association between parent–child religious discord and adolescent reports of parent–child relations has been reported elsewhere (Stokes and Regnerus 2009), but our study is the first to demonstrate that religious discord can partially explain the association between religious heterogamy and paternal engagement.

It is necessary to note some limitations of the present study. First, because it used cross-sectional data, it is impossible to make causal claims regarding the associations among religious heterogamy, marital happiness, and paternal engagement. The quality of some paternal relationships may be due more to the fact that some fathers are simply better at relationships than to the quality of the marriage. Further, it is possible that fathers who have fewer interactions with their children are more likely to have children with different views on religion because they do not get adequate religious

Religions **2019**, *10*, 102

socialization from their fathers. Future work, using longitudinal data, should be done to fully address the direction of causation. Second, this study relied heavily on fathers' self-reports of all study variables. For example, religious heterogamy was measured with fathers' assessment of their own and their wives' religiousness. Although it would be ideal to measure religious heterogamy using both husbands' and wives' reports, our data were not collected at the dyadic level. Paternal engagement was also measured solely from fathers' self-reports. It is possible that fathers overreported their perception and parenting behaviors (Hernandez and Coley 2007, see Wical and Doherty 2005 as well).

In conclusion, the present study suggests that religious heterogamy discourages paternal engagement. In particular, fathers who are more religious than their wives tend to be less involved in their children's lives, as a result of the unhappiness of their marriage. These results point to the importance of understanding father engagement within a dyadic context in which parenting takes place. Future work will shed light on the exact mechanism by which wives influence their highly religious husbands' parenting.

Author Contributions: Y.-I.K. conceived of the study, obtained the data, conducted data analysis, interpreted the results, wrote the introduction, methods, results, discussion and conclusion, and supervised the project. I.S. conducted and wrote the literature review, developed the theory in discussions with Y.-I.K. and wrote the theory section and the references. All authors contributed to the final version of the manuscript.

Funding: This research received no external funding.

Acknowledgments: The authors would like to thank the Institute for Advanced Studies in Culture at the University of Virginia for allowing us to use data from their project, "Culture of American Families," which was funded by the John Templeton Foundation.

Conflicts of Interest: The authors declare no conflict of interest.

Appendix A

Table A1. Descriptive statistics (*n* = 675).

	Mean	*SD*	Min.	Max.
Father–child interaction	5.50	1.25	2	7
Father–child closeness	5.93	1.05	2	7
W, H = religious at the same level	0.54	0.50	0	1
W = more religious	0.29	0.45	0	1
H = more religious	0.17	0.38	0	1
Marital happiness	3.44	0.64	1	4
Father–child religious discord	2.69	1.47	1	7
Religious service attendance	3.33	1.84	1	7
Importance of religion	3.18	1.31	1	5
Evangelical Protestant	0.27	0.44	0	1
Mainline Protestant	0.22	0.42	0	1
Catholic	0.24	0.43	0	1
Jew	0.03	0.17	0	1
Other	0.10	0.30	0	1
Nonaffiliated	0.13	0.34	0	1
Age	44.64	8.07	22	72
white	0.79	0.40	0	1
Black	0.06	0.23	0	1
Hispanic	0.08	0.28	0	1
Other race	0.07	0.25	0	1
Education	3.65	1.03	1	5
Household income	13.83	3.46	1	19
Employed	0.77	0.42	0	1
Having a son	0.76	0.43	0	1
All biological child	0.79	0.41	0	1
Intact family	0.89	0.31	0	1
Number of children	2.23	1.07	1	9
Social support	2.57	1.02	1	4
Father role attitudes	5.13	1.71	1	7

Descriptive statistics are unweighted. W = Wife, H = Husband.

Religions **2019**, *10*, 102

Table A2. Ordinary least squares regression of paternal engagement on religious heterogamy.

	Father–Child Interaction			Father–Child Closeness		
	Model 1	Model 2	Model 3	Model 4	Model 5	Model 6
Control Variables						
Age	−0.18 ***	−0.17 ***	−0.17 ***	−0.20 ***	−0.19 **	−0.20 ***
Black	0.05	0.06	0.05	−0.08	−0.08	−0.09
Hispanic	0.02	−0.00	0.02	0.06	0.04	0.07
Other race	−0.01	−0.01	−0.01	−0.02	−0.02	−0.03
Education	−0.03	−0.05	−0.03	0.04	0.01	0.03
Income	0.04	0.03	0.03	0.12 †	0.11	0.11 †
Employed	−0.00	0.00	0.00	−0.05	−0.05	−0.05
Having a son	0.04	0.04	0.04	0.05	0.05	0.04
All biological child	−0.00	−0.00	−0.00	−0.04	−0.04	−0.04
Intact family	0.11 *	0.12 *	0.10 †	0.03	0.05	0.02
Number of children	−0.04	−0.03	−0.05	−0.08	−0.07	−0.09
Social support	0.16 ***	0.14 **	0.15 **	0.09 †	0.06	0.09 †
Father role attitudes	0.12 *	0.12 *	0.10 *	0.11 *	0.12 *	0.10 †
Religious attendance	0.07	0.05	0.06	0−.09	−0.11	−0.10
Importance of religion	0.00	−0.01	−0.05	0.27 **	0.26 **	0.20 *
Mainline Protestants	−0.04	−0.02	−0.02	0.05	0.08	0.07
Catholic	−0.08	−0.06	−0.06	0.09	0.11 †	0.11 †
Jewish	−0.11 *	−0.10 *	−0.10 *	0.01	0.02	0.02
Other	−0.04	−0.04	−0.03	0.08	0.09	0.09
Nonaffiliated	−0.00	0.00	−0.00	0.12	0.13 †	0.12
Religious Heterogamy						
W = more religious	−0.07	−0.06	−0.06	−0.06	−0.04	−0.05
H = more religious	−0.11 *	−0.08	−0.10 †	−0.10 *	−0.07	−0.09 *
Mediating Variable						
Marital happiness	–	0.13 **	–	–	0.18 ***	–
Religious discord	–	–	−0.14 *	–	–	−0.18 **
Intercept	0.65 ***	0.68 ***	0.66 ***	0.63 ***	0.63 ***	0.63 ***
Adjusted R-squared	0.14	0.15	0.15	0.13	0.15	0.15
N	675	675	675	675	675	675

Standardized beta coefficients are presented in the table. Robust standard errors are omitted due to space constraints. The reference categories are non-Hispanic White, not all male child, not all biological child, not intact, evangelical Protestant, religiously homogamous, † $p < 0.10$, * $p < 0.05$, ** $p < 0.01$, *** $p < 0.001$.

References

Bartkowski, John, and Xiaohe Xu. 2000. Distant Patriarchs or Expressive Dads? The Discourse and Practice of Fathering in Conservative Protestant Families. *The Sociological Quarterly* 41: 465–85. [CrossRef] [PubMed]

Bartkowski, John, Xiaohe Xu, and Martin Levin. 2008. Religion and Child Development: Evidence from the Early Childhood Longitudinal Study. *Social Science Research* 37: 18–36. [CrossRef]

Bengtson, Vern L., Norella M. Putney, and Susan C. Harris. 2013. *Families and Faith: How Religion Is Passed Down across Generations*. New York: Oxford University Press.

Booth, Alan, and Paul R. Amato. 1994. Parental Marital Quality, Parental Divorce, and Relations with Parents. *Journal of Marriage and the Family* 56: 21–34. [CrossRef]

Bowman, Carl Desportes. 2012. *Culture of American Families: A National Survey*. Charlottesville: Institute for Advanced Studies in Culture.

Call, Vaughn, and Tim Heaton. 1997. Religious Influence on Marital Stability. *Journal for the Scientific Study of Religion* 36: 382–92. [CrossRef]

DeMaris, Alfred, Annette Mahoney, and Kenneth Pargament. 2011. Doing the Scut Work of Infant Care: Does Religiousness Encourage Father Involvement? *Journal of Marriage and Family* 73: 354–68. [CrossRef]

Furstenberg, Frank F., and Andrew J. Cherlin. 1991. *Divided Families: What Happens to Children When Parents Part*. Cambridge: Harvard University Press.

Hernandez, Daphne C., and Rebekah Levine Coley. 2007. Measuring Father Involvement within Low-income Families: Who Is a Reliable and Valid Reporter? *Parenting: Science and Practice* 7: 69–97. [CrossRef]

Ishizuka, Patrick. 2018. Social Class, Gender, and Contemporary Parenting Standards in the United States: Evidence from a National Survey Experiment. *Social Forces*. Available online: https://doi.org/10.1093/sf/soy107 (accessed on 7 February 2019).

Kalmijn, Matthijs. 1991. Shifting Boundaries: Trends in Religious and Educational Homogamy. *American Sociological Review* 56: 786–800. [CrossRef]

King, Valarie. 2003. The Influence of Religion on Fathers' Relationships with Their Children. *Journal of Marriage and Family* 65: 382–95. [CrossRef]

King, Valarie. 2010. The Influence of Religion on Ties Between the Generations. In *Religion, Families, and Health: Population-Based Research in the United States*. Edited by Christopher Ellison and Robert Hummer. New Brunswick: Rutgers University Press.

King, Valarie, Maggie Ledwell, and Jennifer Pearce-Morris. 2013. Religion and Ties Between Adult Children and Their Parents. *The Journals of Gerontology: Series B* 68: 825–36. [CrossRef]

LaRossa, Ralph. 1988. Fatherhood and Social Change. *Family Relations* 37: 451–57. [CrossRef]

Lehrer, Evelyn L., and Carmel U. Chiswick. 1993. Religion as a Determinant of Marital Stability. *Demography* 30: 385–404. [CrossRef] [PubMed]

Lofquist, Daphne, Terry Lugalia, Martin O'Connell, and Sarah Feliz. 2012. Households and Families: 2010. US Census Bureau. Available online: https://www.census.gov/prod/cen2010/briefs/c2010br-14.pdf (accessed on 7 February 2019).

Long, J. Scott, and Jeremy Freese. 2006. *Regression Models for Categorical Dependent Variables Using Stata*. College Station: Stata Press.

Mahoney, Annette, Kenneth Pargament, Aaron Murray-Swank, and Nichole Murray-Swank. 2003. Religion and the Sanctification of Family Relationships. *Review of Religious Research* 44: 220–36. [CrossRef]

Myers, Scott. 2006. Religious Homogamy and Marital Quality: Historical and Generational Patterns, 1980–1997. *Journal of Marriage and Family* 68: 292–304. [CrossRef]

Olson, Jonathan, James Marshall, H. Wallace Goddard, and David Schramm. 2015. Shared Religious Beliefs, Prayer, and Forgiveness as Predictors of Marital Satisfaction. *Family Relations* 64: 519–33. [CrossRef]

Pearce, Lisa, and William Axinn. 1998. The Impact of Family Religious Life on the Quality of Mother-Child Relations. *American Sociological Review* 63: 810–28. [CrossRef]

Petts, Richard. 2007. Religious Participation, Religious Affiliation, and Engagement with Children Among Fathers Experiencing the Birth of a New Child. *Journal of Family Issues* 28: 1139–61. [CrossRef]

Petts, Richard. 2011. Parental Religiosity, Religious Homogamy, and Young Children's Well-Being. *Sociology of Religion* 72: 389–414. [CrossRef]

Petts, Richard. 2016. Religious Homogamy, Race/Ethnicity, and Parents' Relationship Stability. *Sociological Focus* 49: 163–79. [CrossRef]

Petts, Richard, and Chris Knoester. 2007. Parents' Religious Heterogamy and Children's Well-Being. *Journal for the Scientific Study of Religion* 46: 373–89. [CrossRef]

Rossi, Alice, and Peter Rossi. 1990. *Of Human Bonding: Parent-Child Relations Across the Life Course*. New York: Transaction Publishers.

Schramm, David, James Marshall, Victor Harris, and Thomas Lee. 2012. Religiosity, Homogamy, and Marital Adjustment: An Examination of Newlyweds in First Marriages and Remarriages. *Journal of Family Issues* 33: 246–68. [CrossRef]

Sechrist, Jori, J. Jill Suitor, Nicholas Vargas, and Karl Pillemer. 2011. The Role of Perceived Religious Similarity in the Quality of Mother-Child Relations in Later Life: Differences Within Families and Between Races. *Research on Aging* 33: 3–27. [CrossRef] [PubMed]

Sobel, Michael E. 1982. Asymptotic Confidence Intervals for Indirect Effects in Structural Equation Models. *Sociological Methodology* 13: 290–312. [CrossRef]

Stokes, Charles E., and Mark D. Regnerus. 2009. When Faith Divides Family: Religious Discord and Adolescent Reports of Parent–child Relations. *Social Science Research* 38: 155–67. [CrossRef] [PubMed]

Vaaler, Margaret, Christopher Ellison, and Daniel Powers. 2009. Religious Influences on the Risk of Marital Dissolution. *Journal of Marriage and Family* 71: 917–34. [CrossRef]

Waite, Linda J., and Evelyn L. Lehrer. 2003. The Benefits from Marriage and Religion in the United States: A Comparative Analysis. *Population and Development Review* 29: 255–75. [CrossRef] [PubMed]

Wical, Kurt A., and William J. Doherty. 2005. How Reliable Are Fathers' Reports of Involvement with their Children?: A Methodological Report. *Fathering* 3: 81–92. [CrossRef]

Wilcox, Bradford. 2002. Religion, Convention, and Paternal Involvement. *Journal of Marriage and Family* 64: 780–92. [CrossRef]

Wildeman, Christopher. 2008. Conservative Protestantism and Paternal Engagement in Fragile Families. *Sociological Forum* 23: 556–74. [CrossRef]

Williams, Richard. 2006. Generalized Ordered Logit/Partial Proportional Odds Models for Ordinal Dependent Variables. *The Stata Journal* 6: 58–82. [CrossRef]

religions

MDPI

Article

Mixed Blessing: The Beneficial and Detrimental Effects of Religion on Child Development among Third-Graders

John P. Bartkowski [1,*], Xiaohe Xu [1,2] and Stephen Bartkowski [3]

[1] Department of Sociology, University of Texas at San Antonio, San Antonio, TX 78249, USA; xiaohe.xu@utsa.edu
[2] The School of Public Administration, Sichuan University, Chengdu 610064, China
[3] Institutional Research and Effectiveness Services, Alamo Colleges District, 201 W. Sheridan, San Antonio, TX 78204, USA; stephenbartkowski@gmail.com
* Correspondence: john.bartkowski@utsa.edu

Received: 9 November 2018; Accepted: 4 January 2019; Published: 9 January 2019

check for updates

Abstract: Previous research has linked parental religiosity to a number of positive developmental characteristics in young children. This study introduces the concept of selective sanctification as a refinement to existing theory and, in doing so, adds to a small but growing body of longitudinal research on this topic. We explore how parents' religious attendance (for fathers, mothers, and couples) and the household religious environment (parent–child religious discussions, spousal conflicts over religion) influence child development among third-graders. Analyses of longitudinal data from the Early Childhood Longitudinal Study (ECLS)-Kindergarten Cohort reveal a mix of salutary (beneficial) and adverse (detrimental) developmental outcomes based on teachers' ratings and standardized test performance scores. Third-graders' psychological adjustment and social competence are enhanced by various religious factors, but students' performance on reading, math, and science tests is hampered by several forms of parental religiosity. We discuss the implications of these findings and suggest several avenues for future research.

Keywords: religion; faith; spirituality; child development; youth; standardized test

1. Introduction

In the last several years, a great deal of attention has been paid to the role of religion in socializing young people (among recent studies, see Chiswick and Mirtcheva 2013; Petts 2011a, 2011b, 2012; Petts and Kysar-Moon 2012; for reviews, see Bartkowski 2007; Hemming and Madge 2011; Holden and Williamson 2014; Nelson 2009). While the bulk of early research had detected the beneficial effects of religion on adolescent dispositions and behaviors (e.g., Smith and Denton 2005), increasing attention is now being given to religion's influence on the development of elementary and middle school-age children (e.g., Bartkowski et al. 2008; Chiswick and Mirtcheva 2013; Miller et al. 1997; Petts 2012; Petts and Kysar-Moon 2012). One of the earliest studies to use national data revealed that parental religiosity, especially the frequency of couples' worship service attendance, was associated with enhanced psychological adjustment and social competence among primary school-age children (Bartkowski et al. 2008). Religious solidarity among couples and parent–child communication about religion were also linked with positive developmental characteristics, while religious conflict among spouses either failed to yield salutary effects or was connected to adverse outcomes. More recent inquiries have revealed that parental religiosity can have beneficial effects on child development even under challenging circumstances, such as within single-mother households (Petts 2012) and among disadvantaged fathers in urban areas (Petts 2011b). In short, religion can be a vital part of a children's developmental foundation.

To date, a handful of studies have used longitudinal data to examine the effects of religion on child development and have revealed a number of salutary effects on internalizing behaviors, externalizing behaviors, and mental health (Chiswick and Mirtcheva 2013; Petts 2011a, 2011b, 2012; Petts and Knoester 2007; Petts and Kysar-Moon 2012). Longitudinal research is valuable inasmuch as it establishes (1) the causal influence of religiosity on child development, which cannot be determined through cross-sectional inquiries, and (2) the enduring impact of parental religiosity on child development as elementary school students grow older. However, there is still much to be learned about this issue. Our study takes a cue from previous research by exploring the effects of religious homogamy and heterogamy on early child development with respect to the frequency of attendance among married spouses.

At the same time, our investigation augments the current body of scholarship in three distinct ways. First, we examine the extent to which the household religious environment, namely, the frequency of parent–child discussions about religion and the frequency of spousal arguments about religion, may affect the development of young children over time. These factors produced significant effects in a previous cross-sectional study (Bartkowski et al. 2008), but have not been examined longitudinally. Second, we explore a wide range of developmental outcomes, including children's (1) psychological adjustment (e.g., self-control, internalizing problem behaviors); (2) social competence (e.g., interpersonal skills, externalizing problem behaviors); and (3) academic performance (i.e., approaches to learning as well as standardized test scores). The last of these domains is particularly important to examine given scholarly inquiries about religion's potential to undermine educational achievement (Darnell and Sherkat 1997), verbal acumen (Sherkat 2010), and scientific literacy (Sherkat 2011). Third, our study combines subjective assessments of child development (rendered by teachers) with objective measures of developmental outcomes (children's performance on standardized tests). Subjective ratings offered by parents, teachers, or others can be subject to bias, thus underscoring the utility of more objective outcome measures.

1.1. Religion and Child Development: Prior Research and Theory

Despite the vast attention paid to structural and cultural predictors of child development (e.g., household income, family composition, race-ethnicity), religion had long been ignored until recently. Significant findings emerged with nationally representative data. Bartkowski et al. (2008) found that parental attendance, and especially high rates of couple attendance, were associated with enhanced self-control, interpersonal skills, and positive learning styles, as well as a diminished incidence of internalizing problem behaviors in children beginning elementary school. These results differed from those observed for older youth (ages 10–17) and young adults (18–23) for whom parents' religious heterogamy did not significantly influence self-esteem or life satisfaction (Petts and Knoester 2007). While findings published in previous research (Bartkowski et al. 2008) were generally more robust for parents' ratings of children's behavior, significant effects also surfaced in teachers' ratings of child development. Moreover, the frequency of parent–child discussions of religion was directly associated with a number of positive parent ratings of children (e.g., self-control, social interaction skills, approaches to learning), though fewer of these findings surfaced in teacher ratings of child development. Likewise, the deleterious effects of spousal conflicts over religion (e.g., diminished self-control, increased emotional problems) were associated with parents' ratings of children but not those of teachers. Bartkowski et al. (2008) were quick to call attention to one significant limitation to their study, namely, the use of cross-sectional data and, hence, their inability to establish causal order in a definitive fashion. They acknowledged that selectivity bias (e.g., the willingness of parents with well-behaved children to attend religious services more frequently) could influence the results in their cross-sectional investigation.

A group of more recent studies, quite notable for their use of longitudinal data, have corroborated and augmented these findings. A series of investigations conducted by Petts (2011b, 2012) have demonstrated that religion is a valuable resource for promoting positive child developmental outcomes within households facing social disadvantage (e.g., single-mother-headed families, urban fathers in economically depressed environments). Moreover, salutary effects of parental religiosity have been observed with other nationally representative data, such that families' religious involvement has been shown to facilitate positive psychological health outcomes among children during their preteen and early teenage years (Chiswick and Mirtcheva 2013). This last study corroborated an earlier investigation that revealed protective effects of religion in the intergenerational transmission of depressive symptoms (Miller et al. 1997).[1]

This is not to say that religion produces uniformly positive developmental outcomes for children and youth. For example, spousal arguments about religion often undermine children's psychological adjustment and social competence, even when controlling for other types of spousal arguments (Bartkowski et al. 2008). And internalizing behaviors are more common when (1) children have two parents or a father with strict religious beliefs, and (2) children are raised in single-parent or cohabiting households in which only one parent believes religion is important (Petts 2011a). Moreover, while only marginally significant, the importance of religion among children ages 6–11 is associated with lower levels of psychological health (Chiswick and Mirtcheva 2013). Finally, cross-national data collected from children, including those in the U.S., revealed that household religion fosters greater empathy among children but is also linked with more punitiveness and less altruism (Decety et al. 2015).

Why would religion have such pronounced effects on the development of young children? On the positive side of the ledger, religion has been shown to enhance the parent–child bond for both mothers (Pearce and Axinn 1998) and fathers (Bartkowski and Xu 2000; King 2003; Wilcox 2002). It is not surprising, then, that religion and spirituality are meaningful to many children (see Bartkowski 2007; Holden and Williamson 2014). Moreover, a principal concern of religious communities entails the provision of resources to parents and families (Mahoney 2010; Mahoney et al. 2001, 2003; Wilcox 2008). For this reason, scholars have underscored religion's sanctification of family relationships (Bartkowski et al. 2008; Mahoney 2010; Mahoney et al. 2003) whereby domestic bonds are imbued with special meaning and significance. As Mahoney and colleagues (2003:221) have argued: "Religion is distinctive because it incorporates peoples' perceptions of the 'sacred' into the search for significant goals and values ... [that] deserve veneration and respect ... Indeed, part of the power of religion lies in its ability to infuse spiritual character and significance into a broad range of worldly concerns," including those in the home. Hence, families can use religion as a cultural resource to enhance cohesion, resolve conflicts, and pursue desired goals. In short, religion casts parental responsibilities as covenantal. However, given prior research on the potentially adverse outcomes associated with religiosity (e.g., Bartkowski et al. 2008; Petts 2011a), sanctification must be understood in a contextually specific fashion. Although religion may serve as a bridge in same-faith homes, it can function as a wedge in mixed-faith families. In households in which couples do not share a common faith or argue about religion, children often have poorer developmental outcomes.

This study therefore provides a ripe opportunity to clarify sanctification theory. The process of sanctification would be expected to produce positive outcomes for child development factors that fall squarely within the province of religiosity but not for those that fall outside of religion's sphere of influence. A great deal of research has indicated that major religions, and Christianity in particular, have a central focus on promoting the well-being of families and children (e.g., Bartkowski 2001; Bartkowski et al. 2008; Bartkowski and Grettenberger 2018; Browning and Clairmont 2007; Browning and Miller-McLemore 2009; Wilcox et al. 2004; see Marks and Dollahite 2017 for a comprehensive

---

[1]   The effects of religion on child development have also been linked to variations in religiously distinctive child discipline techniques and approaches to nurturing. For example, conservative Protestant parents spank their young children more often, but also hug and praise them more frequently (Ellison et al. 2011; Petts and Kysar-Moon 2012).

and accessible review). Such research underscores the prevalence of family ministry programs in American congregations. Moreover, the Bible and other religious scriptures focus extensively on fostering healthy marital unions and parent–child relationships (Bartkowski 2001; Browning and Clairmont 2007; Browning and Miller-McLemore 2009). Therefore, it is reasonable to hypothesize that parental religious involvement would influence young children's psychological adjustment and social competence because religions aim to sanctify family relationships and primary attachments that are often viewed as foundational for young children's personal development. By contrast, outcomes that are beyond the purview of family sanctification, such as academic performance, would be expected to be less subject to the influence of religious involvement or perhaps adversely affected by parental religiosity if religious commitment is stressed at the expense of academic mastery. In short, the remarkably robust institutional synergy that marks that religion–family nexus, including widely prevalent congregational family ministry programs, is manifested across denominational traditions (Wilcox et al. 2004). Yet, this same synergy is not evident with respect to the linkages between religion and other social institutions (Bartkowski and Grettenberger 2018). To be sure, religion can influence educational attainment, economic arrangements, and political circumstances, but not with the same principal focus—some might say preoccupation—directed at families. In fact, religion's extensive focus on family and social relationships may detract attention from other considerations. The argument that religious involvement can undermine children's academic performance and educational attainment has been demonstrated in previous research (Darnell and Sherkat 1997; Sherkat 2010, 2011), thereby hinting at the limits and context-specific nature of sanctification. We therefore introduce the theoretical construct of selective sanctification and anticipate differential effects with respect to religion and particular types of child outcomes. Children's psychological adjustment and social development are expected to be enhanced by parental religiosity while their academic performance will not.

Despite the empirical and theoretical insights to emerge from previous research, there are a number of important questions left unanswered that will be addressed by the present investigation. First, while the publication of several longitudinal studies of religion and child development in recent years is quite welcome, the small size of this research literature could benefit from additional scholarship. Augmenting the few longitudinal studies on this topic is necessary to establish with greater confidence the causal influence and enduring impact of religiosity on child development.[2] Second, very little research has previously examined the extent to which the religious environment within households may affect the development of young children over time. Because religion is best understood as a group property (i.e., a product of social relationships rather than merely an individual attribute), the collective nature of religion clearly needs additional attention. To this end, we examine the longitudinal effects associated with the frequency of parent–child discussions of religion and spousal conflicts over religion. These factors produced significant effects in a previous cross-sectional study (Bartkowski et al. 2008) but have not been examined longitudinally. Finally, our study is able to examine a diverse array of developmental outcomes, including children's psychological adjustment, social competence, and academic performance, thereby complementing subjective ratings of children's behavior with more objective performance measures.

To conduct our study, we use data collected during two different waves of the Early Childhood Longitudinal Study-Kindergarten Cohort (ECLS-K), from baseline (1999) to outcome (2002). Extant research and theory (reviewed above) lead us to generate several hypotheses that are tested in this study. All relationships anticipated in these hypotheses are net of controls, which include child

---

2   We recognize that debates persist about causation and statistical techniques to account for it. See various articles in *Measurement: Interdisciplinary Research & Perspectives* 12[4], 2014 and the Bainter and Bollen (2015) rejoinder. We follow convention in child development research by controlling for child characteristics at baseline to prevent time 1 developmental differences from influencing time 2 developmental patterns observed in this study. In this way, our investigation explores the effect of religion on the child development trajectory, that is, changes in child development characteristics from time 1 to time 2. As an additional precaution, all models were also run without time 1 child development characteristics controlled. These results, available from the authors by request, were largely similar.

development characteristics at baseline, thus providing a more rigorous test of the effects of religious factors.[3]

Hypothesis 1 (H1). *More frequent parental religious attendance at baseline will result in (a) more positive psychological and social child development outcomes over time and (b) more negative academic outcomes over time.*

Hypothesis 2 (H2). *More frequent parent–child discussions of religion at baseline will result in (a) more positive psychological and social child development outcomes over time and (b) more negative academic outcomes over time.*

Hypothesis 3 (H3). *More frequent spousal conflicts over religion at baseline will result in (a) more negative psychological and social child development outcomes over time and (b) more negative academic performance outcomes over time.*

2. Research Methodology

2.1. Data Description

We use data from the Early Childhood Longitudinal Study-Kindergarten Class of 1998–1999 (ECLS-K) (National Center for Education Statistics (NCES) 2018). The authors conducted the study through secondary data analysis and were not involved in the collection of the data. The ECLS-K is a multisource, multimethod study that focuses on children's early childhood and school experiences beginning with kindergarten. Sponsored by the U.S. Department of Education and National Center for Education Statistics, the initial wave of ECLS-K data was collected from a nationally representative sample of 21,260 kindergarteners and first-graders, as well as their parents and teachers, beginning with the 1998–1999 school year (base year of data collection). The primary sampling units (PSUs) were geographical areas composed of counties or groups of counties, with schools serving as second-stage units sampled within PSUs. Students within schools served as the final unit of the multistage sample design. Our study is limited to couples who were in a marital relationship at the time of the first-grade data collection wave because this characteristic permits us to examine various combinations of religious homogamy and heterogamy, which is essential to testing family sanctification. After listwise deletion, our study sample is 10,720.

Several waves of data were collected from the full sample following the base year of data collection. Our study uses baseline data from the Spring 1999 (parent–child discussions and spousal arguments about religion) and Spring 2000 (parental worship service attendance) waves of the ECLS-K (first-graders). Child development outcome measures are drawn from the Spring 2002 survey (third-graders), with cross-sectional ratings of children from baseline (Spring 2000) serving as controls. The Spring 2002 survey features a combination of subjective (teacher ratings) and objective (test performance) measures of child development. This multisource data collection strategy permits children's behavioral, emotional, and cognitive development to be assessed.

2.2. Measures and Analytical Strategies

Dependent Variables: Child Development Assessments of Teachers and Student Standardized Test Scores. In this study, survey assessments from teachers are used to rate several different child

---

[3] As noted elsewhere (Footnote 2), controlling for baseline child development characteristics is warranted and offers a more stringent model for testing the influence of religious factors. Regrettably, the ECLS dataset measures religion only at baseline. Therefore, changes in parental religiosity since baseline or effects of parental religion prior to baseline cannot be controlled and are a study limitation.

development outcomes featured in the Spring 2002 wave of the ECLS-K (children's behavioral, emotional, and cognitive development in third grade). The ECLS-K research team created several different scales designed to tap these developmental domains and conducted appropriate statistical tests to ensure the internal reliability of each rating scale. The rating scales featured in the ECLS-K were administered to teachers concerning the child's dispositions, behaviors, and skills in various domains. For each item used to construct the scales described below, teachers in the ECLS-K were asked how often they observed the child exhibit the disposition, behavior, or skill in question. Teacher respondents could choose from among the following response categories (coded as numbered here): (1) never, (2) sometimes, (3) often, and (4) very often. There was also a "no opportunity to observe this behavior" response option (coded as missing data).

For each scale, higher scores indicate teachers' more frequent observation of the characteristic in question. For the *self-control scale*, teachers were presented with four items that gauged the child's ability to respect the property rights of others, control his/her temper, accept peer ideas for group activities, and respond appropriately to pressure from peers (split-half reliability = 0.79). To gauge the social competence of the child, an *interpersonal skills scale* was administered to teachers. This scale rated the child's skill in forming and maintaining friendships, getting along with people who are different, comforting or helping other children, expressing feelings, ideas, and opinions in a positive way, and showing sensitivity to the feelings of others (split-half reliability = 0.89). An *internalizing behavior problems scale*, an indicator of adverse psychological adjustment, inquired about teachers' observation of anxiety, loneliness, low self-esteem, and sadness as exhibited by the child (split-half reliability = 0.76). Teachers also completed an externalizing behavior problems scale. This scale featured five items that measured acting out behaviors, including the frequency at which the child argues, fights, gets angry, acts impulsively, and disturbs ongoing activities (split-half reliability = 0.89). The *approaches to learning scale* allowed teachers to rate the child's attentiveness, task persistence, eagerness to learn, learning independence, flexibility, and organization (split-half reliability = 0.91). Objective measures of children's school performance were also ascertained. ECLS reports standardized test scores for *reading, math, and science*. All test items came from the ECLS-K third grade direct cognitive assessment battery. Information on specific test items is limited in ECLS documentation due to copyright restrictions but all tests were administered with fidelity and scores on all tests were comparable across administrations (see National Center for Education Statistics 2018).

2.3. Key Independent Variables

Husband's and Wife's Religious Attendance, Couple's Religious Homogamy, and Household Religious Environment. The Spring 1999 and Spring 2000 waves of the ECLS-K provide several religiosity measures. These items include individual measures of parental religiosity (frequency of worship service attendance), which is used to calculate the husband's and wife's attendance, respectively, along with religious attendance homogamy ([dis]parity in father–mother attendance). Parental religiosity is ascertained as an individual measure of the respondent's (typically, mother's) self-reported frequency of attendance at religious services during the past year. The parent respondent also reported his/her spouse/partner's religious attendance during the past year. Response categories for frequency of religious attendance of the husband and wife were coded as numbered: (1) never attend, (2) attend several times a year, (3) attend several times a month, (4) attend once per week, and (5) attend more than once per week.

Because religion is a group property (Bartkowski et al. 2008), religious homogamy for the couple was calculated from the Spring 2000 survey, resulting in six categories: (1) the mother attends more frequently than the father, (2) the father attends more frequently than the mother, (3) both attend sporadically (several times a year), (4) both attend semiregularly (several times a month), (5) both attend frequently (once or more per week), and (6) neither the mother nor the father attend. The first two categories in this recoding scheme are heterogamous, while the last four represent various types of homogamous combinations (frequent, semiregular, sporadic, and no attendance).

The first five categories were dummy-coded with neither parent attending (category 6) serving as the reference. The operationalization of these concepts is consistent with previously published research (Bartkowski et al. 2008).

Finally, two additional ECLS-K measures on the Spring 1999 parent survey gauge the household religious environment. The first of these items is measured by the question, "How often does someone in your family talk with CHILD about your family's religious beliefs or traditions?" The response options include the following: (1) never, (2) almost never, (3) several times a year, (4) several times a month, and (5) several times a week or more (coded as numbered). The second family religious environment measure taps the couple dimension of the family religious environment by asking, "Do you and your current partner often, sometimes, hardly ever, or never have arguments about religion?" Response categories for this item were coded as numbered to reflect the frequency of couples' arguments about religion, and include (1) never, (2) hardly ever, (3) sometimes, and (4) often. Thus, the household religious environment may be characterized by cohesion or conflict, both of which are accounted for using ECLS data.

2.4. Control Variables

Several variables were used as controls in all models to gauge the potentially confounding effects of other social factors: gender and race of the child (with race categorized as white, black, Hispanic, Asian, other race/ethnicity), number of siblings under eighteen years old, family structure (intact family, stepfamily, other family type), family socioeconomic status (family income), region (South, Northeast, Midwest, West), locale (rural–urban), and parents' school involvement. This last indicator is an additive index of parents' involvement in parent–teacher association (PTA) meetings, school events, parent–teacher conferences, open houses, fundraising, and school volunteering. A control for cross-sectional ratings was used for each outcome variable (e.g., teacher ratings of students' self-control in first grade are controlled in longitudinal analyses of self-control), as is gender of the respondent (teacher). The first-grade controls hold constant pre-existing developmental differences, thereby offering the most rigorous assessment of religion's influence on outcomes. Given the large number of dependent and independent variables in this study, the coefficients associated with control variables are not featured in the tables (available upon request). Finally, although parents were surveyed about child discipline, these measures are featured in a separate wave of the survey and thus were not included here.

To conduct this study, multiple linear regression (Ordinary Least Squares) was employed with complex survey design effects controlled. This technique permits an examination of the net effects of the key independent variables (parental religiosity, couples' religious homogamy, and household religious environment) on the dependent variables of interest (child development domains) while holding constant potentially confounding factors. Multiple imputation was performed to maximize the study sample size, and the results were similar prior to and following imputation. Given the large number of statistical controls included in the regression models, adjusted R-squared values were obtained and reported as goodness-of-fit measures.

3. Results

Descriptive statistics for all variables before multiple imputation are presented in Table 1. For each variable, the sample size (n) and percent (for categorical variables) or mean and standard deviation (for continuous variables) are presented. Where teacher ratings of child behavior are concerned, means and standard deviations of child outcomes are within expected ranges, and positive characteristics are more commonly observed on average than negative characteristics. Turning to religious predictors, we find that mothers (mean = 2.97) report attending somewhat more frequently than fathers (mean = 2.65) on the five-point attendance scale. Among couples, it is more common for mothers to attend more frequently (19.71 percent of the sample) than for fathers to attend more (2.51 percent). A minority of couples (17.54 percent) are those in which neither partner attends, as compared with sporadically attending couples (15.20 percent), semiregularly attending couples (13.06 percent), and frequently attending couples (31.99 percent). Discussions of religion are not uncommon (mean = 3.95), and arguments about religion are less common (mean = 1.35), with both measured on a four-point scale.

Table 1. Early Childhood Longitudinal Study (ECLS) 3rd Grade Sample Characteristics before Multiple Imputation.

	n	Percent	Mean	SD	Minimum	Maximum
Dependent variables						
Self-control (3rd grade)	8375	-	3.26	0.59	1.00	4.00
Interpersonal skills (3rd grade)	8360	-	3.15	0.64	1.00	4.00
Internalizing problem behaviors (3rd grade)	8386	-	1.59	0.52	1.00	4.00
Externalizing problem behaviors (3rd grade)	8445	-	1.63	0.57	1.00	4.00
Approaches to learning (3rd grade)	8461	-	3.13	0.66	1.00	4.00
Standardized reading test scores (3rd grade)	10,055	-	52.13	9.38	14.18	83.68
Standardized math test scores (3rd grade)	10,103	-	52.04	9.54	15.95	83.86
Standardized science test scores (3rd grade)	10,090	-	52.23	9.59	20.41	82.15
Religion variables						
Father's religious attendance (1st grade)	10,720	-	2.65	1.34	1.00	5.00
Mother's religious attendance (1st grade)	10,720	-	2.97	1.30	1.00	5.00
Neither parent attends (reference) (1st grade)	1880	17.54	-	-	-	-
Mother attends more (1st grade)	2113	19.71	-	-	0.00	1.00
Father attends more (1st grade)	269	2.51	-	-	0.00	1.00
Both attend sporadically (1st grade)	1629	15.20	-	-	0.00	1.00
Both attend semiregularly (1st grade)	1400	13.06				
Both attend frequently (1st grade)	3429	31.99	-	-	0.00	1.00
Frequency of discussing religion (1st grade)	10,424	-	3.95	1.16	1.00	5.00
Frequency of arguing about religion (1st grade)	9848	-	1.35	0.69	1.00	4.00
Control variables						
Self-control (1st grade)	9454	-	3.24	0.59	1.00	4.00
Interpersonal skills (1st grade)	9440	-	3.17	0.63	1.00	4.00
Internalizing problem behaviors (1st grade)	9424	-	1.55	0.49	1.00	4.00
Externalizing problem behaviors (1st grade)	9467	-	1.59	0.60	1.00	4.00
Approaches to learning (1st grade)	9523	-	3.12	0.68	1.00	4.00
Child is male (3rd grade)	5457	50.90	-	-	0.00	1.00
Child is female (reference) (3rd grade)	5263	49.10	-	-	-	-
Child is white (reference) (3rd grade)	6959	64.97	-	-	-	-
Child is black (3rd grade)	731	6.82	-	-	0.00	1.00
Child is Hispanic (3rd grade)	1816	16.95	-	-	0.00	1.00
Child is Asian (3rd grade)	648	6.05	-	-	0.00	1.00
Child is other race/ethnicity (3rd grade)	558	5.21	-	-	0.00	1.00
Respondent is male (3rd grade)	729	7.29	-	-	0.00	1.00
Respondent is female (reference) (3rd grade)	9266	92.71	-	-	-	-
Biological parent family (3rd grade)	8161	81.65	-	-	0.00	1.00
Other family type (reference) (3rd grade)	1834	18.35	-	-	-	-
Number of siblings under age 18 (3rd grade)	9995	-	2.54	1.09	1.00	12.00
Mother age (3rd grade)	9874	-	38.30	6.01	21.00	76.00
Parental education (1st grade)	10,690	-	5.25	1.95	1.00	9.00
Family socioeconomic status (1st grade)	9995	-	0.14	0.78	−2.49	2.58
Parental school involvement (3rd grade)	9987	-	4.40	1.39	0.00	6.00
Northeast (3rd grade)	1957	19.07	-	-	0.00	1.00
Midwest (3rd grade)	2834	27.61	-	-	0.00	1.00
West (3rd grade)	2318	22.59	-	-	0.00	1.00
South (reference) (3rd grade)	3154	30.73	-	-	-	-
Rural (3rd grade)	2343	23.31	-	-	0.00	1.00
Urban (reference) (3rd grade)	7707	76.69	-	-	-	-

3.1. Children's Psychological and Social Development Outcomes

Tables 2–6 feature the results of regression analyses using teacher ratings. Unstandardized coefficients and significance levels are reported. In each of these tables, the models are presented such that Model 1 features the net effects (i.e., estimated effects net of control variables) of fathers' religious attendance on the child development outcome in question. Model 2 estimates the net effects of mothers' religious attendance. Model 3 features the estimated net effects of various homogamy combinations (with nonattending couples serving as the reference category). In Models 4 and 5, respectively, the net effects of parent–child religious discussions and spousal arguments about religion are estimated. Model 6 (full model) features the estimated effects of all variables on the particular child development measure in question. (Model 6 cannot include the religious attendance of the mother or father due to its collinearity with homogamy measures.) Recall that Hypotheses 1a, 2a, and 3a refer to parental religious effects on children's psychological adjustment and social competence. These hypotheses are treated first (Tables 2–5).

Turning to the first psychological development outcome, Table 2 reports the coefficients of all predictor variables on teachers' ratings of children's self-control in the classroom. Neither the religious attendance of fathers alone (Model 1) nor mothers alone (Model 2) predicts children's self-control. Among couples' attendance variables (Model 3), significantly greater self-control is exhibited by children whose parents attend semiregularly ($p < 0.05$), when compared with their nonattending counterparts (reference category). Neither parent–child discussions (Model 4) nor spousal arguments about religion (Model 5) have a significant relationship with children's self-control. The sole significant effect observed for this outcome—namely, couples' semiregular attendance—persists in the full model ($p < 0.05$, Model 6). Hypothesis 1a, which predicted positive effects from parents' religious attendance, is partially supported. Hypotheses 2a and 3a, which anticipated a positive outcome associated with parent–child religious discussions and an adverse outcome associated with spousal arguments about religion, were not supported.

Teacher ratings of children's internalizing problem behaviors, another indicator of psychological adjustment, reveal two significant effects (Table 3). In Model 1, fathers' attendance is inversely associated with children's internalizing problem behaviors ($p < 0.01$). Similarly, Model 3 shows that parental semiregular attendance is negatively associated with children's internalizing problem behaviors ($p < 0.05$) but this factor is no longer significant in the full model (Model 6). In addition, mothers' attendance approaches significance ($p < 0.10$). Neither parent–child discussions nor spousal arguments about religion are significant, though the former approaches significance ($p < 0.10$). On this outcome, then, Hypothesis 1a is modestly supported. Hypotheses 2a and 3a are unsupported.

Table 4 presents the coefficients for all predictor variables on teachers' ratings of children's interpersonal skills (social competence). Once again, neither fathers' nor mothers' religious attendance alone affects children's interpersonal skills (Models 1 and 2). Significantly more positive outcomes in social competence are again observed for children whose parents attend semiregularly ($p < 0.05$) when compared with their nonattending peers (reference group) (Model 3). Both parents attending frequently ($p < 0.10$) approaches significance. The frequency of parent–child religious discussions ($p < 0.01$) produces a significant salutary effect on children's interpersonal skills, but couples' religious arguments have no effect (Models 4 and 5). In the full model (Model 6), only parent–child discussions remain statistically significant ($p < 0.05$). Thus, for children's interpersonal skills, Hypothesis 1a is partially supported, Hypothesis 2a is strongly supported, and Hypothesis 3a is not supported.

Table 2. Unstandardized coefficients predicting children's self-control (teachers' ratings, n = 10,720) [a].

	Model 1	Model 2	Model 3	Model 4	Model 5	Model 6
Father's religious attendance	0.004					
Mother's religious attendance		0.005				
Mother attends more [b]			0.039			0.026
Father attends more			0.025			0.014
Both attend sporadically			0.044			0.036
Both attend semiregularly			0.078 **			0.069 *
Both attend frequently			0.026			0.015
Frequency of discussing religion				0.011		0.008
Frequency of arguing about religion					0.019	0.017
Adjusted R^2	20.46%	20.47%	20.51%	20.47%	20.45%	20.53%

[a] Design effects are corrected with robust standard errors and weights; [b] Both do not attend is reference. Covariates included are children's self-control reported by teacher in 1st grade, child's and respondent's gender, child's race/ethnicity, mother's age, parental education, number of siblings <18, biological parent family, family SES, region of residence, urban–rural residence, and parental school involvement. Consistent significant control variables: children's self-control reported by teacher in 1st grade (+); child is male (-); child is black (-); child is Asian (+); biological parent family (+); and parental school involvement (+). Note: Parental school involvement is an index variable encompassing parent attendance at (1) PTA meetings, (2) school events, (3) parent–teacher conferences, and (4) open houses; as well as (5) parent participation in fundraising; and (6) parent acting as school volunteer. + $p < 0.10$; * $p < 0.05$; ** $p < 0.01$; *** $p < 0.001$.

Table 3. Unstandardized coefficients predicting children's internalizing problem behaviors (teachers' ratings, n = 10,720) [a].

	Model 1	Model 2	Model 3	Model 4	Model 5	Model 6
Father's religious attendance	−0.016 **					
Mother's religious attendance		−0.011 +				
Mother attends more [b]			0.017			0.029
Father attends more			0.043			0.054
Both attend sporadically			0.001			0.008
Both attend semiregularly			−0.052 *			−0.042
Both attend frequently			−0.035			−0.023
Frequency of discussing religion				−0.011 +		−0.008
Frequency of arguing about religion					−0.012	−0.016
Adjusted R^2	10.22%	10.18%	10.30%	10.17%	10.09%	10.34%

[a] Design effects are corrected with robust standard errors and weights; [b] Both do not attend is reference. Covariates included are children's internalizing problem behaviors reported by teacher in 1st grade, child's and respondent's gender, race/ethnicity, mother's age, parental education, number of siblings <18, biological parent family, family SES, region of residence, urban–rural residence, and parental school involvement. Consistent significant control variables: children's internalizing problem behaviors reported by teacher in 1st grade (+); child is male (+); child is Hispanic (-); child is Asian (-); biological parent family (-); and parental school involvement (-). Note: Parental school involvement is an index variable encompassing parent attendance at (1) PTA meetings, (2) school events, (3) parent–teacher conferences, and (4) open houses; as well as (5) parent participation in fundraising; and (6) parent acting as school volunteer. + $p < 0.10$; * $p < 0.05$; ** $p < 0.01$; *** $p < 0.001$.

Table 4. Unstandardized coefficients predicting children's interpersonal skills (teachers' ratings, n = 10,720) [a].

	Model 1	Model 2	Model 3	Model 4	Model 5	Model 6
Father's religious attendance	0.011					
Mother's religious attendance		0.008				
Mother attends more [b]			0.023			0.003
Father attends more			0.012			−0.004
Both attend sporadically			0.042			0.026
Both attend semiregularly			0.069 *			0.048
Both attend frequently			0.043 +			0.014
Frequency of discussing religion				0.022 **		0.020 *
Frequency of arguing about religion					0.001	−0.001
Adjusted R^2	21.13%	21.13%	21.18%	21.19%	21.06%	21.24%

[a] Design effects are corrected with robust standard errors and weights; [b] Both do not attend is reference. Covariates included are children's interpersonal skills reported by teacher in 1st grade, child's and respondent's gender, child's race/ethnicity, mother's age, parental education, number of siblings <18, biological parent family, family SES, region of residence, urban–rural residence, and parental school involvement. Consistent significant control variables: interpersonal skills reported by teacher in 1st grade (+); child is male (-); child is Asian (+); biological parent family (+); and parental school involvement (+). Note: Parental school involvement is an index variable encompassing parent attendance at (1) PTA meetings, (2) school events, (3) parent–teacher conferences, and (4) open houses; as well as (5) parent participation in fundraising; and (6) parent acting as school volunteer. + $p < 0.10$; * $p < 0.05$; ** $p < 0.01$; *** $p < 0.001$.

Table 5. Unstandardized coefficients predicting children's externalizing problem behaviors (teachers' ratings, n = 10,720) [a].

	Model 1	Model 2	Model 3	Model 4	Model 5	Model 6
Father's religious attendance	0.002					
Mother's religious attendance		0.002				
Mother attends more [b]			−0.001			−0.002
Father attends more			−0.010			−0.003
Both attend sporadically			0.003			0.009
Both attend semiregularly			−0.044			−0.037
Both attend frequently			0.012			0.021
Frequency of discussing religion				−0.005		−0.007
Frequency of arguing about religion					−0.007	−0.005
Adjusted R^2	32.10%	32.10%	32.15%	32.10%	32.08%	32.15%

[a] Design effects are corrected with robust standard errors and weights; [b] Both do not attend is reference. Covariates included are children's externalizing problem behaviors reported by teacher in 1st grade, child's and respondent's gender, race/ethnicity, mother's age, parental education, number of siblings <18, biological parent family, family SES, region of residence, urban–rural residence, and parental school involvement. Consistent significant control variables: children's externalizing problem behaviors reported by teacher in 1st grade (+); child is male (+); child is black (+); child is Asian (-); and biological parent family (-). Note: Parental school involvement is an index variable encompassing parent attendance at (1) PTA meetings, (2) school events, (3) parent–teacher conferences, and (4) open houses; as well as (5) parent participation in fundraising; and (6) parent acting as school volunteer. + $p < 0.10$; * $p < 0.05$; ** $p < 0.01$; *** $p < 0.001$.

No significant effects concerning externalizing problems are observed in Table 5. Hypotheses 1a–3a predicting salutary effects of religious factors are not supported for externalizing problem behaviors. These results were unexpected.

Table 6 displays the regression results for predictor variables on teacher ratings of children's approaches to learning. The effects of parental attendance are again featured in Models 1–3. Fathers' religious attendance ($p < 0.05$) significantly predicts more positive learning dispositions (Model 1), as do both semiregular attendance ($p < 0.05$) and frequent attendance among couples ($p < 0.05$) (Model 3). Parent–child discussions of religion and spousal arguments about religion yield no significant effects on children's approaches to learning. Both parents attending frequently is reduced to just below significance ($p < 0.10$) in Model 6. Therefore, Hypothesis 1a is moderately supported, while Hypotheses 2a and 3a are not.

Table 6. Unstandardized coefficients predicting children's approaches to learning (teachers' ratings, n = 10,720) [a].

	Model 1	Model 2	Model 3	Model 4	Model 5	Model 6
Father's religious attendance	0.017 *					
Mother's religious attendance		0.011				
Mother attends more [b]			0.006			0.001
Father attends more			0.030			0.026
Both attend sporadically			0.035			0.031
Both attend semiregularly			0.067 *			0.062 *
Both attend frequently			0.054 *			0.048 +
Frequency of discussing religion				0.009		0.004
Frequency of arguing about religion					0.002	0.003
Adjusted R^2	35.25%	35.22%	35.28%	35.18%	35.13%	35.29%

[a] Design effects are corrected with robust standard errors and weights; [b] Both do not attend is reference. Covariates included are children's approaches to learning reported by teacher in 1st grade, child's and respondent's gender, child's race/ethnicity, mother's age, parental education, number of siblings <18, biological parent family, family SES, region of residence, urban–rural residence, and parental school involvement. Consistent significant control variables: children's approaches to learning reported by teacher in 1st grade (+); child is male (-); child is Asian (+); biological parent family (+); parental education (+); and parental school involvement (+). Note: Parental school involvement is an index variable encompassing parent attendance at (1) PTA meetings, (2) school events, (3) parent–teacher conferences, and (4) open houses; as well as (5) parent participation in fundraising; and (6) parent acting as school volunteer. + $p < 0.10$; * $p < 0.05$; ** $p < 0.01$; *** $p < 0.001$.

3.2. Children's Academic Performance Outcomes

One contribution of our study entails its analysis of objective measures of children's academic performance. Recall that, consistent with the concept of selective sanctification, Hypotheses 1b–3b anticipated adverse outcomes of parental religiosity on children's standardized test performance. The influence of religious factors on this cognitive development domain is featured in Tables 7–9. Table 7 reveals that parental attendance can have an adverse effect on children's reading proficiency when mothers attend more ($p < 0.05$, Model 6) and when both parents attend sporadically ($p < 0.05$ and $p < 0.01$, Models 3 and 6), in support of Hypothesis 1b. Fathers' religious attendance in Model 1 approaches significance in a positive fashion ($p < 0.10$). Interestingly, parent–child discussions about religion significantly bolster children's reading proficiency ($p < 0.05$, Models 4 and 6), thus contradicting Hypothesis 2b, but are not fully counterintuitive (for reasons explained in the discussion). Hypothesis 3b is not supported given the null effects observed for spousal arguments about religion.

Table 7. Unstandardized coefficients predicting children's standardized reading test scores (n = 10,720) [a].

	Model 1	Model 2	Model 3	Model 4	Model 5	Model 6
Father's religious attendance	0.155 +					
Mother's religious attendance		0.093				
Mother attends more [b]			−0.504			−0.846 *
Father attends more			1.199			0.911
Both attend sporadically			−0.832 *			−1.062 **
Both attend semiregularly			−0.542			−0.828 +
Both attend frequently			0.123			−0.240
Frequency of discussing religion				0.225 *		0.253 *
Frequency of arguing about religion					0.301	0.320 +
Adjusted R^2	25.44%	25.41%	25.47%	25.44%	25.41%	25.51%

[a] Design effects are corrected with robust standard errors and weights; [b] Both do not attend is reference. Covariates included are child's and respondent's gender, child's race/ethnicity, mother's age, parental education, number of siblings <18, biological parent family, family SES, region of residence, urban–rural residence, and parental school involvement. Consistent significant control variables: child is male (-); child is black (-); child is Hispanic (-); child is other race (-); number of young children (-); biological parent family (+); family SES (+); and parental school involvement (+). Note: Parental school involvement is an index variable encompassing parent attendance at (1) PTA meetings, (2) school events, (3) parent–teacher conferences, and (4) open houses; as well as (5) parent participation in fundraising; and (6) parent acting as school volunteer. + $p < 0.10$; * $p < 0.05$; ** $p < 0.01$; *** $p < 0.001$.

Table 8. Unstandardized coefficients predicting children's standardized math test scores (n = 10,720) [a].

	Model 1	Model 2	Model 3	Model 4	Model 5	Model 6
Father's religious attendance	−0.063					
Mother's religious attendance		−0.176 *				
Mother attends more [b]			−1.034 **			−1.143 **
Father attends more			−0.381			−0.472
Both attend sporadically			−0.967 **			−1.043 **
Both attend semiregularly			−1.089 **			−1.186
Both attend frequently			−0.767 *			−0.890 *
Frequency of discussing religion				−0.025		0.086
Frequency of arguing about religion					0.046	0.082
Adjusted R^2	22.18%	22.19%	22.21%	22.17%	22.17%	22.19%

[a] Design effects are corrected with robust standard errors and weights; [b] Both do not attend is reference. Covariates included are child's and respondent's gender, child's race/ethnicity, mother's age, parental education, number of siblings <18, biological parent family, family SES, region of residence, urban–rural residence, and parental school involvement. Consistent significant control variables: child is male (+); child is black (-); child is Hispanic (-); child is other race; number of young children (-); biological parent family (+); family SES (+); rural residence (-); and parental school involvement (+). Note: Parental school involvement is an index variable encompassing parent attendance at (1) PTA meetings, (2) school events, (3) parent–teacher conferences, and (4) open houses, as well as (5) parent participation in fundraising, and (6) parent acting as school volunteer. + $p < 0.10$; * $p < 0.05$; ** $p < 0.01$; *** $p < 0.001$.

Table 9. Unstandardized coefficients predicting children's standardized science test scores (n = 10,720) [a].

	Model 1	Model 2	Model 3	Model 4	Model 5	Model 6
Father's religious attendance	−0.126					
Mother's religious attendance		−0.054				
Mother attends more [b]			−0.330			−0.527
Father attends more			−0.508			−0.683
Both attend sporadically			−0.995 ***			−1.115 ***
Both attend semiregularly			−1.251 ***			−1.393 ***
Both attend frequently			−0.549 +			−0.718 *
Frequency of discussing religion				0.042		0.117
Frequency of arguing about religion					0.302 +	0.299 +
Adjusted R^2	30.52%	30.50%	30.56%	30.49%	30.51%	30.59%

[a] Design effects are corrected with robust standard errors and weights; [b] Both do not attend is reference. Covariates included are child's and respondent's gender, child's race/ethnicity, mother's age, parental education, number of siblings <18, biological parent family, family SES, region of residence, urban–rural residence, and parental school involvement. Note: Parental school involvement is an index variable encompassing parent attendance at (1) PTA meetings, (2) school events, (3) parent–teacher conferences, and (4) open houses, as well as (5) parent participation in fundraising, and (6) parent acting as school volunteer. + $p < 0.10$; * $p < 0.05$; ** $p < 0.01$; *** $p < 0.001$.

As seen in Table 8, children's performance on standardized math tests is adversely predicted by various religious factors, including mothers' attendance ($p < 0.05$, Model 2), mothers attending more than fathers ($p < 0.01$, Model 3), and couples attending sporadically ($p < 0.01$), semiregularly ($p < 0.01$), or frequently ($p < 0.05$) (Model 3). These generally robust results persist in the full model (Model 6), and are consistent with findings anticipated by Hypothesis 1b. Parent–child discussions of religion and spousal arguments about religion have no effect on standardized math test scores, thus lending no support to Hypotheses 2b and 3b.

Finally, Table 9 demonstrates that couples' sporadic ($p < 0.001$, Models 3 and 6), semiregular ($p < 0.001$, Models 3 and 6), and frequent attendance ($p < 0.05$, Model 6) are inversely associated with children's performance on standardized science tests, and these effects remain in the full model (Model 6). No effects are observed for parent–child discussions of religion or for spousal arguments about religion, although the latter measure approaches significance in Models 5 and 6. The attendance findings support the expectations of Hypothesis 1b, with no support observed for Hypotheses 2b and 3b. Table 10 features a summary of all significant effects observed in the study.

Table 10. Summary of Observed Results Relative to Hypothesized Effects.

Psychological and Social Development	H1a: Positive Effect of Parental Religious Attendance	H2a: Positive Effect of Religious Discussions	H3a: Negative Effect of Religious Arguments
Self-control	H1a supported for semiregularly attending couples	H2a not supported	H3a not supported
Internalizing behavior problems	H1a supported for fathers' attendance and semiregularly attending couples	H2a not supported	H3a not supported
Interpersonal skills	H1a supported for semiregularly attending couples	H2a supported	H3a not supported
Externalizing behavior problems	H1a not supported	H2a not supported	H3a not supported
Approaches to learning	H1a supported for fathers' attendance as well as semiregularly and frequently attending couples	H2a not supported	H3a not supported
Academic Performance	**H1b: Negative Effect of Parental Religious Attendance**	**H2b: Negative Effect of Religious Discussions**	**H3b: Negative Effect of Religious Arguments**
Reading proficiency	H1b supported; reading proficiency diminished when mothers attend more and for sporadically attending couples	H2b not supported (opposite effect observed)	H3b not supported
Mathematical acumen	H1b supported; math acumen diminished by mothers' attendance, when mothers attend more, and for sporadically, semiregularly, and frequently attending couples	H2b not supported	H3b not supported
Scientific ability	H1b supported; science ability diminished for sporadically, semiregularly, and frequently attending couples	H2b not supported	H3b not supported

4. Discussion

This study set out to examine the longitudinal effects of parental religiosity (individual and couple worship service attendance) and the household religious environment (parent–child religious discussions, spousal conflicts over religion) on child development outcomes among a nationally representative sample of third-graders. The developmental outcomes investigated here ranged widely to include teachers' ratings of children's psychological adjustment (e.g., self-control) and social competence (e.g., interpersonal skills), as well as objective measures of students' performance on standardized tests (reading, math, and science). This broad set of outcome measures was justified by prior research and permitted us to test a refined version of sanctification theory with a construct we called selective sanctification. Given the salutary effects observed for psychological and social development in earlier research, we hypothesized that parental attendance and parent–child discussions about religion would yield protective effects while spousal religious conflicts would undermine child development. However, prior research on religion and educational outcomes led us to be more circumspect on this score. The process of selective sanctification would prioritize the human relationship facets of social life that are central to religion (psychological adjustment and social competence), while downplaying the importance of academic performance (Darnell and Sherkat 1997; Sherkat 2010, 2011). Thus, selective sanctification led us to expect adverse effects (or possibly null effects) of parental and family religiosity with respect to academic achievement as measured through standardized reading, math, and science test performance.

We controlled for baseline child development characteristics to ensure that our study offered a rigorous test of the religious antecedents on child development. We discovered several important patterns. Concerning teachers' ratings of children's psychological adjustment and social competence, our expectations about the effects of parental attendance were modestly supported. Select measures of parents' attendance were associated with a number of salutary developmental outcomes in children's classroom behavior, including bolstered self-control and interpersonal skills, fewer internalizing problems, and enhanced approaches to learning. Contrary to previous research (Bartkowski et al. 2008), however, the strongest and most consistent effects were not always observed for children whose parents frequently attend worship services. Desirable effects were observed with greater regularity for children of semiregularly attending couples when compared with their nonattending peers (see Table 10). Moreover, the attendance of fathers was inversely associated with internalizing problem behaviors and positively predicted approaches to learning. By controlling for baseline child characteristics, most of our dependent variables measure developmental gains and losses evident among children over a three-year time period.

There seems to be a threshold attendance effect whereby some worship service attendance produces the greatest gains relative to nonattending families (our reference group). It is possible that children in families who attend very frequently (and have consistently done so) did not reap the same magnitude of developmental gains because frequent attendance early in life already provides children with significant advantages that are not statistically evident when controlling for baseline child characteristics (Bartkowski et al. 2008). Thus, the methodological decision to control for baseline child development characteristics could reduce the observed effects for children of frequently attending couples because developmental gains across waves may be less pronounced for this group of children if they were developmentally "ahead" of their counterparts at the outset. Alternatively, it is possible that attributes not included in this study, such as children's integration in positive peer networks, might be especially influential for those whose parents attend semiregularly because such attendance constitutes an important threshold that fosters a critical form of social inclusion, beyond which there may not be discernible effects. In the end, there is a puzzling U-shaped curve that emerged concerning the positive social effects of semiregular parental attendance when compared with the children of nonattending parents. This unanticipated finding, and the lack of positive social attributes for children of frequently attending parents, needs more investigation. Similarly, fathers' attendance seems to be more instrumental in yielding developmental gains for children than is mothers' attendance. This finding may be linked to women's higher average level of religious involvement when compared with that of men.

For standardized test performance, we observed a number of adverse effects for parental attendance. Clearly, the most negative effects of parental attendance were evidenced in math test performance, but similar findings were observed for reading and science test performance. This pattern is consistent with research that has linked religious factors with suboptimal performance in particular domains of academic achievement and intellectual development (Darnell and Sherkat 1997; Sherkat 2010, 2011). Although our study cannot test for the effects of sectarian denominational affiliation or conservative theological beliefs, this facet of our investigation lends additional credence to the conclusion that parents' attendance is not uniformly positive in children's development. That being said, not all forms of religiosity yield adverse outcomes on academic achievement. More frequent parent–child discussions of religion significantly bolstered standardized test scores for reading, thereby suggesting that such conversations—perhaps practiced as scripture study or religious devotionals within the home—might enhance children's literacy. Also, some forms of parental religiosity (fathers' attendance and both spouses attending semiregularly or frequently) produced salutary effects on children's approaches to learning as rated by teachers. Therefore, children's orientations to learning and their achievement on tests are affected somewhat differently by parental religiosity.

Overall, then, what are we to make of these findings? First, religion remains consequential for the development of third-graders, but does not exert a wholly consistent influence at this stage in children's developmental trajectory. Thus, while religion has been shown to be critical in shaping the developmental foundation of very young children (kindergarteners) (Bartkowski et al. 2008), the psychological adjustment, social competence, and academic performance of somewhat older children is likely subject to a mix of religious factors (e.g., parents' attendance) and nonreligious factors (e.g., teachers, peers). If our study is paired with previous research on religion and youth, the profoundly positive influence of religion for very young children (Bartkowski et al. 2008) seems to become more circumscribed by third grade, and then rebounds to yield strongly protective effects during adolescence (Smith and Denton 2005; see also Petts and Knoester 2007).

Second, our study was guided by insights from sanctification theory, which posits that religion creates a strong moral foundation for parenting by casting parent–child relationships as a domain of ultimate concern, that is, a covenantal relationship. It seems that some revision to sanctification theory is in order based on the mixed findings presented here. The empirical process that we have observed is best described as selective sanctification. Parental religiosity yields salutary effects on a number of child development outcomes related to psychological adjustment (e.g., self-control) and social competence (e.g., interpersonal skills). And it can also bolster children's orientations toward learning. However, parental religiosity can also undermine children's academic development in reading, math, and science. In this way, parental religiosity is a mixed blessing in the lives of developing children. Moreover, within the household religious environment, we found that parent–child discussions of religion exhibited generally beneficial effects for developing children with respect to their interpersonal skills and reading scores but that spousal arguments about religion were generally ineffectual (producing null results). Thus, when considering developmental trajectories over time, different facets of the household religious environment yield distinctive effects. In short, this study renders a more complicated portrait concerning the effects of parental and household religion in the lives of young children, such that several salutary outcomes on psychological and social measures are observed alongside a series of mostly adverse effects on academic performance measures. This combination of results is summarized in Table 10. Note that a "positive effect" as described in Table 10 refers to a salutary (that is, a desirable or beneficial) child development outcome. Therefore, more self-control is a positive effect, as are fewer internalizing behavior problems because they are both socially desirable outcomes. A negative effect would be an undesirable outcome. The terms positive and negative in this table do not refer to regression coefficient signs.

Several limitations of our study and promising directions for future research should be kept in mind as work on this important topic proceeds. It should be noted that our study focused on teachers' ratings of children's behavior and actual standardized test performance. Thus, this study was concerned with child development in a particular domain of social life, namely, school. This limitation is important to recognize because religion has been shown to be more influential on children's dispositions and behaviors at home than in school (Bartkowski et al. 2008). So, our findings of inconsistent religious effects at this particular point in the developmental trajectory may be, in part, a product of the school-based outcomes investigated here. They do not rule out the role that religion may play in shaping other facets of children's lives such as relationships with parents and siblings throughout childhood, topics that would certainly benefit from more research.

In addition, it is important to note that the use of a series of separate regression models to conduct these analyses does raise the prospect of a Type I error. A Type I error increases the probability of observing a "false positive," that is, the mistaken discovery of statistically significant effects when the null hypothesis of no significant difference should be accepted. The line of analysis employed in this study was pursued because our investigation extends a previously published article that utilized this methodological approach (Bartkowski et al. 2008). The series of separate regression models was employed in our study with this limitation in mind.

Moreover, the data utilized here did not permit us to investigate denominational differences in child development or parents' theological beliefs (e.g., scriptural inerrancy). Given denominational differences in social outcomes for adolescents (Smith and Denton 2005), this is a noteworthy shortcoming. Until interfaith variations can be investigated (e.g., conservative Protestants versus mainline Protestants versus Catholics), we must be careful not to overstate the conclusions drawn here. Finally, long-term developmental trajectories beyond the roughly three-year span between baseline and outcome data analyzed here need additional scrutiny, as does the prospect of religious change among parents. ECLS data only measure religion at baseline, thus leaving possible changes in attendance patterns and the household religious environment unable to be explored.

Setting aside these limitations, the argument for noteworthy forms of religious influence among elementary school-age children—at least in the classroom setting—is supported by this investigation. Religion affects a range of child development outcomes by age eight. And, while its influence on psychological adjustment and social competence is broadly beneficial for young children, its impact on standardized test performance is generally adverse. Religion is an important influence, generally for good and sometimes for ill, as children navigate their way through the grade school years.

Author Contributions: J.P.B. conceived of the study and wrote the majority of this paper, including the key theoretical and empirical arguments, as well as the interpretation of results. X.X. conducted all data analyses and created tables along with contributing to the interpretation of results. S.B. contributed to the literature review of the study.

Funding: This research received no external funding.

Acknowledgments: The authors are grateful for comments offered by colleagues at public presentations of this research.

Conflicts of Interest: The authors declare no conflict of interest.

References

Bainter, Sierra A., and Kenneth A. Bollen. 2015. Moving Forward in the Debate on Causal Indicators: Rejoinder to Comments. *Measurement* 13: 63–74. [CrossRef]

Bartkowski, John P. 2001. *Remaking the Godly Marriage: Gender Negotiation in Evangelical Families*. New Brunswick: Rutgers University Press.

Bartkowski, John P. 2007. Religious Socialization among American Youth. In *The Sage Handbook of the Sociology of Religion*. Edited by James A. Beckford and N. J. Demerath III. Thousand Oaks: Sage, pp. 511–25. [CrossRef]

Bartkowski, John P., and Susan E. Grettenberger. 2018. *The Arc of Faith-Based Initiatives: Religion's Changing Role in Welfare Service Provision*. Cham: Springer.

Bartkowski, John P., and Xiaohe Xu. 2000. Distant Patriarchs or Expressive Dads? The Discourse and Practice of Fathering in Conservative Protestant Families. *The Sociological Quarterly* 41: 465–85. [CrossRef] [PubMed]

Bartkowski, John P., Xiaohe Xu, and Martin L. Levin. 2008. Religion and Child Development: Evidence from the Early Childhood Longitudinal Study. *Social Science Research* 37: 18–36. [CrossRef]

Browning, Don S., and David A. Clairmont, eds. 2007. *American Religions and the Family: How Faith Traditions Cope with Modernization and Democracy*. New York: Columbia University Press.

Browning, Don S., and Bonnie J. Miller-McLemore. 2009. *Children and Childhood in American Religions*. New Brunswick: Rutgers University Press.

Chiswick, Barry R., and Donka M. Mirtcheva. 2013. Religion and Child Health: Religious Affiliation, Importance, and Attendance and Health Status among American Youth. *Journal of Family and Economic Issues* 34: 120–40. [CrossRef]

Darnell, Alfred, and Darren E. Sherkat. 1997. The Impact of Protestant Fundamentalism on Educational Attainment. *American Sociological Review* 62: 306–15. [CrossRef]

Decety, Jean, Jason M. Cowell, Kang Lee, Randa Mahasneh, Susan Malcolm-Smith, Bilge Selcuk, and Xinyue Zhou. 2015. The Negative Association between Religiousness and Children's Altruism across the World. *Current Biology* 25: 2951–55. [CrossRef] [PubMed]

Ellison, Christopher G., Marc A. Musick, and George W. Holden. 2011. Does Conservative Protestantism Moderate the Association between Corporal Punishment and Child Outcomes? *Journal of Marriage and Family* 5: 946–61. [CrossRef]

Hemming, Peter J., and Nicola Madge. 2011. Researching Children, Youth and Religion: Identity, Complexity, and Agency. *Childhood* 19: 38–51. [CrossRef]

Holden, George W., and Paul Alan Williamson. 2014. Religion and Child Well-Being. In *Handbook of Child Well-Being*. Edited by Asher Ben-Arieh, Ferran Casas, Ivar Frones and Jill E. Korbin. New York: Springer, pp. 1137–69. [CrossRef]

King, Valarie. 2003. The Influence of Religion on Fathers' Relationships with Their Children. *Journal of Marriage and Family* 65: 382–95. [CrossRef]

Mahoney, Annette. 2010. Religion in the Home, 1999–2009: A Relational Spirituality Perspective. *Journal of Marriage and Family* 72: 805–27. [CrossRef]

Mahoney, Annette, Kenneth I. Pargament, Nalini Tarakeshwar, and Aaron B. Swank. 2001. Religion in the Home in the 1980s and 90s: Meta-Analyses and Conceptual Analyses of Links between Religion, Marriage, and Parenting. *Journal of Family Psychology* 15: 559–96. [CrossRef] [PubMed]

Mahoney, Annette, Kenneth I. Pargament, Aaron Murray-Swank, and Nichole Murray-Swank. 2003. Religion and the Sanctification of Family Relationships. *Review of Religious Research* 44: 220–36. [CrossRef]

Marks, Loren D., and David C. Dollahite. 2017. *Religion and Families: An Introduction*. New York: Routledge.

Miller, Lisa, Virginia Warner, Priya Wickramaratne, and Myrna Weissman. 1997. Religiosity and Depression: Ten-Year Follow-Up of Depressed Mothers and Offspring. *Journal of the American Academy of Child and Adolescent Psychiatry* 36: 1416–25. [CrossRef] [PubMed]

National Center for Education Statistics. 2018. Early Childhood Longitudinal Study, Kindergarten Class of 1998–99. Available online: https://nces.ed.gov/ecls/kindergarten.asp (accessed on 1 December 2018).

Nelson, James M. 2009. *Psychology, Religion, and Spirituality*. New York: Springer, ISBN 978-0-387-87573-6.

Pearce, Lisa D., and William G. Axinn. 1998. The Impact of Family Religious Life on the Quality of Mother-Child Relations. *American Sociological Review* 63: 810–28. [CrossRef]

Petts, Richard J. 2011a. Parental Religiosity, Religious Homogamy, and Young Children's Well-Being. *Sociology of Religion* 72: 389–414. [CrossRef]

Petts, Richard J. 2011b. Is Urban Fathers' Religion Important for their Children's Behavior? *Review of Religious Research* 53: 183–206. [CrossRef]

Petts, Richard J. 2012. Single Mothers' Religious Involvement and Early Childhood Behavior. *Journal of Marriage and Family* 74: 251–68. [CrossRef]

Petts, Richard J., and Chris Knoester. 2007. Parent's Religious Heterogamy and Children's Well-Being. *Journal of the Scientific Study of Religion* 46: 373–89. [CrossRef]

Petts, Richard J., and Ashleigh E. Kysar-Moon. 2012. Child Discipline and Conservative Protestantism: Why the Relationship between Corporal Punishment and Child Behavior Problems May Vary by Religious Context. *Review of Religious Research* 54: 445–68. [CrossRef]

Sherkat, Darren E. 2010. Religion and Verbal Ability. *Social Science Research* 29: 2–13. [CrossRef]

Sherkat, Darren E. 2011. Religion and Scientific Literacy in the United States. *Social Science Quarterly* 92: 1134–50. [CrossRef]

Smith, Christian, and Melinda L. Denton. 2005. *Soul Searching: The Religious and Spiritual Lives of American Teenagers*. New York: Oxford University Press, ISBN-13: 978-0195384772.

Wilcox, W. Bradford. 2002. Religion, Convention, and Paternal Involvement. *Journal of Marriage and Family* 64: 780–93. [CrossRef]

Wilcox, W. Bradford. 2008. Focused on Their Families: Religion, Parenting, and Child Well-Being. In *Authoritative Communities: The Scientific Case for Nurturing the Whole Child*. Edited by Kathleen Kovner Kline. New York: Springer, pp. 227–44. [CrossRef]

Wilcox, W. Bradford, Mark Chaves, and David Franz. 2004. Bradford, Mark Chaves, and David Franz 2004. Focused on the Family? Religious Traditions, Family Discourse, and Pastoral Practice. *Journal for the Scientific Study of Religion* 43: 491–504. [CrossRef]

religions

MDPI

Article

Depression, Religiosity, and Parenting Styles among Young Latter-Day Saint Adolescents

Mark D. Ogletree *, W. Justin Dyer, Michael A. Goodman, Courtney Kinneard and Bradley W. McCormick

Department of Church History and Doctrine, Brigham Young University, 270F Joseph Smith Building, Provo, UT 84602, USA; JustinDyer@byu.edu (W.J.D.); professorgoodman@gmail.com (M.A.G.); courtney.kinneard@gmail.com (C.K.); bradley.mccormick4@icloud.com (B.W.M.)
* Correspondence: mark_ogletree@byu.edu

Received: 30 January 2019; Accepted: 8 March 2019; Published: 26 March 2019

check for
updates

Abstract: This study examines depression among Latter-day Saint teens, particularly how religiosity and the parent–child relationship are associated with depressive symptomology. Although there is an abundance of research on adolescent depression and on adolescent religiosity, there is less research addressing the connection between the two. The research questions include: Does religiosity among Latter-day Saint teens reduce their rates of depression? What aspects of religiosity affect depression most significantly? How does religious coping influence depression? How does the parent–child relationship affect depression rates among Latter-day Saint teens? Being a sexual minority and living in Utah were related to higher levels of depression. Greater depression was also associated with more anxiety and poorer physical health. Authoritative parenting by fathers was associated with lower depression for daughters but not sons. Finally, feeling abandoned by God was related to higher depression, while peer support at church was associated with lower depression.

Keywords: depression; religiosity; parenting styles; religious coping; Latter-day Saint adolescents

Research documents a decline in Christian religious affiliation and participation among Americans over the past several decades. Of the silent generation (those born between 1928 and 1945), 85% identified as "Christian" in their religious beliefs. However, of the younger millennial generation (those born between 1990 and 1996), only 56% are affiliated with a Christian religion in the United States (Cooperman et al. 2015). Other researchers have noted a "clear decline in outward religious expression" among young adults (Uecker et al. 2007, p. 1667), and an overall decline in religious participation in adolescents as they move through the teenage years.

One study reported that 43% of eighth graders attended church services regularly, as compared to 33% of twelfth graders (Smith et al. 2002). Another prevalent trend is that more teens and adults are identifying as "nones"—a term suggesting no religious affiliation. In the early 1980s, more than 90% of high school seniors identified with one religious group or another. Only 10% chose "none" as their religious affiliation. However, in 2016, 31% identified religiously as a "none" (Twenge 2017).

Despite these trends, religion still appears to be a significant force in the lives of many American teens and is linked to many positive outcomes. For example, studies have found that religious affiliation and participation are inversely related to juvenile drug, alcohol, and tobacco use, as well as a host of other externalizing or delinquent behaviors (Smith 2003). Adolescents who report higher levels of personal and familial religiosity appear to have greater self-esteem and healthier psychological functioning (Ball et al. 2003). Other studies show that religiosity is negatively related to suicidal ideation, suicide attempts, and actual suicide (Donahue and Benson 1995). Studies have also shown an inverse relationship between religious participation, teenage sexual activity, and pregnancy (Lammers et al. 2000; Whitehead et al. 2001). Adolescent religious participation has been positively associated with physical health (Jessor et al. 1998), family cohesion (Varon and Riley 1999), effective coping (Shortz and Worthington 1994), and academic achievement (Muller and Ellison 2001; Regnerus 2000).

With fewer adolescents participating in religious activities and society becoming more culturally secular, will religion continue to have similar influences in the lives of those involved today—especially in light of what appears to be an increase in mental health challenges, such as anxiety and depression? Furthermore, less is known about the specific aspects of religiosity that may relate to mental health and how these variables might interact with family processes to influence adolescent mental health. We will examine the interaction between four variables: parenting style, religiosity, gender, and mental health. The purpose of the present study was to examine what aspects of their faith and family relate to their mental health within a cohort of Latter-day Saint teens. Although Latter-day Saint adolescents have not drawn the attention of many researchers, they have been called the "spiritual athletes" of their generation because of their spiritual sacrifices, devotion, and energy towards their faith (Dean 2010). These qualities may add further nuance towards the outcomes of the study.

1. Literature Review

A recent study reported that between 2005 and 2014, the prevalence of major depressive episodes among adolescents increased from 8.7% to 11.3% (Mojtabai et al. 2017). The prevalence of depression among adolescents ranged from 5% to 15% and affects one in five people before adulthood (Dew et al. 2010). Other experts have estimated that among high school teens, up to 30% have reported episodes of depression (Arntzen 2017). Furthermore, there appears to be a gender gap associated with major depressive disorder (MDD) in adolescents. *The National Survey on Drug Use and Health* (NSDUH) revealed that 19.5% of adolescent girls but only 5.8% of adolescent boys reported a major depressive episode in 2015 (Bose et al. 2016; see also Lewinsohn et al. 1998).

Because of the deleterious effect of depression on adolescent well-being, it is important we further understand what may increase or mitigate depression. Teenage depression is associated with low academic success and poor psychosocial development (Birmaher et al. 1996). Birmaher et al. (1996) also reported that 70% of youth who experience depression might eventually develop major depressive disorder. These trends become even more concerning when contemplating the possible long-term consequences. Most mental health disorders in adulthood are preceded by an internalizing disorder in adolescence (Pine et al. 1998). If a method exists to prevent or decrease adolescent depression, it may also act as a preventative measure for adult depression. In 1993, the United States spent USD $44 billion on adult depression; working to prevent depression among youth may be more cost effective in the long run and alleviate much suffering (Lewinsohn et al. 1998). This necessitates a better understanding of adolescent depression.

1.1. Correlates of Adolescent Depression

Distinguishing between cause from effect in psychology is often difficult. Diego et al. (2001) identified commonalities between depressed teens. Many spent less time doing homework, had fewer friends, felt lonely, exercised less, had suicidal thoughts, and used marijuana or cocaine. In addition, Diego et al. (2001) also found that very few of these teens had positive relationships with their parents.

Lewinsohn et al. (1998), found that almost half of depressed teens have another mental health disorder and teens who smoked were twice as likely to have depression at some point. This study also identified a prototypical case of depression: a 16-year old female with low self-esteem/poor body image, low feelings of self-worth, pessimistic, overly dependent on others, feels that she is receiving little support from her family, and is coping poorly with both major and minor stressors (such as conflicts with parents, physical illness, poor school performance, and relationship breakups). Birmaher's findings are congruent: 60–70% of adolescents had experienced one or more "severe" stressful life event(s) in the year prior to the onset of the MDD, including loss, divorce, bereavement, and exposure to suicide (1996).

In terms of biological factors, adult twin and adoption studies have shown that genetic factors may account for at least 50% of the variance in the transmission of mood disorders (Birmaher et al. 1996). Other twin studies have reported the positive relationship between heritability and depression (Pinheiro et al. 2018). A meta-analysis documented the "familial" factor with the onset of depression and concluded that this mood disorder is often influenced by genetic influences (Sullivan et al. 2000).

Additionally, the Avon Longitudinal Study of Parents and Children (ALSPAC) found that depression is more prevalent among females who have a family history of depression (Niarchou et al. 2015). One study documented that depression in boys increased by 21% between 2012 and 2015; however, during that same period, depression in girls increased by 50% (Twenge 2017). There are also environmental factors that can influence adolescent depression. One study reported that females who reported low emotional closeness to their parents were 2.3 times more likely to report higher depressive symptoms than those who reported a higher emotional connection. The same study reported that female adolescents are more susceptible to stressors that do not affect males as much (Lewis et al. 2015).

Girgus and Yang (2015) explored gender differences in depression from a developmental perspective. There appears to be few gender differences in younger children—the prevalence of depression being about equal. Beginning in early adolescence; however, rates of female depression begin to increase. By late adolescence, girls are nearly twice as likely as teenage boys to be depressed. One theory that may explain this difference is that females ruminate and coruminate (discuss problems with other people) more than males. Another theory postulates that there are three common ways to react to a negative situation: to ruminate, problem-solve, or engage in distracting behaviors. Boys are supposedly more likely to engage in two of the latter, and therefore have lower rates of depression by later adolescence than girls (Girgus and Yang 2015). It is also possible that depression is equally prevalent among men and women; however, men do not disclose it. Psychiatric drugs are also prescribed more often to women than men (Studd and Morgan 1992).

1.2. Parenting Effects on Depression and Effects of Depression on Parenting

Children are more likely to experience depression if they perceive interactions between their parents and themselves as uncaring, unsupportive, and negative (Diego et al. 2001). In turn, when children are depressed, they often have less in-depth or lengthy communication with their mothers and view their parents as more critical, angry, or sad (Chiariello and Orvaschel 1995). Betts et al. (2009) found that parents who were over-protective with low levels of nurturing, unavailable caregivers, cold, controlling and intrusive were more likely to have depressed children. Lack of nurturance and the lack of parental encouragement of autonomy created an insecure bond between the parent and child, resulting in the adolescent often having low self-confidence and difficulty in establishing trusting and supportive relationships. Such insecurity led to learned helplessness (Betts et al. 2009). Irons and Gilbert (2005) agreed that insecure attachment had negative implications—that children either felt socially inferior or compensated with competition.

Studies have shown that parental depression can have an impact on adolescent depression. Depressed mothers have been found to exercise excessive authority, control, criticism, disapproval, insufficient parental care, nurturance, and support (Chiariello and Orvaschel 1995). Approximately 15 million adolescents in the United States reside with a parent who suffers from depression. These teens are at three to four times greater risk for depression than the general population (Compas et al. 2015). Additional findings in children of depressed mothers included delay in acquiring self-regulation strategies, lower scores on measures of mental and motor development, more school problems, less social competence, lower levels of self-esteem, and higher levels of behavioral problems (Goodman and Gotlib 1999).

1.3. Religiosity and Adolescent Depression

Multiple studies have examined the relationship between depression and religion (Sanders et al. 2015; Stearns et al. 2018; Yonker et al. 2012). For example, individuals who struggle with personal religiosity—whether that includes feelings of abandonment by God, loss of faith, trials, or viewing themselves as unworthy—were shown to have poorer mental health outcomes (Rippentrop et al. 2005). Another study found that religion is positively associated with mental health in adolescents and is a significant predictor of lower levels of depression (Sanders et al. 2015). Similarly, Stearns et al. (2018) found that individuals who reported high levels of religiosity also reported lower levels of depression. Results of a meta-analysis indicated that spirituality and religiosity has a positive effect on psychological outcomes in adolescents and emerging adults (Yonker et al. 2012). Further, attending religious services has been found to be a protective factor against suicide (Anderson et al. 2015).

There are many potential reasons religious adolescents generally fare so well, especially when it comes to depressive symptoms. They are often affiliated with a strong, positive support network, including peers and adults. Their religious doctrines may provide a means to manage stress and maintain a positive outlook on life (Cotton et al. 2006). Further, religious beliefs could provide a means for problem solving and coping. Religion also often inspires adolescents to set goals and to look towards the future optimistically (Cotton et al. 2005). Wright and co-authors found that spirituality and the role of religious beliefs in an adolescent's interactions in life were directly associated with lower levels of depression (Wright et al. 1993). Pearce et al. (2003) reported that if adolescents considered themselves spiritual, and have had positive religious experiences, they reported lower levels of depression. Religion appears to provide adolescents with a framework to navigate difficult circumstances, to interpret difficult experiences more positively, and to have adults and peers as a built-in support system (Pearce et al. 2003).

Anderson et al. (2015) suggested that spirituality should be incorporated in more clinical interventions. Despite lower levels of religiosity among clinicians, many clients in psychotherapy use religious beliefs to cope and want to discuss spirituality (Anderson et al. 2015). The positive effects of religion extend beyond Christianity. A study of patients receiving hemodialysis in Jordan discovered that the more religious Muslims were, the less likely they reported depressive symptoms (Musa et al. 2018). Researchers found that spiritual wellness practices such as fasting, prayer, fostering positive relationships, expressing beliefs through art, and studying religious materials served as protective factors against depression.

However, certain religious beliefs have been associated with distress. For example, those who believed that suffering is caused by a non-benevolent God struggled more with the divine and, in turn, experienced lower levels of well-being and higher levels of distress (Wilt et al. 2016). Studies have highlighted the negative mental health effects that are caused when one feels abandonment by God. These feelings about God may be influenced by the parent-child relationship. A study conducted by Exline et al. (2013) found that how a child views their parent has a large influence on the child's feelings of abandonment by God. The more the child views their parents as cruel, the more they felt abandoned by God and saw God as cruel. These feelings were then related to feelings of anger towards the divine. Another study found that those who experienced sexual abuse growing up also experienced feelings of being abandoned by God. For these victims, the feeling of abandonment brought out anger and increased doubt in God and his promises (Rudolfsson and Tidefors 2014). Other studies among various religious groups have established the strong relationship between depression and negative religious coping such as feeling abandoned by God. (Braam et al. 2010).

1.4. Possible Construct Interaction

The extant literature clearly shows a relationship between religiosity, parenting style, gender and depression. Based on Bronfenbrenner's bioecological model (Bronfenbrenner 1999), we theorized that there were likely interactions between these well-established correlates to depression. Bronfenbrenner's theory focuses on how proximal processes (i.e., direct, reciprocal, enduring, increasingly complex interactions) become the driving force behind developmental changes in adolescence. Proximal processes are the first of four interrelated aspects of the process–person–context–time (PPCT) model for understanding how adolescents internalize influences (Bronfenbrenner 1995). Family religiosity and parenting practices are examples of a proximal process which likely influences the development of children. However, in Bronfenbrenner's bioecological theory, that influence will likely differ based on person-level constructs such as gender, temperament, and even biological issues. Each of these processes and person-level characteristics are also contained within a specific context such as a family or a religious community. Finally, the impact of these constructs likely varies over time. Rather than examining each construct independently, the bioecological model encourages researchers to examine the processes, person-level characteristics, contexts, and time variables of interest simultaneously. One way to do this is to look for interactions between the constructs already known to influence depression.

1.5. Latter-Day Saint Youth as an Important Understudied Sample

Although there has been a significant amount of research dedicated to how religious participation affects internalizing and externalizing behaviors of protestant adolescents, fewer studies have examined Latter-day Saint (LDS) teens. The Church of Jesus Christ of Latter-day Saints has a total church membership of 16,118,169—presently there are 6.6 million Latter-day Saints in the United States (Mormon Newsroom 2018).

In July 2002, Christian Smith and his team of researchers began the *National Study of Youth and Religion* (NSYR), a national, random digit-dial telephone survey. Findings indicated that activity rates and outcomes for LDS youth (also known as Mormons) generally compared favorably to other religious youth. For example, 40% of all youth surveyed attend church services at least weekly compared to 71% of LDS youth (Smith and Denton 2005, p. 37). LDS youth also appeared strongly motivated by their religion. When asked, "Would you attend Church if it were totally up to you?" Almost 70% of LDS youth responded "Yes" to that query, with 47% of Protestant youth, and 40% of Catholic teens responding in the same manner (Smith and Denton 2005, p. 37). Smith and Denton summarized their research on LDS youth stating, "when belief and 'social outcomes' are measured, 'Mormon kids tend to be on top'" (Dean 2010, p. 47). In addition, Kenda Creasy Dean, a professor at Princeton Theological Seminary summarized, "Mormon teenagers tend to be the 'spiritual athletes' of their generation, conditioning for an eternal goal with an intensity that requires sacrifice, discipline, and energy" (Dean 2010, p. 51).

However, these LDS youth are still susceptible to the problems and challenges common to adolescents. Indeed, Utah (a state that has over 50% Latter-day Saints) has a higher than national rate of teen suicide, which has increased substantially over the last decade, leading many to examine what factors in Utah may exacerbate or ameliorate mental health problems (Annor et al. 2017). The purpose of this study is to examine the prevalence of depression among Latter-day Saint teens and how religiosity and the parent–child relationships are associated with depressive symptomology. This study focuses on the following specific research questions: Does religiosity among Latter-day Saint teens reduce their rates of depression? If so, what aspects of religiosity affect depression most significantly? For example, we hypothesize that the more daily spiritual experiences an individual has, the less depressed they will be. Moreover, we hypothesize that positive religious coping, peer and leader support at Church, and family religious practices will protect and insulate adolescents from depressive symptoms.

We also examined how religiosity and parenting may combine as they relate to teen depression. As referenced earlier, when parents are harsh, teens may develop a negative, punitive view of God. Combined with family religious activities, it may be that harsh parenting has an even greater negative effect given that harshness is associated with religious activities and, hence, the teen may develop even more negative views of God. We therefore examined whether the relationship between family religious practices and depression is moderated by parenting style.

Given gender differences in rates of depression and religiosity, it may influence how parenting and religion are associated with depression. We therefore examined gender as a moderator in our analyses.

2. Methods

2.1. Measures

For each scale we employed confirmatory factor analysis to create a factor score for use in analyses. By using factor scores rather than summing or averaging the items in a scale, measurement error is reduced. We calculated reliability of factor scores using Rakov's maximal reliability method (MR; Raykov 2012).

Depression. Teen depression was assessed using the 10-item self-report Center for Epidemiological Studies Depression Scale for Children—10 (CES-D—10; Bjorck et al. 2010). Participants respond by rating the degree to which they have experienced each item in the past week (e.g., "I felt lonely", "I felt depressed"), with a Likert-type response scale ranging from 1 ("not at all") to 4 ("a lot"). The MR for this scale was excellent, at 0.99

Daily Spiritual Experiences. A subscale of the National Institute on Aging/Fetzer Religion and Spirituality Scale (Idler et al. 2003; Underwood and Teresi 2002) was used to examine the regularity with which teens felt some connection with God/spirituality with response categories being 1 = "never or almost never" to 6 = "many times a day". Items include "I feel God's love for me" and "I feel guided by God." The MR for this scale was 0.97.

Positive Religious Coping and Abandonment by God. Both positive and negative religious coping were measured using the religious coping scale of Pargament et al. (2011). For positive coping, participants were asked to think of how they deal with problems in their life and then asked the degree to which they used various strategies to cope (e.g., "Sought God's love and care", and "Looked for a stronger connection with God"). Responses range from 0 ("not at all") to 3 ("a great deal"). The MR for this scale was 0.96.

For negative coping, participants were asked how often they did things that indicated tension, conflict, and struggle with the sacred (e.g., "Questioned God's love for me", "Wondered whether God had abandoned me"). We conceptualized this construct as "Abandonment by God." A question regarding church support within this scale was omitted to keep this scale conceptually distinct from the separate church support scale (see below). The MR for this scale was 0.97.

Parenting Style. Parenting behaviors and styles of parenting were measured using the Parenting Styles and Dimensions Questionnaire—Short Version (PSDQ; Robinson et al. 2001). Children reported on both parents, and the parent reported on their own parenting, as well as the parenting of the other parent. Thus, there are two reports for each parent, one from a child and one from a parent. Responses are on a five-point Likert-type scale ranging from 1 ("never") to 5 ("always"), with higher scores indicating higher levels of the respective parenting styles and/or specific dimension of parenting behavior.

The authoritative subscale is 15 items and includes question such as "My parent is responsive to my feelings" and "My parent takes my desires into account". The authoritarian subscale is 12 items and includes question such as "My parent explodes in anger toward me" and "My parent scolds and criticizes to make me improve." Items were rephrased when parents responded about themselves or about the other parent. The MR was good (0.96 and above) for all reports of authoritative and authoritarian parents.

Private religious practices. Six items from the work of Smith and Denton (2005) were used to measure private religious practices. These include question about private prayer, meditation, scripture reading, listening to various types of religious media, and fasting. Responses ranged from 1 ("not in the past year") to 9 ("more than once a day"). The MR for this scale was acceptable at 0.75.

Support at church. Two scales were used to measure support at church, one regarding the support of peers at church and the other regarding support from church leaders. These come from the

Multi-Faith Religious Support Scale (Bjorck et al. 2017). Items included "I am valued by other teens [religious leaders] in my religious group" and "Other teens [leaders] in my religious group care about my life and situation." Responses ranged from 1 ("strongly disagree") to 4 ("strongly agree"). The MR for both of these scales was 0.98.

Controls. Several controls were added to the model including the child's age, their gender (1 = female, 0 = male), whether they lived in Utah or Arizona, their physical health (rated on a five-point scale from "poor" to "excellent"), family income, race (1 = white, 0 = other), and whether the parents were married (1 = married, 0 = not married). Sexual orientation was also included. Less than 2% identified as gay or lesbian, with 3% responding they were "questioning" their gender. This variable was dichotomized with 1 = heterosexual, 0 = other (heterosexual, n = 764; not heterosexual, n = 32). Parent depression was also controlled. The CES-D—10 was also used for parents and had good reliability (MR = 0.99). Finally, to get a more direct measure of depression, we controlled for child anxiety which was measured with the six-item Spence Children's Anxiety Scale (Spence 1998).

2.2. Sample

Participants were taken from Wave 2 of the Family Foundations of Youth Development project, a longitudinal study of families with adolescents. This project has a strong emphasis on adolescent faith and mental health development with detailed scales on numerous related issues such as internalizing and externalizing problems and pro-social behaviors and beliefs. The project also has extensive scales examining family processes and influences. Data for the second wave were collected from Utah and Arizona (the first wave included only families in Utah). Families were recruited using the *InfoUSA* national database which contains over 80 million households across the United States. Contact information was obtained for households with children between the ages of 12 and 16. To recruit, potential participants were sent letters with follow-up phone calls. One teen and one parent filled out the survey, with the teen being compensated USD $30 and the parent compensated USD $40. For the current study, we selected only LDS youth for a total n of 796 with 251 in Arizona and 545 in Utah. Mean age of teens was 14.21 (SD = 1.09) with a range from 11 to 17. The majority of children in the study came from homes with two married biological parents (93%). Ninety-one percent of the sample identified as white, with the other 9% split between Hispanic, "mixed," Asian, Black, and "other." Median yearly household income was relatively high at USD $100,000. The lower 15% of the parents made less than USD $60,000 a year and the higher 15% of the parents made above USD $150,000. Forty-six percent of the teens were male. The vast majority had married parents (97%). Paternal data were imputed for those who did not report they had a father. While this imputation may seem counterintuitive, allowing those who did not have a father to remain in the sample allows the analyses to be more representative, particularly as we can control for having a father or not. However, the analyses are substantively identical when excluding those who did not have fathers. The only difference is that the interaction between being female and family religious practices becomes significant when fitting the model excluding those without fathers (n = 11; it was very close to significance prior to the 11 being removed). However, because the three-way interaction is present, this is only interpretable in context of the three-way interaction. Prototypical plots for females (estimated at +/− 1 standard deviation from the mean) revealed no significant differences in depression for females across family religiosity. Thus, whether we remove or retain the 11 teens without fathers, the results are substantively identical.

3. Analysis Plan

Analyses were conducted in the program Stata 15 (StataCorp 2018). Missing data were minimal (0 to 3.6%) and a single imputation was conducted using the Stata procedure ICE to produce a complete dataset for analysis (Royston 2005). Regarding missing data, the only restriction was that the youth had to indicate they were currently a Latter-day Saint. With minimal amount of missingness, we used single imputation to impute missing values.

A regression was constructed with teen depression as the dependent variable with family, religious, and control variables specified as independent variables. After the initial regression model, a series of models were tested to examine whether the relationship between the independent variables and depression varied by child gender. This was done with Stata's ibn. prefix on gender which, for each independent variable, gave the value of its relationship to depressions separately for males and females. An interaction was considered if, for males or females, the relationship between the independent variable and depression was significant for one gender but not both. We also examined whether the relationship between family religious practices and depression was moderated by parenting style. Finally, we examined whether this differed by child gender. That is, we examined whether the interaction between parenting style and religiosity differed by child gender. When a control variable was not significantly related to the depression at $p < 0.10$, it was dropped for the sake of parsimony and power.

4. Results

Correlations. In Table 1, all independent variables and controls were significantly related to depression except for parents' perceptions of their authoritarian parenting and the teen's race.

Regression models. Table 2 contains final model results. Significant relationships not moderated by child gender included peer support at church (B(SE) = −0.09(0.03), $p < 0.001$) and abandonment by God (B(SE) = 0.18(0.02), $p < 0.001$). These relationships were in the hypothesized direction such that greater peer church support was related to less depression and greater abandonment by God was related to more depression. Significant controls were teen anxiety (B(SE) = 0.21(.02), $p < 0.001$), being from Utah (B(SE) = 0.05(0.02), $p < 0.01$), teens' physical health (B(SE) = −0.03(0.01), $p < 0.001$), and the teen being heterosexual (B(SE) = −0.08(0.04), $p < 0.05$). Parent income, marital status, and teen race were not related to depression at $p < 0.10$ and were therefore dropped from the model.

Several effects were moderated by gender. These included females experiencing less depression when they reported their father was more authoritative (B(SE) = −0.05(0.02), $p < 0.01$) and males reporting more depression the more private religious practices they engaged in (B(SE) = 0.02(0.01), $p < 0.05$). There was also a three-way interaction between gender, parent report of authoritative parenting by the father, and family religious practices. That is, the two-way interaction between authoritative parenting by the father and family religious practices is significant for males (B(SE) = −0.03(0.03), $p < 0.05$) but not for females. A graph of this interaction was produced (see Figure 1). In this interaction, estimated depression does not appear associated with family religious practices when father authoritative parenting is low (i.e., at low authoritative parenting, there is almost no difference in depression whether the family religious practices were high or low). In contrast, when father authoritative parenting is high, depression is substantially less *when family religious practices are also high*. In other words, the combination of an authoritative father and high family religious (religiosity) was related to lower levels of teen depression.

Table 1. Correlations and descriptives (*n* = 796).

	1	2	3	4	5	6	7	8	9	10	11	12	13	14	15	16	17	18
(1) Teen depression	-																	
(2) Parent depression	0.09*	1.00																
(3) Mom authoritative C	-0.27*	-0.11*	1.00															
(4) Mom authoritative P	-0.08*	-0.19*	0.28*	1.00														
(5) Dad authoritative C	-0.27*	-0.15*	0.68*	0.19*	1.00													
(6) Dad authoritative P	-0.08*	-0.24*	0.17*	0.42*	0.35*	1.00												
(7) Mom authoritarian C	0.22*	0.08*	-0.32*	-0.12*	-0.20*	-0.11*	1.00											
(8) Mom authoritarian P	0.06	0.22*	-0.19*	-0.35*	-0.11*	-0.20*	0.38*	1.00										
(9) Dad authoritarian C	0.19*	0.09*	-0.19*	-0.12*	-0.31*	-0.23*	0.64*	0.28*	1.00									
(10) Dad authoritarian P	0.05	0.17*	-0.08*	-0.16*	-0.25*	-0.49*	0.23*	0.39*	0.43*	1.00								
(11) Private religious practices	-0.11*	-0.08*	0.29*	0.04	0.28*	0.09*	-0.11*	-0.04	-0.05	-0.04	1.00							
(12) Family religious practices	-0.15*	-0.15*	0.18*	0.02	0.20*	0.07*	-0.04	-0.06	-0.09*	-0.07*	0.44*	1.00						
(13) Daily spiritual experiences	-0.23*	-0.04	0.35*	0.07	0.32*	0.11*	-0.14*	-0.02	-0.07*	-0.03	0.60*	0.29*	1.00					
(14) Peer church support	-0.35*	-0.07*	0.32*	0.01	0.30*	0.05	-0.12*	-0.01	-0.10*	-0.01	0.34*	0.25*	0.42*	1.00				
(15) Leader church support	-0.30*	-0.10*	0.34*	0.05	0.31*	0.09*	-0.16*	-0.06	-0.13*	-0.05	0.37*	0.27*	0.41*	0.78*	1.00			
(16) Abandonment by God	0.46*	0.07*	-0.18*	-0.09*	-0.18*	-0.09*	0.21*	0.07*	0.16*	0.05	-0.11*	-0.15*	-0.28*	-0.24*	-0.26*	1.00		
(17) Positive religious. coping	-0.14*	-0.04	0.36*	0.06	0.31*	0.09*	-0.16*	-0.04	-0.06	-0.05	0.60*	0.31*	0.63*	0.36*	0.37*	-0.10*	1.00	
(18) Teen female	0.11*	0.01	0.07	0.08*	0.01	0.02	-0.15*	-0.10*	-0.10*	-0.04	0.08*	-0.06	0.06	-0.01	0.01	0.04	0.12*	1.00
Mean	2.03	1.97	3.58	3.86	3.40	3.48	1.77	1.62	1.76	1.67	5.01	5.03	1.93	2.93	3.16	1.43	2.79	0.46
SD	0.29	0.25	0.70	0.42	0.83	0.70	0.49	0.29	0.57	0.41	10.55	10.13	0.62	0.49	0.48	0.38	0.67	0.50

C Child report, P Parent report.

Table 2. Predicting teen depression (*n* = 796).

Predictor	Teen Depression	
	B(SE)	β
Constant		
Females	1.73(0.19) ***	–
Males	1.74(0.19) ***	–
Mom authoritative [C]	−0.03(0.02)	−0.07
Mom authoritative [P]	0.00(0.02)	0.00
Dad authoritative [C]		
Females	−0.05(0.02) **	−0.11
Males	−0.01(0.02)	−0.02
Dad authoritative [P]		
Females	0.04(0.02) *	0.08
Males	−0.03(0.02)	−0.04
Family religious practices		
Females	0.02(0.01)	0.05
Males	−0.02(0.01)	−0.06
Dad authoritative [P] *		
Family religious practices		
Females	−0.01(0.01)	−0.02
Males	−0.03(0.03) *	−0.05
Mom authoritarian [C]	0.04(0.02)	0.06
Mom authoritarian [P]	−0.00(0.03)	−0.00
Dad authoritarian [C]	0.00(0.02)	0.01
Dad authoritarian [P]	−0.00(0.02)	−0.01
Private religious practices		
Females	0.01(0.01)	0.06
Males	0.02(0.01) *	0.07
Daily spiritual experiences	−0.00(0.02)	−0.00
Peer church support	−0.09(0.03) ***	−0.15
Leader church support	−0.00(0.03)	−0.00
Abandonment by God	0.18(0.02) ***	0.24
Positive religious coping	−0.02(0.02)	−0.04
Controls		
Anxiety	0.21(0.02) ***	0.38
Parent depression	0.05(0.03)	0.04
Utah	0.05(0.02) **	0.08
Physical health	−0.03(0.01) ***	−0.11
Heterosexual	−0.08(0.04) *	−0.05
Age	0.01(0.01)	0.05
Adjusted R^2	0.47	

* $p < 0.05$. ** $p < 0.01$. *** $p < 0.001$. [C] Child report, [P] Parent report.

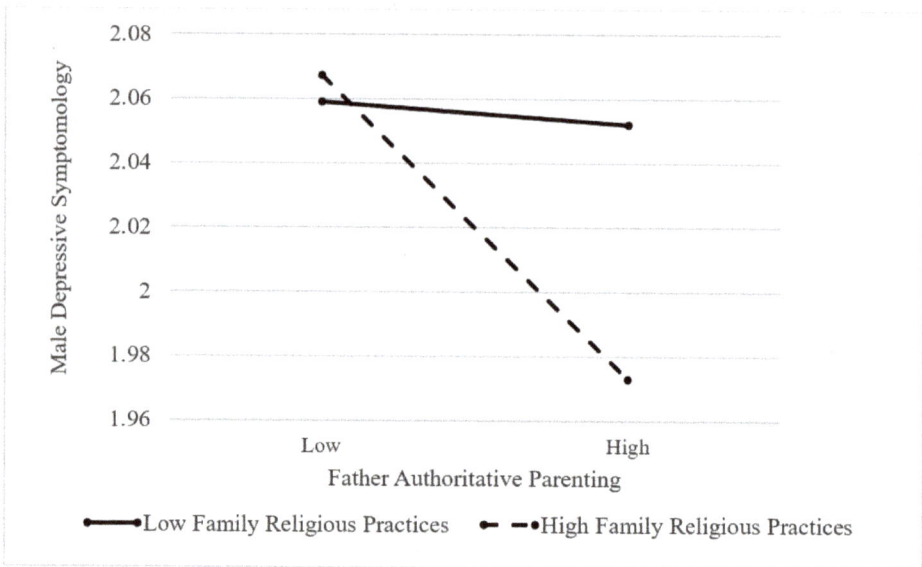

Figure 1. Interaction between paternal authoritative parenting and family religious practices for male teens.

5. Discussion

This study examined the relationship between family, faith, and depression in a sample of Latter-day Saint adolescents and identified factors indicative of greater depression. This enables us to better identify those who may be at greatest risk for depressive symptoms. Furthermore, this study also illuminates how faith and family may interact in their association with risk. This goes beyond simply controlling for faith or family factors, but rather employs a more comprehensive conceptualization by examining whether the impact of family and faith may, in part, be dependent on one another.

For basic demographics, youth in Utah reported higher depression compared to adolescents in Arizona. The U.S. Department of Health and Human Services cite two studies of adolescent depression in both states with conflicting findings. A 2018 study measured depression with a single question that asked how often youth felt sad or hopeless. In this study, Utah adolescents appeared to experience less depression (33% of Utah adolescents experienced depressive symptoms compared to 36% of Arizona youth; both groups however had higher values than the United States average of 31%). However, a 2017 study that measured adolescent depression found Utah adolescents experienced more depression than Arizona adolescents, 14% to 12%, with the United States average being 13% (Arizona Adolescent Mental Health Facts 2018). The measure used to assess depression in the current study from the CES-D−10 more closely aligned with the measure used in the 2017 study mentioned above, which also had Utah adolescents experiencing higher levels of depression. Since there are more LDS youth in Utah than Arizona, it could be argued that something about the LDS faith is driving the slightly higher depression rates in Utah. However, the fact that LDS youth in Arizona have lower levels of depression than LDS youth in Utah raises the possibility that there are other personal-level, or contextual influences besides the LDS faith that are driving the higher Utah depression rates. Our measures do not provide enough detail to know for sure. One possible contributing factor might be elevation. Higher altitude has been associated with a higher suicide rate (Betz et al. 2011; Brenner et al. 2011) with some suggesting greater depression as a possible mechanism (Gamboa et al. 2011). Indeed, in examining the counties from which the sample was primarily drawn, the Utah counties have between three and seven times the elevation of the Arizona counties.

The National Alliance on Mental Health states that LGBTQ youth experience almost three times more mental health conditions than heterosexual youth (LGBTQ/NAM, 2019). Other national and international studies have found similar outcomes (Mustanski et al. 2010; Shenkman and Shmotkin 2011). Studies have found that these negative outcomes stem from several causes including prejudice and stigma, higher levels of substance abuse, higher suicidality, and even disparities in care (Russell and Fish 2016).

In addition, and not surprisingly, depression was associated with greater anxiety and physical health problems. Further, as has been found in other research (e.g., Petterson et al. 2017), those who identified as heterosexual reported lower levels of depression than those identifying as gay, lesbian, bisexual, or questioning.

Regarding religiosity, two aspects had main effects on depression: abandonment by God and support at church from teens. Previous research has found that individuals who perceive God has abandoned them often report depressive symptoms (Rippentrop et al. 2005; Dew et al. 2010) and that church support is related to fewer depressive symptoms (Nooney and Woodrum 2002). Interestingly, these are both relational constructs. That is, when teens feel cared about by God and/or their peers at church, their depression is lower. This may indicate that, for depression, a key protective factor within religion is whether the individual's religious experiences facilitate connections with the divine and with others. This fits well with Bronfenbrenner's theory that: "The developmental power of proximal processes (in this case religious practices) are substantially enhanced when they occur within the context of a relationship between persons who have developed a strong emotional attachment to each other" (Bronfenbrenner 2000, p. 130). Thus, if adolescents feel disconnected from a close relationship with their family or God, they may be more susceptible to depression. Given the current study uses cross-sectional data we cannot determine whether individuals who are depressed distance themselves (and/or perceive more distance) from God and peers or whether poor connections with God and peers increases depression. Likely the relationship between religious connections and depression is transactional, with each affecting the other. In any case, given they are at increased risk for depressive symptomology, it would be important for church organizations to identify those lower on these connections and attempt to foster those connections for their members.

Contrary to hypotheses, positive religious coping was not significantly related to depression. It may be that more nuanced measures of coping are needed. There are other types of coping that we did not examine. For example, Pargament et al. (2001) developed a model that looked at three religious coping styles: self-directed coping, collaborative coping, and deferring coping. These three styles of coping may relate to depression. In one study on adolescent religious coping, the researchers found that the collaborative religious coping style served as a protective factor against negative mental health outcomes (Molock et al. 2006). Therefore, for religious adolescents, encouraging a collaborative relationship with God can minimize the effects of negative mental health outcomes. Although there has been a significant amount of research in the areas of adolescents, religious coping, and serious medical conditions, more research will need to be conducted in the arena of religious coping and mental health.

Regarding parenting, paternal authoritative parenting was associated with lower depression in daughters but not sons, indicating a differential impact of the person-level construct of gender—both the gender of the parent and the gender of the child. Other research has found unique effects of paternal involvement on the psychological wellbeing of daughters (e.g., Flouri and Buchanan 2003), though without longitudinal data it is unclear whether this is a father effect (the father's authoritative parenting reducing daughter's depression), a daughter effect (fathers being more authoritative towards daughters who are less depressed), or whether there is a third explanation. Whatever the explanation, a father's less authoritative behaviors may be a signal of greater mental difficulties for their daughter(s).

The significant three-way interaction between gender, family religious practices, and paternal authoritative parenting is suggestive of the conditions under which family and faith may exert a more pronounced influence. In this instance, when either family religious practices (a proximal process) or paternal authoritative parenting (both a process and a context) were low, neither one appeared related to depression. That is, depression was essentially the same across levels of authoritative fathering when family religious practices were low. Further, when paternal authoritative parenting was low, there was no significant difference in depression across levels of family religious practices. However, when both paternal authoritative parenting and religious practices were high, there was an associated lower level of depression. It is possible that regular family religious practices provide a forum in which the positive parenting can occur. This connects with Bronfenbrenner's theory that "to be effective, the interaction must occur on a fairly regular basis over extended periods of time" (Bronfenbrenner 1999, p. 5).

Family religious practices may provide a regular and enduring context for authoritative parenting to have an effect. Why this would be the case only for male children is not entirely clear given, as noted earlier, fathering has typically been related more strongly to daughters' mental wellbeing than sons'. It is possible, as suggested by our findings, that paternal authoritative behaviors exert more of an influence on sons when in combination with other positive family practices, whereas for daughters the effect ranges across a variety of family contexts.

Although there are many studies that suggest religion can be a positive influence on physical and mental health, religion can also exacerbate problems (see Pruyser 1977; Pargament et al. 2001). Research from this study reveals that sometimes, religion can be detrimental to an individual's well-being. For example, religiosity has been found to discourage individuals from seeking mental health help (Blank et al. 2002).

6. Conclusions

This study confirms findings from prior research in several areas. Being a sexual minority and experiencing higher levels of anxiety were associated with greater depression. Contrary to hypotheses, church leader support, positive religious coping, and daily spiritual experiences were unrelated to depression. Religion and spirituality were not uniformly associated with lower depression as many studies have found. For this sample, peer church support was associated with lower depression but feeling abandoned by God was related to higher levels of depression. There was also evidence that fathers' authoritative parenting has a main effect on depression for daughters. Further, father authoritative parenting interacted with family religious practices predicting adolescent depression for sons. That is, if both authoritative parenting and family religious practices were high, depression levels were low in sons. However, if both were not high, neither was related to depression levels in a significant way.

7. Limitations

The sample used in the current study is homogenous, being primarily White and all LDS. Furthermore, 92% of our sample represented intact families, with a mother and father present in the home. In order for our findings to be generalizable, in the future, our participants in the study will need to be more diverse. Further, as mentioned, this study is unable to examine the direction of effects. It may be that the effects flow from depression to the family and religious variables. Still, the study does identify factors that can help identify teens that may be at most risk for depression.

Author Contributions: Conceptualization, M.D.O., M.A.G., & W.J.D.; Methodology, W.J.D. and M.A.G.; Formal Analysis, W.J.D.; Resources, M.D.O., M.A.G., and W.J.D.; Data Curation, W.J.D.; Writing—Original Draft Preparation, M.D.O., M.A.G., C.K., B.W.M.; Writing—Review and Editing, M.D.O., M.A.G., C.K., B.W.M.; Supervision, M.D.O.; Project Administration, M.D.O., W.J.D.; Funding Acquisition, W.J.D., M.D.O., M.A.G.

Funding: This research received no external funding.

Conflicts of Interest: The authors declare no conflicts of interest.

References

Anderson, Naomi, Suzanne Heywood-Everett, Najma Siddiqi, Judy Wright, Jodi Meredith, and Dean McMillian. 2015. Faith-adapted psychological therapies for depression and anxiety: Systematic review and meta-analysis. *Journal of Affective Disorders* 176: 183–96. [CrossRef] [PubMed]

Annor, Francis, Amanda Wilkinson, and Marissa Zwald. 2017. *Epi-Aid # 2017–2019: Undetermined Risk Factors for Suicide among Youth Aged 10–17 Years—Utah, 2017*. Atlanta: Centers for Disease Control and Prevention.

Arizona Adolescent Mental Health Facts. 2018. Text, HHS.gov. Available online: https://hhs.gov/oah/facts-and-stats/national-and-state-data-sheets/adolescent-mental-health-fact-sheets/arizona/index.html (accessed on 14 November 2018).

Arntzen, Elsie. 2017. 2017 Montana Youth Risk Behavior Survey 14. Available online: http://opi.mt.gov/portals/182/page%20files/yrbs/17mt_yrbs_fullreport.pdf (accessed on 25 March 2019).

Ball, Joanna, Lisa Armistead, and Barbara-Jeanne Austin. 2003. The relationship between religiosity and adjustment among African-American, female, urban adolescents. *Journal of Adolescence* 26: 431–46. [CrossRef]

Betts, Jennifer, Eleonora Gullone, and Janice Allen. 2009. An examination of emotion regulation, temperament, and parenting style as potential predictors of adolescent depression risk status: A correlational study. *British Journal of Developmental Psychology* 27: 473–85. [CrossRef] [PubMed]

Betz, Marian E., Morgan A. Valley, Steven R. Lowenstein, Holly Hedegaard, Deborah Thomas, Lorann Stallones, and Benjamin Honigman. 2011. Elevated suicide rates at high altitude: Sociodemographic and health issues may be to blame. *Suicide and Life-Threatening Behavior* 41: 562–73. [CrossRef]

Birmaher, Boris, Neal Ryan, Douglas Williamson, David Brent, Joan Kaufman, Ronald Dahl, James Perel, and Beverly Nelson. 1996. Childhood and adolescent depression: A review of the past 10 years. *Journal of the American Academy of Child and Adolescent Psychiatry* 35: 1427–39. [CrossRef]

Bjorck, Jeffrey, Robert Braese, Joseph Tadie, and David Gililland. 2010. The Adolescent Religious Coping Scale: Development, validation, and cross-validation. *Journal of Child and Family Studies* 19: 343–59. [CrossRef]

Bjorck, Jeffrey, Grace Kim, Dawna Cunha, and Robert Braese. 2017. Assessing religious support in Christian adolescents: Initial validation of the Multi-Faith Religious Support Scale-Adolescent (MFRSS-A). In *Psychology of Religion and Spirituality, Advance Online Publication*. No Pagination Specified-No Pagination Specified. [CrossRef]

Blank, Michael, Marcus Mahmood, Jeanne Fox, and Thomas Guterbock. 2002. Alternative mental health services: The role of the Black church in the South. *American Journal of Public Health* 92: 1668–72. [CrossRef]

Bose, Jonaki, Sara Hedden, Rachel Lipari, and Eunice Park-Lee. 2016. *Key Substance Use and Mental Health Indicators in the United States: Results from 2015 National Survey of Drug Use and Health*; North Bethesda: Center for Behavioral Health Statistics and Quality, Substance Abuse and Mental Health Services Administration.

Braam, Arjan, Agnes Schrier, Wilco Tuinebreijer, Aartjan Beekman, Jack Dekker, and Matty De Wit. 2010. Religious coping and depression in multicultural Amsterdam: A comparison between native Dutch citizens and Turkish, Moroccan and Surinamese/Antillean migrants. *Journal of Affective Disorders* 125: 269–78. [CrossRef] [PubMed]

Brenner, Barry, David Cheng, Sunday Clark, and Carlos A. Camargo Jr. 2011. Positive association between altitude and suicide in 2584 U.S. counties. *High Altitude Medicine & Biology* 12: 31–35. [CrossRef]

Bronfenbrenner, Urie. 1995. Developmental ecology through space and time: A future perspective. In *Examining Lives in Context: Perspectives on the Ecology of Human Development*. Edited by Phillis Moen, Glenn H. Elder and Kurt Luscher. Washington: American Psychological Association, pp. 619–47.

Bronfenbrenner, Urie. 1999. Environments in developmental perspective: Theoretical and operational models. In *Measuring Environment Across the Life Span: Emerging Methods and Concepts*. Edited by Sarah L. Friedman and Theodore D. Wachs. Washington: American Psychological Association, pp. 3–28.

Bronfenbrenner, Urie. 2000. Ecological systems theory. In *Encyclopedia of Psychology*. Edited by Alan E. Kazdin and Alan E. Kazdin. Washington and New York: American Psychological Association Oxford University Press, vol. 3, pp. 129–33.

Chiariello, Mary, and Helen Orvaschel. 1995. Patterns of parent-child communication: Relationship to depression. *Clinical Psychology Review* 15: 395–407. [CrossRef]

Compas, Bruce, Rex Forehand, Jennifer Thigpen, Emily Hardcastle, Emily Garai, Laura McKee, and Sonya Sterba. 2015. Efficacy and moderators of a family group cognitive–behavioral preventive intervention for children of parents with depression. *Journal of Consulting and Clinical Psychology* 83: 541–53. [CrossRef] [PubMed]

Cooperman, Alan, Gregory Smith, and Katherine Ritchey. 2015. *America's Changing Religious Landscape*. Washington: Pew Research Center, vol. 11.

Cotton, Sian, Elizabeth Larkin, Andrea Hoopes, Barbara Cromer, and Susan Rosenthal. 2005. The impact of adolescent spirituality on depressive symptoms and health risk behaviors. *Journal of Adolescent Heath* 36: 529e7–529e14. [CrossRef]

Cotton, Sian, Kathy Zebracki, Susan Rosenthal, Joel Tsevat, and Dennis Drotar. 2006. Religion, spirituality and adolescent health outcomes: A review. *Journal of Adolescent Health* 38: 472–80. [CrossRef]

Dean, Kenda C. 2010. *Almost Christian: What the Faith of Our Teenagers is Telling the American Church*. New York: Oxford University Press.

Dew, Rachel, Stephanie S. Daniel, David B. Goldston, William V. McCall, Margatha N. Kuchibhatla, Charlie Schleifer, Mary F. Triplett, and Harold G. Koenig. 2010. A prospective study of religion/spirituality and depressive symptoms among adolescent psychiatric patients. *Journal of Affective Disorders* 120: 149–57. [CrossRef]

Diego, Miguel, Christopher Sanders, and Tiffany Field. 2001. Adolescent depression and risk factors. *Adolescence* 36: 491–98.

Donahue, Michael, and Peter L. Benson. 1995. Religion and the well-being of adolescents. *Journal of Social Issues* 51: 145–160. [CrossRef]

Exline, Julie J., Stephanie J. Homolka, and Joshua B. Grubbs. 2013. Negative views of parents and struggles with God: An exploration of two mediators. *Journal of Psychology and Theology* 41: 200–12. [CrossRef]

Flouri, Eirini, and Ann Buchanan. 2003. The role of father involvement in children's later mental health. *Journal of Adolescence* 26: 63–78. [CrossRef]

Gamboa, Jorge L., Ricardo Caceda, and Alberto Arregui. 2011. Is depression the link between suicide and high altitude? *High Altitude Medicine & Biology* 12: 403–4.

Girgus, Joan, and Kaite Yang. 2015. Gender and Depression. *Current Opinion in Psychology* 4: 43–60. [CrossRef]

Goodman, Sherryl, and Ian Gotlib. 1999. Risk for psychopathology in the children of depressed mothers: A developmental model for understanding mechanisms of transmission. *Psychological Review* 106: 458–90. [CrossRef] [PubMed]

Idler, Elen, Marc Musick, Christopher Ellison, Linda George, Neal Krause, Marcia Ory, and David Williams. 2003. Measuring multiple dimensions of religion and spirituality for health research: Conceptual background and findings from the 1998 General Social Survey. *Research on Aging* 25: 327–65. [CrossRef]

Irons, Chris, and Paul Gilbert. 2005. Evolved mechanisms in adolescent anxiety and depression symptoms: the role of the attachment and social rank systems. *Journal of Adolescence* 28: 325–41. [CrossRef] [PubMed]

Jessor, Richard, Mark Turbin, and Frances Costa. 1998. Risk and protection in successful outcomes among disadvantaged adolescents. *Applied Developmental Science* 2: 194–208. [CrossRef]

Lammers, Cristina, Marjorie Ireland, Michael Resnick, and Robert Blum. 2000. Influences on adolescents' decision to postpone onset of sexual intercourse: A survival analysis of virginity among youths aged 13–18 years. *Journal of Adolescent Health* 26: 42–48.

Lewinsohn, Peter, Paul Rohde, and John Seely. 1998. Major depressive disorder in older adolescents: Prevalence, risk factors, and clinical implications. *Clinical Psychology Review* 18: 765–94. [CrossRef]

Lewis, Andrew, Peter Kremer, Kim Douglas, John W. Toumbourou, Mohajer A. Hameed, George C. Patton, and Joanne Williams. 2015. Gender differences in adolescent depression: Differential female susceptibility to stressors affecting family functioning. *Australian Journal of Psychology* 67: 131–39. [CrossRef]

Mojtabai, Ramin, Mark Olfson, and Beth Han. 2017. National trends in the prevalence and treatment of depression in adolescents and young adults. *Pediatrics* 138: 1–10. [CrossRef]

Molock, Sherry, Rupa Puri, Samantha Matlin, and Crystal Barksdale. 2006. Relationship between religious coping and suicidal behaviors among African American adolescents. *Journal of Black Psychology* 32: 366–89. [CrossRef]

Mormon Newsroom. 2018. LDS Statistics and Church Facts | Total Church Membership. Available online: https://www.mormonnewsroom.org/facts-and-statistics (accessed on 12 January 2019).

Muller, Chandra, and Christopher Ellison. 2001. Religious involvement, social capital, and adolescents' academic progress: Evidence from the National Longitudinal Study of 1988. *Sociological Focus* 341: 55–183. [CrossRef]

Musa, Ahmad, David Pevalin, and Murad Al Khalaileh. 2018. Spiritual well-being, depression, and stress among hemodialysis patients in Jordan. *Journal of Holistic Nursing* 36: 354–65. [CrossRef]

Mustanski, Brian, Robert Garofalo, and Erin Emerson. 2010. Mental health disorders, psychological distress, and suicidality in a diverse sample of lesbian, gay, bisexual, and transgender youths. *American Journal of Public Health* 100: 2426–32. [CrossRef] [PubMed]

Niarchou, Maria, Stanley Zammit, and Glyn Lewis. 2015. The Avon longitudinal study of parents and children (ALSPAC) birth cohort as a resource for studying psychopathology in childhood and adolescence: A summary of findings for depression and psychosis. *Social Psychiatry & Psychiatric Epidemiology* 50: 1017–27.

Nooney, Jennifer, and Eric Woodrum. 2002. Religious coping and church-based social support as predictors of mental health outcomes: Testing a conceptual model. *Journal for the Scientific Study of Religion* 41: 359–68. [CrossRef]

Pargament, Kenneth, Nalini Tarakeshwar, Christopher Ellison, and Keith Wulff. 2001. Religious coping among the Religious: The Relationships between Religious Coping and Well-being in a National sample of Presbyterian Clergy, Elders, and Members. *Journal for the Scientific Study of Religion* 40: 497–513. [CrossRef]

Pargament, Kenneth, Margaret Feuilleand, and Donna Burdzy. 2011. The Brief RCOPE: Current psychometric status of a short measure of religious coping. *Religions* 2: 51–76. [CrossRef]

Pearce, Michelle, Todd Little, and John Perez. 2003. Religiousness and depressive symptoms among adolescents. *Journal of Clinical Child Adolescent Psychology* 32: 267–76. [CrossRef] [PubMed]

Petterson, Lanna, Doug VanderLaan, Tonje Persson, and Paul Vasey. 2017. The relationship between indicators of depression and anxiety and sexual orientation in Canadian women. *Archives of Sexual Behavior* 40: 1173–82. [CrossRef]

Pine, Daniel, Patricia Cohen, Diana Gurley, Judith Brook, and Yuju Ma. 1998. The risk for early-adulthood anxiety and depressive disorders in adolescents with anxiety and depressive disorders. *Archives of General Psychiatry* 55: 56–64. [CrossRef]

Pinheiro, Marina, Jose Morosoli, Lucia Colodro-Conde, Paulo Ferreira, and Juan Ordoñana. 2018. Genetic and environmental influences to low back pain and symptoms of depression and anxiety: A population-based twin study. *Journal of Psychosomatic Research* 105: 92–98. [CrossRef]

Pruyser, Paul W. 1977. The seamy side of current religious beliefs. *Bulletin of the Menniger Clinic* 41: 329–48. [CrossRef]

Raykov, Tenko. 2012. Scale construction and development using structural equation modeling. In *Handbook of Structural Equation Modeling*. Edited by Rick H. Hoyle. New York: Guilford, pp. 472–92.

Regnerus, Mark. 2000. Shaping schooling success: Religious socialization and educational outcomes in urban public schools. *Journal for the Scientific Study of Religion* 39: 363–70. [CrossRef]

Rippentrop, Elizabeth, Elizabeth Altmaier, Joseph Chen, Ernest Found, and Valerie Keffala. 2005. The relationship between religion/spirituality and the physical health, mental health, and pain in a chronic pain population. *Pain* 116: 311–21. [CrossRef]

Robinson, Clyde, Barbara Mandleco, Susan Olsen, and Craig Hart. 2001. The Parenting Styles and Dimensions Questionnaire (PSQD). In *Handbook of Family Measurement Techniques*. Edited by John Touliatos, Barry F. Perlmutter and George W. Holden. Thousand Oaks: Sage, vol. 3, pp. 319–21.

Royston, Patrick. 2005. Multiple imputation of missing values: Update. *Stata Journal* 5: 188–201. [CrossRef]

Rudolfsson, Lisa, and Inga Tidefors. 2014. I have cried to him a thousand times, but it makes no difference: Sexual abuse, faith, and images of God. *Mental Health, Religion & Culture* 17: 910–22. [CrossRef]

Russell, Stephen, and Jessica Fish. 2016. Mental health in Lesbian, Gay, Bisexual, and Transgender (LGBT) youth. *Annual Review of Clinical Psychology* 12: 465–87. [CrossRef]

Sanders, Peter, Kawika Allen, Lane Fischer, Morgan Richards, David Potts, and Richard Potts. 2015. Intrinsic religiousness and spirituality as predictors of mental health and positive psychological functioning in Latter-day Saint adolescents and young adults. *Journal of Religion and Health* 54: 871–87. [CrossRef] [PubMed]

Shenkman, Geva, and Dov Shmotkin. 2011. Mental health among Israeli homosexual adolescents and young adults. *Journal of Homosexuality, Suicide, Mental Health, and Youth Development* 58: 97–116. [CrossRef] [PubMed]

Shortz, Joianne, and Everett Worthington. 1994. Young adults' recall of religiosity, attributions, and coping in parental divorce. *Journal for the Scientific Study of Religion* 33: 172–79. [CrossRef]

Smith, Christian. 2003. Theorizing religious effects among American adolescents. *Journal for the Scientific Study of Religion* 42: 17–30. [CrossRef]

Smith, Christian, and Melinda Denton. 2005. *Soul Searching: The Religious and Spiritual Lives of American Teenagers.* New York: Oxford University Press.

Smith, Christian, Melinda Denton, Robert Faris, and Mark Regnerus. 2002. Mapping American adolescent religious participation. *Journal for the Scientific Study of Religion* 41: 597–612. [CrossRef]

Spence, Susan H. 1998. A measure of anxiety symptoms among children. *Behaviour Research and Therapy* 36: 545–66. [CrossRef]

StataCorp. 2018. *Stata Statistical Software: Release 15.1.* College Station: StataCorp LP.

Stearns, Melanie, Danielle Nadorff, Ethan Lantz, and Ian McKay. 2018. Religiosity and depressive symptoms in older adults compared to younger adults: Moderation by age. *Journal of Affective Disorders* 238: 522–25. [CrossRef] [PubMed]

Studd, John, and Jaquelinem Morgan. 1992. Gender and depression. *The Lancet* 340: 8822. [CrossRef]

Sullivan, Patrick, Michael C. Neale, and Kenneth S. Kendler. 2000. Genetic epidemiology of major depression: Review and meta-analysis. *The American Journal of Psychiatry* 157: 1552–62. [CrossRef]

Twenge, Jean. 2017. *IGen: Why Today's Super-Connected Kids Are Growing up Less Rebellious, More Tolerant, Less Happy—And Completely Unprepared for Adulthood (122–123).* New York: Atria Books.

Uecker, Jeremy E., Mark D. Regnerus, and Margaret L. Vaaler. 2007. Losing my religion: The social sources of religious decline in early adulthood. *Social Forces* 85: 1667–92. [CrossRef]

Underwood, Lynn G., and Jeanne A. Teresi. 2002. The daily spiritual experience scale: Development, theoretical description, reliability, exploratory factor analysis, and preliminary construct validity using health-related data. *Annals of Behavioral Medicine* 24: 22–33. [CrossRef]

Varon, Stuart R., and Anne W. Riley. 1999. Relationship between maternal church attendance and adolescent mental health and social functioning. *Psychiatric Services* 50: 799–805. [CrossRef] [PubMed]

Whitehead, Barbara D., Brian Wilcox, and Sharon Rostosky. 2001. *Keeping the Faith: The Role of Religious and Faith Communities in Preventing Teen Pregnancy.* Washington: National Campaign to Prevent Teen Pregnancy.

Wilt, Joshua A., Julie J. Exline, Joshua B. Grubbs, Crystal L. Park, and Kenneth I. Pargament. 2016. God's role in suffering: Theodicies, divine struggle, and mental health. *Psychology of Religion and Spirituality* 8: 352–62. [CrossRef]

Wright, Loyd S., Christopher J. Frost, and Stephen J. Wisecarver. 1993. Church attendance, meaningfulness of religion, and depressive symptomology among adolescents. *Journal of Youth Adolescence* 22: 559–68. [CrossRef]

Yonker, Julie E., Chelsea A. Schnabelrauch, and Laura G. DeHaan. 2012. The relationship between spirituality and religiosity on psychological outcomes in adolescents and emerging adults: A meta-analytic review. *Journal of Adolescence* 35: 299–314. [CrossRef]

religions

MDPI

Article

Secrets and Lies: Adolescent Religiosity and Concealing Information from Parents

Scott A. Desmond

Department Information, Indiana University Purdue University Columbus, 4601 Central Avenue, Columbus, IN 47203, USA; sadesmon@iupuc.edu

Received: 15 January 2019; Accepted: 20 February 2019; Published: 23 February 2019

check for
updates

Abstract: There is very little research on the relationship between adolescent religiosity and concealing information from parents, although research on religiosity and family life is plentiful. Therefore, I used the second wave of the National Study of Youth and Religion to examine the relationship between adolescent religiosity and lying to parents and keeping secrets from parents. The results suggest that adolescents who attend religious services more often are less likely to keep secrets from parents, whereas adolescents who believe that religion is important are both less likely to lie to parents and keep secrets from parents. Being spiritual, but not religious, is not related to lying to parents or keeping secrets from parents. Results also suggest that primarily alcohol use, substance using peers, and morality mediate the effect of adolescent religiosity on lying to parents and keeping secrets from parents. Adolescents who attend religious services often and believe that religion is important are less likely to use alcohol, less likely to have friends that use substances, and are more likely to believe that moral rules should not be broken, which helps to explain why they are less likely to lie to parents and keep secrets from parents.

Keywords: information management; lying; secrets; adolescents

---

1. Introduction

Parental knowledge of adolescent activities, such as knowing what adolescents are doing, where they are going, and whom they are with, has been linked to many beneficial outcomes for adolescents, including lower rates of delinquency and substance use (Soenens et al. 2006; Yun et al. 2016). Parental knowledge is also related to several aspects of subjective well being, such as depression, low self-esteem, and stress (Frijns et al. 2005). Research suggests that parents can increase their knowledge of adolescent activities by fostering loving relationships with their children (Smetana 2009; Yun et al. 2016). Other aspects of parenting, such as parental control, authority, solicitation, and trust, may also facilitate greater parental knowledge of adolescent activities (Hawk et al. 2013; Smetana 2009; Soenens et al. 2006; Tilton-Weaver 2014).

Although parental monitoring can increase parental knowledge, recent studies have determined that parental knowledge depends more on the willingness of adolescents to disclose information than on the efforts of parents (Kerr and Stattin 2000; Darling and Tilton-Weaver 2019; Stattin and Kerr 2000). For example, one longitudinal study regarding parental monitoring found that adolescent disclosure was significantly related to parental knowledge, but neither parental control nor parental solicitation contributed to greater parental knowledge (Kerr et al. 2010). As Grigoryeva (2018, p. 227) argues, "child disclosure and secrecy—not parental attempts at monitoring and supervision—generate the knowledge that parents require to discipline children and prevent them from engaging in delinquency". Therefore, in contrast to a passive view of adolescents, recent research suggests "adolescents actively contribute to their own socialization by choosing how much information to share with and keep from their parents" (Darling and Tilton-Weaver 2019, p. 9).

Given the importance of adolescent information management strategies (i.e., full disclosure, omitting details, lying) for parental knowledge and the beneficial effects of parental knowledge on a host of adolescent outcomes, researchers have attempted to identify the conditions under which adolescents are more likely to disclose or conceal information from their parents. In contrast to the parent-adolescent relationship, which has been the focus of much research, with the exception of sex and age, few studies have examined the effect of individual characteristics (or "individual differences") on adolescent information management. Given religious teachings regarding the authority of parents (e.g., "honor thy father and mother") and the importance of honesty (e.g., "thou shall not bear false witness"), religious adolescents should be less likely to conceal information from their parents by lying and keeping secrets. Despite decades of research on religion and family life, we know very little about the relationship between adolescent religiosity and concealing information from parents. Are religious adolescents less likely to conceal information from their parents by lying and keeping secrets? Furthermore, if religious adolescents are less likely to conceal information from their parents, what are the mechanisms that help to explain the relationship between religiosity and lying to parents and keeping secrets from parents?

2. Background

2.1. Adolescent Information Management

Although parental monitoring is an important concept in many theories of adolescent development, Stattin and Kerr (2000) observed that parental monitoring is often measured while using items that assess parental knowledge (i.e., where is the adolescent, who is the adolescent with, what is the adolescent doing). It was traditionally assumed that parental knowledge was the byproduct of parental behaviors, such as direct supervision or asking questions to gain greater knowledge. From this perspective, a lack of parental knowledge was considered to be the result of neglectful parents. In contrast, Stattin and Kerr (2000) argued that parental knowledge also depends on how willing adolescents are to disclose information to their parents (see also Kerr and Stattin 2000). The results of their study confirmed the importance of child disclosure to parental knowledge. Stattin and Kerr (Stattin and Kerr 2000, p. 1072) concluded that "tracking and surveillance is not the best prescription for parental behavior and that a new prescription must rest on an understanding of the factors that determine child disclosure".

Following the publication of Stattin and Kerr (2000) influential study, researchers have focused on developing a greater understanding of adolescent information management (Smetana 2009). Adolescents use a variety of passive and active strategies to manage the information that their parents have about their activities, such as full disclosure, omitting details, avoiding the issue unless asked, keeping secrets, and lying (Laird et al. 2013; Smetana et al. 2009; Tasopoulos-Chan et al. 2009). Research suggests that disclosing and concealing should be considered to be two separate (but related) concepts, rather than two ends of a continuum (Darling and Tilton-Weaver 2019; Frijns et al. 2010; Jaggi et al. 2016). As Darling and Tilton-Weaver (2019, p. 1) argue "revealing and concealing strategies are conceptually distinct from one another: an adolescent can reveal a great deal of information to parents about school activities while concealing their drinking". Previous research also suggests that the relationship between information management and adolescent outcomes is primarily the result of concealing strategies (Frijns et al. 2010; Jaggi et al. 2016). In other words, concealing strategies have a strong negative effect on adolescent outcomes, whereas disclosing strategies have a weak positive effect on adolescent outcomes. Therefore, the disclosure-adjustment link may primarily be the result of a concealment-maladjustment link (Frijns et al. 2010).

Previous research suggests that the domain of behavior (routine, personal, prudential, moral, and/or multifaceted) influences disclosing and concealing. Adolescents are less willing to accept parental authority, and they are most willing to engage in deception, when it comes to personal activities (Gingo et al. 2017), but more willing to accept parental authority for prudential activities

(Perkins and Turiel 2007). Adolescents also conceal information from their parents for a variety of reasons. Adolescents engage in deception in order to avoid punishment or restrictions that might be imposed by parents (e.g., can't associate with certain friends), but also because they want to maintain their autonomy or avoid upsetting their parents (Marshall et al. 2005).

2.2. Religiosity and Concealing Information from Parents

Although the parent-adolescent relationship has an important influence on whether adolescents disclose or conceal information from their parents, several authors have called for more attention to individual characteristics among adolescents that might also be related to disclosure and concealment. Previous research suggests that adolescent religiosity influences many aspects of the parent-adolescent relationship (Pearce and Axinn 1998; Stokes and Regnerus 2009). Most relevant to this study, Desmond and Kraus (2012) found that adolescents who believe that religion is important less often lie to their parents, but the more frequently adolescents attend religious services, the more often they lie to their parents.

Why might religious adolescents be less likely to conceal information from their parents? In addition to a direct effect of religiosity on concealing information from parents, previous research suggests that the effect of religiosity could be mediated by self-control, morality, peer behaviors, and adolescent substance use. First, although adolescents may be very strategic in what they conceal from their parents, research suggests that lying and secrecy may also be the result of low self-control (Frijns et al. 2005; Grigoryeva 2018). In other words, rather than being the product of "rational decision-making or future planning on the part of children (i.e., agency)", lying to parents and keeping secrets from parents is the result of impulsivity, an inability to delay gratification or consider long-term consequences, and/or a tendency to engage in spontaneous, and often risky, behavior (Grigoryeva 2018, p. 226). Research suggests that religiosity helps adolescents to develop stronger self-control (McCullough and Willoughby 2009). Therefore, in addition to a direct effect, religiosity may also indirectly contribute to less lying and secrecy by fostering greater self-control.

In addition to self-control, religiosity may also reduce lying to parents and keeping secrets from parents by encouraging a strong sense of morality. Judgements regarding the acceptability of lying to parents and keeping secrets from parents are influenced by moral considerations (Perkins and Turiel 2007). Adolescents with a strong sense of morality may find it harder to rationalize or justify lying to their parents or keeping secrets from their parents. In support of this argument, research suggests that adolescent religiosity contributes to a strong sense of morality (i.e., adolescents are more likely to believe that certain behaviors are wrong), which partially explains the effect of religiosity on adolescent misbehavior (Desmond et al. 2009).

In addition to monitoring their adolescents, parents try to gain information about their adolescents' friends. The most common source of information about adolescents' friends is the adolescents themselves (Bourdeau et al. 2011). Obtaining information from their children is also the most frequent strategy that is used by parents to obtain information about the substance use of their adolescents' friends (Bourdeau et al. 2011). One important part of adolescent friendships is trust, however, and in order to maintain the trust of friends, adolescents may have to keep their substance use private by lying to parents or by keeping their substance use a secret. Given that religious adolescents are less likely to associate with substance using peers (Desmond et al. 2011), they may have fewer reasons to lie to parents to cover up the misbehavior of their friends.

Finally, previous research suggests that adolescent substance use contributes to concealing information from parents (Marshall et al. 2005). Darling and Tilton-Weaver (2019), for example, found that adolescents who used more alcohol kept more secrets from their parents. Adolescents are more likely to conceal information that they consider to be personal. In contrast to parents, research suggests that adolescents are more likely to consider substance use a personal issue than a prudential issue, and this is especially the case for adolescents who more often use drugs (Nucci et al. 1991, p. 847). Research suggests that religious adolescents are less likely to engage in substance use, so they should have fewer reasons to lie to their parents and keep secrets from their parents. Consistent with this argument, Desmond and Kraus (2012) found that adolescents who believe that religion is important are less likely to lie to their parents, because they are less likely to drink alcohol and smoke marijuana.

Although research shows that religiosity is consistently related to more honesty, several studies also suggest that some measures of religiosity, perhaps under certain conditions, may contribute to greater dishonesty (Desmond and Kraus 2012). Research suggests that some attempts at parental control may be experienced as intrusive, because they are interpreted by adolescents as infringing on their autonomy or as an invasion of their privacy. If adolescents feel that they are being coerced to engage in religious activities by their parents, then attending religious services and/or religious classes may lead to greater dishonesty. Additionally, adolescents are less willing to accept parental interference and are most willing to engage in deception, when it comes to personal activities (Gingo et al. 2017). If attending religious services and/or religious classes is considered by adolescents to be a matter of personal choice, then adolescents may consider parental authority in this area to be illegitimate, which tends to be related to more deception (Gingo et al. 2017).

2.3. Present Study

Given the lack of research on individual characteristics that might contribute to adolescents concealing information from their parents, in this research, I examine the effect of religious service attendance and importance of religion on adolescent information management. Because previous research suggests that the relationship between information management and adolescent outcomes is primarily the result of negative consequences from concealing strategies, rather than the positive effect of disclosing strategies (Frijns et al. 2010); in this research, I focus on two concealing strategies, lying to parents and keeping secrets from parents. Based on previous research, I expect that importance of religion will reduce lying to parents and keeping secrets from parents. The relationship between religious service attendance and lying to parents and keeping secrets from parents is harder to predict, given that previous research suggests that religious service attendance might be related to increased lying to parents (Desmond and Kraus 2012). In addition to examining the direct effects of adolescent religiosity on lying to parents and keeping secrets from parents, I also examine the indirect effects of adolescent religiosity on lying to parents and keeping secrets from parents through self-control, morality, substance using and delinquent peers, and adolescent substance use. For the analysis, I use the second wave of the National Study of Youth and Religion.

3. Methods

3.1. Data

The National Study of Youth and Religion (NSYR) is a nationally representative survey of American youth. The NSYR began in 2002 with telephone surveys of randomly selected English and Spanish speaking adolescents between 13 and 17 years of age. There were a total of 3370 parent-child respondents who participated in the study (81% response rate). In 2005, English speaking adolescents who participated in wave 1 were contacted during a second wave of data collection. Of the eligible wave 1 participants, 2581 respondents completed wave 2 of the study (78% response rate). Because some of the questions that were used for the analysis were not included in wave 1 of the NSYR (e.g., risk taking), I used the 2581 wave 2 survey respondents (age 16–20).

3.2. Measures

3.2.1. Lying and Keeping Secrets from Parents

For the dependent variables, I used two items to measure concealing information from parents, lying to parents and keeping secrets from parents. First, adolescents were asked: "In the last year, how often, if ever, did you lie to a parent (0 = never to 5 = very often)?" Although the majority of adolescents (86.3%) reported lying to a parent in the last year, adolescents did not report lying to their parents frequently (37.9% reported "rarely" lying to a parent, which was the most common response). Second, adolescents were asked: "In the last year, how often, if ever, did you do things that you hoped your parent would never find out about (0 = never to 5 = very often)?" Similar to the results for lying to a parent, the majority of adolescents kept secrets from their parents (90.2%), but not frequently (32.3% reported rarely keeping secrets from parents).

3.2.2. Religiosity

The first measure of religion, religious affiliation, consisted of nine categories: Evangelical Protestant, mainline Protestant, Black Protestant, Catholic, Jewish, Latter-day Saints (LDS), other religion, indeterminate religion, and no religion (contrast category). To measure public religion, I used a measure of religious service attendance. Adolescents were asked, "About how often do you attend religious services?" The responses ranged from 0 = never to 6 = more than once a week. I used a question about the importance of religion in daily life to measure private religiosity. Adolescents were asked "How important or unimportant is religious faith in shaping how you live your daily life?" Responses ranged from 0 = not important at all to 4 = extremely important. Finally, to measure spirituality, the adolescents were asked, "Some people say that they are 'spiritual but not religious'. How true or not would you say that is of you?" Responses were coded as 2 = very true, 1 = somewhat true, 0 = not true at all (contrast category)?

3.2.3. Mediating Variables

In addition to testing the direct effects of religious service attendance and importance of religion on concealing information from parents, I also tested the indirect effects of religious service attendance and the importance of religion on concealing information from parents through self-control, morality, substance using and delinquent peers, and adolescent substance use. First, self-control was measured using an item regarding risk taking. Adolescents were asked to agree or disagree (strongly agree = 0 to strongly disagree = 4) with the statement "you like to take risks" (higher scores indicate greater self-control or less willingness to take risks). Second, adolescents were asked about the permissibility of breaking moral rules: "Some people believe that it is sometimes okay to break moral rules if it works to your advantage and you can get away with it" (1 = strongly agree to 5 = strongly disagree). Third, peer associations were measured using two different items, one for substance use and the other for delinquency. Associating with substance using peers was measured using an item that asked young people how many of their five closest friends "do drugs or use a lot of alcohol?" Delinquent peers was measured using a similar item that asked how many of their five closest friends "have been in trouble for cheating, fighting, or skipping classes" (0 = no friends and 5 = all five friends). Finally, adolescent substance use was measured using three separate items. The adolescents were asked how often they drank alcohol, used marijuana, and smoked cigarettes (0 = never to 6 = once a day or more).

3.2.4. Control Variables

Previous research suggests that sex, race, age, education, family structure, and close relationships with parents are significantly related to lying to parents and keeping secrets from parents (Desmond and Kraus 2012; Jensen et al. 2004; Keijsers et al. 2010; Smetana et al. 2009; Tasopoulos-Chan et al. 2009). Accordingly, I included these variables as controls. Sex was measured as a dichotomous variable (1 = female and 0 = male). Race was measured using a series of dummy variables: White, African American, Hispanic, and other race (contrast category). Age was an interval-level variable that ranged from 16–20. Education was measured as a series of dummy variables: some college, high school graduate (no college), currently in high school, and high school dropout (contrast category). Family structure was also measured as a series of dummy variables: biological/adoptive parents, stepfamily, single-parent family, and other family structure (contrast category). Finally, I included a measure of closeness to mother and closeness to father, both of which combined two items: "How close or not do you feel to [mother/father]?" and "In general, how well do you and [mother/father] get along?" Table 1 includes the descriptive statistics for all variables that were included in the analysis.

Table 1. Descriptive statistics.

	Mean	SD	Minimum	Maximum
Sex	0.51	0.50	0.00	1.00
White	0.66	0.48	0.00	1.00
African American	0.17	0.38	0.00	1.00
Hispanic	0.11	0.32	0.00	1.00
Other	0.06	0.23	0.00	1.00
Age	17.70	1.36	16.00	20.00
College	0.22	0.42	0.00	1.00
High School Graduate	0.27	0.45	0.00	1.00
In High School	0.46	0.50	0.00	1.00
High School Dropout	0.04	0.21	0.00	1.00
Biological Family	0.48	0.50	0.00	1.00
Stepfamily	0.14	0.35	0.00	1.00
Single Parent Family	0.22	0.41	0.00	1.00
Other Family Structure	0.16	0.37	0.00	1.00
Close to Mother	7.35	2.27	0.00	10.00
Close to Father	5.37	3.53	0.00	10.00
Evangelical Protestant	0.28	0.45	0.00	1.00
Mainline Protestant	0.10	0.30	0.00	1.00
Black Protestant	0.07	0.26	0.00	1.00
Catholic	0.17	0.38	0.00	1.00
Jewish	0.03	0.18	0.00	1.00
LDS	0.02	0.15	0.00	1.00
Other Religion	0.03	0.16	0.00	1.00
Indeterminate	0.04	0.19	0.00	1.00
No Religion	0.25	0.43	0.00	1.00
Religious Attendance	2.55	2.22	0.00	6.00
Importance of Religion	2.27	1.23	0.00	4.00
Very Spiritual	0.12	0.32	0.00	1.00
Somewhat Spiritual	0.48	0.50	0.00	1.00
Not Spiritual	0.40	0.50	0.00	1.00
Self-control	1.13	0.68	0.00	3.00
Break Moral Rules	2.08	0.95	1.00	5.00
Substance Using Peers	1.78	1.80	0.00	5.00
Delinquent Peers	1.32	1.62	0.00	5.00
Drink Alcohol	1.79	1.77	0.00	6.00
Marijuana Use	0.74	1.61	0.00	6.00
Smoke	1.26	2.25	0.00	6.00
Lied to Parents	1.84	1.37	0.00	5.00
Secrets from Parents	2.17	1.46	0.00	5.00

3.3. Analytic Strategy

Three conditions must be met in order to establish mediation or an indirect relationship (Baron and Kenny 1986): (1) the independent variables (religious service attendance and importance of religion) must have a significant effect on the mediating variables (self-control, morality, peers, and substance use), (2) the independent variables must have a significant effect on the dependent variable (lying to parents and keeping secrets), and (3) the mediating variables must have a significant effect on the dependent variable. Given the three conditions for establishing mediation, I started by examining the relationship between religious service attendance and the mediating variables, self-control, morality, substance using and delinquent peers, and adolescent substance use. Second, I examined the relationship between religious service attendance and the importance of religion and the first dependent variable, lying to parents. After modeling the direct effect of religious service attendance and importance of religion on lying to parents, in subsequent models I determined whether the effect of religious service attendance and importance of religion on lying to parents is mediated by self-control, morality, substance using and delinquent peers, and adolescent substance use. Finally, I replicated the analysis (direct effects and mediation) for the second dependent variable, keeping secrets from parents.

4. Results

4.1. Intervening Variables: Self-control, Morality, Peers, and Substance Use

Religious adolescents might be less likely to conceal information from their parents because they have greater self-control, a stronger sense of morality, associate with fewer substance using and delinquent peers, and/or engage in less substance use. If these hypotheses are accurate, then adolescent religiosity should be significantly related to each intervening variable. The results for the analysis of adolescent religiosity and the hypothesized intervening variables are depicted in Table 2.

First, the results for religiosity and self-control suggest that religious service attendance and the importance of religion are not significantly related to self-control. Therefore, contrary to expectations, adolescents who reported greater religious service attendance and importance of religion do not have greater self-control. Additionally, adolescents who identified as being spiritual, but not religious, had lower self-control.

Second, both religious service attendance and the importance of religion were significantly related to morality. Adolescents who reported greater attendance at religious services, and adolescents who considered religion more important, indicated that it was less acceptable to break moral rules. In contrast, adolescents who identified as being spiritual, but not religious, indicated that it was more acceptable to break moral rules.

Third, adolescents who reported attending religious services more often were significantly less likely to associate with substance using peers, but religious service attendance was not related to associating with delinquent peers. On the other hand, the importance of religion was significantly related to associating with both substance using and delinquent peers. Therefore, adolescents who believe that religion is important are less likely to have friends that use substances and/or engage in delinquency. Adolescents who identified as being spiritual, but not religious, were no more likely to associate with substance using peers, but they were more likely to associate with delinquent peers.

Finally, adolescents who reported greater attendance at religious services were less likely to use alcohol, marijuana, and smoke. On the other hand, adolescents who believed that religion was more important were less likely to use alcohol. Adolescents who considered themselves spiritual, but not religious, were more likely to use marijuana, but they were not more likely to use alcohol or smoke.

These results suggest that, if attending religious services reduces concealing information from parents, then it is most likely the result of morality, having fewer friends that use substances, or less adolescent substance use, since religious service attendance was unrelated to self-control and associating with delinquent peers. In contrast, the importance of religion was significantly related to morality, associating with substance using and delinquent peers, and adolescent drinking. Finally, adolescents who identified as being spiritual, but not religious, reported lower self-control, a greater willingness to break moral rules, more delinquent peers, and more frequent marijuana use.

Table 2. OLS Regression of Potential Mediators on Religion (Standard Errors).

	Self-Control	Morality	Substance Using Peers	Delinquent Peers	Alcohol	Marijuana	Smoking
Sex	0.162 (0.032) **	−0.196 (0.042) **	−0.416 (0.083) **	−0.442 (0.076) **	−0.316 (0.077) **	−0.351 (0.074) **	−0.346 (0.100) **
Age	0.030 (0.021)	−0.040 (0.029)	0.100 (0.054)	0.048 (0.053)	0.075 (0.053)	0.029 (0.052)	0.315 (0.071) **
White	−0.048 (0.064)	−0.037 (0.097)	0.054 (0.185)	−0.074 (0.173)	0.276 (0.165)	0.199 (0.141)	0.568 (0.186) **
African American	0.065 (0.086)	0.060 (0.120)	−0.249 (0.228)	0.477 (0.222) *	−0.334 (0.215)	0.123 (0.185)	−0.120 (0.233)
Hispanic	−0.078 (0.085)	0.077 (0.126)	−0.195 (0.225)	0.016 (0.214)	−0.112 (0.209)	0.093 (0.178)	0.016 (0.244)
College	0.204 (0.080) *	−0.146 (0.137)	−0.378 (0.214)	−1.274 (0.242) **	0.258 (0.256)	−0.525 (0.267) *	−2.308 (0.357) **
High School Graduate	0.131 (0.081)	−0.122 (0.135)	−0.449 (0.201) *	−0.676 (0.239) **	−0.070 (0.251)	−0.429 (0.269)	−1.335 (0.352) **
In High School	0.155 (0.090)	−0.065 (0.151)	−0.633 (0.207) *	−0.670 (0.250) **	−0.520 (0.271)	−0.543 (0.290)	−1.492 (0.368) **
Biological Family	0.110 (0.044)	−0.014 (0.066)	−0.249 (0.129)	−0.320 (0.115) **	−0.492 (0.129) **	−0.285 (0.118) *	−0.735 (0.164) **
Stepfamily	0.101 (0.060)	−0.132 (0.075)	−0.305 (0.150) *	−0.121 (0.146)	−0.547 (0.141) **	−0.138 (0.150)	−0.285 (0.197)
Single Parent Family	0.102 (0.052) *	−0.012 (0.077)	−0.263 (0.140)	−0.246 (0.134)	−0.497 (0.138) **	−0.277 (0.145)	−0.308 (0.193)
Close to Mother	0.009 (0.007)	−0.022 (0.010) *	−0.067 (0.018) **	−0.054 (0.017) **	−0.056 (0.017) **	−0.036 (0.017) *	−0.063 (0.024) **
Close to Father	0.001 (0.006)	−0.023 (0.008) **	−0.020 (0.014)	−0.028 (0.013) *	−0.022 (0.014)	−0.033 (0.013) *	−0.023 (0.018)
Evangelical Protestant	0.068 (0.063)	−0.019 (0.089)	0.042 (0.163)	−0.106 (0.155)	0.101 (0.164)	−0.139 (0.164)	0.249 (0.209)
Mainline Protestant	0.066 (0.075)	0.0716 (0.099)	0.702 (0.199) **	−0.267 (0.159)	0.549 (0.179) **	0.008 (0.173)	0.208 (0.237)
Black Protestant	−0.047 (0.094)	0.164 (0.129)	0.087 (0.229)	0.002 (0.237)	0.298 (0.226)	−0.110 (0.208)	−0.106 (0.252)
Catholic	0.042 (0.056)	0.178 (0.083) *	0.216 (0.157)	0.072 (0.142)	0.507 (0.148) **	−0.038 (0.157)	0.149 (0.196)
Jewish	−0.068 (0.125)	−0.064 (0.212)	0.171 (0.358)	−0.524 (0.202) *	0.058 (0.312)	−0.112 (0.313)	−0.786 (0.257) **
LDS	0.072 (0.108)	−0.219 (0.115)	−0.179 (0.257)	0.032 (0.249)	−0.643 (0.229) **	−0.198 (0.226)	−0.431 (0.289)
Other Religion	0.104 (0.139)	0.203 (0.175)	0.364 (0.296)	0.302 (0.283)	0.520 (0.303)	0.021 (0.296)	0.640 (0.371)
Indeterminate	0.053 (0.066)	0.084 (0.088)	0.152 (0.167)	0.097 (0.157)	0.202 (0.157)	−0.033 (0.174)	0.021 (0.201)
Religious Attendance	−0.005 (0.010)	−0.036 (0.013) **	−0.105 (0.026) **	−0.040 (0.024)	−0.102 (0.026) **	−0.105 (0.022) **	−0.145 (0.033) **
Importance of Religion	0.034 (0.017)	−0.132 (0.023) **	−0.224 (0.046) **	−0.096 (0.045) *	−0.228 (0.046) **	−0.082 (0.045)	−0.082 (0.060)
Very Spiritual	−0.218 (0.051) **	0.164 (0.077) *	0.122 (0.139)	0.336 (0.132) **	0.260 (0.134)	0.435 (0.152) **	0.357 (0.183)
Somewhat Spiritual	−0.089 (0.034)	0.052 (0.045)	0.003 (0.090)	0.154 (0.080)	−0.007 (0.084)	−0.002 (0.076)	−0.060 (0.108)
R-Square	0.051	0.119	0.147	0.128	0.209	0.102	0.168
N	2468	2476	2462	2449	2477	2466	2477

* p < 0.05; ** p < 0.01.

4.2. Lying to Parents

Table 3 depicts the results for the analysis of adolescent religiosity and lying to parents. The results suggest that adolescents who believe that religion is important are significantly less likely to lie to their parents (model 1). In contrast, religious service attendance is not significantly related to lying to parents. Being spiritual, but not religious, is also not related to lying to parents.

Self-control has a significant, negative effect on lying to parents (model 2). Adolescents with high self-control are less likely to lie to their parents. When self-control is added to the model the effect of importance of religion on lying to parents is reduced by 8% (from −0.154 to −0.142). Given that the importance of religion was not significantly related to self-control, and including self-control in the model does not reduce the effect of importance of religion on lying to parents by much, the results suggest that self-control does not explain the effect of importance of religion on lying to parents.

Similar to self-control, morality is significantly related to lying to parents (model 3). Adolescents who have a strong sense of morality are less likely to lie to their parents. When morality is added to the model, the effect of importance of religion on lying to parents is reduced by 25% (from −0.154 to −0.116). The importance of religion had a significant effect on morality, and including morality in the model leads to a noticeable reduction in the effect of importance of religion on lying to parents. Therefore, the results suggest that adolescents who believe that religion is important are less likely to lie to their parents, in part, because they are more likely to believe that moral rules should not be broken.

Both associating with substance using and delinquent peers are significantly related to lying to parents (model 4). As expected, when adolescents have more friends who use substances and engage in delinquency, they are more likely to lie to their parents. When peer associations are added to the model, the effect of importance of religion on lying to parents decreases by 23% (from −0.154 to −0.119). Supplemental analysis (not shown) suggests that substance using friends (coefficient change from −0.154 to −0.124, a 19% reduction) does more to mediate the effect of importance of religion on lying to parents than delinquent friends (coefficient change from −0.154 to −0.136, a 12% reduction), perhaps because substance use is far more common than delinquent activities (such as theft and violence) or is more difficult than delinquent activities to conceal.

Drinking alcohol, using marijuana, and smoking are all significantly related to lying to parents (model 5). Therefore, adolescents who engage in substance use are more likely to lie to their parents. Including substance use in the model reduces the effect of importance of religion on lying to parents by 27% (from −0.154 to −0.113). Supplemental analysis (not shown) suggests that alcohol use (coefficient change from −0.154 to −0.111, a 28% reduction) mediates the effect of private religiosity on lying more than marijuana use (coefficient change from −0.154 to −0.143, a 19% reduction) or smoking (coefficient change from −0.154 to −0.146, a 6% reduction). The importance of religion was significantly related to adolescent alcohol use, and including alcohol use in the model reduces the effect of importance of religion on lying to parents more than any other variable (28%). Therefore, the results suggest that adolescents who believe that religion is important lie to their parents less often, in part, because they are less likely to use alcohol.

All of the potential intervening variables were included in the final model (model 6). The results suggest that adolescents with greater self-control and a stronger sense of morality are less likely to lie to their parents, whereas adolescents who associate with delinquent peers, drink more alcohol, and use more marijuana are more likely to lie to their parents. With all of the intervening variables in the model, the effect of importance of religion is considerably diminished (from −0.154 to −0.079, a 49% reduction) and it is no longer significantly related to lying to parents.

Table 3. OLS Regression of Lying to Parents on Religion and Mediators (Standard Errors).

	Model 1	Model 2	Model 3	Model 4	Model 5	Model 6
Sex	−0.004 (0.063)	0.043 (0.064)	0.053 (0.063)	0.100 (0.063)	0.083 (0.063)	0.177 (0.062) **
Age	−0.088 (0.044) *	−0.079 (0.044)	−0.077 (0.043)	−0.102 (0.043) *	−0.110 (0.042) **	−0.089 (0.041) *
White	−0.081 (0.120)	−0.093 (0.119)	−0.072 (0.119)	−0.080 (0.114)	−0.163 (0.115)	−0.140 (0.112)
African American	0.018 (0.166)	0.029 (0.165)	0.001 (0.163)	−0.026 (0.161)	0.055 (0.156)	−0.003 (0.153)
Hispanic	0.179 (0.160)	0.159 (0.159)	0.156 (0.159)	0.180 (0.156)	0.198 (0.157)	0.151 (0.155)
College	−0.083 (0.185)	−0.015 (0.185)	−0.042 (0.185)	0.134 (0.201)	0.023 (0.205)	0.176 (0.209)
High School Graduate	0.067 (0.181)	0.106 (0.181)	0.102 (0.181)	0.207 (0.192)	0.168 (0.200)	0.245 (0.199)
In High School	0.011 (0.194)	0.063 (0.193)	0.027 (0.192)	0.174 (0.200)	0.207 (0.213)	0.266 (0.208)
Biological Family	0.204 (0.101) *	0.228 (0.100) *	0.209 (0.099) *	0.270 (0.101) **	0.317 (0.099) **	0.321 (0.098) **
Stepfamily	0.069 (0.119)	0.095 (0.119)	0.104 (0.117)	0.111 (0.117)	0.149 (0.115)	0.162 (0.114)
Single Parent Family	−0.277 (0.118) *	−0.253 (0.118) *	−0.275 (0.117) *	−0.206 (0.119)	−0.178 (0.115)	−0.170 (0.116)
Close to Mother	−0.098 (0.015) **	−0.095 (0.015) **	−0.092 (0.015) **	−0.085 (0.015) **	−0.083 (0.014) **	−0.077 (0.014) **
Close to Father	−0.058 (0.012) **	−0.059 (0.012) **	−0.052 (0.012) **	−0.051 (0.012) **	−0.051 (0.012) **	−0.044 (0.012) **
Evangelical Protestant	0.140 (0.129)	0.154 (0.127)	0.140 (0.127)	0.163 (0.128)	0.113 (0.127)	0.139 (0.124)
Mainline Protestant	0.095 (0.143)	0.107 (0.139)	0.072 (0.141)	0.076 (0.142)	−0.001 (0.141)	0.045 (0.139)
Black Protestant	0.105 (0.192)	0.100 (0.191)	0.054 (0.185)	0.092 (0.193)	0.075 (0.187)	0.024 (0.184)
Catholic	0.163 (0.116)	0.166 (0.114)	0.110 (0.114)	0.147 (0.112)	0.079 (0.112)	0.065 (0.110)
Jewish	−0.127 (0.236)	−0.152 (0.230)	−0.135 (0.226)	−0.054 (0.234)	−0.093 (0.225)	−0.070 (0.221)
LDS	−0.183 (0.206)	−0.171 (0.201)	−0.126 (0.205)	−0.162 (0.192)	−0.066 (0.191)	−0.063 (0.185)
Other Religion	0.176 (0.251)	0.199 (0.240)	0.114 (0.238)	0.105 (0.224)	0.061 (0.228)	0.041 (0.213)
Indeterminate	0.195 (0.131)	0.203 (0.132)	0.165 (0.129)	0.169 (0.127)	0.164 (0.129)	0.144 (0.126)
Religious Attendance	−0.020 (0.020)	−0.021 (0.020)	−0.009 (0.020)	−0.002 (0.020)	0.011 (0.020)	0.017 (0.020)
Importance of Religion	−0.154 (0.036) **	−0.142 (0.036) **	−0.116 (0.036) **	−0.119 (0.035) **	−0.113 (0.034) **	−0.079 (0.035)
Very Spiritual	0.130 (0.109)	0.071 (0.107)	0.083 (0.105)	0.076 (0.106)	0.047 (0.103)	−0.016 (0.100)
Somewhat Spiritual	0.053 (0.067)	0.029 (0.067)	0.036 (0.066)	0.038 (0.065)	0.058 (0.065)	0.025 (0.065)
Self-control		−0.294 (0.049) **				−0.164 (0.048) **
Morality			0.283 (0.035) **			0.202 (0.036) **
Substance Using Peers				0.092 (0.021) **		0.005 (0.024)
Delinquent Peers				0.143 (0.024) **		0.106 (0.026) **
Alcohol Use					0.140 (0.022) **	0.100 (0.024) **
Marijuana Use					0.083 (0.025) **	0.055 (0.027) *
Smoking					0.049 (0.017) **	0.030 (0.017)
R-Square	0.088	0.107	0.121	0.138	0.151	0.191
N	2479	2468	2476	2442	2466	2418

* $p < 0.05$; ** $p < 0.01$.

Desmond and Kraus (2012) tested for an interaction effect between religious service attendance and importance of religion on lying to parents. The results of their study suggested that religious service attendance was related to more lying to parents, but only when adolescents did not believe that religion was important. In supplemental analysis (not shown), I also tested for an interaction effect between religious service attendance and importance of religion, but the interaction term was not significant.

4.3. Keeping Secrets from Parents

Table 4 depicts the results of the analysis for keeping secrets from parents. In contrast to the results for lying to parents, when none of the intervening variables are included in the model (model 1), both religious service attendance and the importance of religion are significantly related to keeping secrets from parents. Adolescents who report greater religious service attendance, and adolescents who believe that religion is important, are significantly less likely to keep secrets from their parents. Being spiritual, but not religious, is not related to keeping secrets from parents. Given that spiritual, but not religious, was also unrelated to lying to parents, it appears that forms of spirituality, as separated from religion, are not related to concealing information from parents.

Consistent with the results for lying to parents, self-control is significantly related to keeping secrets from parents (model 2). Adolescents with higher self-control are less likely to keep secrets from parents. When self-control is included in the model, the effect of religious service attendance on keeping secrets from parents is not reduced, whereas the effect of importance of religion on lying to parents is reduced by 9% (from −0.139 to −0.126). Similar to the results on lying to parents, since religious service attendance and importance of religion were not significantly related to self-control, and including self-control in the model reduces the effect of religious service attendance and importance of religion on keeping secrets from parents very little, it is unlikely that self-control explains the effect of adolescent religiosity on keeping secrets from parents.

Morality is also significantly related to keeping secrets from parents (model 3). Adolescents who have a strong sense of morality are less likely to keep secrets from parents. When morality is included in the model, the effect of religious service attendance on keeping secrets from parents is reduced by 17% (from −0.066 to −0.055), and the effect of importance of religion on keeping secrets from parents is reduced by 29% (from −0.139 to −0.098). Given that both religious service attendance and the importance of religion were significantly related to morality, and including morality in the model reduces the effect of both religious service attendance and importance of religion on keeping secrets from parents, the results suggest that adolescents are less likely to keep secrets from their parents in part because they have a strong sense of morality.

Adolescents who associate with substance using peers and delinquent peers are both more likely to keep secrets from parents (model 4). When peer relationships are included in the model, the effect of religious service attendance on keeping secrets from parents is reduced by 41% (from −0.066 to −0.039) and it no longer has a significant effect on keeping secrets from parents. In comparison, when peer relationships are included in the model, the effect of importance of religion on keeping secrets from parents is reduced by 37% (from −0.139 to −0.087), but it still has a significant effect on keeping secrets from parents. Supplemental analysis (not shown) suggests that substance using friends (coefficient change from −0.066 to −0.040, a 39% reduction) does much more to mediate the effect of religious service attendance on keeping secrets from parents than delinquent friends (coefficient change from −0.066 to −0.059, an 11% reduction). Substance using friends (coefficient change from −0.139 to −0.091, a 35% reduction) also mediates more of the effect of importance of religion on keeping secrets from parents than delinquent friends (coefficient change from −0.139 to −0.119, a 14% reduction). Religious service attendance and the importance of religion both had a significant effect on associating with substance using peers, and including substance using peers in the models reduces the effect of both measures of religiosity considerably (and much more than associating with delinquent peers), suggesting that one main reason that religious adolescents are less likely to keep secrets from their parents is because they are less likely to have friends who use drugs and alcohol.

Table 4. OLS Regression of Keeping Secrets from Parents on Religion and Mediators (Standard Errors).

	Model 1	Model 2	Model 3	Model 4	Model 5	Model 6
Sex	-0.147 (0.067) *	-0.097 (0.067)	-0.088 (0.066)	-0.003 (0.065)	-0.020 (0.063)	0.073 (0.063)
Age	-0.069 (0.045)	-0.058 (0.044)	-0.056 (0.044)	-0.089 (0.042) *	-0.094 (0.041) *	-0.070 (0.041)
White	0.075 (0.139)	0.058 (0.138)	0.081 (0.134)	0.068 (0.133)	-0.028 (0.129)	-0.008 (0.126)
African American	0.137 (0.178)	0.154 (0.180)	0.120 (0.174)	0.127 (0.174)	0.185 (0.166)	0.162 (0.166)
Hispanic	0.128 (0.171)	0.108 (0.171)	0.104 (0.167)	0.153 (0.167)	0.146 (0.165)	0.122 (0.162)
College	0.475 (0.191) *	0.540 (0.190) **	0.514 (0.194) **	0.713 (0.194) **	0.586 (0.212) **	0.710 (0.212) **
High School Graduate	0.304 (0.189)	0.342 (0.188)	0.338 (0.193)	0.474 (0.188) *	0.439 (0.208) *	0.509 (0.205) *
In High School	0.244 (0.203)	0.301 (0.202)	0.262 (0.209)	0.468 (0.199) *	0.511 (0.221) *	0.589 (0.218) **
Biological Family	0.014 (0.109)	0.048 (0.108)	0.021 (0.109)	0.090 (0.106)	0.171 (0.100)	0.171 (0.101)
Stepfamily	-0.073 (0.129)	-0.030 (0.127)	-0.043 (0.129)	0.008 (0.125)	0.049 (0.116)	0.085 (0.117)
Single Parent Family	-0.361 (0.125) **	-0.323 (0.124) **	-0.361 (0.125) **	-0.284 (0.122) *	-0.213 (0.116)	-0.210 (0.117)
Close to Mother	-0.090 (0.015) **	-0.087 (0.015) **	-0.085 (0.015) **	-0.069 (0.015) **	-0.069 (0.014) **	-0.060 (0.014) **
Close to Father	-0.042 (0.012) **	-0.042 (0.012) **	-0.036 (0.012) **	-0.035 (0.012) **	-0.032 (0.012) **	-0.027 (0.012) *
Evangelical Protestant	0.271 (0.138) *	0.288 (0.136) *	0.264 (0.135)	0.288 (0.134) *	0.263 (0.129) *	0.280 (0.128) *
Mainline Protestant	0.383 (0.152) *	0.398 (0.151) *	0.355 (0.151) *	0.298 (0.141) *	0.264 (0.136)	0.275 (0.136) *
Black Protestant	0.470 (0.210) *	0.426 (0.213) *	0.413 (0.205) *	0.428 (0.202) *	0.439 (0.194) *	0.328 (0.194)
Catholic	0.317 (0.126) *	0.314 (0.126) *	0.261 (0.124) *	0.270 (0.121) *	0.219 (0.114)	0.185 (0.114)
Jewish	-0.152 (0.259)	-0.177 (0.256)	-0.136 (0.238)	-0.109 (0.243)	-0.121 (0.225)	-0.105 (0.216)
LDS	-0.066 (0.236)	-0.051 (0.224)	-0.017 (0.234)	-0.026 (0.228)	0.110 (0.210)	0.102 (0.208)
Other Religion	0.169 (0.230)	0.195 (0.228)	0.102 (0.221)	0.063 (0.223)	0.048 (0.226)	0.018 (0.222)
Indeterminate	0.256 (0.136)	0.268 (0.138)	0.217 (0.134)	0.208 (0.130)	0.230 (0.125)	0.197 (0.125)
Religious Attendance	-0.066 (0.021) **	-0.067 (0.021) **	-0.055 (0.021) *	-0.039 (0.021)	-0.024 (0.021)	-0.015 (0.021)
Importance of Religion	-0.139 (0.038) **	-0.126 (0.038) **	-0.098 (0.038) *	-0.087 (0.037) *	-0.077 (0.035) *	-0.045 (0.036)
Very Spiritual	0.068 (0.117)	0.005 (0.115)	0.022 (0.114)	0.000 (0.113)	-0.065 (0.108)	-0.109 (0.107)
Somewhat Spiritual	-0.004 (0.072)	-0.033 (0.072)	-0.023 (0.071)	-0.023 (0.070)	-0.006 (0.068)	-0.038 (0.067)
Self-control		-0.331 (0.051) **				-0.155 (0.049) **
Morality			0.282 (0.040) **			0.167 (0.039) **
Substance Using Peers				0.188 (0.021) **		0.065 (0.024) **
Delinquent Peers				0.133 (0.025) **		0.085 (0.025) **
Alcohol Use					0.202 (0.024) **	0.148 (0.026) **
Marijuana Use					0.163 (0.026) **	0.122 (0.028) **
Smoking					0.033 (0.018)	0.014 (0.018)
R-Square	0.069	0.091	0.098	0.157	0.191	0.226
N	2478	2467	2475	2441	2465	2417

* $p < 0.05$; ** $p < 0.01$.

Similar to the results for lying to parents, drinking alcohol, and using marijuana (but not smoking) is significantly related to keeping secrets from parents. Adolescents who drink alcohol and use marijuana are more likely to keep secrets from parents. When adolescent substance use is added to the model (model 5), the effect of religious service attendance is reduced by 64% (from -0.066 to -0.024) and it no longer has a significant effect on keeping secrets from parents. When adolescent substance use is added to the model the effect of importance of religion is reduced by 45% (from -0.139 to -0.077), but the importance of religion still has a significant effect on keeping secrets from parents. Supplemental analysis (not shown) suggests that alcohol use (coefficient change from -0.066 to -0.038, a 42% reduction) and marijuana use (coefficient change from -0.066 to -0.039, a reduction of 41%) mediate more of the effect of religious service attendance on keeping secrets from parents than smoking (coefficient change from -0.066 to -0.049, a 26%reduction). Additionally, alcohol use (coefficient change from -0.139 to -0.076, a 45% reduction) mediates much more of the effect of importance of religion on keeping secrets from parents than marijuana use (coefficient change from -0.139 to -0.118, a 15% reduction) or smoking (coefficient change from -0.139 to -0.128, an 8% reduction). Both religious service attendance and the importance of religion had significant effects on alcohol use (only religious service attendance was significantly related to marijuana use and smoking) and including alcohol use in the model diminishes the effect of religious service attendance and importance of religion on keeping secrets from parents. Therefore, similar to the results for substance using peers, the results suggest that religious adolescents are less likely to keep secrets from their parents, in part, because they are less likely to use substances, especially alcohol.

All of the potential intervening variables—self-control, morality, peer associations, and adolescent substance use—were included in the final model (model 6). Consistent with the results for lying to parents, adolescents with greater self-control and a stronger sense of morality are less likely to keep secrets from parents. Adolescents who associate with substance using and delinquent peers and adolescents who drink alcohol and use marijuana are more likely to keep secrets from parents. When all of the potential intervening variables are included in the model, the effect of religious service attendance on keeping secrets from parents is reduced by 77% (from -0.066 to -0.015) and no longer has a significant effect on keeping secrets from parents. Similar to the results regarding religious service attendance, the effect of importance of religion on keeping secrets from parents is reduced by 68% (from -0.139 to -0.045) and it no longer has a significant effect on keeping secrets from parents, when all of the intervening variables are included in the model.

Given that previous research (Desmond and Kraus 2012) revealed a significant interaction between religiosity service attendance and the importance of religion on lying to parents, I tested for an interaction between religious service attendance and importance of religion on keeping secrets from parents. Similar to the results for lying to parents in supplemental analysis (not shown), the interaction between religious service attendance and the importance of religion was not significant. Therefore, the effect of religious service attendance on keeping secrets from parents does not seem to depend on beliefs regarding the importance of religion (and vice versa).

5. Discussion

Although parental knowledge of adolescent activities has traditionally been considered to be the product of efforts by parents to monitor their children, such as direct supervision or soliciting adolescents for information about their activities, research suggests that parental knowledge is primarily the result of adolescents' willingness to disclose or conceal information (Kerr and Stattin 2000; Kerr et al. 2010; Stattin and Kerr 2000). Previous research has focused on how the parent-adolescent relationship contributes to more adolescent disclosing and less concealing. The results of this research suggest that individual characteristics, such as adolescent religiosity, may also influence adolescent disclosing and concealing of information from their parents. In particular, consistent with previous research (Desmond and Kraus 2012), the results suggest that adolescents who believe that religion is important are less likely to lie to their parents. Building on previous research, the results also suggest that adolescents who attend religious services more often, and adolescents who believe that religion is more important, are less likely to keep secrets from their parents. Being spiritual, but not religious, is not related to lying to parents or keeping secrets from parents either.

Why do adolescents who believe that religion is important lie less often to parents and keep fewer secrets from parents? Based on the mediation analysis, adolescents who believe that religion is important are less likely to lie to parents and to keep secrets from parents primarily because they are less likely to drink alcohol. The effect of importance of religion on lying to parents was reduced by 28%, and the effect on keeping secrets from parents by 45%, when alcohol use was added to the model. Other forms of substance use, such as using marijuana and smoking, did not mediate as much of the effect of importance of religion on lying to parents and keeping secrets from parents. Therefore, amongst adolescent misbehaviors, the results suggest that drinking alcohol is the most likely to lead adolescents to lying and keeping secrets from parents, perhaps because drinking alcohol is more common than other delinquent activities (such as violence and theft) and alcohol use is harder to conceal (trying to hide the smell of alcohol or the effects of being drunk).

Although the effect of importance of religion on lying to parents and keeping secrets from parents is explained primarily by adolescent alcohol use, morality and peer associations may also mediate part of the effect of importance of religion on concealing information from parents. In particular, morality reduced the effect of importance of religion on lying to parents by 25% and the effect of importance of religion on keeping secrets from parents by 29%. In addition to concealing their own alcohol use, adolescents may also lie to their parents and keep secrets from parents in order to conceal the substance use of their friends. Substance using peers reduced the effect of importance of religion on lying to parents by 19% and keeping secrets from parents by 35%.

Unlike the importance of religion, religious service attendance was only significantly related to keeping secrets from parents. Similar to importance of religion, adolescents who attend religious services often are less likely to keep secrets from parents, primarily because they are less likely to use substances, associate with substance using peers, and have a strong sense of morality. The effect of religious service attendance on keeping secrets from parents was reduced by 42% when alcohol use was added to the model. Marijuana use also mediated more of the effect of religious service attendance on keeping secrets from parents (reduced 41%) than the importance of religion (reduced 15%). In addition to substance use, the effect of religious service attendance on keeping secrets from parents was reduced by 39% when substance using peers was added to the model and 17% when morality was added to the model. As a whole, the results suggest that adolescents who attend religious services often and believe that religion is important are less likely to lie to their parents and keep secrets from their parents, primarily because they engage in less substance use (especially drinking alcohol) and associate with fewer friends who use substances.

Unlike much previous research on religion and adolescent behavior, I also examined the effect of spirituality (spiritual, but not religious) on lying to parents and keeping secrets from parents. The results suggest that spirituality, absent religiosity, is not related to lying to parents or keeping secrets from parents. When compared to religiosity (especially importance of religion), being spiritual, but not religious, had a very different relationship with the intervening variables that were used in the analysis. Adolescents who reported being spiritual, but not religious, had lower self-control, thought that it was more acceptable to break moral rules, were more likely to associate with delinquent peers, and were more likely to use marijuana. Therefore, spirituality, absent a religious foundation, may not have the protective effects of religiosity. It is also possible that the item for spiritual, but not religious is a better measure of "not religious" than being spiritual.

Although this study contributes to existing research on adolescent information management, there are several limitations that suggest directions for future research. First, previous research suggests that many of the variables that were included in the model are reciprocally related (Tilton-Weaver 2014). For example, adolescent substance use and delinquency contributes to concealing information from parents (Jaggi et al. 2016), but a tendency to conceal information from parents also seems to be significantly related to further substance use and delinquency (Frijns et al. 2005; Jaggi et al. 2016). Adolescents who have low self-control may conceal more from their parents, but (based on the "muscle" or "strength" model of self-control) concealing information from parents may also reduce the capacity for self-control (Frijns et al. 2005). Also, lying to parents and keeping secrets from parents may depend on different domains of behavior (Perkins and Turiel 2007; Smetana et al. 2009) and the items that are used to measure lying to parents and keeping secrets from parents do not differentiate between these domains (e.g., private, prudential). Finally, previous research suggests that adolescents have different relationships with their mothers and fathers (Tasopoulos-Chan et al. 2009), but the items that were used to measure lying to parents and keeping secrets from parents do not distinguish between mothers and fathers.

In conclusion, previous research has revealed that parental knowledge of adolescent activities is determined more by adolescents' willingness to disclose or conceal information than parental monitoring (i.e., parental knowledge is determined more by the behavior of adolescents than the behavior of parents). Previous research has primarily focused on characteristics of the parent-adolescent relationship that influence adolescent disclosing and concealing. Although the parent-adolescent relationship provides an important context for information management strategies, the results of this study suggest that adolescent disclosing and concealing can also be influenced by individual characteristics, such as adolescent religiosity. In particular, religious service attendance and importance of religion can reduce lying to parents and keeping secrets from parents by reducing the acceptability of concealing information from parents (morality) and the necessity to conceal information from parents (peers and substance use).

Funding: This research received no external funding.

Conflicts of Interest: The author declares no conflicts of interest.

References

Baron, Reuben M., and David A. Kenny. 1986. The Moderator-Mediator Variable Distinction in Social Psychological Research: Conceptual, Strategic, and Statistical Considerations. *Journal of Personality and Social Psychology* 31: 1173–82. [CrossRef]

Bourdeau, Beth, Brenda A. Miller, Michael R. Duke, and Genevieve M. Ames. 2011. Parental Strategies for Knowledge of Adolescents' Friends: Distinct from Monitoring? *Journal of Child and Family Studies* 20: 814–21. [CrossRef] [PubMed]

Darling, Nancy, and Lauree Tilton-Weaver. 2019. All in the Family: Within-Family Differences in Parental Monitoring and Adolescent Information Management. *Developmental Psychology* 55: 390–402. [CrossRef] [PubMed]

Desmond, Scott A., and Rachel Kraus. 2012. Liar, Liar: Adolescent Religiosity and Lying to Parents. *Interdisciplinary Journal of Research on Religion* 8: 1–26.

Desmond, Scott A., Sarah E. Soper, and Rachel Kraus. 2011. Religiosity, Peers, and Delinquency: Does Religiosity Reduce the Effect of Peers on Delinquency? *Sociological Spectrum* 31: 665–94. [CrossRef]

Desmond, Scott A., Sarah E. Soper, David J. Purpura, and Elizabeth Smith. 2009. Religiosity, Moral Beliefs, and Delinquency: Does the Effect of Religiosity on Delinquency Depend on Moral Beliefs? *Sociological Spectrum* 29: 51–71. [CrossRef]

Frijns, Tom, Catrin Finkenauer, Ad A. Vermulst, and Rutger C. M. E. Engels. 2005. Keeping Secrets from Parents: Longitudinal Associations of Secrecy in Adolescence. *Journal of Youth and Adolescence* 34: 137–48. [CrossRef]

Frijns, Tom, Loes Keijers, Susan Branje, and Wim Meeus. 2010. What Parents Don't Know and How it May Effect Their Children: Qualifying the Disclosure-Adjustment Link. *Journal of Adolescence* 33: 261–70. [CrossRef] [PubMed]

Gingo, Matthew, Alona D. Roded, and Elliot Turiel. 2017. Authority, Autonomy, and Deception: Evaluating the Legitimacy of Parental Authority and Adolescent Deceit. *Journal of Research on Adolescence* 27: 862–77. [CrossRef] [PubMed]

Grigoryeva, Maria S. 2018. Strategic Action or Self-control? Adolescent Information Management and Delinquency. *Social Science Research* 72: 225–39. [CrossRef] [PubMed]

Hawk, Skyler, Loes Keijsers, Tom Frijns, William H. Hale, Susan Branje, and Wim Meeus. 2013. I Still Haven't Found What I'm Looking for: Parental Privacy Invasion Predicts Reduced Parental Knowledge. *Developmental Psychology* 49: 1286–98. [CrossRef] [PubMed]

Jaggi, Lena, Tess K. Drazdowski, and Wendy Kilewer. 2016. What Parents Don't Know: Disclosure and Secrecy in a Sample of Urban Adolescents. *Journal of Adolescence* 53: 64–74. [CrossRef] [PubMed]

Jensen, Lene Arnett, Jeffrey Jensen Arnett, S. Shirley Feldman, and Elizabeth Cauffman. 2004. The Right to Do Wrong: Lying to Parents among Adolescents and Emerging Adults. *Journal of Youth and Adolescence* 33: 101–12. [CrossRef]

Keijsers, Loes, Susan J. T. Branje, Tom Frijns, Catrin Finkenauer, and Wim Meeus. 2010. Gender Differences in Keeping Secrets. *Developmental Psychology* 46: 293–98. [CrossRef] [PubMed]

Kerr, Margaret, and Hakan Stattin. 2000. What Parents Know, How They Know It, and Several Forms of Adolescent Adjustment: Further Support for a Reinterpretation of Monitoring. *Developmental Psychology* 36: 366–80. [CrossRef] [PubMed]

Kerr, Margaret, Hakan Stattin, and William J. Burk. 2010. A Reinterpretation of Parental Monitoring in Longitudinal Perspective. *Journal of Research on Adolescence* 20: 39–64. [CrossRef]

Laird, Robert D., Matthew D. Marrero, Jessica A. Melching, and Emily S. Kuhm. 2013. Information Management Strategies in Early Adolescence: Developmental Change in Use and Transactional Associations with Psychological Adjustment. *Developmental Psychology* 49: 928–37. [CrossRef] [PubMed]

Marshall, Sheila K., Lauree C. Tilton-Weaver, and Lara Bosdet. 2005. Information Management: Considering Adolescents' Regulation of Parental Knowledge. *Journal of Adolescence* 28: 633–47. [CrossRef] [PubMed]

McCullough, Michael E., and Brian L. B. Willoughby. 2009. Religion, Self-Regulation, and Self Control: Associations, Explanations, and Implications. *Psychological Bulletin* 135: 69–93. [CrossRef] [PubMed]

Nucci, Larry, Nancy Guerra, and John Lee. 1991. Adolescent Judgements of the Personal, Prudential, and Normative Aspects of Drug Usage. *Developmental Psychology* 27: 841–48. [CrossRef]

Pearce, Lisa D., and William G. Axinn. 1998. The Impact of Family Religious Life on the Quality of Mother-Child Relations. *American Sociological Review* 63: 810–28. [CrossRef]

Perkins, Serena A., and Elliot Turiel. 2007. To Lie or Not to Lie: To Whom and Under What Circumstances. *Child Development* 78: 609–21. [CrossRef] [PubMed]

Smetana, Judith G. 2009. It's 10 O'clock: Do You Know Where Your Children Are? Recent Advances in Understanding Parental Monitoring and Adolescents' Information Management. *Child Development Perspectives* 2: 19–25. [CrossRef]

Smetana, Judith G., Myriam Villalobos, Marina Tasopoulos-Chan, Denise C. Gettman, and Nicole Campione-Barr. 2009. Early and Middle Adolescents' Disclosure to Parents about Activities in Different Domains. *Journal of Adolescence* 32: 693–713. [CrossRef] [PubMed]

Soenens, Bart, Maarten Vansteenkiste, Koen Luycks, and Luc Goossens. 2006. Parenting and Adolescent Problem Behavior: An Integrated Model with Adolescent Self-Disclosure and Perceived Parental Knowledge as Intervening Variables. *Developmental Psychology* 42: 305–18. [CrossRef] [PubMed]

Stattin, Hakan, and Margaret Kerr. 2000. Parental Monitoring: A Reinterpretation. *Child Development* 71: 1072–85. [CrossRef] [PubMed]

Stokes, Charles E., and Mark D. Regnerus. 2009. When Faith Divides Family: Religious Discord and Adolescent Reports of Parent-Child Relations. *Social Science Research* 38: 155–67. [CrossRef] [PubMed]

Tasopoulos-Chan, Marina, Judith G. Smetana, and Jenny P. Yau. 2009. How Much Do I Tell Thee?: Strategies for Managing Information to Parents Among American Adolescents from Chinese, Mexican, and European Backgrounds. *Journal of Family Psychology* 23: 364–74. [CrossRef] [PubMed]

Tilton-Weaver, Lauree. 2014. Adolescents' Information Management: Comparing Ideas About Why Adolescents Disclose to or Keep Secrets from Parents. *Journal of Youth and Adolescence* 43: 803–13. [CrossRef] [PubMed]

Yun, Hye-Jung, Ming Cui, and Bethany L. Blair. 2016. The Mediating Roles of Adolescent Disclosure and Parental Knowledge in the Association between Parental Warmth and Delinquency among Korean Adolescents. *Journal of Child and Family Studies* 25: 2395–2404. [CrossRef]

religions

MDPI

Article

Paternity Leave, Father Involvement, and Parental Conflict: The Moderating Role of Religious Participation

Richard J. Petts

Department of Sociology, Ball State University, North Quad 222, Muncie, IN 47306, USA; rjpetts@bsu.edu

Received: 24 August 2018; Accepted: 21 September 2018; Published: 22 September 2018

check for
updates

Abstract: Numerous studies show that taking paternity leave is associated with increased father involvement. However, fewer studies have explored contextual factors that may increase (or diminish) the likelihood that paternity leave-taking provides benefits to families. Using data from the Fragile Families and Child Wellbeing Study, this study examines the associations between paternity leave, fathers' religious participation, father involvement, and parental conflict, and whether fathers' religious participation moderates the associations between paternity leave, father involvement, and parental conflict. Results suggest that paternity leave-taking, length of paternity leave, and fathers' religious participation are associated with increased father involvement but are unrelated to parental conflict. Results also suggest that religious participation may enhance the association between paternity leave and family outcomes; paternity leave-taking and length of paternity leave are only associated with lower levels of parental conflict among families in which fathers attend religious services frequently. Moreover, fathers who take leave and attend religious services frequently are more likely to be involved with their child than fathers who take leave but do not attend religious services.

Keywords: paternity leave; fatherhood; religious participation; father involvement; parental conflict

There has been increased interest in parental leave within the U.S. Six states and Washington, DC have passed legislation providing paid family leave, more companies than ever offer paid parental leave, and most Americans are supportive of paid parental leave (Horowitz et al. 2017; Petts et al. 2018; National Partnership for Women and Families 2018). Relatedly, scholars have also begun to examine the potential consequences of paternity leave-taking for American families, finding that paternity leave is associated with greater father involvement (Petts and Knoester 2018; Pragg and Knoester 2017). Combined with results from European studies that also demonstrate a link between paternity leave and stronger parental relationships (Kotsadam and Finseraas 2011), evidence largely suggests that taking paternity leave and longer periods of leave provides benefits to families.

Despite increased attention to the predictors and potential consequences of paternity leave-taking, more work in this area is needed. For example, scholars have yet to extensively consider the contexts surrounding leave-taking and whether the relationship between paternity leave and family outcomes may vary by these contextual factors. One factor that is important to consider is religion. Religion encourages fathers to be more involved in their family life and provides fathers with social support and guidance that may help them to become more engaged parents and partners (Palkovitz 2002; Wilcox 2004). Indeed, there is evidence suggesting that fathers increase their religious participation after the birth of a child, and religious fathers are more likely to be involved in their children's lives than nonreligious fathers (King 2003; Petts 2007, 2011). Evidence also suggests that fathers' religious participation is associated with more favorable relationship outcomes with mothers (Mahoney 2010; Wolfinger and Wilcox 2008). Thus, fathers' religious participation may moderate the relationships between paternity leave, father involvement, and parental relationships. That is, actively religious fathers may receive greater social support and be more likely to sanctify their family relationships while on leave (Mahoney et al. 2003), which may be associated with more frequent father involvement and fewer parental arguments relative to less religious fathers.

The current study builds on previous research linking paternity leave-taking to father involvement and parental relationships by examining whether fathers' religious participation moderates these relationships. In doing so, this study contributes to a growing literature on the potential consequences of paternity leave-taking by assessing whether fathers' religious participation is one contextual factor that may be associated with the degree to which fathers become more invested in their family life after taking leave.

1. Conceptual Framework

1.1. Paternity Leave

The United States is an outlier in regard to family leave policy; the U.S. is one of only a few countries throughout the world that does not have a statutory paid parental leave entitlement, and most OECD countries also guarantee paid leave to fathers (Blum et al. 2017; Raub et al. 2018). However, the only national leave policy in the U.S. is the Family and Medical Leave Act (FMLA), which allows employees who meet eligibility requirements to take up to 12 weeks of unpaid leave after childbirth (Blum et al. 2017). In addition, four states provide paid family leave to new parents and three additional states have passed legislation to implement paid family leave in the future (National Partnership for Women and Families 2018). Some workers may also have access to employer-based leave programs, but these are relatively rare and are more commonly found in high-paying occupations (Albiston and O'Connor 2016). Overall, the piecemeal structure of leave in the U.S. makes it challenging for many workers to take leave after having a child; 40% of employees are not eligible for leave under FMLA, statutory paid leave is not available to fathers in 46 states, and only 16% of workers have access to paid parental leave from their employer (Blum et al. 2017; Bureau of Labor Statistics 2018).

In addition to lack of access to leave, fathers also face social and cultural barriers to leave-taking. For example, many workplaces are structured around the ideal worker norm that assumes employees prioritize work above all else (Williams 2000). Fatherhood norms also continue to emphasize fathers' roles as economic providers, despite an increase in men expressing a desire to spend more time with their families (Marsiglio and Roy 2012; McGill 2014). These expectations provide benefits to men within the workplace, but can also lead men who take leave to be stigmatized (Killewald 2013; Rudman and Mescher 2013; Williams et al. 2013). Indeed, taking leave is associated with negative consequences such as lower performance ratings and lower earnings for men (Coltrane et al. 2013; Rege and Solli 2013).

Despite the challenges U.S. fathers face in taking leave, most fathers take at least some time off work after the birth of a child (Petts and Knoester 2018; Pragg and Knoester 2017). Some fathers may use sick or personal days, whereas others may take unpaid time off, but evidence suggests that few fathers use FMLA for paternity leave and less than half of fathers are able to take paid time off (Harrington et al. 2014; Klerman et al. 2012; Petts et al. 2018). Perhaps not surprisingly, American fathers take relatively short periods of leave, with average leaves lasting one week or less (Petts et al. 2018; Petts and Knoester 2018; Pragg and Knoester 2017).

1.2. Paternity Leave, Father Involvement, and Parental Conflict

Understanding the current structure and usage of paternity leave in the U.S. is important because it may have implications for fathers' engagement in their family life. Fathers increasingly state that being actively engaged in their children's lives is important to them, but they often find it challenging to meet these desires due to expectations at work and pressures of being an economic provider (Aumann et al. 2011; Doucet 2013; McGill 2014). The time off of work provided by paternity leave may enable fathers to act on their desires and be an engaged parent from birth (Rehel 2014;

Tanaka and Waldfogel 2007). Fathers may be able to establish early bonds with their child as well as have a focused period of time in which to learn how to be a parent (Rehel 2014; Tanaka and Waldfogel 2007). By having this time, fathers may become more attached to their child as well as become a more confident parent. In doing so, fathers who take paternity leave (and longer leaves) may develop stronger father identities and be perceived as competent parents by themselves and others (Petts and Knoester 2018; Pragg and Knoester 2017; Rehel 2014). As a result, paternity leave may help to facilitate father involvement.

Indeed, evidence from both the U.S. and Europe suggests that fathers who take longer periods of paternity leave are more engaged with their children both in infancy and later in childhood (Haas and Hwang 2008; Huerta et al. 2014; Nepomnyaschy and Waldfogel 2007; Petts and Knoester 2018; Pragg and Knoester 2017; Tanaka and Waldfogel 2007). However, studies have not yet considered contextual factors that may enhance (or diminish) the likelihood that fathers utilize the time provided by paternity leave to become actively involved parents. Since father involvement is associated with positive outcomes for children (Lamb 2010; Sarkadi et al. 2008), it is important to further explore the link between paternity leave and father involvement.

Similarly, relationship conflict has important implications for couples and children. For example, high levels of conflict between partners, and negative communication during conflict, is associated with a higher risk of divorce or separation (Birditt et al. 2010; Carrère and Gottman 1999). Relationship conflict between parents is also associated with lower well-being among children (Grych and Fincham 1990). Thus, it is also important to consider factors that may help to promote parental relationship quality.

Paternity leave-taking may also help to facilitate stronger parental relationships. Similar to the idea that fathers may use the time off provided by paternity leave to focus on their relationship with their new child, fathers may also use this time to focus on their relationship with their coparent. Having a child is a significant life event, and parents may be able to strengthen their relationship with each other by having time together after the birth of a child. Fathers' use of paternity leave may also enable parents to set parenting expectations and learn to coparent together (Almqvist and Duvander 2014; Bünning 2015; Rehel 2014). Having dedicated time to learn how to divide parenting tasks in a way that both parents will be comfortable with may be particularly important as more couples espouse egalitarian ideals (Gerson 2010; Pedulla and Thébaud 2015), as egalitarianism is positively associated with relationship quality between partners (Carlson et al. 2016; Carlson et al. 2018; Frisco and Williams 2003). There is also evidence that paternity leave-taking increases fathers' participation in domestic tasks, which is associated with fewer conflicts and an increased likelihood of perceiving the division of household labor as equitable (Almqvist and Duvander 2014; Bünning 2015). Therefore, taking paternity leave (and longer periods of leave) may be associated with stronger parental relationships and lower levels of conflict (Kotsadam and Finseraas 2011).

1.3. Religious Participation, Father Involvement, and Parental Conflict

A sizeable body of literature also suggests that religion may promote positive family outcomes (Mahoney 2010; Mahoney et al. 2001). Religious organizations generally emphasize the importance of family life, and provide teachings and guidelines for parents (Edgell 2006; King 2003; Wilcox 2004). Religious institutions may also provide social support for fathers, and encourage them to be engaged parents and partners (Dollahite 1998; Petts 2007). In addition, religion may also provide men with a sense of meaning and purpose in life, as well as a framework for dealing with any stresses associated with becoming a new parent (Ellison and Levin 1998; Palkovitz 2002). Moreover, active involvement in religion may increase the likelihood that fathers sanctify—or place a high level of [spiritual] meaning or significance on—their family relationships (Mahoney et al. 2003). Overall, fathers who attend religious services frequently may be more likely to hear messages about the importance of family life, more likely to feel supported by a religious community, and more likely to internalize these ideas to sanctify family relationships. Consequently, religious participation by fathers may be associated with positive family outcomes such as more frequent father involvement and lower parental conflict.

Indeed, evidence largely suggests that religiously active fathers are more likely to be engaged in their children's lives than less religious fathers. Specifically, studies suggest that religious fathers report higher quality relationships with their children, are more involved in activities with their child and youth activities more generally, and report higher levels of parental supervision than less religious fathers (Bartkowski and Xu 2000; King 2003; Petts 2007; Roggman et al. 2002; Wilcox 2004). Greater involvement by religious fathers may be due to sanctification, as highly religious fathers feel their role as a parent is "sanctified" and that religion supports their goal of being an involved father (Lynn et al. 2016).

Similarly, religious participation is associated with higher quality, more stable relationships. That is, religious participation is associated with increased marital stability, a lower risk of divorce, and higher relationship satisfaction between partners (Call and Heaton 1997; Mahoney 2010). There is also evidence that fathers' religious participation, in particular, contributes to higher relationship quality (Wilcox and Wolfinger 2008; Wolfinger and Wilcox 2008). Higher relationship quality and lower levels of conflict among religious parents may also be due, at least in part, to the sanctification of family relationships; viewing relationships as having spiritual significance decreases the likelihood of engaging in hurtful, negative behaviors, and increases the likelihood of working together to resolve conflict (Kusner et al. 2014; Mahoney et al. 1999; Wilcox and Wolfinger 2008).

1.4. Religious Participation as a Moderator

In addition to evidence suggesting that religious participation is associated with greater father involvement and lower relationship conflict, it is also possible that religious participation moderates the associations between paternity leave-taking (and length of leave) and father involvement and relationship conflict. That is, among fathers who take leave, father involvement may be higher and parental conflict may be lower for fathers with high levels of religious participation than for fathers with low levels of religious participation. Religiously active fathers may be more likely to sanctify their family relationships (Mahoney et al. 2003). In doing so, actively religious fathers may find greater meaning in these relationships, and may place more importance on interacting with their children and coparents in positive ways than less religious fathers (Mahoney et al. 2003; Mahoney 2005).

Periods of paternity leave are generally short in the U.S. (Petts et al. 2018; Petts and Knoester 2018; Pragg and Knoester 2017), which may leave fathers with only a limited period of time to bond with their child and establish coparenting expectations. By believing that family relationships have spiritual significance, actively religious fathers may be particularly motivated to utilize whatever [little] time they may have while on leave. Because fathers' religious participation is associated with greater father involvement and higher quality relationships with romantic partners (Bartkowski and Xu 2000; King 2003; Petts 2007; Roggman et al. 2002; Wilcox 2004; Wilcox and Wolfinger 2008; Wolfinger and Wilcox 2008), it is also possible that these associations persist for fathers who take paternity leave.

2. Hypotheses

Three hypotheses grounded in the conceptual framework guide this study:

Hypothesis 1. *Paternity-leave taking and length of paternity leave will be positively associated with father involvement and negatively associated with relationship conflict.*

Hypothesis 2. *Father's religious participation will be positively associated with father involvement and negatively associated with relationship conflict.*

Hypothesis 3. *The relationships between paternity leave, father involvement, and relationship conflict will be moderated by fathers' religious participation. That is, among fathers who take paternity leave (and longer periods of leave), fathers with higher levels of religious participation will more involved in their children's lives, and argue less frequently with mothers, than fathers with lower levels of religious participation.*

3. Data and Methods

3.1. Sample

Data for this study is taken from the Fragile Families and Child Wellbeing Study (FFCW). The FFCW is a longitudinal birth cohort study that follows 4898 children born between 1998 and 2000 and their parents. Fragile families are defined as unmarried parents and their children, and these data consist of an urban sample with high percentages of low-income, minority, and unmarried parents. Data was collected from parents shortly after the birth of their child (W1), and follow-up interviews were conducted when children were approximately one (W2), three (W3), five (W4), nine (W5), and fifteen years old (W6).

For this study, the first two waves are used to assess whether paternity leave is associated with father involvement and parental conflict in the year following a child's birth, and whether religious participation moderates these relationships. The sample is restricted to families in which mothers and fathers were interviewed in the first two waves, families in which fathers were employed at W1 to be eligible for paternity leave, and families in which fathers answered the questions about leave. These restrictions result in a final sample size of 2109 families.

3.2. Paternity Leave

For this study, paternity leave is defined as taking time off for the birth of a child. In the W2 survey, fathers reported on whether they took any time off of work after the birth of the focal child, and how many weeks of leave they took. These questions were used to construct two indicators. Paternity leave-taking indicates whether fathers took leave (1 = *yes*). Length of paternity leave indicates whether fathers took no leave, one week, two weeks, or more than two weeks of leave.

3.3. Religious Participation

Fathers reported on how often they attended religious services in the W1 survey. Religious participation indicates whether fathers never attend, hardly attend, attend several times/year, attend several times/month, or attend services at least weekly.

3.4. Father Involvement and Parental Relationship Conflict

Father involvement and parental relationship conflict are used as the outcomes of interest in this study because measures are available at both W1 and W2, which helps to account for levels of father involvement and parental conflict before or at the time of the child's birth. Although other indicators of parental relationships are included in the W2 survey (e.g., relationship quality, coparenting quality), these indicators are not available in the W1 survey.[1]

Father involvement is taken from the W2 survey, and indicates how many days per week fathers reported engaging in eight activities such as reading, singing songs, telling stories, and playing with their child ($\alpha = 0.83$). The mean is used as the indicator. In the W1 survey, fathers were asked about their involvement in activities prior to the birth of the child. Prenatal involvement indicates whether fathers (a) gave the mother money to buy things for the baby during the pregnancy and (b) helped in other ways such as providing transportation to the prenatal clinic or helping with chores. Parental conflict is taken from the W2 survey, and indicates how often mothers report arguing with fathers about things that are important (1 = *never* to 5 = *always*). In the W1 survey, mothers report how often (1 = *never* to 3 = *often*) they argue with fathers about money, spending time together, sex, the pregnancy, drinking or drug use, and being faithful ($\alpha = 0.61$). The mean is used as the indicator.

---

[1] These variables were included in supplementary analyses. Although there were instances in which paternity leave and/or religious participation were associated with these outcomes, the relationship between paternity leave and these outcomes did not vary by religious participation.

3.5. Control Variables

A number of variables taken from W1 were included as controls. Fathers' religious affiliation is indicated by whether fathers identify as (a) Catholic, (b) conservative Protestant, (c) mainline Protestant, (d) other Protestant, (e) other religious affiliation, or (f) no religious affiliation (used as reference group) using the classification scheme from Steensland et al. (2000) as a guide. Relationship status at W1 is categorized as (a) married (used as reference category), (b) cohabiting, and (c) nonresident father. Controls are also included for fathers' educational attainment (1 = *did not complete high school* to 4 = *college degree*), fathers' income (0 = *less than $10,000* to 8 = *$75,000 or more*), mothers' income (0 = *less than $5000* to 4 = *$20,000 or more*), fathers' age, whether father was born in the U.S., number of other children, child's age (at W2, in months), child gender (1 = *male*), and length of time that the mother took off of work following the child's birth (taken from the W2 survey). Father's work hours are categorized as (a) part-time (less than 35 h a week), (b) full-time (35–44 h a week, used as reference category), and (c) more than full time (45 h a week or more). Fathers' occupation type is categorized as (a) professional, (b) labor (used as reference category), (c) service, (d) sales, or (e) other occupational type. Father's race/ethnicity is coded as (a) White (used as reference category), (b) Black, (c) Latino, or (d) other race/ethnicity. Three additional controls assess fathers' attitudes. Positive father attitudes are indicated by fathers' level of agreement at (1 = *strongly disagree* to 4 = *strongly agree*) on whether (a) being a father and raising children is one of the most fulfilling experiences for a man, (b) I want people to know that I have a new child, and (c) not being a part of my child's life would be one of the worst things that could happen to me ($\alpha = 0.73$). The mean response is used. Fathers were also asked to identify which fathering role (provide regular financial support, teach child about life, provide direct care, show love and affection to the child, provide protection for the child, or serve as an authority figure and discipline the child) was most important, and engaged father attitudes indicates fathers who identified either providing direct care or showing love and affection to the child as most important. Traditional gender attitudes indicates whether fathers agree that it is much better for everyone if the man earns the main living and the woman takes care of the home and family.

3.6. Analytic Strategy

Ordinary least squares (OLS) regression models were used in this study. First, OLS models were used to assess whether paternity leave-taking, length of paternity leave, and father's religious participation are associated with father involvement and parental conflict in separate models. Second, interaction terms were included in separate models to assess whether the relationships between paternity leave, father involvement, and parental conflict were moderated by religious participation. Missing data were accounted for using multiple imputation, and combined results from ten imputed models are presented here.

4. Results

Summary statistics for all variables are reported in Table 1. Consistent with previous research, most fathers take paternity leave (79%), but take short leaves, on average (approximately one week). Mean values also suggest that fathers engage in activities with their child approximately four days a week (M = 4.35), mothers report arguing with fathers between "rarely" and "sometimes" (M = 2.80), and fathers report attending religious services several times a year on average (M = 1.91).

Table 1. Summary Statistics at W1.

Variables	M	SD	Min	Max
Dependent Variables				
Father Involvement	4.35	1.59	0	7
Relationship Conflict	2.80	0.90	1	5
Key Variables				
Paternity Leave	0.79	-	0	1
Length of Paternity Leave	1.07	0.78	0	3
Religious Participation	1.91	1.35	0	4
Controls				
Catholic	0.30	-	0	1
Conservative Protestant	0.27	-	0	1
Mainline Protestant	0.05	-	0	1
Other Protestant	0.18	-	0	1
Other Religious Affiliation	0.09	-	0	1
No Religious Affiliation *	0.11	-	0	1
Married *	0.34	-	0	1
Cohabiting	0.41	-	0	1
Nonresident	0.25	-	0	1
Number of Other Children	1.02	1.18	0	5
Education	2.31	1.00	1	4
Works Part-Time	0.08	-	0	1
Works Full-Time *	0.49	-	0	1
Works more than Full-Time	0.43	-	0	1
Professional Occupation	0.17	-	0	1
Labor Occupation *	0.49	-	0	1
Sales Occupation	0.08	-	0	1
Service Occupation	0.24	-	0	1
Other Occupation	0.02	-	0	1
Income	3.36	2.18	0	8
Mother's Income	1.17	1.63	0	4
Age	28.18	6.93	18	57
White *	0.27	-	0	1
Black	0.42	-	0	1
Latino	0.26	-	0	1
Other Race	0.05	-	0	1
U.S. Native	0.84	-	0	1
Child Age	15.60	3.90	5	30
Child is Male	0.52	-	0	1
Length of Maternity Leave	2.46	3.14	0	12
Positive Father Attitudes	3.76	0.40	1	4
Engaged Father Attitudes	0.66	-	0	1
Traditional Gender Attitudes	0.39	-	0	1
Prenatal Involvement	0.93	-	0	1
W1 Relationship Conflict	1.40	0.35	1	3

$N = 2109$. * Used as reference category.

Results examining the relationships between paternity leave, religious participation, and father involvement are presented in Table 2. Consistent with the first two hypotheses, paternity leave and religious participation are both positively associated with father involvement. As shown in Model 1, taking paternity leave is associated with engaging in activities with children just under one-half day more frequently per week compared to not taking leave ($b = 0.40$, $p < 0.001$). Similarly, as shown in Model 3, longer periods of paternity leave are associated with more frequent father involvement ($b = 0.23$, $p < 0.001$). Moreover, as shown in both Models 1 and 3, more frequent attendance at religious services is associated with more frequent involvement with young children ($b = 0.06$, $p < 0.05$).

Table 2. Results from OLS regression models predicting father involvement.

Variable	1		2		3		4	
	b	SE *b*	*B*	SE *b*	*b*	SE *b*	*b*	SE *b*
Paternity Leave-Taking	0.40	0.09 ***	0.21	0.14				
Length of Paternity Leave					0.23	0.04 ***	0.16	0.08 *
Religious Participation	0.06	0.03 *	−0.02	0.06	0.06	0.03 *	0.02	0.04
Catholic	0.18	0.13	0.18	0.13	0.19	0.13	0.19	0.13
Conservative Protestant	0.00	0.13	0.01	0.13	0.01	0.13	0.02	0.13
Mainline Protestant	−0.04	0.18	−0.04	0.18	−0.04	0.18	−0.04	0.18
Other Protestant	0.00	0.13	0.01	0.13	0.02	0.13	0.03	0.13
Other Religious Affiliation	0.12	0.16	0.12	0.16	0.12	0.16	0.13	0.16
Cohabiting	−0.10	0.09	−0.09	0.09	−0.09	0.09	−0.08	0.09
Nonresident	−0.72	0.11 ***	−0.71	0.11 ***	−0.71	0.11 ***	−0.71	0.11 ***
Number of Other Children	−0.09	0.03 **	−0.09	0.03 **	−0.09	0.03 **	−0.09	0.03 **
Education	−0.01	0.04	−0.01	0.04	−0.02	0.04	−0.02	0.04
Works Part-Time	−0.21	0.13	−0.21	0.13	−0.22	0.13	−0.21	0.13
Works more than Full-Time	−0.01	0.08	−0.01	0.08	−0.01	0.08	−0.00	0.08
Professional Occupation	0.05	0.11	0.06	0.11	0.03	0.11	0.03	0.11
Sales Occupation	0.17	0.13	0.17	0.13	0.18	0.13	0.18	0.13
Service Occupation	−0.03	0.08	−0.03	0.08	−0.05	0.08	−0.05	0.08
Other Occupation	−0.22	0.26	−0.23	0.26	−0.24	0.26	−0.25	0.26
Income	−0.01	0.02	−0.01	0.02	−0.01	0.02	−0.01	0.02
Mother's Income	0.01	0.02	0.01	0.02	0.01	0.02	0.01	0.02
Age	−0.00	0.01	−0.00	0.01	−0.00	0.01	−0.00	0.01
Black	0.08	0.10	0.07	0.10	0.07	0.10	0.07	0.10
Latino	0.01	0.11	0.01	0.11	−0.01	0.11	−0.01	0.11
Other Race	0.10	0.18	0.10	0.18	0.07	0.18	0.07	0.18
U.S. Native	0.35	0.11 **	0.35	0.11 **	0.35	0.11 **	0.35	0.11 **
Child Age	−0.00	0.01	−0.00	0.01	−0.00	0.01	−0.00	0.01
Child is Male	0.07	0.07	0.07	0.07	0.07	0.07	0.07	0.07
Length of Maternity Leave	0.01	0.01	0.01	0.01	0.01	0.01	0.01	0.01
Positive Father Attitudes	0.26	0.08 **	0.26	0.08 **	0.25	0.08 **	0.25	0.08 **
Engaged Father Attitudes	0.08	0.07	0.08	0.07	0.08	0.07	0.08	0.07
Traditional Gender Attitudes	0.00	0.07	0.00	0.07	0.02	0.07	0.02	0.07
Prenatal Involvement	0.59	0.14 ***	0.59	0.14 ***	0.61	0.14 ***	0.61	0.14 ***
Leave-Taking × Religious Participation			0.11	0.06 †				
Length of Leave × Religious Participation							0.04	0.03
R^2	0.10		0.10		0.11		0.11	

$N = 2109.$ † $p < 0.10.$ * $p < 0.05.$ ** $p < 0.01.$ *** $p < 0.001.$

Results assessing whether religious participation moderates the relationships between paternity leave and father involvement are included in Models 2 and 4 of Table 2. Although the interaction term for length of paternity leave and religious participation is not significant (Model 4), there is some evidence that religious participation moderates the relationship between paternity leave-taking and father involvement (Model 2). Consistent with hypothesis 3, religious participation is especially likely to be associated with greater father involvement among fathers who take paternity leave ($b = 0.11$, $p < 0.10$), although this interaction term is only marginally significant. This relationship is illustrated in Figure 1, which shows predicted values of father involvement calculated from the estimates in Model 2 of Table 2. As shown in Figure 1, more frequent attendance at religious services is associated with more frequent involvement among fathers who take paternity leave. In contrast, among fathers who do not take paternity leave, religious participation is largely unrelated to father involvement.

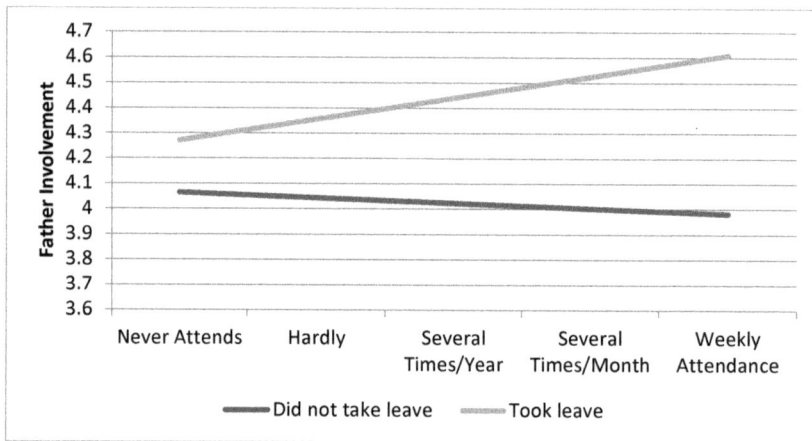

Figure 1. Predicted values of the relationships between paternity leave-taking, religious participation, and father involvement.

Results examining the relationships between paternity leave, religious participation, and parental conflict are presented in Table 3. In contrast to the first two hypotheses, none of the key variables—paternity leave-taking, length of paternity leave, and religious participation—are associated with parental conflict, as shown in Models 1 and 3. However, when interaction terms are included in Models 2 and 4, there is some evidence in support of hypothesis 3. First, as shown in Model 2, religious participation is especially likely to be associated with less frequent conflict within families in which fathers take paternity leave ($b = -0.08$, $p < 0.05$). This relationship is illustrated in Figure 2. As shown in Figure 2, more frequent attendance at religious services is associated with less frequent conflict when fathers take paternity leave. In contrast, when fathers do not take paternity leave, religious participation is positively associated with parental conflict.

Table 3. Results from OLS regression models predicting relationship conflict.

Variable	1		2		3		4	
	b	SE *b*	*b*	SE *b*	*b*	SE *b*	*b*	SE *b*
Paternity Leave-Taking	−0.04	0.05	0.10	0.08				
Length of Paternity Leave					−0.04	0.03	0.03	0.05
Religious Participation	−0.02	0.02	0.04	0.03	−0.02	0.02	0.02	0.03
Catholic	−0.02	0.08	−0.02	0.08	−0.02	0.08	−0.02	0.08
Conservative Protestant	−0.09	0.08	−0.10	0.08	−0.09	0.08	−0.09	0.08
Mainline Protestant	−0.09	0.11	−0.10	0.11	−0.09	0.11	−0.10	0.11
Other Protestant	−0.02	0.09	−0.03	0.09	−0.03	0.09	−0.03	0.09
Other Religious Affiliation	−0.12	0.09	−0.13	0.09	−0.12	0.09	−0.13	0.09
Cohabiting	0.09	0.06	0.09	0.06	0.09	0.06	0.08	0.06
Nonresident	0.15	0.06 *	0.15	0.06 *	0.15	0.06*	0.15	0.06*
Number of Other Children	0.01	0.02	0.01	0.02	0.01	0.02	0.01	0.02
Education	0.01	0.03	0.01	0.03	0.01	0.03	0.01	0.03
Works Part-Time	0.05	0.08	0.05	0.08	0.05	0.08	0.05	0.08
Works more than Full-Time	−0.01	0.06	−0.01	0.06	−0.01	0.06	−0.02	0.06
Professional Occupation	−0.04	0.07	−0.04	0.07	−0.03	0.07	−0.03	0.07
Sales Occupation	−0.13	0.07 †	−0.13	0.07 †	−0.13	0.07 †	−0.14	0.07 †
Service Occupation	−0.05	0.05	−0.05	0.05	−0.05	0.05	−0.05	0.05
Other Occupation	0.16	0.15	0.16	0.15	0.16	0.15	0.16	0.15
Income	−0.00	0.01	−0.00	0.01	−0.00	0.01	−0.00	0.01
Mother's Income	0.01	0.01	0.01	0.01	0.01	0.01	0.01	0.01

Table 3. *Cont.*

Variable	1		2		3		4	
	b	SE *b*	*b*	SE *b*	*b*	SE *b*	*b*	SE *b*
Age	−0.01	0.00	−0.01	0.00	−0.01	0.00	−0.01	0.00
Black	0.06	0.06	0.07	0.06	0.06	0.06	0.07	0.06
Latino	0.01	0.07	0.01	0.07	0.01	0.07	0.01	0.07
Other Race	0.05	0.15	0.04	0.15	0.05	0.15	0.05	0.15
U.S. Native	0.01	0.06	0.01	0.06	0.01	0.06	0.00	0.06
Child Age	0.00	0.01	0.00	0.01	0.00	0.01	0.00	0.01
Child is Male	−0.04	0.04	−0.04	0.04	−0.04	0.04	−0.04	0.04
Length of Maternity Leave	−0.01	0.01	−0.01	0.01	−0.01	0.01	−0.01	0.01
Positive Father Attitudes	0.01	0.05	0.01	0.05	0.01	0.05	0.01	0.05
Engaged Father Attitudes	−0.04	0.04	−0.04	0.04	−0.04	0.04	−0.04	0.04
Traditional Gender Attitudes	0.08	0.04 †	0.08	0.04 *	0.08	0.04 †	0.08	0.04 †
Prenatal Involvement	−0.02	0.09	−0.02	0.09	−0.02	0.09	−0.02	0.09
W1 Relationship Conflict	0.63	0.06 ***	0.62	0.06 ***	0.62	0.06***	0.62	0.06***
Leave-Taking × Religious Participation			−0.08	0.04 *				
Length of Leave × Religious Participation							−0.04	0.02 †
R^2	0.10		0.10		0.10		0.10	

$N = 2109$. † $p < 0.10$. * $p < 0.05$. ** $p < 0.01$. *** $p < 0.001$.

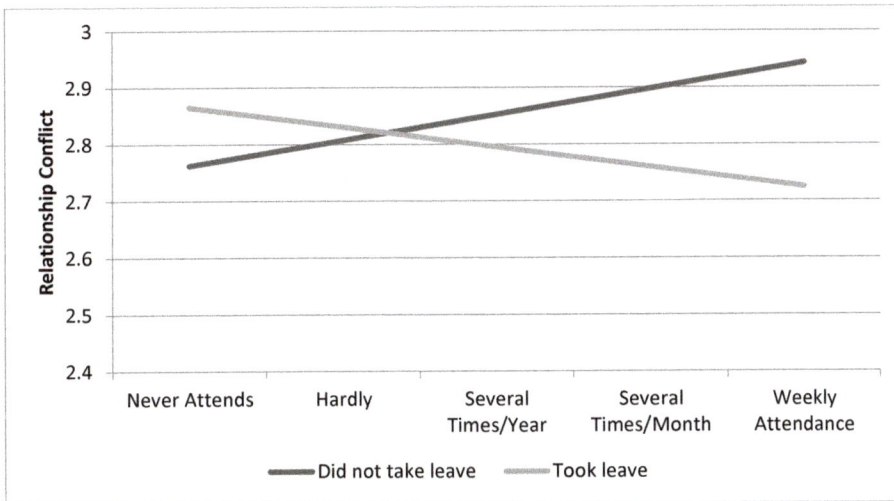

Figure 2. Predicted values of the relationships between paternity leave-taking, religious participation, and relationship conflict.

In addition, as shown in Model 4 of Table 3, there is evidence that religious participation moderates the relationship between length of paternity leave and parental conflict ($b = −0.04$, $p < 0.10$), although this relationship is only marginally significant. This relationship is illustrated in Figure 3. As shown in Figure 3, religious participation is associated with a slight increase in parental conflict when fathers do not take leave. In contrast, more frequent religious participation is associated with less frequent conflict when fathers take paternity leave, with longer periods of leave being associated with lower levels of conflict when religious participation is higher.

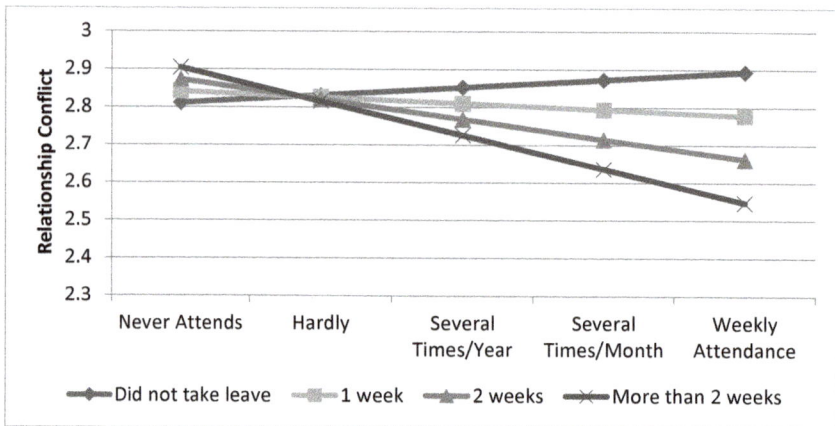

Figure 3. Predicted values of the relationships between length of paternity leave, religious participation, and relationship conflict.

5. Discussion

Despite increased attention on paternity leave in the U.S., few studies have focused on factors that may contextualize the associations between paternity leave-taking and family outcomes. This study advances our understanding of factors that may contextualize the relationships between paternity leave, father involvement, and parental conflict by focusing on fathers' religious participation. Overall, results provide some evidence suggesting that paternity leave-taking (and length of leave) and fathers' religious participation are independently associated with father involvement, and also that fathers' religious participation moderates the relationships between paternity leave, father involvement, and parental conflict.

Consistent with previous research, results from this study suggest that paternity leave-taking and length of paternity leave are associated with more frequent father involvement (Haas and Hwang 2008; Huerta et al. 2014; Nepomnyaschy and Waldfogel 2007; Petts and Knoester 2018). Having time off when a child is born may provide fathers with time to feel comfortable performing parenting tasks as well as to bond with their newborn child (Rehel 2014; Tanaka and Waldfogel 2007). These early experiences may increase attachments between fathers and children, strengthening men's identities as fathers and increasing the likelihood that fathers maintain a high level of involvement throughout the child's life (Cabrera et al. 2008; Petts and Knoester 2018).

However, results from this study did not support the hypothesis that paternity leave-taking (and length of leave) would be associated with parental conflict. The transition to parenthood (or having an additional child) is often challenging, as parents need to adapt to their new roles (Twenge et al. 2003). Consequently, parental relationship quality declines after having a new child and conflict often increases (Cowan et al. 1985; Twenge et al. 2003). Although paternity leave may provide parents with time to figure out how to coparent together, it may also provide additional time for parents to argue with each other as they figure out their new roles. As such, any positive benefits of paternity leave for parents (such as symbolizing a commitment by fathers to be an engaged parent) may be offset by additional time to experience conflict. This may also help to explain why relatively few studies have found an influence of paternity leave on parental relationships (Kotsadam and Finseraas 2011), whereas a large body of literature has noted the benefits of paternity leave (and length of leave) for father involvement.

Similar to the findings for paternity leave (and length of leave), results from this study also showed that fathers' religious participation is positively associated with father involvement but unrelated to parental conflict. Consistent with previous research, actively religious fathers may receive messages about the importance of family life as well as social support that encourages and enables them to be involved parents (King 2003; Petts 2007; Wilcox 2004). Thus, fathers who attend religious services frequently may be motivated to be engaged in their children's lives early on, as evidence from this study and previous research suggests (Bartkowski and Xu 2000; Petts 2007; Roggman et al. 2002). However, although previous research suggests that religious participation is associated with lower family conflict (Mahoney et al. 1999; Wilcox and Wolfinger 2008), this relationship may be offset by the increases in conflict that often occur after having a new child (Cowan et al. 1985; Twenge et al. 2003).

It is also somewhat surprising that religious affiliation was unrelated to both father involvement and parental conflict. There was some evidence that Catholic fathers were more involved in their children's lives than unaffiliated fathers and that conservative Protestant fathers reported less parental conflict than religiously unaffiliated fathers ($p < 0.10$) in supplementary analyses, but these variations disappeared after accounting for fathers' religious participation. As such, religious participation appears to be more important than affiliation in these data. Yet, it is also possible that the lack of significant findings on religious affiliation may be due to competing expectations for religiously affiliated fathers (especially fathers who are more religiously conservative). That is, religiously conservative fathers may be perceived as the spiritual head of the household and thus may place particular importance on sanctifying family relationships (Gallagher and Smith 1999). However, conservative denominations are also more likely to encourage traditional gender roles within families, which may reduce the likelihood that fathers are highly engaged parents (DeMaris et al. 2011; Denton 2004). These competing expectations may offset one another, resulting in no relationship between religious affiliation, father involvement, and parenting conflict. Future research should further explore variations by religious affiliation.

Although there were no direct associations between paternity leave or fathers' religious participation and parental conflict, there is some evidence that the association between paternity leave and parental conflict varies by how frequently fathers attend religious services. At low levels of religious participation, paternity leave-taking and length of paternity leave are largely unrelated to parental conflict. In contrast, when fathers attend religious services frequently, taking paternity leave (and longer periods of leave) is associated with lower levels of parental conflict. Specifically, among fathers who attend religious services weekly, there is approximately a 1/3 standard deviation difference in parental conflict between those who take more than two weeks of leave and those who do not take leave.

Similarly, there is also some evidence that fathers' religious participation may enhance the association between paternity leave-taking and father involvement (although this relationship is only marginally significant). Although fathers who take paternity leave report higher levels of father involvement regardless of how frequently they attend religious services, the gap in involvement between fathers who take leave and those who do not increases at higher levels of religious participation. Specifically, among fathers who attend religious services weekly, those who take leave engage with their child over one-half day more frequently (0.4 standard deviations) than fathers who do not take leave.

These findings suggest that religious participation may be one contextual factor that may motivate fathers to become more invested in their family life while on leave. Fathers who attend religious services frequently may sanctify their family relationships and find more meaning in learning and performing parenting tasks after the birth of a new child compared to less religious fathers (Mahoney et al. 2003). Actively religious fathers may also be more willing to collaborate with mothers during this time, and perhaps focus more on the positive aspects of being a new parent as opposed to the frustrations and stresses that can also occur (Mahoney 2005; Mahoney et al. 1999). As such, fathers who attend religious services frequently may have fewer arguments with mothers while on leave compared to fathers who attend religious services less frequently. Due to the lack of a national paid family leave policy as well as other barriers to leave-taking for fathers, most fathers take relatively short periods of time off when a child is born (Albiston and O'Connor 2016; Petts et al. 2018). Results from this study suggest that involvement in a religious community may encourage fathers to make the most of the limited time at home they have, resulting in an increased likelihood of being engaged in their child's life one year later and a decreased likelihood of arguing with mothers (Bartkowski and Xu 2000; King 2003; Wilcox and Wolfinger 2008).

There are also some limitations to acknowledge in this study. First, the data contains limited information about how fathers were able to take time off for the birth of their child. Fathers in these data may be using workplace paternity (or parental) leave programs, unpaid time off through FMLA, or other forms of leave (using sick, personal, or vacation days). The publicly available data also does not contain information about the state or region that respondents reside in, which is important given state variations in paid family leave. Knowing exactly what type of leave fathers have access to and are using is essential to get an accurate assessment of the consequences of paternity leave, as well as to better understand potential barriers to paternity leave-taking.

Second, the moderating influence of religious participation on the associations between paternity leave, father involvement, and parental conflict is speculated to be due to religiously active fathers sanctifying their family relationships. Unfortunately, the indicators of religiosity available in the data are limited, and there are no questions that allow for an assessment of the role sanctification plays in these processes. or the extent to which fathers are exposed to religious messages about the importance of family life. Future studies should incorporate additional measures of religiosity—and measures of sanctification in particular—to better understand whether and how religion shapes fathers' decisions and actions while on paternity leave.

Third, this study focuses on a sample of urban families that are relatively disadvantaged. Although this dataset has been used extensively to study various outcomes associated with fathers' religious participation (e.g., Petts 2007, 2011; Wolfinger and Wilcox 2008), the findings uncovered here may differ for fathers within different socioeconomic and regional contexts. Future studies should explore the role of religion in decisions about, and consequences of, paternity leave in other contexts (rural, higher SES, etc.).

Despite these limitations, this study contributes to the areas of religion and family life by exploring whether fathers' religious participation moderates the associations between paternity leave, father involvement, and parental conflict. Although previous studies have found evidence that paternity leave-taking and religious participation may both be associated with family outcomes, this study is the first to examine whether fathers' religious participation may contextualize the experience of paternity leave. Overall, there is some evidence suggesting that taking paternity leave, and longer periods of leave, is more likely to be associated with more frequent father involvement and lower parental conflict among fathers who attend religious services frequently than among fathers who attend less frequently. Future studies should continue to examine the intersection of family and religion in predicting family outcomes, and the role religion may play in fathers' decisions about, and behaviors during, paternity leave to better understand the context of paternity leave within the United States.

Funding: Research was supported by the Eunice Kennedy Shriver National Institute of Child Health & Human Development of the National Institutes of Health under Award Number R03HD087875. The content is solely the responsibility of the author and does not necessarily represent the official views of the National Institutes of Health.

Conflicts of Interest: The authors declare no conflicts of interest.

References

Albiston, Catherine, and Lindsey Trimble O'Connor. 2016. Just Leave. *Harvard Women's Law Journal* 39: 1–65.
Almqvist, Anna-Lena, and Ann-Zofie Duvander. 2014. Changes in Gender Equality? Swedish Fathers' Parental Leave, Division of Childcare and Housework. *Journal of Family Studies* 20: 19–27. [CrossRef]
Aumann, Kerstin, Ellen Galinsky, and Kenneth Matos. 2011. *The New Male Mystique*. New York: Families and Work Institute.
Bartkowski, John P., and Xiaohe Xu. 2000. Distant Patriarchs or Expressive Dads? The Discourse of Fathering in Conservative Protestant Families. *The Sociological Quarterly* 41: 465–85. [CrossRef] [PubMed]

Birditt, Kira S., Edna Brown, Terri L. Orbuch, and Jessica M. McIlvane. 2010. Marital Conflict Behaviors and Implications for Divorce Over 16 Years. *Journal of Marriage and Family* 72: 1188–204. [CrossRef] [PubMed]

Blum, Sonja, Alison Koslowski, and Peter Moss, eds. 2017. *International Review of Leave Policies and Research 2017*. Available online: http://www.leavenetwork.org/lp_and_r_reports/ (accessed on 1 August 2018).

Bünning, Mareike. 2015. *European Sociological Review* 31: 738–48.

Bureau of Labor Statistics. 2018. Access to Paid Personal Leave, December 2017. Available online: https://www.bls.gov/ebs/paid_personal_leave_122017.htm (accessed on 1 August 2018).

Cabrera, Natasha J., Jay Fagan, and Danielle Farrie. 2008. Explaining the Long Reach of Fathers' Prenatal Involvement on Later Paternal Engagement. *Journal of Marriage and Family* 70: 1094–107. [CrossRef] [PubMed]

Call, Vaughn R. A., and Tim B. Heaton. 1997. Religious Influence on Marital Stability. *Journal for the Scientific Study of Religion* 36: 382–92. [CrossRef]

Carlson, Daniel L., Sarah Hanson, and Andrea Fitzroy. 2016. The Division of Child Care, Sexual Intimacy, and Relationship Quality in Couples. *Gender & Society* 30: 442–66.

Carlson, Daniel L., Amanda J. Miller, and Sharon Sassler. 2018. Stalled for whom? Change in the division of particular housework tasks and their consequences for middle- to low-income couples. *Socius* 4. [CrossRef]

Carrère, Sybil, and John Mordechai Gottman. 1999. Predicting Divorce among Newlyweds from the First Three Minutes of a Marital Conflict Discussion. *Family Process* 38: 293–301. [CrossRef] [PubMed]

Coltrane, Scott, Elizabeth C. Miller, Tracy DeHaan, and Lauren Stewart. 2013. Fathers and the Flexibility Stigma. *Journal of Social Issues* 69: 279–302. [CrossRef]

Cowan, Carolyn Pape, Philip A. Cowan, Gertrude Heming, Ellen Garrett, William S. Coysh, Harriet Curtis-Boles, and Abner J. Boles III. 1985. Transitions to Parenthood: His, Hers, and Theirs. *Journal of Family Issues* 6: 451–81. [CrossRef] [PubMed]

DeMaris, Alfred, Annette Mahoney, and Kenneth I. Pargament. 2011. Doing the Scut Work of Infant Care: Does Religiousness Encourage Father Involvement? *Journal of Marriage and Family* 73: 354–68. [CrossRef] [PubMed]

Denton, Melinda Lundquist. 2004. Gender and Marital Decision Making: Negotiating Religious Ideology and Practice. *Social Forces* 82: 1151–80. [CrossRef]

Dollahite, David C. 1998. Fathering, Faith, and Spirituality. *Journal of Men's Studies* 7: 3–16. [CrossRef]

Doucet, Andrea. 2013. Gender Roles and Fathering. In *Handbook of Father Involvement: Multidisciplinary Perspectives*. Edited by Natasha J. Cabrera and Catherine S. Tamis-Lemonda. New York: Routledge, pp. 297–319.

Edgell, Penny. 2006. *Religion and Family in a Changing Society*. Princeton: Princeton University Press.

Ellison, Christopher G., and Jeffrey S. Levin. 1998. The Religion-Health Connection: Evidence, Theory, and Future Directions. *Health Education and Behavior* 25: 700–20. [CrossRef] [PubMed]

Frisco, Michelle L., and Kristi Williams. 2003. Perceived Housework Equity, Marital Happiness, and Divorce in Dual-Earner Households. *Journal of Family Issues* 24: 51–73. [CrossRef]

Gallagher, Sally K., and Christian Smith. 1999. Symbolic Traditionalism and Pragmatic Egalitarianism: Contemporary Evangelicals, Families, and Gender. *Gender & Society* 13: 211–33.

Gerson, Kathleen. 2010. *The Unfinished Revolution: How a New Generation Is Reshaping Family, Work, and Gender in America*. New York: Oxford University Press.

Grych, John H., and Frank D. Fincham. 1990. Marital Conflict and Children's Adjustment: A Cognitive-Contextual Framework. *Psychological Bulletin* 108: 267–90. [CrossRef] [PubMed]

Haas, Linda, and C. Philip Hwang. 2008. The Impact of Taking Parental Leave on Fathers' Participation in Childcare and Relationships with Children: Lessons from Sweden. *Community, Work, and Family* 11: 85–104. [CrossRef]

Harrington, Brad, Fred Van Deusen, Jennifer Sabatini Fraone, Samantha Eddy, and Linda Haas. 2014. *The New Dad: Take Your Leave*. Boston: Boston College Center for Work and Family.

Horowitz, Juliana, Kim Parker, Nikki Graf, and Gretchen Livingston. 2017. *Americans Widely Support Paid Family and Medical Leave, but Differ Over Specific Policies*. Washington: Pew Research Center.

Huerta, Maria C., Willem Adema, Jennifer Baxter, Wen-Jui Han, Mette Lausten, RaeHyuck Lee, and Jane Waldfogel. 2014. Fathers' Leave and Fathers' Involvement: Evidence from Four OECD Countries. *European Journal of Social Security* 16: 308–46. [CrossRef] [PubMed]

Killewald, Alexandra. 2013. A Reconsideration of the Fatherhood Premium: Marriage, Coresidence, Biology, and Fathers' Wages. *American Sociological Review* 78: 96–116. [CrossRef]

King, Valerie. 2003. The Influence of Religion on Father's Relationships with Their Children. *Journal of Marriage and Family* 65: 382–95. [CrossRef]

Klerman, Jacob Alex, Kelly Daley, and Alyssa Pozniak. 2012. *Family and Medical Leave in 2012: Technical Report.* Cambridge: ABT Associates.

Kotsadam, Andreas, and Henning Finseraas. 2011. The State Intervenes in the Battle of the Sexes: Causal Effects of Paternity Leave. *Social Science Research* 40: 1611–22. [CrossRef]

Kusner, Katherine G., Annette Mahoney, Kenneth I. Pargament, and Alfred DeMaris. 2014. Sanctification of Marriage and Spiritual Intimacy Predicting Observed Marital Interactions Across the Transition to Parenthood. *Journal of Family Psychology* 28: 604–14. [CrossRef] [PubMed]

Lamb, Michael E., ed. 2010. How do Fathers Influence Children's Development? Let me Count the Ways. In *The Role of the Father in Child Development*, 5th ed. Hoboken: Wiley, pp. 1–26.

Lynn, Mark G., John H. Grych, and Gregory M. Fosco. 2016. Influences on Father Involvement: Testing for Unique Contributions of Religion. *Journal of Child and Family Studies* 25: 3247–59. [CrossRef]

Mahoney, Annette. 2005. Religion and Conflict in Marital and Parent-Child Relationships. *Journal of Social Issues* 61: 689–706. [CrossRef]

Mahoney, Annette. 2010. Religion in Families, 1999–2009: A Relational Spirituality Framework. *Journal of Marriage and Family* 72: 805–27. [CrossRef] [PubMed]

Mahoney, Annette, Kenneth I. Pargament, Tracey Jewell, Aaron B. Swank, Eric Scott, Erin Emery, and Mark Rye. 1999. Marriage and the Spiritual Realm: The Role of Proximal and Distal Religious Constructs in Marital Functioning. *Journal of Family Psychology* 13: 321–38. [CrossRef]

Mahoney, Annette, Kenneth I. Pargament, Nalini Tarakeshwar, and Aaron B. Swank. 2001. Religion in the Home in the 1980s and 1990s: A Meta-Analytic Review and Conceptual Analysis of Links between Religion, Marriage, and Parenting. *Journal of Family Psychology* 15: 559–96. [CrossRef] [PubMed]

Mahoney, Annette, Kenneth I. Pargament, Aaron Murray-Swank, and Nichole Murray-Swank. 2003. Religion and the Sanctification of Family Relationships. *Review of Religious Research* 44: 220–36. [CrossRef]

Marsiglio, William, and Kevin Roy. 2012. *Nurturing Dads: Social Initiatives for Contemporary Fatherhood.* New York: Russell Sage Foundation.

McGill, Brittany S. 2014. Navigating New Norms of Involved Fatherhood: Employment, Fathering Attitudes, and Father Involvement. *Journal of Family Issues* 35: 1089–106. [CrossRef]

National Partnership for Women and Families. 2018. State Paid Family and Medical Leave Laws, July 2018. Washington, D.C. Available online: http://www.nationalpartnership.org/research-library/work-family/paid-leave/state-paid-family-leave-laws.pdf (accessed on 30 August 2018).

Nepomnyaschy, Lenna, and Jane Waldfogel. 2007. Paternity Leave and Fathers' Involvement with their Young Children. *Community, Work and Family* 10: 427–53. [CrossRef]

Palkovitz, Rob. 2002. *Involved Fathering and Men's Adult Development: Provisional Balances.* Mahwah: Lawrence Erlbaum Associates.

Pedulla, David S., and Sarah Thébaud. 2015. Can We Finish the Revolution? Gender, Work-Family Ideals, and Institutional Constraint. *American Sociological Review* 80: 116–39. [CrossRef] [PubMed]

Petts, Richard J. 2007. Religious Participation, Religious Affiliation, and Engagement with Children Among Fathers Experiencing the Birth of a New Child. *Journal of Family Issues* 28: 1139–61. [CrossRef]

Petts, Richard J. 2011. Is Urban Fathers' Religion Important for their Children's Behavior? *Review of Religious Research* 53: 183–206. [CrossRef]

Petts, Richard J., and Chris Knoester. 2018. Paternity Leave-Taking and Father Engagement. *Journal of Marriage and Family* 80: 1144–62. [CrossRef] [PubMed]

Petts, Richard J., Chris Knoester, and Qi Li. 2018. Paid Paternity Leave-Taking in the United States. *Community, Work & Family* 14: 1–22. [CrossRef]

Pragg, Brianne, and Chris Knoester. 2017. Parental Leave Usage among Disadvantaged Fathers. *Journal of Family Issues* 38: 1157–85. [CrossRef] [PubMed]

Raub, Amy, Arijit Nandi, Nicolas De Guzman Chorny, Elizabeth Wong, Paul Chung, Priya Batra, Adam Schickedanz, Bijetri Bose, Judy Jou, Daniel Franken, and et al. 2018. *Paid Parental Leave: A Detailed Look at Approaches Across OECD Countries*. Los Angeles: WORLD Policy Analysis Center.

Rege, Mari, and Ingeborg F. Solli. 2013. The Impact of Paternity Leave on Fathers' Future Earnings. *Demography* 50: 2255–77. [CrossRef] [PubMed]

Rehel, Erin M. 2014. When Dad Stays Home Too: Paternity Leave, Gender, and Parenting. *Gender and Society* 28: 110–32. [CrossRef]

Roggman, Lori A., Lisa K. Boyce, Gina A. Cook, and Jerry Cook. 2002. Getting Dads Involved: Father Involvement in Early Head Start and with their Children. *Infant Mental Health Journal* 23: 62–78. [CrossRef]

Rudman, Lauri A., and Kris Mescher. 2013. Penalizing Men who Request a Family Leave: Is Flexibility Stigma a Femininity Stigma? *Journal of Social Issues* 69: 322–40. [CrossRef]

Sarkadi, Anna, Robert Kristiansson, Frank Oberklaid, and Sven Bremberg. 2008. Fathers' Involvement and Children's Developmental Outcomes: A Systematic Review of Longitudinal Studies. *Acta Paediatrica* 97: 153–58. [CrossRef] [PubMed]

Steensland, Brian, Jerry Z. Park, Mark D. Regnerus, Lynn D. Robinson, W. Bradford Wilcox, and Robert D. Woodberry. 2000. The Measure of American Religion: Toward Improving the State of the Art. *Social Forces* 79: 291–318. [CrossRef]

Tanaka, Sakiko, and Jane Waldfogel. 2007. Effects of Parental Leave and Working Hours on Fathers' Involvement with their Babies: Evidence from the UK Millennium Cohort Study. *Community, Work, and Family* 10: 409–26. [CrossRef]

Twenge, Jean M., W. Keith Campbell, and Craig A. Foster. 2003. Parenthood and Marital Satisfaction: A Meta-Analytic Review. *Journal of Marriage and Family* 65: 574–83. [CrossRef]

Wilcox, W. Bradford. 2004. *Soft Patriarchs, New Men: How Christianity Shapes Fathers and Husbands*. Chicago: The University of Chicago Press.

Wilcox, W. Bradford, and Nicholas H. Wolfinger. 2008. Living and Loving 'Decent': Religion and Relationship Quality among Urban Parents. *Social Science Research* 37: 828–43. [CrossRef] [PubMed]

Williams, Joan C. 2000. *Unbending Gender: Why Family and Work Conflict and What to Do about It*. Oxford: Oxford University Press.

Williams, Joan C., Mary Blair-Loy, and Jennifer L. Berdahl. 2013. Cultural Schemas, Social Class, and the Flexibility Stigma. *Journal of Social Issues* 69: 209–34. [CrossRef]

Wolfinger, Nicholas H., and W. Bradford Wilcox. 2008. Happily Ever After? Religion, Marital Status, Gender, and Relationship Quality in Urban Families. *Social Forces* 86: 1311–37. [CrossRef]

religions

MDPI

Article

Parent's Just Don't Understand: Parental Support, Religion and Depressive Symptoms among Same-Race and Interracial Relationships

Andrea K. Henderson * and Mia J. Brantley

Department of Sociology, University of South Carolina, 911 Pickens Street Columbia, SC 29208, USA; miab@email.sc.edu
* Correspondence: ahenderson@sc.edu

Received: 29 January 2019; Accepted: 28 February 2019; Published: 6 March 2019

check for updates

Abstract: Research finds that individuals in interracial relationships have poorer mental health than those in same-race relationships. Family support, or lack thereof, may play an important role in explaining the psychological risks for such individuals. Growing attention has focused on the complex interplay between religion, health, and family life, particularly the stress-buffering role of religious involvement. However, little attention has been given to the possible mitigating effects of religion in the face of limited family support among same-race and interracial couples. Using data from the National Longitudinal Study of Adolescent to Adult Health (Add Health), this study addresses two important questions: (1) Is weak family support associated with depressive symptoms among individuals in same-race and interracial relationships?; and (2) Does religious involvement buffer the association between weak family support and depressive symptoms for individuals engaged in these romantic ties? Results suggest that weak parental support is associated with depressive symptoms for individuals in both same-race and interracial relationships, however we find limited support of religion protecting against weak parental support for individuals in interracial unions. The results highlight the complex interplay between religion, health, and family in contemporary American life.

Keywords: Religion; health; family support; race

1. Introduction

Recent increases in the rate of interracial relationships, both in dating and marriage, suggest it has garnered greater social acceptance (Carroll 2007; Herman and Campbell 2012). As of 2015, nearly 17% of new marriages were between partners of a different race compared to less than 1% in 1970 (Pew Research Center 2017). A growing literature, however, also describes the persistent challenges interracial couples encounter, including negative reactions from strangers and diminished support from family and friends (Childs 2005; Dalmage 2000). Familial support continues to be an important and vital part of young adult adjustment (Arnett and Schwab 2013; Fingerman et al. 2012), and in its absence many young adults are vulnerable to psychological distress (B. Miller 2017). Findings from several recent studies suggest that when compared to their same-race counterparts, individuals in interracial relationships report higher rates of distress and anxiety (B. Miller 2017; Lykke 2017; Bratter and Eschbach 2006; Miller and Kail 2016; Kroeger and Williams 2011). There is mixed evidence that parental support helps to explain the differences in the association between depressive symptoms and interracial and same-race relationships (Tillman and Miller 2017). Surprisingly, limited work has identified social and cultural factors that may protect the mental well-being of individuals in interracial relationships from the loss of social support.

One such factor may be religion. First, several decades of work have documented the health-promoting effects of religiosity (Ellison and Levin 1998). Religious involvement is positively associated with better psychological well-being, including lower depression and anxiety and higher levels of self-esteem (McCullough and Larson 1999; Krause 1995; Shreve-Neiger and Edelstein 2004). Moreover, religion often plays a salient role in facilitating effective coping, and more favorable outcomes in the face of problematic life events and chronic stress, including financial hardship, role strain, discrimination, and other challenging events (Bradshaw and Ellison 2010; Henderson 2016; Bierman 2006; Sherkat and Re 1992). Second, there is evidence surrounding a religion-family connection, such that religion is often identified as a salient force in the formation, quality, and preservation of romantic relationships (for reviews see Marks 2006; Mahoney 2010). Yet much of what we know about the role of religion in romantic relationships is centered on same-race, largely non-Hispanic white, unions (Mahoney 2010; Edgell 2013; Myers 2006; Vaaler et al. 2009). Little is known about how religion may work in the context of other, more diverse relationships. Religion, however, may play an important role across a variety of relationship contexts, including homosexual couples (Oswald et al. 2008; Rostosky et al. 2008), dating and cohabiting couples (Henderson et al. 2018; Freitas 2008), and "fragile" families (Wilcox and Wolfinger 2008; Sullivan 2008). Lastly, while the relationship between religion and attitudes and behaviors toward interracial relationships is complex (Perry 2013a, 2013b), there is some recent evidence to suggest that certain dimensions of religious involvement are positively related to interracial unions. Recent work by Perry (2013a), finds that more proximal dimensions of religious involvement—i.e., participation in private devotional practices and integrated churches—may incline individuals towards a more favorable attitude in interracial marriage. However, examining *if* and *how* religion works in the context of such romantic relationships has largely been ignored. More work on the interplay between religion, stress, and mental health in the context of romantic relationships, especially interracial couples, remains an unexplored avenue of research.

The aim of the present study is to help fill the gap in this area. Using Wave IV data from the National Longitudinal Study of Adolescent to Adult Health (Add Health), this study addresses two important questions: (1) Is weak parental support associated with depressive symptoms among individuals in same-race and interracial relationships?; and (2) Does religious involvement moderate (i.e., buffer) the association between weak parental support and depressive symptoms among individuals engaged in these relationships? We generate two conceptual models, including the stress-buffering model, to examine these research questions. Findings are discussed in terms of the research on religion and health, as well as the broader research on the relationship between religion, health, and family life. Study limitations are identified and several fruitful directions for further investigation are proposed.

2. Theoretical and Empirical Background

2.1. Depression in Same-Race and Interracial Relationships

Young adults involved in romantic relationships are more likely to experience symptoms of depression than their peers who remain romantically unattached (Connolly and McIsaac 2011; Davila 2008; Joyner and Udry 2000; Welsh et al. 2003). A variety of causes and consequences for the association has been posited. One such explanation includes the stress and coping model (Davila 2008), which suggests young adults in romantic relationships face unnavigated challenges and stress, including negotiation of partner's needs, sexual feelings and desires, relationship conflict, and issues surrounding breakups and rejection (Larson et al. 1999; Davila 2008). Such challenges increase one's risk for distress and poor psychological adjustment (Davila 2008; Connolly and McIsaac 2011). However, recent evidence suggests that individuals in interracial, versus same-race relationships, face additional burdens that may place them at greater risk for psychological distress (Childs 2005; Dalmage 2000; Tillman and Miller 2017; Wong and Penner 2018). Although interracial ties have become more accepted, a substantial portion of Americans continue to disapprove of interracial romance (Carroll 2007; Herman and Campbell 2012; Skinner and Hudac 2017). Consequently, individuals in interracial relationships are likely to face microaggressions, discrimination, and stigma from people who disapprove of their union (Solsberry 1994; Bonilla-Silva and Forman 2000; Skinner and Hudac 2017). For example, Dalmage (2000) finds that many interracially dating White youth report experiencing racism in ways that undermines their ideas of fairness and equality, and many young adults engaged in interracial unions report hiding their relationship from friends and family (Wang et al. 2006). Such maltreatment, whether real or perceived, may adversely affect psychological well-being (Pascoe and Smart Richman 2009). Consequently, a substantial body of work finds that couple's racial composition—same-race versus interracial—is a robust predictor of psychological well-being in young adulthood (B. Miller 2017; Lykke 2017; Bratter and Eschbach 2006; Miller and Kail 2016; Kroeger and Williams 2011).

2.2. Parents, Depression and Same-Race and Interracial Relationships

Family of origin, particularly parental support, is recognized as a salient factor in young adult psychological adjustment (Davila et al. 2009; Lorenzo-Blanco et al. 2013; B. C. Miller 2002; Whitbeck et al. 1993). Supportive parental relationships may protect against the negative effects of stress, including stress associated with romantic ties, on mental health (Hartnett et al. 2013; House et al. 1988). Therefore, in the absence of parental support young adults may experience elevated risk of distress for several reasons, including increased loneliness and a reduced sense of belonging, a withdrawal of instrumental aid, as well as a loss of emotional support in navigating the challenges of romantic ties. Indeed, research suggests that young adults who view their parents as warm and supportive (Jessor and Jessor 1975), and who feel there is open communication with their parents report better mental health and are less likely to engage in behaviors that risk their well-being (Fox 1980; Diiorio et al. 2003). A poor parent-child relationship, characterized by low instrumental and emotional support, has been found to be associated with risky sexual behavior and depression (Jessor and Jessor 1977). For example, Steinberg and Davila (2008) found that the link between dating and depressive symptoms is stronger for individuals who perceive their parents as emotionally unavailable.

In addition to health, parents play a significant role in the formation and quality of the romantic relationships their children experience as adults (Collins and Read 1990; Del Toro 2012; Xia et al. 2018). Parents offer children a foundation, via parental practices and family climate, on which to build future relationships that influence the quality, function, and health of young adult romantic ties (Raby et al. 2015; Xia et al. 2018). The loss of parental support, perhaps as a consequence of a child's relationship, may result in unfavorable health consequences. Surprisingly, little is known about how partner characteristics, including partner's race, influence parental support (for exception see Yahirun 2019). As previously suggested, however, there is some evidence that family opposition is a salient factor in interracial relationships. Individuals in interracial unions often report feeling ostracized from their family (Gaines 2001). Some have even argued that parental objection is the most prominent obstacle in pursuing and maintaining an interracial relationship (Mok 1999; Childs 2005; Dalmage 2000). A brief review of the historical and cultural norms surrounding interracial relationships in the United States may shed light on why parents may choose to withdraw their support from such unions, thereby placing their children at greater risk of distress.

For much of American history, the idea of an interracial union, particularly a Black/White partnership, was repugnant (de Guzman and Nishina 2017). Stemming from our nation's history of slavery, which reinforced unequal race relations as natural, marriages between individuals of different races was often illegal and morally objectionable (de Guzman and Nishina 2017; Foeman and Nance 1999). The 1967 Supreme Court ruling, i.e., Loving v. Virginia, 388 U.S. 1967, overturning miscegenation laws, which barred sex or marriage between Blacks and Whites, substantially changed the cultural environment surrounding interracial relationships (Lombardo 1987). Today, interracial dating and marriage are often used to gauge the level of integration or assimilation for minority groups into the larger culture. Frequently more young adults are engaging in interracial romantic ties. Approximately 12% to 19% of young adults report they have been in at least one interracial romantic relationship (Kreager 2008; Wang et al. 2006) and marriage among different race partners continues to rise (Pew Research Center 2017). Yet despite these changes, individuals in interracial unions continue to face a series of obstacles that unfairly challenge their relationships and health (Childs 2005; Dalmage 2000; B. Miller 2017; Bratter and Eschbach 2006; Miller and Kail 2016; Kroeger and Williams). Identifying and understanding the tools and resources individuals in both interracial and same-race relationships use in the face of such challenges is needed.

2.3. Religion, Weak Parental Support and Depression

The stress and coping model used to explain the risk for elevated distress among individuals engaged in romantic experiences rarely investigates the coping-related mechanisms that may protect against the harmful effects of stress (Davila 2008). A growing body of evidence, however, suggests religion that may be a salient resource and strategy in protecting mental health (Ellison and Levin 1998; Koenig and Larson 2001; Koenig 2009). Various dimensions of religious involvement have been found to be positively associated with better psychological well-being, including lower depression and anxiety, and better self-concept (Levin et al. 1995; Ellison 1993; Koenig 2009). Moreover, religious involvement has been found to reduce the noxious effects of stress, including discrimination, family role strain, and loss of social ties, on psychological well-being (Bierman 2006; Bradshaw and Ellison 2010; Henderson 2016; Sherkat and Re 1992).

Several decades of work have embraced the approach of defining religion as a complex multi-dimensional phenomenon, including organizational, non-organizational and subjective religiosity, which may exert direct and indirect effects on the mental health of individuals in same-race and interracial relationships (Levin et al. 1995; Mahoney 2010). First, organizational religious involvement, often measured via the frequency of religious services attendance (Ellison and Levin 1998), may cultivate well-being by establishing and reinforcing social networks of support and guidance. Religious congregations offer frequent opportunities to develop friendships and relationships that aid individuals in times of trouble (Ellison and Levin 1998; Krause 2006). Via both formal, e.g., sermons and official religious directives, and informal means, e.g., emotional support and practical guidance from coreligionists, religious service attendance brings together like-minded individuals who share faith commitments and values on a regular basis (Ellison and Levin 1998). Such opportunities often build solidarity among religious communities that contributes to a shared sense of meaning and purpose, promotes positive cognitions and emotions, and diverts attention from personal problems or challenges (Krause 2006; Strawbridge et al. 2001) Individuals in same-race and interracial relationships may receive messages from religious officials and co-religionists that reinforce their relationship, but also provide opportunities for personal development and spiritual growth that encourages well-being (Wilcox and Wolfinger 2008; Strawbridge et al. 2001; Rasic et al. 2011). The social support offered by organizational religious involvement may be particularly salient for individuals struggling with the loss of family support. However, for individuals in interracial relationships, who may be experiencing interpersonal sanctioning from other social sources, religious communities may offer a unique opportunity to provide support that encourages and promotes psychological well-being.

Although organizational religious involvement may positively influence the mental health of individuals dealing with the absence of parental support in the ways outlined above, it may be reasonable to expect that formal religious involvement may also negatively influence the health of individuals engaged in interracial unions specifically. Organized religion has a complex history with race and intimacy in which it has often played an unfortunate role in the stigmatization of interracial marriage and relationships in the U.S. (Coates 2015). American Christianity, via formal and unofficial church doctrine, historically prohibited interracial relationship formation, often vilifying such unions as being "unequally yoked" (Botham 2009). Although few churches today would openly admit to such beliefs and practices, most churches continue to be tightly constructed along racial lines (Emerson and Kim 2003). A small minority of churches and congregations are truly multiethnic (Yancey and Emerson 2003; Edwards et al. 2013). Therefore, individuals in interracial relationships, who remain involved in organized religion, may be the target of either real or perceived sanctioning as a result of their relationship that may negatively influence their mental well-being (Perry 2014). Therefore, religious attendance may have less (or even a negative) influence on the health of individuals in interracial relationships compared to their peers in monoracial relationships.

Second, religious coping, best conceptualized as a multidimensional construct involving the use of religious cognitions and behaviors, including private prayer, religious support and guidance (Taylor et al. 2003; Pargament et al. 1998), may also influence health and well-being (Siegel et al. 2001; Pargament and Brant 1998; Fabricatore et al. 2004). For example, through prayer, individuals may develop a close, personal relationship with God (or a divine other), who is thought to offer comfort and solace during difficult times (Pollner 1989; Kirkpatrick 2005). Such private activities may cultivate a belief of being a "child of God" that results in feelings of dignity and worth that alters the perception, experience, and reaction to negative events, including the loss of social support (Cooper-Lewter and Mitchell 1986). Such relationships often result in feelings of closeness and personal attachment, in which people are particularly likely to turn to God (or a divine other) during events perceived as stressful (Kirkpatrick 2005). Indeed, research suggests people often turn to prayer during difficult emotional states, such as loss, anger or fear (Ai et al. 2007). In this context, prayer may help to alleviate strong negative emotions and facilitates open communication and forgiveness in interpersonal relationships that results in better psychological well-being (Lambert et al. 2010). In this context, religious coping provides protection and security, and is therefore likely to reduce distress (Krause 2006).

Lastly, subjective religiosity is a dimension of religious involvement distinct from both public and private forms of religious belief and behavior. Subjective religiosity, generally conceived of as the personal importance or self-assessed strength of one's religious identity, emphasizes an internalized (i.e., intrinsic) religious commitment (Allport and Ross 1967; Chatters et al. 2008). Although individual intentions for engaging in religious behavior may vary, those who are intrinsically motivated may find greater psychological benefits from their religious identity (Ryan et al. 1993). Additionally, subjective religiosity may influence health by offering a comprehensive framework for assigning attributions or explanations to mundane affairs, and chronic challenges that reduces psychological distress (Pargament et al. 1998). For example, intrinsic religiosity has been found to be associated with lower levels of anxiety and depression in response to negative life events, including events described as uncontrollable (Park et al. 1990). Among individuals in interracial relationships, subjective religiosity may be particularly helpful by creating opportunities to establish an identity based on internal qualities, such as spirituality, kindness, and generosity that may reduce the salience of external, racial differences. Work on multiracial congregations suggests participation in multiethnic religious communities may lead to *ethnic transcendence* (Marti 2008), or an alternative identity framed around religious interests instead of a race-ethnic identity. Perhaps it is the case that intrinsically religious individuals—i.e., committed to applying and living out their faith in all areas of their lives—in interracial unions are able to build a (shared) religious identity that transcends race and protects them in the face of stress and challenges related to their romantic union. For these reasons, subjective religiosity, or the salience of religion in one's life, may results in higher levels of psychological well-being, even in the face of stressful situations like lack of family support.

Investigating similarities and differences in the role of religion in same-race and interracial relationships is largely an unexplored avenue of research. Surprisingly, little is known about how religion may influence the health and family life of individuals engaged in interracial relationships. Nevertheless, there may be some reasons to expect that such individuals may be less inclined toward religion when compared to their peers in same-race relationships. Research on the social factors that predict engagement in interracial romantic ties generally find these individuals are younger, politically liberal, live in urban areas, come from racially diverse backgrounds, and have higher incomes and education (Herman and Campbell 2012; Johnson and Jacobson 2005; Perry 2013a; Fujino 1997). Such factors are also associated with lower levels of religious involvement

(Levin and Chatters 1998; Krause 2004). For these reasons it may be that individuals in interracial unions may be less likely to use and engage in religion in established ways, thereby distinguishing them from their peers in same-race relationships. However, theories surrounding resource substitution suggest social and interpersonal resources may be exchanged for one another in the face of loss or threat of loss (Ross and Mirowsky 2006). In the face of weak parental support, individuals in same-race and interracial relationships, who engage religion in the ways described above may indeed find themselves better off than their less religiously involved peers.

2.4. Conceptual Models

Based on the theory and research reviewed to this point, two conceptual models guide the way(s) in which weak parental support and religious involvement may be linked to the depressive symptoms of individuals in same-race and interracial relationships. In the first model, weak parental support is posited to have a positive association with depressive symptoms, while multiple dimensions of religious involvement are expected to have an inverse association with depressive symptoms. The effects of weak parental support and religious involvement, however, are thought to be largely or completely independent of one another. In the second model, or the *stress-buffering* model, we expect that religion will help reduce the impact of weak parental support on depressive symptoms. That is, religious involvement is expected to moderate, i.e., buffer or mitigate, the deleterious effects of weak parental support on depressive symptoms among individuals in same-race and interracial relationships. The buffering (or moderating) model is formulated as one involving an interaction—or cross-product term—between weak parental support and religion (i.e., weak parental support × religion; Ellison and Henderson 2011).

3. Data and Methods

Data come from the National Longitudinal Study of Adolescent to Adult Health (Add Health), a school-based study of a nationally representative sample of adolescents in grades 7–12 in 1994–1995 in the US. The Add Health used a multistage, stratified, school-based cluster sampling design and involves four waves of data collection. Add Health focuses on the social, economic, psychological and physical well-being of adolescents to young adulthood, and provides unique opportunities to study how social environments and behaviors, including families, romantic relationships, and religion, are linked to health. In 1994–95, Wave I data yielded a sample of 20,745 respondents with a response rate of 79% from all participating schools. Wave IV was a follow-up study of the individuals from Wave I conducted in 2008, in which respondents were 24–32 years old, and yielded approximately 75% of the original Wave 1 respondents (n = 15,701). The sampling methods of the Add Health have been described in detail elsewhere (Harris 2011).

3.1. Dependent Variable: Depressive Symptoms

Depressive symptoms was measured using nine items derived from the Center for Epidemiologic Studies Depression Scale (CES-D) (Radloff 1977). Respondents were asked how often in the past week (7 days) they: (1) were bothered by things, (2) could not shake off the blues, (3) felt as good as others, (4) had trouble concentrating, (5) felt depressed, (6) felt too tired, (7) enjoyed life, (8) felt sad, and (9) felt disliked. Responses ranged from 0 = "never or rarely (less than one day)" to 3 = "most or all of the time (5–7 days)." Per convention, responses were reverse-coded where necessary and the items were summed with a range of 0 to 27. The Cronbach's alpha is 0.83.

3.2. Key Independent Variables

Weak Parental Support. Parental support was constructed by first averaging across four items regarding the respondent's maternal and paternal figure. Specifically, the respondent was asked the following questions: (1) Are you satisfied with the way you and your mother [and father] figure communicate?; and (2) How close to do you feel to your mother [and father] figure? Responses to the questions were 1 = "strongly disagree," to 5 = "strongly agree," and 1 = "not at all" to 5 = "very much," respectively. Responses were reverse coded so that higher scores reflect weak parental support; the original measure ranged of 2–20. However, due to the skewed distribution of the original index, we then dichotomized the index at the mean (x = 6.36), such that: 1 = "weak parental support (i.e., x $\geq$ 6.36)" and 0 = "high parental support (x < 6.36)."[1] Respondents missing on both the mother and father support questions were dropped from the analysis (i.e., no parental figure present). The current measure of parental support is consistent with prior studies using Add Health data (LeCloux et al. 2017).

Religious Involvement. Three distinct aspects of religious involvement were included in the analysis. Organizational religious involvement was assessed by asking about the frequency of worship service attendance in the past 12 months (i.e., *religious attendance*). Responses ranged from 0 = "never" to 5 = "more than once a week." *Religious coping* was assessed by standardizing and averaging the responses of two questions: (1) How often do you pray privately, that is, when you are alone in places other than a religious assembly?" and (2) "How often do you turn to your religious or spiritual beliefs for help when you have personal problems, or problems at school or work?" Responses to the questions ranged from 0 = "never" to 7 = "more than once a day;" and 0 = "never" to 4 = "very often," respectively. The Pearson correlation coefficient for the two items is 0.76, $p < 0.001$. Lastly, one item assessed *subjective religiosity*, in which respondents were asked: "How important (if at all) is your spiritual life to you?" Responses ranged from 1 = "not important" to 4 = "more important than anything else." Higher scores on all three religious involvement items reflect higher levels of the religious attendance, religious coping, and subjective religiosity.

Covariates.[2] In addition, the models control for: race (measured in a series of dummy variables, including 1 = Black, 1 = Hispanic, 1 = Asian vs. 0 = White, non-Hispanic), gender (1 = female vs. 0 = male), age (measured in years), respondent's marital status (measured in a series of dummy variables, 1 = dating, 1 = cohabitation, vs. 0 = married serving as the reference category), parental status (1=current living child(ren) vs. 0 = all other) and socioeconomic status (SES). Respondent SES is a composite index constructed from three standardized measures of the respondent's education, occupation, and poverty threshold (i.e., income in relation to the federal poverty level for a given household size) measured in Wave IV. We also control for depressive symptoms at Wave I to account for previous mental health that may confound the relationship between weak parental support, religious involvement, and young adult depressive symptoms.

Our analytical sample was limited to those who participated in Wave IV in-home interview, reported being in a romantic relationship at the time of the interview, reported their partner's race, and self-identified their race/ethnicity as either non-Hispanic white, non-Hispanic Black, Hispanic, or Asians. Respondents who reported their race as "other" were excluded from the analysis, resulting in an n = 13,044. After listwise deletion of missing cases (n = 873, <7%), including reports of no mother or father figure, the analytical sample is n = 12,171. The sample was stratified across individuals in same-race (n = 9789) and interracial (n = 2382) relationships.

---

[1] We ran the analysis using the original, continuous measure of weak parental support (range 2–20; mean 6.36), as well as an additional cut-off point of one standard deviation above the mean. We found virtually the same results presented here using the described dichotomized measure of weak parental support. Due to the focus of the paper on weak parental support and the skewed distribution of the original variable, we made the decision to dichotomize the original variable. Analysis available upon request.

[2] Previous research suggest there may be significant differences by racial composition of marital stability (Wang et al. 2006) and health (Bratter and Eschbach 2006) for individuals in interracial relationships. These results suggest that non-Hispanic whites partnered with racial minorities, particularly Blacks, face unique challenges (Kroeger and Williams 2011). Taking this literature into account, we included a series of dummy variables of the racial composition of the interracial relationship as an additional covariate: respondent white/partner minority (RW/PM), respondent minority/partner minority (RM/PM), and respondent minority/partner white (RM/PW). In our sample, 46.9% of interracial couples were composed of RW/PM, 24.81% were RM/PM, and 28.34% were RM/PW. However, no statistically significant results were found and for the sake of parsimony these variables were removed from the analysis. Analysis available upon request.

3.3. Analytical Strategy

The data analysis progressed in several steps, and all analyses were stratified by same-race and interracial relationships. First, descriptive statistics are presented in Table 1. To examine the proposed frameworks, we ran a series of five linear regression models. Model 1 reports the estimated net effects of weak parental support on depressive symptoms. Model 2 adds the key independent variables of religious involvement—attendance, religious coping and subjective religiosity—to Model 1. Models 3 through 5 introduce separate interaction terms between weak parental support and our three religious involvement variables (e.g., weak parental support × religion) across both same-race and interracial samples. Continuous variables were mean-centered before estimating interaction terms to reduce collinearity (Aiken and West 1991).

Table 1. Sample Characteristics by Same-race and Interracial Relationship, Add Health [a].

Variable	Range	Same-Race Relationship (n = 9789)		Interracial Relationship (n = 2382)	
		Mean (%)	St. Error	Mean (%)	St. Error
Dependent Variable					
Adult Depressive Symptoms	0–27	5.26	0.08	5.90 [a]	0.15
Key Independent Variables					
Weak Parental Support	0–1	(40)		(45) [a]	
Religious Attendance	0–5	1.57	0.04	1.29 [a]	0.04
Religious Salience	0–3	2.48	0.03	2.35 [a]	0.03
Religious Coping	−1.53–1.23	−0.06	0.03	−0.20 [a]	0.03
Covariates					
NH White	0–1	(72)		(59)	
NH Black	0–1	(15)		(15)	
Hispanic	0–1	(11)		(19)	
Asian/Pacific Islander	0–1	(2)		(7)	
Age (in years)	24–33	28.4	0.12	28.36	0.13
Female	0–1	(49)		(49)	
Parent	0–1	(51)		(47) [a]	
Respondent SES	−2.37–1.12	−0.07	0.03	−0.08	0.04
Married	0–1	(46)		(34) [a]	
Cohabiting	0–1	(20)		(23) [a]	
Dating	0–1	(34)		(43) [a]	
Depressive symptoms, WI	0–27	5.63	0.08	5.97 [a]	0.14

Note: All data are weighted. [a] Mean differences between same-race and interracial relationship are significant at $p < 0.05$.

4. Results

Summary statistics for all variables are reported in Table 1 stratified by same-race and interracial relationships. Young adults in interracial relationships report more depressive symptoms relative to individuals in same-race relationships (values of 5.9 vs. 5.3, $p < 0.05$, respectively). Additionally, a higher percentage of individuals in interracial relationships report weak parental support (45% vs. 40%, $p < 0.05$). Of particular interest are the observed differences in religious involvement by relationship type. Specifically, individuals in same-race relationships appear to report higher levels of religious involvement across all three measures used in the analyses compared with their peers in interracial relationships. There appears to be few significant differences in our sociodemographic characteristics by relationship type, except for relationship status, where a higher percentage of individuals in interracial relationships appear to be dating (43% vs. 34%, $p < 0.05$) and cohabiting (23% vs. 20%, $p < 0.05$) and are less likely to be married (34% vs. 46, $p < 0.05$) compared to those in same-race relationships.

Table 2 shows the results of the multivariate regression models predicting depressive symptoms by weak parental support and religious involvement for same-race couples. As predicted, weak parental support is positively associated with depressive symptoms (Model 1: b = 0.87, $p < 0.001$) net of covariates. That is, compared to individuals with high levels of parental support, those who reported weak parental support also report significantly higher levels of depressive symptoms. In model 2, we find mixed support for our hypotheses regarding religious involvement. After the inclusion of our religion measures, weak parental support remains positively associated with depressive symptoms net of covariates (Model 2: b = 0.88, $p < 0.001$). Religious attendance is inversely related to depressive symptoms (Model 2: b = -0.26, $p < 0.001$). However, surprisingly, religious coping is positively associated with depressive symptoms (Model 2: b = 0.59, $p < 0.001$) among individuals in same-race relationships. We found no significant interactions between weak parental support and our measures of religious involvement, suggesting religion does little to protect against the deleterious effects of weak parental support on depression among individuals in same-race relationships.

Table 2. Estimated for Weighted Linear Regression Models Predicting Depressive Symptoms, Same-Race (n = 9789), Add Health.

	Model 1	Model 2	Model 3	Model 4	Model 5
	b (SE)	b (SE)	b (SE)	b (SE)	b (SE)
Weak parental support	0.87 (0.12) ***	0.88 (0.12) ***	0.88 (0.12) ***	0.88 (0.12) ***	0.88 (0.12) ***
Religious attendance		-0.26 (0.05) ***	-0.24 (0.06) ***	-0.26 (0.05) ***	-0.26 (0.05) ***
Religious coping		0.59 (0.13) ***	0.59 (0.13) ***	0.58 (0.13) ***	0.59 (0.13) ***
Subjective religiosity		-0.20 (0.13)	-0.20 (0.13)	-0.20 (0.13)	-0.17 (0.13)
Black, Non-Hispanic [a]	0.67 (0.20) ***	0.58 (0.21) **	0.58 (0.21) **	0.58 (0.21) **	0.58 (0.21) **
Hispanic [a]	0.03 (0.20)	-0.01 (0.21)	-0.01 (0.21)	-0.01 (0.21)	-0.01 (0.21)
Asian [a]	0.73 (0.29) **	0.79 (0.29) **	0.80 (0.30) **	0.79 (0.29) **	0.80 (0.29) **
Age	0.06 (0.03)	-0.01 (0.03)	-0.01 (0.03)	-0.01 (0.03)	-0.01 (0.03)
Female	1.00 (0.11) ***	0.89 (0.11) ***	0.88 (0.11) ***	0.89 (0.11) ***	0.89 (0.08) ***
Parent	-0.22 (0.12)	-0.22 (0.12)	-0.22 (0.12)	-0.22 (0.12)	-0.22 (0.12)
Cohabiting [b]	0.33 (0.14) *	0.25 (0.15)	0.25 (0.15)	0.25 (0.15)	0.25 (0.15)
Dating [b]	0.53 (0.13) ***	0.49 (0.14) ***	0.49 (0.14) ***	0.49 (0.14) ***	0.49 (0.14) ***
SES	-0.92 (0.08) ***	-0.89 (0.08) ***	-0.89 (0.08) ***	-0.89 (0.08) ***	-0.89 (0.08) ***
Depressive symptoms WI	0.27 (0.01) ***	0.27 (0.01) ***	0.27 (0.01) ***	0.27 (0.01) ***	0.27(0.01) ***
Interactions [c]					
Weak parental support × Religious attendance			-0.04 (0.07)		
Weak parental support × Religious coping				-0.03 (0.13)	
Weak parental support × Religious salience					-0.07 (0.11)
Intercept		2.83 (0.89) **	3.92 (0.88) ***	3.88 (0.88) ***	3.92 (0.88) ***	3.84 (0.87) ***
Adj. R^2	0.16	0.17	0.17	0.17	0.17

Notes: * $p < 0.05$; ** $p < 0.01$; *** $p < 0.001$. [a] Reference category is Non-Hispanic White; [b] Reference category is married; and [c] Components of interaction terms are zero-centered as recommended by Aiken and West (1991) and are entered independently.

Table 3 shows the multivariable regression estimates for individuals in interracial relationships. In Model 1, weak parental support is not significantly associated with depressive symptoms among individuals in interracial relationships net of covariates. However, in Model 2, once the religion variables and covariates are held constant, a curious suppressor pattern emerges, in which weak parental support becomes significantly associated with depressive symptoms among individuals in interracial relationships (Model 2: 32; $p < 0.05$). Counter to our hypotheses, none of our religious involvement variables are significantly related to depressive symptoms among individuals in interracial relationships. Turning to our models examining the stress-buffering effects of religious involvement, it appears we find limited support for our hypotheses. Religious coping appears to protect against the harmful effects of weak parental support on depressive symptoms among individuals in interracial relationships based on the negative regression coefficient (Model 4: -0.51, $p < 0.05$). We present the interaction graphically in Figure 1. The vertical axis indicates depressive symptoms and presents the predicted probabilities. On the horizontal axis is religious coping, ranging from low to high. The lines in the figures show how the effect of religious coping depends on parental support. According to the figure, it appears that at low levels of religious coping, individuals in interracial relationships with weak parental support also report significantly higher levels of depressive symptoms compared with individuals reporting high parental support. The slope of the line for weak parental support, however, remains flat as religious coping increases. At the highest levels of religious coping there is a crossover effect, where individuals reporting weak parental support now report slightly lower levels of depressive symptoms than individuals reporting high levels of parental support. Surprisingly, however, our results suggest individuals in interracial unions with strong parental support, experience elevated symptoms of distress as religious coping increases. We found no significant interactions between weak parental support and religious attendance and subjective religiosity.

Table 3. Estimated for Weighted Linear Regression Models Predicting Depressive Symptoms, Interracial Relationships (n = 2382), Add Health.

	Model 1	Model 2	Model 3	Model 4	Model 5
	b (SE)	b (SE)	b (SE)	b (SE)	b (SE)
Weak parental support	0.34 (0.22)	0.32 (0.22) *	0.32 (0.22)	0.31 (0.22) *	0.31 (0.22)
Religious attendance		−0.22 (0.11)	−0.16 (0.14)	−0.23 (0.11) *	−0.22 (0.11) *
Religious coping		0.35 (0.20)	0.34 (0.20)	0.56 (0.21) **	0.35 (0.20)
Subjective religiosity		−0.15 (0.22)	−0.14 (0.22)	−0.12 (0.22)	−0.46 (0.29)
Black, Non-Hispanic [a]	1.11 (0.39) **	1.08 (0.39) **	1.07 (0.39) **	1.09 (0.39) **	1.07 (0.38) **
Hispanic [a]	0.49 (0.29)	0.52 (0.28)	0.51 (0.28)	0.52 (0.29)	0.52 (0.29)
Asian [a]	0.46 (0.38)	0.49 (0.37)	0.49 (0.38)	0.48 (0.38)	0.53 (0.29)
Age	−0.05 (0.06)	−0.05 (0.06)	−0.05 (0.06)	−0.05 (0.06)	−0.05 (0.06)
Female	1.19 (0.24) ***	1.13 (0.25) ***	1.14 (0.25) ***	1.16 (0.24) ***	1.15 (0.25) ***
Parent	−0.31 (0.28)	−0.31 (0.28)	−0.30 (0.28)	−0.29 (0.28)	−0.31 (0.28)
Cohabiting [b]	0.20 (0.32)	0.10 (0.32)	0.10 (0.32)	0.08 (0.32)	0.08 (0.32)
Dating [b]	0.71 (0.28) **	0.67 (0.28) *	0.68 (0.27) *	0.67 (0.27) *	0.66 (0.27) *
SES	−1.15 (0.18) ***	−1.13 (0.18) ***	−1.12 (0.18) ***	−1.12 (0.18) ***	−1.12 (0.17) ***
Depressive symptoms WI	0.27 (0.03) ***	0.27 (0.03) ***	0.27 (0.03) ***	0.27 (0.03) ***	0.27 (0.03) ***
Interactions [c]					
Weak parental support x Religious attendance			−0.13 (0.14)		
Weak parental support x Religious coping				−0.51 (0.24) *	
Weak parental support x Religious salience					−0.46 (0.29)
Intercept	3.99 (1.79) *	4.61 (1.81) *	4.55 (1.81) *	4.63 (1.82) *	4.06 (1.87) *
Adj. R^2	0.16	0.16	0.16	0.17	0.16

Notes: * $p < 0.05$; ** $p < 0.01$; *** $p < 0.001$. [a] Reference category is Non-Hispanic White; [b] Reference category is married; and [c] Components of interaction terms are zero-centered as recommended by Aiken and West (1991) and are entered independently.

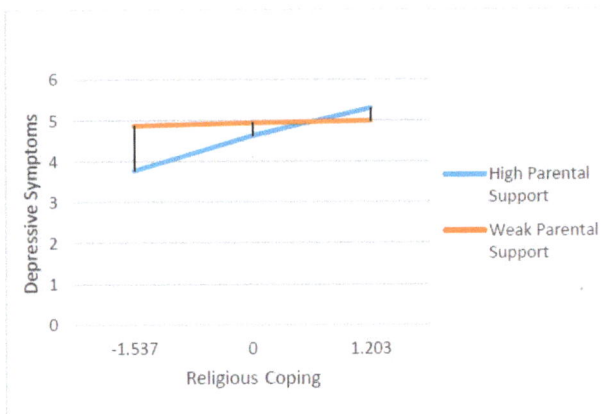

Figure 1. Predicted Depressive Symptoms by Weak Parental Support and Religious Coping, Interracial Relationships.

Ancillary Analysis

In ancillary analysis (not shown, but available upon request), we examined our results for differences by relationship status (i.e., dating, cohabiting and married). There is some evidence to suggest that relationship status is related to depressive symptoms, particularly among interracial couples (Connolly and McIsaac 2011; Bratter and Eschbach 2006), and parental support may also vary according to the level of commitment of the child's romantic relationship. We found no significant differences in the relationship between weak parental support and religion by relationship status across both our same-race and interracial couples. Additionally, we examined our data for differences by racial composition[2] among individuals in our interracial relationship sample. Research suggests that white, minority couples may experience greater disapproval from peers and family than other combinations (e.g., minority, minority relationships; B. Miller 2017; Bratter and Eschbach 2006). However, we found no significant differences in our relationships of interest by couples' racial composition.

5. Discussion

This research contributes to a growing literature on the mental health of individuals in same-race and interracial relationships. We examine weak parental support as a distinct psychosocial stressor and religious involvement as a coping-related mechanism in these romantic relationships. Our results suggest that indeed weak parental support acts as psychosocial stressor for individuals in both same-race and interracial relationships that increases their risk of depressive symptoms. These results are consistent with previous research on the importance of parental support in the psychological adjustment of young adults (Davila et al. 2009; Lorenzo-Blanco et al. 2013; B. C. Miller 2002; Whitbeck et al. 1993). Although there is little research surrounding the specific mechanisms, the absences of parental support may increase the risk of distress in young adults by increasing loneliness and isolation.

We find mixed support for our hypotheses on the main effects of religious involvement on depressive symptoms. Specifically, our results suggest that religious involvement, specifically religious attendance, is inversely related to distress for individuals in same-race relationships, but not individuals in interracial unions. A growing body of research indeed finds that social relationships within churches tend to be especially close and highly supportive, especially during times of trouble (Krause 2006; Nooney and Woodrum 2002). Organizational religious involvement offers opportunities for formal and informal social support (Krause 2006). Regular religious service participation may encourage beliefs and behaviors that promote and enhance the help-giving process (i.e., role models and shared beliefs on forgiveness and acceptance, etc.), which may be particularly helpful for those suffering from the absence of parental guidance. Contrary to our hypotheses, religious coping is positively associated with depressive symptoms among individuals in same-race relationships. What might explain this unexpected finding? Research finds that religion influences the formation of romantic relationships among young adults (Regnerus 2007). Religion has been identified as an important source in opposition to non-marital cohabitation and sex (Lehrer and Chiswick 1993; Barkan 2006; Regnerus 2007). Perhaps religious young adults engaged in romantic ties—especially if the union is not sanctioned by parents—experience elevated feelings of distress. Surprisingly, we find no significant main effects of religion on depression among individuals in interracial relationships. However, our results suggest such individuals are less likely to be religious. Recent work by Perry (2013b) finds that in some contexts, some dimensions of religious involvement are inversely related to interracial dating in adulthood. Such findings suggest that the relationship between religion, health, and family may be more complex among individuals engaged in interracial ties.

We find limited support for our hypotheses concerning the stress-buffering role of religious involvement on weak parental support and depressive symptoms. Specifically, while it appears that religious coping moderates the association between poor parental support and depressive symptoms for individuals in interracial unions, on closer examination it is among individuals with strong parental support that mental well-being declines as they seek comfort via private prayer and religious guidance. This finding is somewhat surprising, and an explanation may be beyond the scope of this paper. However, one possible explanation may be the issue of religious homogamy (Seshadri and Knudson-Martin 2013; Heaton and Pratt 1990; Kalmijn 1998). Religious homogamy, i.e., similarities between partners in religiosity, has been found to influence well-being and relationship quality among married and nonmarried couples (Heaton and Pratt 1990; Lehrer and Chiswick 1993). Perhaps highly religious individuals in interracial unions, with close family ties, experience distress if their partner is less religiously involved. Although such individuals may be able to turn to their parents for support, they may also feel guilt over the differences in their partner's religious commitment, which leads to distress. Unfortunately, no measures of partners' religiosity are available in Wave IV of Add Health. Future work should investigate these relationships at the couple-level.

Although this study addresses an important gap in the literature, it is also characterized by several notable limitations. First, while consistent with previous measures of parental support using Add Health (LeCloux et al. 2017), the items used to construct parental support do not directly reflect attitudes or feelings regarding the child's romantic relationship. Future work should seek to incorporate a distinctive measure of parental support that reflects thoughts and attitudes about of the romantic relationship in which their child is engaged, particularly in the context of an interracial relationship. Second, due to the small sample sizes of some combinations, this study was also unable to investigate differences by specific racial dyads (e.g., Asian–Black)[3]. Third, while we control for prior mental health, the use of longitudinal, panel data to explore these relationships may also prove insightful for understanding the role of stress and coping across the life course among individuals in both same-race and interracial unions. Lastly, this study relies on the responses of a single partner. As previously discussed, future research should attempt to replicate these findings by examining relational spirituality (i.e., shared religious beliefs, shared affiliation and joint attendance; Mahoney 2010) via data from both partners on their shared religious involvement.

Despite these limitations this study has made a significant contribution to the research literature on the relationship between health and intimate relationships. Considerable evidence reveals romantic ties in young adulthood leads to worse mental health (Connolly and McIsaac 2011; Davila 2008; Joyner and Udry 2000; Welsh et al. 2003), particularly for those involved in interracial unions (B. Miller 2017; Lykke 2017; Bratter and Eschbach 2006; Miller and Kail 2016; Kroeger and Williams 2011). It is also clear parents play a critical role in the psychological adjustment of young adults (Davila et al. 2009; Lorenzo-Blanco et al. 2013; B. C. Miller 2002; Whitbeck et al. 1993). However, the potential influence of religious involvement as a protective factor in the absence of parental support has been widely neglected by researchers interested in understanding the health of individuals in same-race and interracial unions. This work adds to the research on the stress-buffering role of religious involvement (Ellison and Henderson 2011). Clearly, the potential influence of religious factors in such relationships is more complex and potentially important than previously recognized. Further investigation along the lines suggested above may clarify the connections between religion, health, and family among a diversity of relationships in the contemporary U.S.

Author Contributions: A.K.H. conceived of the study and was in charge of the overall direction and planning. M.J.B. conducted the statistical analysis under the supervision of the first author. A.K.H. wrote the manuscript with input from all authors.

Funding: This research received no external funding.

Conflicts of Interest: The authors declare no conflicts of interest.

References

Ai, Amy L., Christopher Peterson, Terrence N. Tice, Bu Huang, Willard Rodgers, and Steven F. Bolling. 2007. The influence of prayer coping on mental health among cardiac surgery patients: the role of optimism and acute distress. *Journal of Health Psychology* 12: 580–96. [CrossRef] [PubMed]

Aiken, Leona S., and Stephen G. West. 1991. *Multiple Regression: Testing and Interpreting Interactions.* Newbury Park: Sage.

Allport, Gordon W., and J. Michael Ross. 1967. Personal religious orientation and prejudice. *Journal of Personality and Social Psychology* 5: 432. [CrossRef] [PubMed]

---

3   See Footnote 2 for additional information on couple's racial composition among interracial unions.

Arnett, Jeffrey Jensen, and Joseph Schwab. 2013. *The Clark University Poll of Emerging Adults: Thriving, Struggling, and Hopeful*. Worcester: Clark University.

Barkan, Steven E. 2006. Religiosity and premarital sex in adulthood. *Journal for the Scientific Study of Religion* 45: 407–17. [CrossRef]

Bierman, Alex. 2006. Does religion buffer the effects of discrimination on mental health? Differing effects by race. *Journal for the Scientific Study of Religion* 45: 551–65. [CrossRef]

Bonilla-Silva, Eduardo, and Tyrone A. Forman. 2000. "I Am Not a Racist But...": Mapping White College Students' Racial Ideology in the USA. *Discourse & Society* 11: 50–85.

Botham, Fay. 2009. *Almighty God Created the Races: Christianity, Interracial Marriage, & American Law*. Chapel Hill: University of North Carolina Press.

Bradshaw, Matt, and Christopher G. Ellison. 2010. Financial hardship and psychological distress: Exploring the buffering effects of religion. *Social Science & Medicine* 71: 196–204.

Bratter, Jenifer L., and Karl Eschbach. 2006. 'What about the couple?' Interracial marriage and psychological distress. *Social Science Research* 35: 1025–47. [CrossRef]

Carroll, Joseph. 2007. Most Americans Approve of Interracial Marriages. *Gallup News Service*. Available online: https://news.gallup.com/poll/28417/most-americans-approve-interracial-marriages.aspx (accessed on 19 December 2018).

Chatters, Linda M., Robert Joseph Taylor, Kai M. Bullard, and James S. Jackson. 2008. Spirituality and Subjective Religiosity among African Americans, Caribbean Blacks, and Non-Hispanic Whites. *Journal for the Scientific Study of Religion* 47: 725–37. [CrossRef] [PubMed]

Childs, Erica Chito. 2005. *Navigating Interracial Borders: Black-White Couples and Their Social Worlds*. New Brunswick: Rutgers University Press.

Coates, Julie. 2015. When Culture Becomes Theology: Interracial Marriage in the American Church. Available online: http://www.harvardichthus.org/2015/04/when-culture-becomes-theology-interracial-marriage-in-the-american-church/ (accessed on 10 December 2018).

Collins, Nancy L., and Stephen J. Read. 1990. Adult attachment, working models, and relationship quality in dating couples. *Journal of Personality and Social Psychology* 58: 644–63. [CrossRef] [PubMed]

Connolly, Jennifer, and Caroline McIsaac. 2011. Romantic relationships in adolescence. *Social Development: Relationships in Infancy, Childhood, and Adolescence* 3: 180–203.

Cooper-Lewter, Nicholas C., and Henry H. Mitchell. 1986. *Soul Theology: The Heart of American Black Culture*. New York: Harper Collins Publishers.

Dalmage, Heather M. 2000. *Tripping on the Color Line: Black-White Multiracial Families in a Racially Divided World*. New Brunswick: Rutgers University Press.

Davila, Joanne. 2008. Depressive symptoms and adolescent romance: Theory, research, and implications. *Child Development Perspectives* 2: 26–31. [CrossRef]

Davila, Joanne, Catherine B. Stroud, Lisa R. Starr, Melissa Ramsay Miller, Athena Yoneda, and Rachel Hershenberg. 2009. Romantic and sexual activities, parent–adolescent stress, and depressive symptoms among early adolescent girls. *Journal of Adolescence* 32: 909–24. [CrossRef] [PubMed]

de Guzman, Natalie S., and Adrienne Nishina. 2017. 50 Years of Loving: Interracial Romantic Relationships and Recommendations for Future Research. *Journal of Family Theory & Review* 9: 557–71.

Del Toro, Monica. 2012. The influence of parent-child attachment on romantic relationships. *McNair Scholars Research Journal* 8: 5.

Diiorio, Colleen, Erika Pluhar, and Lisa Belcher. 2003. Parent-child communication about sexuality: A review of the literature from 1980–2002. *Journal of HIV/AIDS Prevention & Education for Adolescents & Children* 5: 7–32.

Edgell, Penny. 2013. *Religion and Family in a Changing Society*. Princeton: Princeton University Press, vol. 57.

Edwards, Korie L., Brad Christerson, and Michael O. Emerson. 2013. Race, religious organizations, and integration. *Annual Review of Sociology* 39: 211–28. [CrossRef]

Ellison, Christopher G. 1993. Religious involvement and self-perception among black Americans. *Social Forces* 71: 1027–55. [CrossRef]

Ellison, Christopher G., and Andrea K. Henderson. 2011. Religion and mental health: Through the lens of the stress process. In *Toward a Sociological Theory of Religion And health*. Edited by Anthony Blasi. Leiden: Brill, pp. 11–44.

Ellison, Christopher G., and Jeffrey S. Levin. 1998. The religion-health connection: Evidence, theory, and future directions. *Health Education & Behavior* 25: 700–20.

Emerson, Michael O., and Karen Chai Kim. 2003. Multiracial congregations: An analysis of their development and a typology. *Journal for the Scientific Study of Religion* 42: 217–27. [CrossRef]

Fabricatore, Anthony N., Paul J. Handal, Doris M. Rubio, and Frank H. Gilner. 2004. Stress, religion, and mental health: Religious coping in mediating and moderating roles. *The International Journal for the Psychology of Religion* 14: 91–108. [CrossRef]

Fingerman, Karen L., Yen-Pi Cheng, Eric D. Wesselmann, Steven Zarit, Frank Furstenberg, and Kira S. Birditt. 2012. Helicopter parents and landing pad kids: Intense parental support of grown children. *Journal of Marriage and Family* 74: 880–96. [CrossRef] [PubMed]

Foeman, Anita Kathy, and Teresa Nance. 1999. From miscegenation to multiculturalism: Perceptions and stages of interracial relationship development. *Journal of Black Studies* 29: 540–57. [CrossRef]

Fox, Greer Litton. 1980. The mother-adolescent daughter relationship as a sexual socialization structure: A research review. *Family Relations* 29: 21–28. [CrossRef]

Freitas, Donna. 2008. *Sex and the soul: America's College Students Speak out about Hookups, Romance, and Religion on Campus*. Oxford: Oxford University Press.

Fujino, Diane C. 1997. The rates, patterns and reasons for forming heterosexual interracial dating relationships among Asian Americans. *Journal of Social and Personal Relationships* 14: 809–28. [CrossRef]

Gaines, Stanley O., Jr. 2001. Coping with prejudice: Personal relationship partners as sources of socioemotional support for stigmatized individuals. *Journal of Social Issues* 57: 113–28. [CrossRef]

Harris, Kathleen M. 2011. *Design Features of Add Health*. Chapel Hill: University of North Carolina.

Hartnett, Caroline Sten, Frank F. Furstenberg, Kira S. Birditt, and Karen L. Fingerman. 2013. Parental Support During Young Adulthood: Why Does Assistance Decline with Age? *Journal of Family Issues* 34: 975–1007. [CrossRef] [PubMed]

Heaton, Tim B., and Edith L. Pratt. 1990. The effects of religious homogamy on marital satisfaction and stability. *Journal of Family Issues* 11: 191–207. [CrossRef]

Henderson, Andrea K. 2016. Jesus didn't teach us to juggle: Religious involvement, work–family conflict, and life satisfaction among African Americans. *Journal of Family* 37: 1558–84. [CrossRef]

Henderson, Andrea K., Christopher G. Ellison, and Norval D. Glenn. 2018. Religion and relationship quality among cohabiting and dating couples. *Journal of Family* 39: 1904–32. [CrossRef]

Herman, Melissa R., and Mary E. Campbell. 2012. I wouldn't, but you can: Attitudes toward interracial relationships. *Social Science Research* 41: 343–58. [CrossRef] [PubMed]

House, James S., Karl R. Landis, and Debra Umberson. 1988. Social relationships and health. *Science* 241: 540–45. [CrossRef] [PubMed]

Jessor, Shirley L., and Richard Jessor. 1975. Transition from virginity to nonvirginity among youth: A social-psychological study over time. *Developmental Psychology* 11: 473–84. [CrossRef]

Jessor, Richard, and Shirley L. Jessor. 1977. *Problem Behavior and Psychosocial Development: A Longitudinal Study of Youth*. Cambridge: Academic Press.

Johnson, Bryan R., and Cardell K. Jacobson. 2005. Contact in context: An examination of social settings on whites' attitudes toward interracial marriage. *Social Psychology Quarterly* 68: 387–99. [CrossRef]

Joyner, Kara, and J. Richard Udry. 2000. You don't bring me anything but down: Adolescent romance and depression. *Journal of Health and Social Behavior* 41: 369–91. [CrossRef] [PubMed]

Kalmijn, Matthijs. 1998. Intermarriage and homogamy: Causes, patterns, trends. *Annual Review of Sociology* 24: 395–421. [CrossRef] [PubMed]

Kirkpatrick, Lee A. 2005. *Attachment, Evolution, and the Psychology of Religion*. New York: Guilford Press.

Koenig, Harold G. 2009. Research on religion, spirituality, and mental health: A review. *The Canadian Journal of Psychiatry* 54: 283–91. [CrossRef] [PubMed]

Koenig, Harold, and David B. Larson. 2001. Religion and mental health: Evidence for an association. *International Review of Psychiatry* 13: 67–78. [CrossRef]

Krause, Neal. 1995. Religiosity and self-esteem among older adults. *The Journals of Gerontology Series B: Psychological Sciences and Social Sciences* 50: P236–P246. [CrossRef]

Krause, Neal. 2004. Religion, aging, and health: exploring new frontiers in medical care. *Southern Medical Journal* 97: 1215–23. [CrossRef] [PubMed]

Krause, Neal. 2006. Exploring the stress-buffering effects of church-based and secular social support on self-rated health in late life. *The Journals of Gerontology Series B: Psychological Sciences and Social Sciences* 61: S35–S43. [CrossRef]

Kreager, Derek A. 2008. Guarded borders: Adolescent interracial romance and peer trouble at school. *Social Forces* 87: 887–910. [CrossRef]

Kroeger, Rhiannon A., and Kristi Williams. 2011. Consequences of black exceptionalism? Interracial unions with blacks, depressive symptoms, and relationship satisfaction. *The Sociological Quarterly* 52: 400–20. [CrossRef] [PubMed]

Lambert, Nathaniel M., Frank D. Fincham, Tyler F. Stillman, Steven M. Graham, and Steven R. H. Beach. 2010. Motivating change in relationships: Can prayer increase forgiveness? *Psychological Science* 21: 126–32. [CrossRef] [PubMed]

Larson, Reed W., Gerald L. Clore, and Gretchen A. Wood. 1999. The emotions of romantic relationships: Do they wreak havoc on adolescents. In *The Development of Romantic Relationships in Adolescence*. New York: Cambridge University Press, pp. 19–49.

LeCloux, Mary, Peter Maramaldi, Kristie A. Thomas, and Elizabeth A. Wharff. 2017. A longitudinal study of health care resources, family support, and mental health outcomes among suicidal adolescents. *Analyses of Social Issues and Public Policy* 17: 319–38. [CrossRef]

Lehrer, Evelyn L., and Carmel U. Chiswick. 1993. Religion as a determinant of marital stability. *Demography* 30: 385–404. [CrossRef] [PubMed]

Levin, Jeffrey S., and Linda M. Chatters. 1998. Religion, health, and psychological well-being in older adults: Findings from three national surveys. *Journal of Aging and Health* 10: 504–31. [CrossRef] [PubMed]

Levin, Jeffrey S., Robert Joseph Taylor, and Linda M. Chatters. 1995. A multidimensional measure of religious involvement for African Americans. *The Sociological Quarterly* 36: 157–73. [CrossRef]

Lombardo, Paul A. 1987. Miscegenation, eugenics, and racism: Historical footnotes to Loving Virginia. *UC Davis Law Review* 21: 421.

Lorenzo-Blanco, Elma I., Cristina B. Bares, and Jorge Delva. 2013. Parenting, family processes, relationships, and parental support in multiracial and multiethnic families: An exploratory study of you perceptions. *Family Relations* 62: 125–39. [CrossRef]

Lykke, Lucia Christine. 2017. Health Associations with Interracial and Inter-ethnic Marital, Cohabiting, and Dating Relationships in the United States. Ph.D. dissertation, University of Maryland, College Park, MD, USA.

Mahoney, Annette. 2010. Religion in families, 1999–2009: A relational spirituality framework. *Journal of Marriage and Family* 72: 805–27. [CrossRef] [PubMed]

Marks, Loren. 2006. Religion and family relational health: An overview and conceptual model. *Journal of Religion and Health* 45: 603–18. [CrossRef]

Marti, Gerardo. 2008. Fluid ethnicity and ethnic transcendence in multiracial churches. *Journal for the Scientific Study of Religion* 47: 11–16. [CrossRef]

McCullough, Michael E., and David B. Larson. 1999. Religion and depression: a review of the literature. *Twin Research and Human Genetics* 2: 126–36. [CrossRef]

Miller, Brent C. 2002. Family influences on adolescent sexual and contraceptive behavior. *Journal of Sex Research* 39: 22–26. [CrossRef] [PubMed]

Miller, Byron. 2017. What are the odds: An examination of adolescent interracial romance and risk for depression. *Youth & Society* 49: 180–202.

Miller, Byron, and Ben Lennox Kail. 2016. Exploring the effects of spousal race on the self-rated health of intermarried adults. *Sociological Perspectives* 59: 604–18. [CrossRef]

Mok, Teresa A. 1999. Asian American dating: Important factors in partner choice. *Cultural Diversity and Ethnic Minority Psychology* 5: 103. [CrossRef] [PubMed]

Myers, Scott M. 2006. Religious homogamy and marital quality: Historical and generational patterns, 1980–1997. *Journal of Marriage and Family* 68: 292–304. [CrossRef]

Nooney, Jennifer, and Eric Woodrum. 2002. Religious coping and church-based social support as predictors of mental health outcomes: Testing a conceptual model. *Journal for the Scientific Study of Religion* 41: 359–68. [CrossRef]

Oswald, Ramona Faith, Abbie Goldberg, Kate Kuvalanka, and Eric Clausell. 2008. Structural and moral commitment among same-sex couples: Relationship duration, religiosity, and parental status. *Journal of Family Psychology* 22: 411. [CrossRef] [PubMed]

Pargament, Kenneth I., and Curtis R. Brant. 1998. Religion and coping. In *Handbook of Religion and Mental Health*. Cambridge: Academic Press, pp. 111–28.

Pargament, Kenneth I., Bruce W. Smith, Harold G. Koenig, and Lisa Perez. 1998. Patterns of positive and negative religious coping with major life stressors. *Journal for the Scientific Study of Religion* 37: 710–24. [CrossRef]

Park, Crystal, Lawrence H. Cohen, and Lisa Herb. 1990. Intrinsic religiousness and religious coping as life stress moderators for Catholics versus Protestants. *Journal of Personality and Social Psychology* 59: 562. [CrossRef] [PubMed]

Pascoe, Elizabeth A., and Laura Smart Richman. 2009. Perceived discrimination and health: a meta-analytic review. *Psychological Bulletin* 135: 531. [CrossRef] [PubMed]

Perry, Samuel L. 2013a. Religion and whites' attitudes toward interracial marriage with African Americans, Asians, and Latinos. *Journal for the Scientific Study of Religion* 52: 425–42. [CrossRef]

Perry, Samuel L. 2013b. Religion and interracial romance: The effects of religious affiliation, public and devotional practices, and biblical literalism. *Social Science Quarterly* 94: 1308–27. [CrossRef]

Perry, Samuel L. 2014. More like us: How religious service attendance hinders interracial romance. *Sociology of Religion* 75: 442–62. [CrossRef]

Pew Research Center. 2017. In the U.S. Metro Areas, Huge Variation in Intermarriage Rates. Available online: http://www.pewresearch.org/fact-tank/2017/05/18/in-u-s-metro-areas-huge-variation-in-intermarriage-rates/ (accessed on 15 December 2018).

Pollner, Melvin. 1989. Divine relations, social relations, and well-being. *Journal of Health and Social Behavior* 30: 92–104. [CrossRef] [PubMed]

Raby, K. Lee, Glenn I. Roisman, R. Chris Fraley, and Jeffry A. Simpson. 2015. The enduring predictive significance of early maternal sensitivity: Social and academic competence through age 32 years. *Child Development* 86: 695–708. [CrossRef] [PubMed]

Radloff, Lenore Sawyer. 1977. The CES-D scale: A self-report depression scale for research in the general population. *Applied Psychological Measurement* 1: 385–401. [CrossRef]

Rasic, Daniel, Jennifer A. Robinson, James Bolton, O. Joseph Bienvenu, and Jitender Sareen. 2011. Longitudinal relationships of religious worship attendance and spirituality with major depression, anxiety disorders, and suicidal ideation and attempts: Findings from the Baltimore epidemiologic catchment area study. *Journal of Psychiatric Research* 45: 848–54. [CrossRef] [PubMed]

Regnerus, Mark. 2007. *Forbidden Fruit: Sex & Religion in the Lives of American Teenagers*. Kettering: Oxford University Press.

Ross, Catherine E., and John Mirowsky. 2006. Sex differences in the effect of education on depression: Resource multiplication or resource substitution? *Social Science & Medicine* 63: 1400–13.

Rostosky, Sharon S., Melanie D. Otis, Ellen D. B. Riggle, Sondra Kelly, and Carolyn Brodnicki. 2008. An exploratory study of religiosity and same-sex couple relationships. *Journal of GLBT Family Studies* 4: 17–36. [CrossRef]

Ryan, Richard M., Scott Rigby, and Kristi King. 1993. Two types of religious internalization and their relations to religious orientations and mental health. *Journal of Personality and Social Psychology* 65: 586–96. [CrossRef] [PubMed]

Seshadri, Gita, and Carmen Knudson-Martin. 2013. How couples manage interracial and intercultural differences: Implications for clinical practice. *Journal of Marital and Family Therapy* 39: 43–58. [CrossRef] [PubMed]

Sherkat, Darren E., and Mark D. Re. 1992. The effects of religion and social support on self-esteem and depression among the suddenly bereaved. *Social Indicators Research* 26: 259–75. [CrossRef]

Shreve-Neiger, Andrea K., and Barry A. Edelstein. 2004. Religion and anxiety: A critical review of the literature. *Clinical Psychology Review* 24: 379–97. [CrossRef] [PubMed]

Siegel, Karolynn, Stanley J. Anderman, and Eric W. Schrimshaw. 2001. Religion and coping with health-related stress. *Psychology and Health* 16: 631–53. [CrossRef]

Skinner, A. L., and C. M. Hudac. 2017. "Yuck, you disgust me!" Affective bias against interracial couples. *Journal of Experimental Social Psychology* 68: 68–77. [CrossRef]

Solsberry, Priscilla Wilson. 1994. Interracial couples in the United States of America: Implications for mental health counseling. *Journal of Mental Health Counseling* 16: 304–17.

Strawbridge, William J., Sarah J. Shema, Richard D. Cohen, and George A. Kaplan. 2001. Religious attendance increases survival by improving and maintaining good health behaviors, mental health, and social relationships. *Annals of Behavioral Medicine* 23: 68–74. [CrossRef] [PubMed]

Steinberg, Sara J., and Joanne Davila. 2008. Romantic functioning and depressive symptoms among early adolescent girls: The moderating role of parental emotional availability. *Journal of Clinical Child & Adolescent Psychology* 37: 350–62.

Sullivan, Susan Crawford. 2008. Unaccompanied children in churches: Low-income urban single mothers, religion, and parenting. *Review of Religious Research* 50: 157–75.

Taylor, Robert Joseph, Linda M. Chatters, and Jeff Levin. 2003. *Religion in the Lives of African Americans: Social, Psychological, and Health Perspectives*. Thousand Oaks: Sage Publications.

Tillman, Kathryn Harker, and Byron Miller. 2017. The role of family relationships in the psychological wellbeing of interracially dating adolescents. *Social Science Research* 65: 240–52. [CrossRef] [PubMed]

Vaaler, Margaret L., Christopher G. Ellison, and Daniel A. Powers. 2009. Religious influences on the risk of marital dissolution. *Journal of Marriage and Family* 71: 917–34. [CrossRef]

Wang, Hongyu, Grace Kao, and Kara Joyner. 2006. Stability of interracial and intraracial romantic relationships among adolescents. *Social Science Research* 35: 435–53. [CrossRef]

Welsh, Deborah P., Catherine M. Grello, and Melinda S. Harper. 2003. When love hurts: Depression and adolescent romantic relationships. In *Adolescent Romantic Relations and Sexual Behavior Theory, Research, and Practical Implications*. London: Routledge.

Whitbeck, Les B., Rand D. Conger, and Meei-Ying Kao. 1993. The influence of parental support, depressed affect, and peers on the sexual behaviors of adolescent girls. *Journal of Family Issues* 14: 261–78. [CrossRef]

Wilcox, W. Bradford, and Nicholas H. Wolfinger. 2008. Living and loving "decent": Religion and relationship quality among urban parents. *Social Science Research* 37: 828–43. [CrossRef] [PubMed]

Wong, Jaclyn S., and Andrew M. Penner. 2018. Better Together? Interracial Relationships and Depressive Symptoms. *Socius* 4: 1–11. [CrossRef]

Xia, Mengya, Gregory M. Fosco, Melissa A. Lippold, and Mark E. Feinberg. 2018. A Developmental Perspective on Young Adult Romantic Relationships: Examining Family and Individual Factors in Adolescence. *Journal of Youth and Adolescence* 47: 1499–516. [CrossRef] [PubMed]

Yahirun, Jenjira J. 2019. Intermarriage and mother-child relationships. *Social Science Research* 78: 203–14. [CrossRef] [PubMed]

Yancey, George, and Michael Emerson. 2003. Integrated Sundays: An exploratory study into the formation of multiracial churches. *Sociological Focus* 36: 111–26. [CrossRef]

religions

MDPI

Article

Family Religiosity, Parental Monitoring, and Emerging Adults' Sexual Behavior

Deirdre A. Quinn [1,*] **and Amy Lewin** [2]

[1]   Center for Health Equity Research and Promotion (CHERP), VA Pittsburgh Healthcare System, University Drive C, Pittsburgh, PA 15240, USA
[2]   Department of Family Science, University of Maryland School of Public Health, College Park, MD 20742, USA; alewin@umd.edu
*   Correspondence: deirdrequinn81@gmail.com

Received: 31 December 2018; Accepted: 10 February 2019; Published: 16 February 2019

check for updates

Abstract: The processes through which families play a role in the religious and sexual socialization of children are varied and complex. Few studies have considered the impact of parental or family religiosity on young people's sexual behaviors, either directly or through influence on adolescents' own religiosity. This study of college students at a large, public university in the mid-Atlantic uses multidimensional measures to examine the relationships among family religiosity, parental monitoring during adolescence, students' religiosity, and students' specific sexual behaviors. Results suggest that greater family religiosity is associated with a decreased likelihood of engaging in certain sex acts, but for students who do engage, family religiosity is not associated with any differences in the timing of sexual onset or in the numbers of partners with whom students engaged. Results also suggest that parental monitoring may mediate the relationship between family religiosity and some sexual risk behavior. Greater individual religiosity is associated with a lower likelihood of having engaged in any sexual activity, and a higher likelihood of condom use for students who have had vaginal sex. This study offers valuable insights into the role that religiosity, at both the family and the individual level, plays in college students' sexual behavior.

Keywords: family; religiosity; emerging adults; sexual behavior

1. Introduction

Religion plays an important role in many people's lives, and can impact both physical and mental health. A growing body of research has examined potential links between religiosity and health behaviors, particularly sexual risk behaviors, in adolescents and young adults. Risky sexual behavior is common among college students, as campus "hook-up" culture promotes casual and unplanned sexual encounters (Burdette et al. 2009; Grello et al. 2006). Students often perceive certain risky behaviors, such as oral and/or anal sex, to be less intimate (and therefore more allowable) than vaginal sexual intercourse (Chambers 2007; Kelly and Kalichman 2002; Lyons et al. 2013). It is important to note that oral and/or anal sex are not inherently riskier than vaginal sex; they are classified in most studies as risk behaviors specifically because of the high likelihood that they will occur without protection against STIs (American College Health Association 2015; Boekeloo and Howard 2002; Brückner and Bearman 2005; Moore and Smith 2012).

Parents have consistently been identified as the most important source of religious influence, both in childhood and adolescence, and into adulthood (Lambert and Dollahite 2010; Smith 2003a; Smith and Denton 2005; Smith et al. 2003). Parental religiosity in particular has been associated with adolescents being less involved in problematic risk behaviors such as alcohol and drug use (Foshee and Hollinger 1996; Hayatbakhsh et al. 2014; Pearce and Haynie 2004). In terms of sexual risk, overall family environment has been shown to play a protective role in adolescent reproductive health decisions (Manlove et al. 2008). However, few studies have considered the specific impact of parental or family religiosity on adolescent sexual behavior, either directly or through influence on adolescents' own religiosity. Those that do exist have used single variables, such as parents' report of religious involvement or of specific beliefs, as a proxy for family religiosity (Manlove et al. 2008; Manlove et al. 2006). Further research is needed to inform a more complete understanding of the mechanisms by which multiple dimensions of family religiosity may impact adolescents' own religiosity and their sexual health decision-making.

The current study extends the literature in order to improve our understanding of the relationships between multi-dimensional aspects of family and college students' religiosity and sexual behavior. This study contributes to existing literature in several unique ways. First, it identifies multiple dimensions of potential religious influence, rather than the one-dimensional measure of religious attendance that is typically used. Second, it considers multiple indicators within the broader context of sexual behavior, allowing for the possibility to observe different avenues of influence by specific sexual act or practice. And third, it considers both family-level and individual-level influences on college students' behavior, acknowledging that these different spheres may be congruent or may contradict one another.

2. Background

2.1. Religion and the Family

Existing literature suggests that the most important determinant of adult religiosity is religious beliefs and participation between the ages of 18 and 20 (Stolzenberg et al. 1995; Wilson and Sherkat 1994), and that parents are one of the strongest socialization influences on adolescent religiosity (Smith and Denton 2005). Religious upbringing is perhaps the most important source of an individual's religious capital (familiarity with a religion's doctrine, rituals, traditions, and members), and is a major determinant of religious belief and behavior (Iannaccone 1990). Most of children's religious capital is built up in a context regulated and favored by their parents; this capital enhances individual satisfaction with religious participation, and so increases the likelihood of later participation (Iannaccone 1990; Stolzenberg et al. 1995). The importance that parents attach to religion is a significant predictor of adolescents' attendance at religious services, the importance they place on religion, their frequency of prayer, and their sense of their religion's doctrine as sacred (Bader and Desmond 2006). College students' retrospective views of their childhood faith activities have been found to be related to their current religious orientations, prayer frequency, and prayer meaning; family faith practices in the home during a child's upbringing are ingrained in each family member, even after they leave the home (Lambert and Dollahite 2010). In a qualitative study of highly religious families from a range of religious denominations, families identified religious conversations as the most meaningful religious activity, even when compared with service attendance or family prayer. Parents and adolescents both named religious conversation as the primary method of sharing their faith (Dollahite and Thatcher 2008). The current study further illuminates pathways between family religiosity during childhood and early adolescence and college students' reports of their current religiosity.

2.2. Religion and Adolescent Sexual Beliefs and Behavior

Religious affiliation has frequently been associated with moral and behavioral attitudes. Multiple studies have found that greater religious participation, irrespective of denomination, is associated with negative attitudes about sex (McKelvey et al. 1999; Pearce and Thornton 2007). Among college students at a large public university in the Eastern US, individuals for whom religion was more a part of their daily lives, and those who adhered to their religion's teachings on sexual behaviors, tended to have more conservative sexual attitudes, were less likely to believe that condoms could prevent negative outcomes such as pregnancy or STIs, and tended to perceive more barriers to condom use (Lefkowitz et al. 2004). Interestingly, the same study found that students who attended services more frequently had less fear about HIV, but students who reported religion playing a more important role in their daily lives tended to have more fear about HIV, implying that attendance at religious services and the 'importance of religion' may be completely separate phenomena, at least in relation to sexual knowledge and attitudes (Lefkowitz et al. 2004).

A large body of research offers evidence that religiosity, both family and individual, is related not only to sexual attitudes but also to sexual behavior. Higher levels of family religiosity and parental religious attendance have been associated with delayed sexual onset (Manlove et al. 2006) and having fewer sexual partners (Manlove et al. 2008). Religious adolescents are less likely to ever have had sex than non-religious adolescents (Adamczyk and Felson 2006), while frequent attendance at religious services has a strong effect on delaying first intercourse (Jones et al. 2005). Emerging adults with high levels of personal religiosity were the least likely to engage in sexual intercourse, even within a committed (non-marital) relationship (Barry et al. 2015). Data from the National Longitudinal Survey of Youth (NLSY) suggest that denominational affiliation is not as important a predictor of adolescent sexual behavior as religious attendance (Manlove et al. 2006), supporting the idea that religious networks reinforce moral directives and discourage risky behaviors (Regnerus 2010).

The abovementioned research suggests that religiosity is protective against sexual activity, in particular early sexual onset and number of sexual partners. Previous work also suggests, however, that religiosity may increase young adults' sexual risk-taking. Certain religious traditions advocate for the delay of sexual initiation until marriage; popular 'virginity pledge' programs, which constitute a promise by the pledger to remain abstinent until marriage, are on the rise (Landor and Simons 2014; Regnerus 2007). Research demonstrates that though they do tend to be older than non-pledgers at sexual debut, a significant number of virginity pledgers still engage in premarital sex (Bearman and Bruckner 2001; Landor and Simons 2014), and may be at greater risk of negative sexual consequences (e.g., unplanned pregnancy or STIs) due to a lack of condom use at first sex and a higher likelihood of engaging in unprotected non-coital sexual encounters, including oral and anal sex (Brückner and Bearman 2005; Landor and Simons 2014). Other studies have found that strong parental religious beliefs and participation in family religious activities are associated with lower odds of using contraception at first sex (Manlove et al. 2006), and that frequent religious service participation is associated with a reduced likelihood of young women accessing contraceptive or STI services (Hall et al. 2012).

Existing evidence is strong that family religiosity influences individual adolescent and emerging adult religiosity, and that individual religiosity can play a role in sexual decision-making. What remains unknown, however, is how these constructs interact. Based on our understanding of college students as belonging to the unique developmental stage of emerging adulthood, characterized by burgeoning independence, intellectual experimentation, and physical and emotional sensation-seeking (Arnett 2000, 2007, 2011), we hypothesize that the impact of family religiosity on sexual behavior will be stronger when emerging adults have strong ties to those family values and teachings (that is, when they are more religious themselves).

2.3. Parental Monitoring

Parental monitoring, defined as rule-setting and vigilant oversight of a child's friend group and activities (Barnes et al. 2006; Chilcoat and Anthony 1996; Li et al. 2000), has been identified as protective against adolescent risk behaviors. Among parents, weekly attendance at religious services is associated with a higher likelihood of monitoring their children's friendships and imposing higher expectations about sexual morality (Kim and Wilcox 2014). Adolescents who report higher levels of parental monitoring are more likely than others to delay sexual onset (DiIorio et al. 2004; Karofsky et al. 2001), and to have fewer partners if they are sexually active (DiClemente et al. 2001; Huebner and Howell 2003). Higher levels of parental monitoring are also associated with less favorable adolescent attitudes about initiating sexual intercourse, and lower intentions to engage in intercourse (Sieverding et al. 2005).

Family religiosity has also been associated with parental monitoring. Data from the National Survey of Parents and Youth suggest that greater religious participation increases parents' supervision of their adolescent children (Smith 2003b). An examination of late adolescents' perceptions of parental religiosity and parenting behavior found that adolescents who perceived their parents as more religious also reported higher levels of parental monitoring behavior (Snider J.B. and Vazsonyi 2004). And data from the National Longitudinal Survey of Youth found that more frequent engagement in family religious activities was associated with higher parental monitoring (Farmer et al. 2008). These prior findings suggest that parental monitoring may play a role on the pathway between family religiosity and adolescent sexual behavior.

The above research supports the conclusion that religiosity (both family and individual) is associated with emerging adults' sexual behavior; however, there remain substantial gaps in our understanding of how these various constructs are related. Existing studies fail to distinguish between different sex acts, implicitly equating sexual activity or involvement (ever having had sex, age at sexual debut, and number of sexual partners) with risk behavior, often while ignoring avenues of actual sexual risk (inconsistent contraceptive use, ever having had oral and/or anal sex, and frequency of condom use for each of these behaviors). In addition, much of this research is more than a decade old. Adolescents and college students today may be less well-informed about the specific sexual values of their individual religions, and younger people, even those who identify as religious, may not adhere to their faiths' doctrines on human sexuality as strictly as older generations (Prothero 2007; Regnerus 2007).

The current study examined potential pathways of influence from family religiosity to emerging adults' religiosity and sexual behaviors. We hypothesized that: (1) greater family religiosity would be associated with decreased sexual activity (early sexual onset and number of sexual partners) and increased sexual risk (including lack of contraceptive use at last vaginal sex, and higher likelihood of students' having had unprotected oral, vaginal, or anal sex) among college students,; (2) that parental monitoring would mediate the relationship between family religiosity and students' sexual behavior; and (3) that students' current religiosity would act as a moderator, strengthening the relationship between family religiosity and students' sexual behavior.

3. Methods

3.1. Sample

This study used a cross-sectional survey design to explore the relationships among family religiosity, parental monitoring, students' religiosity, and students' sexual behavior. Participants were a convenience sample of undergraduate students at a large, public university in the mid-Atlantic. Previous studies have shown the validity of adolescents' self-reported sexual behavior (Davoli et al. 1992; Orr et al. 1997; Schrimshaw et al. 2006; Shew et al. 1997), but a review of the literature calls attention to multiple recommendations for improving the reliability of adolescents' self-report. The current study integrates many of these recommendations. To reduce socially desirable responding, the survey was administered through an anonymous online link. A guarantee of participant confidentiality was repeated before each set of 'sensitive' questions, and the need for accurate reporting for the improvement of knowledge about college students' health was stressed multiple times throughout the survey (Alexander et al. 1993; DiClemente 2015; DiClemente et al. 2013; Weinhardt et al. 1998). All study procedures were reviewed and approved by the university's Institutional Review Board before data collection began. Anonymous online surveys were collected from 684 undergraduate students; cases with too many missing data were removed ($n = 72$), as were four cases representing outliers in terms of age (and therefore, for the purposes of this study, not in the developmental stage of interest), resulting in the final analytic sample, $n = 608$.

3.2. Measures

3.2.1. Family Religiosity

Family religiosity was measured by the 9-item Faith Activities in the Home Scale (FAITHS - short version) (Lambert and Dollahite 2010). Each of 9 family faith activities (e.g., family prayer, family religious conversations) was rated for frequency (0–6, 'never or not applicable' to 'more than once a day') and importance (0–4, 'not important or not applicable' to 'extremely important'). The two summed total scores were highly correlated in this sample (r = 0.852, *p* < 0.001), so subsequent analyses used only the frequency score (Lambert and Dollahite 2010). Because the continuous FAITHS frequency score was positively skewed, we transformed it into a categorical variable with two groups (Never/Infrequent and Frequent) for subsequent analyses.

3.2.2. Parental Monitoring

Parental monitoring was measured using a 9-item scale (Arria et al. 2008) that assesses respondents' perceptions of the level of monitoring and supervision they received during their last year of high school (Pinchevsky et al. 2012). A total parental monitoring score was constructed by summing a participant's responses on all 9 items, with higher scores representing a higher level of parental monitoring.

3.2.3. Student Religiosity

Student religiosity was measured using 4 domains from the Brief Multidimensional Measure of Religiousness/Spirituality (BMMRS), a tool developed specifically for use in health research (John E. Fetzer Institute 2003): (1) Overall self-ranking/Religious Intensity (e.g., to what extent do you consider yourself a religious person?), (2) Private Religious Practices (e.g., how often do you pray privately in places other than at church, synagogue, or other place of worship?), (3) Forgiveness (e.g., I know that God forgives me), and (4) Organizational Religiousness (e.g., how often do you go to religious services?). Each item in the BMMRS uses Likert scale response options, with lower scores indicating a greater 'amount' of the item being measured (e.g., closeness to God). Each subscale receives a separate score; for analytic purposes, the subscale scores can be used individually, or summed together for a total religiosity score. For ease of interpretation, scores on each domain were recoded so that lower scores indicate a lower 'amount' of the item being measured.

3.2.4. Student Sexual Behaviors

The primary outcome variables of student sexual activity and risk were measured using the 9-item sexual behaviors scale from the 2015 *Youth Risk Behavior Survey (YRBS)* (CDC 2015), which evaluates sexual behaviors that contribute to unintended pregnancy and sexually transmitted infections (CDC 2016); students reported age at first sex, number of sexual partners, substance use before last sex, and condom use and/or contraceptive use at last vaginal sex. Participants were asked additional questions about ever having had oral sex or anal sex; if they answered yes, participants were prompted to report whether or not they had ever had the previously reported sexual encounter (oral and/or anal sex) without using a condom.

3.2.5. Covariates

Demographic variables that are theoretically or empirically related to emerging adults' sexual behaviors, including gender, race, religion, sexual relationship status, parents' education, parents' birthplace, and household composition (i.e., single or dual-parent household), were assessed as potential covariates.

3.3. Analyses

Preliminary frequencies and descriptive statistics were performed. We conducted chi-square tests of association and simple logistic regressions to examine the relationships between family and student religiosity, parental monitoring, and student sexual behaviors. Independent variables with a significant bivariate association ($p < 0.05$) with the outcome variables were included in a series of multivariate logistic regression models which produced adjusted odds ratios (aORs). To assess mediation, we first assessed the relationships among family religiosity, parental monitoring, and sexual behavior outcomes; we then used Hayes' PROCESS tool (Hayes 2017) to estimate the indirect effect of parental monitoring on sexual behavior outcomes. Bias-corrected accelerated bootstrapping with 1000 replications was used to obtain 95% confidence intervals (CIs) around the indirect effects. To assess moderation, we created centered interaction terms between family religiosity and each of five possible student religiosity scores (four domain scores and one total score); we then built hierarchical models to test the effect of each interaction term on the relationship between family religiosity and each sexual behavior outcome. Data analyses were conducted in SPSS v25 (IBM Corp 2017).

4. Results

Demographic characteristics of the analytic sample are presented in Table 1. Nearly 77 percent ($n = 467$) of the sample identified as female, and slightly more than half ($n = 318$, 52.3%) as White, with a median age of 21 years old. Religious affiliation was distributed across six separate groups, with a majority of the sample identifying as Christian (non-Catholic) ($n = 158$, 26.2%), Roman Catholic ($n = 136$, 22.5%), or Atheist/Agnostic ($n = 130$, 21.4%). Students were most likely to describe themselves as being currently uninvolved in a sexual relationship ($n = 253$, 41.6%) or involved with one serious (monogamous) sexual partner ($n = 244$, 40.1%) (for reference, only 8 students reported being married).

Students reported high levels of sexual activity and sexual risk behaviors; students' participation in certain sex acts and use of pregnancy and STI prevention methods are highlighted in Figures 1 and 2. Among students who have participated in any sexual activity (oral, vaginal, or anal), more students ($n = 282$, 57%) delayed their first sexual activity until age 17 or later and slightly more than half ($n = 276$, 56%) have had four or more sexual partners.

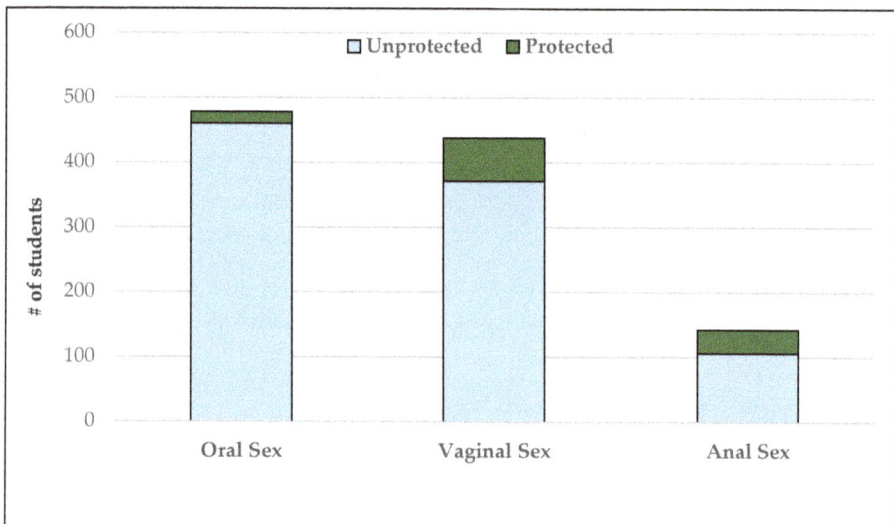

Figure 1. Students' Sexual Activity: Ever Unprotected vs. Always Protected ($n = 608$).

Table 1. Characteristics (%) of Analytic Sample (*n* = 608).

Age, Mean (SD) [a]	20.64 (1.79)
Race	
White	52.3
Black/African American	15.3
Hispanic/Latino	6.1
Asian	15.3
Other (includes Multiple Races)	11
Gender	
Female	76.8
Male	22.7
Transgender	0.5
Which of the following best describes you?	
Heterosexual (straight)	89.6
Gay or Lesbian	2
Bisexual	6.9
Not Sure	1.5
Sexual Relationship Status	
No current sexual relationship	41.6
One casual partner	12.2
One serious (monogamous) partner	40.1
Multiple partners	6.1
Religious Affiliation [b]	
Roman Catholic	22.5
Christian (non-Catholic)	26.2
Jewish	14.5
Muslim	4.4
Other Non-Christian	10.7
Atheist/Agnostic	21.4
First Generation College Student [c]	
No	78.1
Yes	21.9
Parents' Birthplace [d]	
Both parents born in the U.S.	55.7
One or both parents born outside the U.S.	44.2
Single Parent Household (during HS)	
No	81.4
Yes	18.6

SD, standard deviation; HS, high school. [a] *n* = 3 missing; [b] *n* = 4 missing; [c] *n* = 10 missing; [d] *n* = 1 missing.

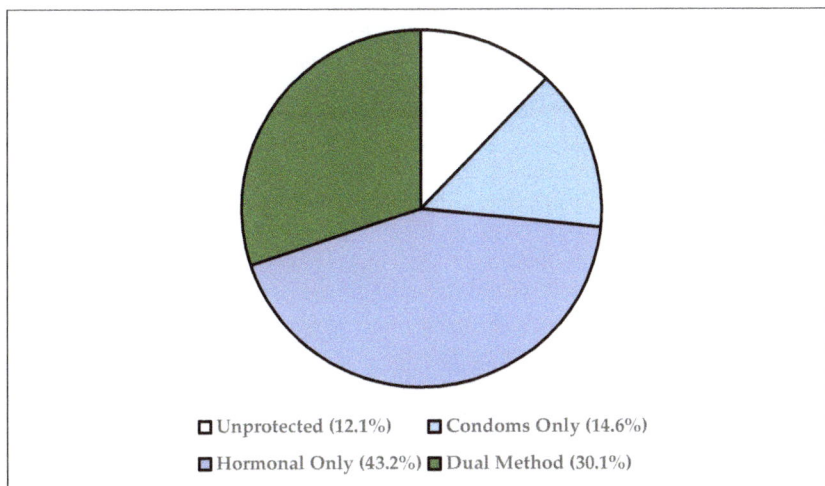

Figure 2. Pregnancy and STI Prevention at Last Vaginal Sex (*n* = 438).

Unprotected (12.1%) Condoms Only (14.6%) Hormonal Only (43.2%) Dual Method (30.1%)

Overall, students reported low family religiosity during their childhood and adolescence (Table 2). The mean *FAITHS* frequency score was 10.56 (possible scores ranged from 0 to 54, with a higher score indicating greater frequency. Average scores in the 'never' or 'yearly' category were categorized as 'infrequent' (61%); average scores in the 'monthly' category or higher were categorized as 'frequent' (39%). Scores on each of the four domains of student religiosity, as well as total student religiosity scores, were low to moderate, indicating a low overall degree of current religiosity in this sample. However, students reported a moderate to high degree of parental monitoring during high school, with female students reporting significantly greater parental monitoring than male students.

Table 2. Summary score statistics (*n* = 608).

	M	**SD**	**Min**	**Max**
Family Religiosity (Frequency) [a]	10.56	11.31	0	54
Parental Monitoring [b]	23.29	6.78	0	36
Student Religiosity—Overall Self-Ranking	2.61	1.75	0	6
Student Religiosity—Private Practice [c]	9.0	8.337	0	35
Student Religiosity—Forgiveness [d]	4.95	2.95	0	9
Student Religiosity—Organizational Religiousness	2.79	2.79	0	10
Student Religiosity—Total Score [e]	19.41	14.03	0	60

SD, standard deviation. [a] *n* = 22 missing; [b] *n* = 148 missing; [c] *n* = 1 missing; [d] *n* = 5 missing; [e] *n* = 6 missing.

Bivariate results. Unadjusted associations between family religiosity and sexual behaviors were computed first for the total sample (Table 3) and then stratified by religious group (tables not shown). Subsequent analyses consider degree of religiosity across groups for the total sample, rather than by denomination. Students who reported frequent family religiosity were less likely ever to have had oral sex, vaginal sex, and anal sex than were those who reported infrequent family religiosity. Among students who reported ever having had vaginal sex, students who reported frequent family religiosity were less likely ever to have had it unprotected.

Parental monitoring differed significantly by family religiosity, with students reporting frequent family religiosity also reporting a higher degree of parental monitoring (M = 24.98, SD = 6.484) than students who reported infrequent family religiosity (M = 22.18, SD = 6.680), $t(443) = -4.317$, $p < 0.001$. Students who reported greater parental monitoring were less likely to have had four or more lifetime partners (OR = 0.959, 95% CI: 0.929, 0.989), less likely ever to have had anal sex (OR = 0.950, 95% CI: 0.920, 0.980), and less likely ever to have had unprotected vaginal sex (OR = 0.921, 95% CI: 0.874, 0.971). They were more likely to have used any effective method of pregnancy prevention at last vaginal sex (OR = 1.075, 95% CI: 1.023, 1.131), and more likely specifically to have used a condom at last vaginal sex (OR = 1.049, 95% CI: 1.014, 1.084).

Associations were also computed between the independent variable of family religiosity and the potential moderator of student religiosity (Table 4); students who reported frequent family religiosity scored significantly higher on every domain of individual religiosity than did students who reported infrequent family religiosity.

Table 3. Unadjusted associations between family religiosity, parental monitoring, and student religiosity and emerging adults' sexual behaviors (n = 608).

Sexual Behavior Outcomes	Family Religiosity (Frequent)			Key Predictors Parental Monitoring			Student Religiosity (Total Score)		
	OR	95% CI	p Value	OR	95% CI	p Value	OR	95% CI	p Value
Age at first sex (oral, vaginal, or anal) (17 or older)	1.167	0.795, 1.714		1.009	0.979, 1.039		1.012	0.997, 1.026	
Four or more lifetime sexual partners	0.848	0.579, 1.241		0.959	0.929, 0.989	0.008	0.978	0.965, 0.992	0.003
Ever had oral sex [a]	0.333	0.221, 0.503	<0.001	0.993	0.959, 1.029		0.949	0.935, 0.963	<0.001
Ever had unprotected oral sex	0.788	0.299, 2.075		0.995	0.910, 1.089		0.980	0.948, 1.014	
Ever had vaginal sex	0.390	0.270, 0.564	<0.001	0.984	0.953, 1.015		0.956	0.944, 0.969	<0.001
Ever had unprotected vaginal sex [b]	0.563	0.329, 0.962	0.036	0.921	0.874, 0.971	0.002	0.982	0.963, 1.002	
Ever had anal sex	0.601	0.399, 0.908	0.015	0.950	0.920, 0.980	0.001	0.972	0.957, 0.986	<0.001
Ever had unprotected anal sex	1.107	0.475, 2.581		0.993	0.928, 1.063		1.003	0.971, 1.036	
Substance use before last sex (oral, vaginal, or anal)	0.762	0.511, 1.134		0.987	0.957, 1.018		0.989	0.974, 1.003	
Condom use at last vaginal sex [c]	1.438	0.953, 2.168		1.049	1.014, 1.084	0.005	1.017	1.002, 1.033	0.031
Pregnancy prevention [d] at last vaginal sex	1.307	0.649, 2.633		1.075	1.023, 1.131	0.005	0.990	0.967, 1.014	

OR, unadjusted odds ratio; CI, confidence interval; p values reported only for variables significant at $p < 0.05$. [a] n = 607; [b] n = 438 (only students who report having had vaginal sex); [c] n = 415 (only students who report having had vaginal sex, n = 23 missing); [d] Pregnancy prevention at last vaginal sex includes condom use and/or use of hormonal birth control methods (pill, patch, ring, intrauterine device, or implant).

Table 4. Student religiosity by family religiosity (frequency).

	Infrequent Family Religiosity		Frequent Family Religiosity			
	M	**SD**	**M**	**SD**	*t*-Test	*df*
Overall self-ranking/religious intensity	1.80	1.441	3.76	1.472	−15.885 ***	584
Private religious practices	5.97	5.560	15.68	8.066	−17.235 ***	583
Forgiveness	4.01	2.994	6.28	2.277	−9.783 ***	579
Organizational religiousness	1.55	1.920	4.55	2.824	−15.309 ***	584
Student Religiosity Total Score	12.36	9.983	29.25	12.49	−18.010 ***	578

*** $p < 0.001$.

Multivariate results. Tables 5 and 6 present the results of multivariate analyses. After controlling for relevant individual- and family-level covariates, we found that students who reported frequent family religiosity were significantly less likely ever to have had oral sex (aOR = 0.429, 95% CI: 0.239, 0.771) and ever to have had vaginal sex (aOR = 0.551, 95% CI: 0.323, 0.942) (Table 4). Among students who reported having had vaginal sex, students with frequent family religiosity remained significantly less likely ever to have had unprotected vaginal sex (aOR = 0.470, 95% CI: 0.262, 0.841).

Table 5. Binary logistic regression models predicting emerging adults' sexual behaviors.

Sexual Behavior Outcomes	Key Predictor: Family Religiosity (Frequent)		
	aOR	95% CI	*p* Value
Age at first sex (oral, vaginal, or anal) (17 or older)	1.034	0.687, 1.556	
Four or more lifetime sexual partners	0.897	0.596, 1.348	
Ever had oral sex [a]	0.429	0.239, 0.771	0.005
Ever had unprotected oral sex	1.100	0.333, 3.004	
Ever had vaginal sex [b]	0.551	0.323, 0.942	0.029
Ever had unprotected vaginal sex [c]	0.470	0.262, 0.841	0.011
Ever had anal sex	0.693	0.431, 1.116	
Ever had unprotected anal sex	1.137	0.455, 2.838	
Substance use before last sex (oral, vaginal, or anal)	0.805	0.530, 1.222	
Condom use at last vaginal sex [d]	1.592	1.033, 2.453	0.035
Pregnancy prevention [e] at last vaginal sex	1.740	0.827, 3.661	

aOR, adjusted odds ratio; CI, confidence interval; *p* values reported only for multivariate models significant at *p* < 0.05. [a] *n* = 607; model adjusted for race, religion, sexual relationship status, parents' birthplace, and single parent household during high school. [b] *n* = 608; model adjusted for age, race, religion, sexual relationship status, parents' birthplace, first generation college student, and single parent household during high school. [c] *n* = 438 (only students who report having had vaginal sex); model adjusted for age and sexual relationship status. [d] *n* = 415 (only students who report having had vaginal sex, *n* = 23 missing); model adjusted for sexual relationship status. [e] Pregnancy prevention at last vaginal sex includes condom use and/or use of hormonal birth control methods (pill, patch, ring, intrauterine device, or implant).

Only one outcome variable, ever having had unprotected vaginal sex, had a statistically significant relationship with both the independent variable of family religiosity (OR = 0.563, 95% CI: 0.329, 0.962) and with the potential mediator of parental monitoring (OR = 0.921, 95% CI: 0.874, 0.971); subsequent tests for mediation using hierarchical logistic regression were conducted on this outcome variable. After controlling for relevant individual-level characteristics, results suggest that, as hypothesized, there was a significant indirect effect of family religiosity on college students' ever having had unprotected vaginal sex through parental monitoring (*b* = −0.261, BCa CI: −0.515, −0.085).

To test for possible moderation by student religiosity, we built separate hierarchical logistic regression models for each sexual behavior outcome and the interaction of family religiosity with each of five possible student religiosity scores (four domain scores and one total score). Results from these regressions (tables not shown) indicate that none of the five domains of student religiosity moderate the relationship between family religiosity and student sexual activity or sexual risk. Student religiosity was subsequently explored as an independent predictor of students' sexual activity and sexual risk. After controlling for relevant individual-level and family-level characteristics, higher students' total religiosity score was significantly associated with less likelihood of having had four or more sexual partners (aOR = 0.985, 95% CI: 0.970, 1.000), ever having had oral sex (aOR = 0.972, 95% CI: 0.952, 0.993), ever having had vaginal sex (aOR = 0.973, 95% CI: 0.953, 0.993), and ever having had anal sex (aOR = 0.979, 95% CI: 0.960, 0.998). In addition, students with a higher religiosity score were more likely to have used a condom at last vaginal sex (aOR = 1.017, 95% CI: 1.001, 1.034) (Table 5).

Table 6. Binary logistic regression models predicting emerging adults' sexual behaviors.

Sexual Behavior Outcomes	Key Predictor: Student Religiosity (Total Score)		
	aOR	95% CI	*p* Value
Age at first sex (oral, vaginal, or anal) (17 or older)	1.005	0.989, 1.022	
Four or more lifetime sexual partners [a]	0.984	0.969, 1.000	0.043
Ever had oral sex [b]	0.972	0.952, 0.993	0.008
Ever had unprotected oral sex	0.990	0.949, 1.033	
Ever had vaginal sex [c]	0.973	0.953, 0.993	0.009
Ever had unprotected vaginal sex	0.985	0.965, 1.006	
Ever had anal sex [d]	0.979	0.960, 0.998	0.034
Ever had unprotected anal sex	0.999	0.963, 1.036	
Substance use before last sex (oral, vaginal, or anal)	0.992	0.977, 1.007	
Condom use at last vaginal sex [e]	1.017	1.001, 1.034	0.039
Pregnancy prevention [f] at last vaginal sex	1.007	0.982, 1.034	

aOR, adjusted odds ratio; CI, confidence interval; *p* values reported only for multivariate models significant at $p < 0.05$. [a] $n = 485$ (only students who report having had oral, vaginal, or anal sex, $n = 10$ missing); model adjusted for age, sexual relationship status, and parents' birthplace. [b] $n = 607$ ($n = 1$ missing); model adjusted for race, religion, sexual relationship status, parents' birthplace, and single parent household during high school. [c] $n = 608$; model adjusted for age, race, religion, sexual relationship status, parents' birthplace, first generation college student, and single parent household during high school. [d] $n = 585$ ($n = 23$ missing); model adjusted for age and sexual relationship status. [e] $n = 415$ (only students who report having had vaginal sex, $n = 23$ missing); model adjusted for sexual relationship status. [f] Pregnancy prevention at last vaginal sex includes condom use and/or use of hormonal birth control methods (pill, patch, ring, intrauterine device, or implant).

5. Discussion

Findings from this study suggest that religiosity, both family and individual, may play a role in emerging adults' sexual behavior. Greater family religiosity was associated with a decreased likelihood of students' engaging in certain sex acts (ever having had oral or vaginal sex), but for students who did choose to engage, family religiosity was not associated with any differences in the timing of sexual onset or in the students' number of partners. This finding confirms previous work and implies that family religiosity may influence some students' decisions whether or not to have sex; but for students who do choose to have sex, the break from religious teachings about sex may already have occurred, so family religiosity no longer had a role to play in decisions like when to begin having sex, or whether or not to have sex with more than one partner. It is also possible that students who internalized religious messages about refraining from sexual activity might be more likely to characterize their families as being highly religious than would students for whom those religious messages were less salient.

Contrary to our expectation, higher family religiosity was associated with a decreased likelihood of risk behaviors, rather than an increased likelihood of risk. Within the context of the previous finding, it may be that students who have chosen to be sexually active, in contradiction to family religious teachings about sexual activity, would be more likely to take extra precautions so as not to be found out (through pregnancy or STIs) by their parents or other family members. Previous research on adolescents active in their church community found that participants' parents had regularly reinforced the idea that going against biblical principles related to sexual activity would increase the likelihood of negative consequences that could derail future goals and opportunities (Moore et al. 2014). Fear that a negative consequence like unplanned pregnancy may lead to parental disappointment or shame may drive students to protect themselves from risk by avoiding unprotected vaginal sex to maintain the secrecy of sexual activity.

Though more frequent family religiosity was associated with higher student religiosity, none of the four domains of student religiosity (overall self-ranking, private practice, forgiveness, or organizational religiosity), nor the total student religiosity score, served to moderate the relationship between family religiosity and students' sexual behaviors. The finding that higher family religiosity is associated with higher student religiosity was expected; growing up in an environment that values religious participation and religious teachings is likely to instill an appreciation for, or sense of obligation to, those religious traditions. The lack of moderation by students' current religiosity on the relationship between family religiosity and students' sexual behaviors suggests that, rather than family religiosity exerting influence in the form of a parent's voice in a student's head or memories of a family's religious teachings, a more thorough transmission of beliefs may occur in highly religious families, so that students now view those beliefs as their own, rather than as a holdover from parental influence in childhood. Having a high degree of personal religiosity is independently associated with certain student sexual behaviors, but that association does not change the original relationship between family religiosity and students' behaviors; whether or not a student has internalized religious messages remains separate from the potential internalizing of other standards of behavior or sexual expectations.

Students in more religious families report a higher degree of parental monitoring, and also a significantly lower likelihood of ever having had unprotected vaginal sex (among students who have had vaginal sex). This finding seems to support earlier findings in this study and the possibility that fear of parents finding out about sexual activity may be a strong motivator for students from highly religious families to avoid sexual risk-taking. Parents in more religious families are paying more attention to students' whereabouts and behaviors. If the family's messaging around sex is religiously motivated and focused on abstinence or 'saving oneself for marriage', it is likely that students' fear of negative consequences (like pregnancy or sexually transmitted infections) is leading them to use condoms during vaginal sex. Avoiding pregnancy or sexually transmitted infections may ensure that parents never learn about students' sexual activity or behaviors.

It is also possible that the desire to maintain individual and family reputation within a close religious community acts as further motivation to avoid risk. Hill et al. (2014) suggest that an individual may be more likely to engage in a behavior like premarital sex if feelings of shame or embarrassment associated with that behavior were lower. In a highly religious family that is part of a larger religious community, stigma around premarital sex and the potential to bring community shame upon and one's family may further motivate sexually active students to avoid unprotected vaginal sex that could result in an unintended pregnancy.

This study has certain limitations that must be considered when interpreting the results. Because participants were assessed at only one time point, causal inferences cannot be made using these cross-sectional data. In addition, because we only had access to students and not to their parents or families, family religiosity was measured by students' retrospective report. It is possible that students' recall of family religious activities may not be consistent with perceptions of other family members. Because religiosity (both family and individual) was low overall in this sample, it is possible that we may not be fully capturing the relationship between religiosity and emerging adults' sexual behaviors; however, the strength and direction of certain findings related to religiosity, despite low report overall in the sample, suggest that we may be underestimating, rather than overestimating, the potential role of religiosity in emerging adults' sexual behaviors.

A final limitation of this study relates to the fluid nature of sexual activity and sexual relationships during the developmental stages of late adolescence and emerging adulthood. An abundance of literature suggests that emerging adults develop intimate relationships and acquire new sexual experiences at a rapid pace (e.g., Alexander et al. 2015; Meier and Allen 2009; Tanner et al. 2009), often through casual hook-up encounters (Allison and Risman 2014, 2017; Stinson et al. 2014). Dating, love, and romantic exploration are different during emerging adulthood, with a focus on individual identity exploration as well as the potential for physical and emotional intimacy (Arnett 2000). Given the rapid pace of change during this developmental stage, it is important to recognize that the data reported in this study only provide one snapshot of students' sexual behaviors and do not account for the complexities inherent in emerging adult sexual encounters.

Despite these limitations, findings from this study contribute to the study of religion and family life by illuminating potential relationships between family-level influences and emerging adults' sexual behaviors and highlighting the complex nature of religiosity and its long arm of influence. Overall, there is some evidence that both family and individual religiosity are associated with emerging adults' sexual behavior, though the two play independent roles in the relationship, and parent religiosity seems to exert influence primarily through increased parental monitoring of adolescents.

Author Contributions: D.A.Q. and A.L. conceived of the study in discussion together. D.A.Q. conducted all data analyses, preliminary interpretations, and wrote the original draft. A.L. edited multiple versions of the manuscript and contributed to theory development, model building, and interpretation of results. Both authors contributed to the final version of the manuscript.

Funding: This research received no external funding.

Acknowledgments: This work was partially supported by a postdoctoral fellowship to D.A. Quinn through the Department of Veterans Affairs Office of Academic Affiliations and the Center for Health Equity Research and Promotion at the VA Pittsburgh Healthcare System. The opinions expressed in this work are the authors' and do not reflect those of the institutions, the Department of Veterans Affairs, or the U.S. government.

Conflicts of Interest: The authors declare no conflicts of interest.

References

Adamczyk, Amy, and Jacob Felson. 2006. Friends' religiosity and first sex. *Social Science Research* 35: 924–47. [CrossRef]

Alexander, Cheryl S., Mark R. Somerfield, Margaret E. Ensminger, Karin E. Johnson, and Young J. Kim. 1993. Consistency of adolescents' self-report of sexual behavior in a longitudinal study. *Journal of Youth and Adolescence* 22: 455–71. [CrossRef]

Alexander, Kamila A., Loretta S. Jemmott, Anne M. Teitelman, and Patricia D'Antonio. 2015. Addressing sexual health behaviour during emerging adulthood: A critical review of the literature. *Journal of Clinical Nursing* 24: 4–18. [CrossRef]

Allison, Rachel, and Barbara J. Risman. 2014. It goes hand in hand with the parties. *Sociological Perspectives* 57: 102–23. [CrossRef]

Allison, Rachel, and Barbara J. Risman. 2017. Marriage delay, time to play? Marital horizons and hooking up in college. *Sociological Inquiry* 87: 472–500. [CrossRef]

American College Health Association. 2015. *NCHA-ACHA II Spring 2015 Reference Group Data Report*. Hanover: ACHA, Available online: http://www.acha-ncha.org/docs/NCHA-IIWEB_SPRING_2015_REFERENCE_GROUP_DATA_REPORT.pdf (accessed on 8 August 2018).

Arnett, Jeffrey Jensen. 2000. Emerging adulthood: A theory of development from the late teens through the twenties. *American Psychologist* 55: 469–80. [CrossRef] [PubMed]

Arnett, Jeffrey Jensen. 2007. Emerging adulthood: What is it, and what is it good for? *Child Development Perspectives* 1: 68–73. [CrossRef]

Arnett, Jeffrey Jensen. 2011. Emerging adulthood(s): The cultural psychology of a new life stage. In *Bridging Cultural and Developmental Approaches to Psychology: New Syntheses in Theory, Research, and Policy*. Edited by Lene Arnett Jensen. Oxford: Oxford University Press, pp. 255–75.

Arria, Amelia M., Vanessa Kuhn, Kimberly M. Caldeira, Kevin E. O'Grady, Kathryn B. Vincent, and Eric D. Wish. 2008. High school drinking mediates the relationship between parental monitoring and college drinking: A longitudinal analysis. *Substance Abuse Treatment, Prevention, And Policy* 3: 6. [CrossRef]

Bader, Christopher D., and Scott A. Desmond. 2006. Do as I say and as I do: The effects of consistent parental beliefs and behaviors upon religious transmission. *Sociology of Religion* 67: 313–29. [CrossRef]

Barnes, Grace M., Joseph H. Hoffman, John W. Welte, Michael P. Farrell, and Barbara A. Dintcheff. 2006. Effects of parental monitoring and peer deviance on substance use and delinquency. *Journal of Marriage and Family* 68: 1084–104. [CrossRef]

Barry, Carolyn McNamara, Brian J. Willoughby, and Kirsten Clayton. 2015. Living your faith: Associations between family and personal religious practices and emerging adults' sexual behavior. *Journal of Adult Development* 22: 159–72. [CrossRef]

Bearman, Peter S., and Hannah Bruckner. 2001. Promising the future: Virginity pledges and first intercourse. *American Journal of Sociology* 106: 859–912. [CrossRef]

Boekeloo, Bradley O., and Donna E. Howard. 2002. Oral sexual experience among young adolescents receiving general health examinations. *American Journal of Health Behavior* 26: 306–14. [CrossRef] [PubMed]

Brückner, Hannah, and Peter Bearman. 2005. After the promise: The STD consequences of adolescent virginity pledges. *Journal of Adolescent Health* 36: 271–78. [CrossRef] [PubMed]

Burdette, Amy M., Terrence D. Hill, Christopher G. Ellison, and Norval D. Glenn. 2009. "Hooking up" at college: Does religion make a difference. *Journal for the Scientific Study of Religion* 48: 535–51. [CrossRef]

CDC. 2015. 2015 National Youth Risk Behavior Survey. Centers for Disease Control and Prevention. Available online: ftp://ftp.cdc.gov/pub/data/yrbs/2015/2015_xxh_questionnaire.pdf (accessed on 7 January 2017).

CDC. 2016. *2015 YRBS Data User's Guide*. Atlanta: CDC. [CrossRef]

Chambers, Wendy C. 2007. Oral sex: Varied behaviors and perceptions in a college population. *The Journal of Sex Research* 44: 28–42. [CrossRef] [PubMed]

Chilcoat, Howard D., and James C. Anthony. 1996. Impact of parent monitoring on initiation of drug use through late childhood. *Journal of the American Academy of Child and Adolescent Psychiatry* 35: 91–100. [CrossRef]

Davoli, Marina, Carlo A. Perucci, Massimo Sangalli, Giovanna Brancato, and Giovanni Dell'Uomo. 1992. Reliability of sexual behavior data among high school students in Rome. *Epidemiology* 3: 531–35. [CrossRef]

DiClemente, Ralph J. 2015. Validity of self-reported sexual behavior among adolescents: Where do we go from here? *AIDS and Behavior* 20: 2–4. [CrossRef]

DiClemente, Ralph J., Gina M. Wingood, Richard Crosby, Brenda K. Cobb, Kathy Harrington, and Susan L. Davies. 2001. Parent-adolescent communication and sexual risk behaviors among African American adolescent females. *The Journal of Pediatrics* 139: 407–12. [CrossRef]

DiClemente, Ralph J., Andrea L. Swartzendruber, and Jennifer L. Brown. 2013. Improving the validity of self-reported sexual behavior: No easy answers. *Sexually Transmitted Diseases* 40: 111–12. [CrossRef] [PubMed]

DiIorio, Colleen, William N. Dudley, Johanna E. Soet, and Johanna E. McCarty. 2004. Sexual possibility situations and sexual behaviors among young adolescents: The moderating role of protective factors. *Journal of Adolescent Health* 35: 11–20. [CrossRef] [PubMed]

Dollahite, David C., and Jennifer Y. Thatcher. 2008. Talking about religion: How highly religious youth and parents discuss their faith. *Journal of Adolescent Research* 23: 611–41. [CrossRef]

Farmer, Antoinette Y., Jill Witmer Sinha, and Emmett Gill. 2008. The effects of family religiosity, parental limit-setting, and monitoring on adolescent substance use. *Journal of Ethnicity in Substance Abuse* 7: 428–50. [CrossRef] [PubMed]

Foshee, Vangie A., and Bryan R. Hollinger. 1996. Maternal religiosity, adolescent social bonding, and adolescent alcohol use. *Journal of Early Adolescence* 16: 451–68. [CrossRef]

Grello, Catherine M., Deborah P. Welsh, and Melinda S. Harper. 2006. No strings attached: The nature of casual sex in college students. *The Journal of Sex Research* 43: 255–67. [CrossRef] [PubMed]

Hall, Kelli Stidham, Caroline Moreau, and James Trussell. 2012. Lower use of sexual and reproductive health services among women with frequent religious participation, regardless of sexual experience. *Journal of Women's Health* 21: 739–47. [CrossRef]

Hayatbakhsh, Reza, Alexandra Clavarino, Gail M. Williams, and Jake M. Najman. 2014. Maternal and personal religious engagement as predictors of early onset and frequent substance use. *American Journal on Addictions* 23: 363–70. [CrossRef]

Hayes, Andrew F. 2017. *Introduction to Mediation, Moderation, and Conditional Process Analysis: A Regression-Based Approach*, 2nd ed. New York: The Guilford Press.

Hill, Nicholas J., Mxolisi Siwatu, and Alexander K. Robinson. 2014. "My religion picked my birth control": The influence of religion on contraceptive use. *Journal of Religion and Health* 53: 825–33. [CrossRef]

Huebner, Angela J., and Laurie W. Howell. 2003. Examining the relationship between adolescent sexual risk-taking and perceptions of monitoring, communication, and parenting styles. *Journal of Adolescent Health* 33: 71–78. [CrossRef]

Iannaccone, Laurence R. 1990. Religious practice: A human capital approach. *Journal for the Scientific Study of Religion* 29: 297–314. [CrossRef]

IBM Corp. 2017. *IBM SPSS Statistics for Macintosh, Version 25.0*. Armonk: IBM.

John E. Fetzer Institute. 2003. *Measurement of Religiousness/Spirituality for Use in Research*. A Report of the Fetzer Institute/National Institute on Aging Working Group. Kalamazoo: John E. Fetzer Institute, pp. 1–103.

Jones, Rachel K., Jacqueline E. Darroch, and Susheela Singh. 2005. Religious differentials in the sexual and reproductive behaviors of young women in the United States. *Journal of Adolescent Health* 36: 279–88. [CrossRef] [PubMed]

Karofsky, Peter S., Lan Zeng, and Michael R. Kosorok. 2001. Relationship between adolescent-parental communication and initiation of first intercourse by adolescents. *Journal of Adolescent Health* 28: 41–45. [CrossRef]

Kelly, Jeffrey A., and Seth C. Kalichman. 2002. Behavioral research in HIV/AIDS primary and secondary prevention: Recent advances and future directions. *Journal of Consulting and Clinical Psychology* 70: 626–39. [CrossRef] [PubMed]

Kim, Young, and W. Bradford Wilcox. 2014. Religious identity, religious attendance, and parental control. *Review of Religious Research* 56: 555–80. [CrossRef]

Lambert, Nathaniel M., and David C. Dollahite. 2010. Development of the Faith Activities in the Home Scale (FAITHS). *Journal of Family Issues* 31: 1442–64. [CrossRef]

Landor, Antoinette M., and Leslie Gordon Simons. 2014. Why virginity pledges succeed or fail: The moderating effect of religious commitment versus religious participation. *Journal of Child and Family Studies* 23: 1102–13. [CrossRef]

Lefkowitz, Eva S., Meghan M. Gillen, Cindy L. Shearer, and Tanya L. Boone. 2004. Religiosity, sexual behaviors, and sexual attitudes during emerging adulthood. *The Journal of Sex Research* 41: 150–59. [CrossRef]

Li, Xiaoming, Bonita Stanton, and Susan Feigelman. 2000. Impact of perceived parental monitoring on adolescent risk behavior over 4 years. *The Journal of Adolescent Health* 27: 49–56. [CrossRef]

Lyons, Heidi, Wendy Manning, Peggy Giordano, and Monica Longmore. 2013. Predictors of heterosexual casual sex among young adults. *Archives of Sexual Behavior* 42: 585–93. [CrossRef]

Manlove, Jennifer S., Elizabeth Terry-Humen, Erum N. Ikramullah, and Kristin A. Moore. 2006. The role of parent religiosity in teens' transitions to sex and contraception. *Journal of Adolescent Health* 39: 578–87. [CrossRef] [PubMed]

Manlove, Jennifer S., Cassandra Logan, Kristin A. Moore, and Erum N. Ikramullah. 2008. Pathways from family religiosity to adolescent sexual activity and contraceptive use. *Perspectives on Sexual and Reproductive Health* 40: 105–17. [CrossRef] [PubMed]

McKelvey, Robert S., John A. Webb, Loretta V. Baldassar, Suzanne M. Robinson, and Geoff Riley. 1999. Sex knowledge and sexual attitudes among medical and nursing students. *Australian and New Zealand Journal of Psychiatry* 33: 260–66. [CrossRef] [PubMed]

Meier, Ann, and Gina Allen. 2009. Romantic relationships from adolescence to young adulthood: Evidence from the National Longitudinal Study of Adolescent Health. *The Sociological Quarterly* 50: 308–35. [CrossRef] [PubMed]

Moore, Erin W., and William E. Smith. 2012. What college students do not know: Where are the gaps in sexual health knowledge? *Journal of American College Health: J of ACH* 60: 436–42. [CrossRef] [PubMed]

Moore, Erin, Jannette Berkley-Patton, Alexandria Bohn, Starlyn Hawes, and Carole Bowe-Thompson. 2014. Beliefs about sex and parent-child-church sex communication among church-based African American youth. *Journal of Religion and Health* 54: 1810–25. [CrossRef]

Orr, Donald P., Dennis J. Fortenberry, and Margaret J. Blythe. 1997. Validity of self-reported sexual behaviors in adolescent women using biomarker outcomes. *Sexually Transmitted Diseases* 24: 261–66. [CrossRef]

Pearce, Lisa D., and Dana L. Haynie. 2004. Intergenerational religious dynamics and adolescent delinquency. *Social Forces* 82: 1553–72. [CrossRef]

Pearce, Lisa D., and Arland Thornton. 2007. Religious identity and family ideologies in the transition to adulthood. *Journal of Marriage and Family* 69: 1227–43. [CrossRef]

Pinchevsky, Gillian M., Amelia M. Arria, Kimberly M. Caldeira, Laura M. Garnier-Dykstra, Kathryn B.Vincent, and Kevin E. O'Grady. 2012. Marijuana exposure opportunity and initiation during college: Parent and peer influences. *Prevention Science* 13: 43–54. [CrossRef]

Prothero, Stephen. 2007. Worshiping in Ignorance. *The Chronicle of Higher Education* 53: B6–B7.

Regnerus, Mark D. 2007. *Forbidden Fruit: Sex and Religion in the Lives of American Teenagers*. New York: Oxford University Press.

Regnerus, Mark D. 2010. Religion and adolescent sexual behavior. In *Religion, Families, and Health*. Edited by Robert A. Hummer and Christopher G. Ellison. New Brunswick: Rutgers University Press, pp. 61–85.

Schrimshaw, Eric W., Margaret Rosario, Heino F. L. Meyer-Bahlburg, and Alice A. Scharf-Matlick. 2006. Test-retest reliability of self-reported sexual behavior, sexual orientation, and psychosexual milestones among gay, lesbian, and bisexual youths. *Archives of Sexual Behavior* 35: 225–34. [CrossRef] [PubMed]

Shew, Marcia L., Gary J. Remafedi, Linda H. Bearinger, Patricia L. Faulkner, Barbara A. Taylor, Sandra J. Potthoff, and Michael D. Resnick. 1997. The validity of self-reported condom use among adolescents. *Sexually Transmitted Diseases* 24: 503–10. [CrossRef] [PubMed]

Sieverding, John A., Nancy Adler, Stephanie Witt, and Jonathan Ellen. 2005. The influence of parental monitoring on adolescent sexual initiation. *Archives of Pediatrics and Adolescent Medicine* 159: 724–29. [CrossRef] [PubMed]

Smith, Christian. 2003a. Religious participation and network closure among American adolescents. *Journal for the Scientific Study of Religion* 42: 259–67. [CrossRef]

Smith, Christian. 2003b. Religious participation and parental moral expectations and supervision of American youth. *Review of Religious Research* 44: 414–24. [CrossRef]

Smith, Christian, and Melina Lundquist Denton. 2005. *Soul Searching: The Religious and Spiritual Lives of American Teenagers*. New York: Oxford University Press.

Smith, Christian, Robert Faris, Melinda Lundquist Denton, and Mark Regnerus. 2003. Mapping American adolescent subjective religiosity and attitudes of alienation toward religion: A research report. *Sociology of Religion* 64: 111–33. [CrossRef]

Snider J.B., Andrea Clements, and Alexander T. Vazsonyi. 2004. Late adolescent perceptions of parent religiosity and parenting processes. *Family Process* 43: 489–502. [CrossRef]

Stinson, Rebecca D., Lauren B. Levy, and Marcus Alt. 2014. "They're just a good time and move on": Fraternity men reflect on their hookup experiences. *Journal of College Student Psychotherapy* 28: 59–73. [CrossRef]

Stolzenberg, Ross M., Mary Blair-Loy, and Linda J. Waite. 1995. Religious participation in early adulthood: Age and family life cycle effects on church membership. *American Sociological Review* 60: 84–103. [CrossRef]

Tanner, Jennifer L., Jeffrey Jensen Arnett, and Julie A. Leis. 2009. Emerging Adulthood: Learning and development during the first stage of adulthood. In *Handbook of Research on Adult Learning and Development*. Edited by M. Cecil Smith and Nancy DeFrates-Densch. New York: Routledge, pp. 34–67.

Weinhardt, Lance S., Andrew D. Forsyth, Michael P. Carey, Beth C. Jaworski, and Lauren E. Durant. 1998. Reliability and validity of self-report measures of HIV-related sexual behavior: Progress since 1990 and recommendations for research and practice. *Archives of Sexual Behavior* 27: 155–80. [CrossRef] [PubMed]

Wilson, John, and Darren E. Sherkat. 1994. Returning to the fold. *Journal for the Scientific Study of Religion* 33: 148–61. [CrossRef]

religions

MDPI

Article

Marital Sanctification and Spiritual Intimacy Predicting Married Couples' Observed Intimacy Skills across the Transition to Parenthood

Emily Padgett, Annette Mahoney *, Kenneth I. Pargament and Alfred DeMaris

Department of Psychology, Bowling Green State University, Bowling Green, OH 43403, USA;
emily.a.padgett@gmail.com (E.P.); kpargam@bgsu.edu (K.I.P.); ademari@bgsu.edu (A.D.)
* Correspondence: amahone@bgsu.edu; Tel.: +1-419-372-0282

Received: 15 January 2019; Accepted: 28 February 2019; Published: 11 March 2019

check for
updates

Abstract: This study examined the extent to which 164 married heterosexuals' reports of the sanctification of marriage and spiritual intimacy during pregnancy predicted the trajectory of the couples' observed intimacy skills during late pregnancy and when their first child was 3, 6, and 12 months old. At each time point, couples were videotaped in their homes for 10 min discussing their fears and vulnerabilities about becoming and being a new parent. Separate teams of three coders rated the four interactions and each spouse's intimacy skills, including disclosure of feelings of vulnerability about becoming or being a new parent, and supportive comments and positive non-verbal responses to each other. Using a multi-level dyadic discrepancy approach to growth curve modeling, both husbands' and wives' observed intimacy skills displayed a curvilinear trajectory over the first year of parenthood, with wives consistently displaying more emotional intimacy skills than husbands. Consistent with hypotheses, higher endorsement of the sanctification of marriage and spiritual intimacy between spouses at home predicted higher observed intimacy skills across time. No variation in these associations emerged due to parent gender. Thus, this longitudinal study identifies two specific spiritual processes within marriages that may motivate spouses to share their vulnerabilities and provide one another with valuable emotional support in coping with the transition to parenthood.

Keywords: sanctification; spiritual intimacy; parents; parenting; transition to parenthood; religion

1. Introduction

The psychological literature on the transition to parenthood (TtP) has documented that heterosexual couples, on average, develop more conflict and negative marital communication patterns, and less marital satisfaction when adjusting to first-time parenthood compared to prenatal marital functioning (for reviews see, Doss and Rhoades 2017; Mitnick et al. 2009). Marked variability, however, exists in couples' adaptation to the TtP (Doss and Rhoades 2017), with much less steep declines in marital satisfaction for some than others (Don and Mickelson 2014) and a minority of couples growing closer as they respond to the challenges of integrating an infant into their family unit (Holmes et al. 2013). Greater constructive communication during pregnancy is a fairly consistent predictor of less deterioration in post-birth marital functioning (Doss et al. 2009; Rholes et al. 2014; Trillingsgaard et al. 2014). Yet couples with the highest levels of prenatal relationship positives, such as emotional intimacy, exhibit the largest decreases in marital well-being following biological births and adoption (Doss and Rhoades 2017). Thus, adaptive dyadic coping resources need to be identified that help couples sustain emotionally supportive dialogues across the TtP (Rholes et al. 2014). Specific spiritual or religious (S/R) resources centered on marriage represent an understudied, but potentially important, set of factors that may facilitate marital well-being across the TtP (Mahoney 2010, 2013). This longitudinal study therefore investigated whether greater sanctification of marriage (i.e., perceiving one's marriage as having sacred qualities and/or being a manifestation of God/higher power) and spiritual intimacy (i.e., disclosing and being supportive of the spouse's disclosures about spirituality) during pregnancy predicted the trajectory of couples' observed emotional intimacy skills at pregnancy and when the couples' first child was 3, 6, and 12 months old.

1.1. Marital Adaptation Across the TtP

1.1.1. Variation in Marital Adjustment

A large body of literature on the TtP highlights that, on average, heterosexual couples experience decreases in marital satisfaction and increases in negative marital interactions from the time of pregnancy through the first years of their child's life (Doss and Rhoades 2017; Mitnick et al. 2009; Ryan and Padilla 2019). For example, overall marital quality diminishes for around 60–80% of couples, and many experience decreases in general conversation and the frequency of sex (Doss and Rhoades 2017; Don and Mickelson 2014). New parents also often report increased conflict over physical intimacy, finances, division of household labor, family and in-laws, shared leisure time, and life goals (Kluwer and Johnson 2007). In addition, childrearing emerges as a potentially new source of friction, with wives typically taking on a disproportional amount of infant care and couples often discovering they disagree about coparenting (Cowan and Cowan 1992; Ryan and Padilla 2019). In observational studies, couples' interactions also tend to deteriorate after the TtP, with an increase in hostile, critical comments and a decrease in positivity during problem-solving focused discussions (Cox et al. 1999; Trillingsgaard et al. 2014; Houts et al. 2008; Ryan and Padilla 2019). Despite these clear trends, a minority of couples report increased marital satisfaction (Doss and Rhoades 2017) and feeling closer to one another after their infant enters their lives (Holmes et al. 2013).

Given the marked variation in marital adjustment across the TtP, researchers have called for more attention to be paid to adaptive communication skills that could facilitate marital adjustment as couples cope with the strains of new parenthood (Mitnick et al. 2009; Rholes et al. 2014). Such calls dovetail with a growing emphasis in couples' literature to identify specific marital resources that could help couples sustain the quality and stability of their unions (Bradbury et al. 2000). In particular, Vulnerability Stress Adaptation (VSA) models of relationship dynamics expand the theoretical lens of couples' research beyond dysfunctional problem-solving interactions exhibited by clinic-referred couples; VSA models also strive to identify adaptive dyadic coping strategies that help generally non-distressed couples successfully navigate stressful, yet normative, challenges in daily life and accommodate the enduring psychological vulnerabilities that each partner possesses (Falconier et al. 2015; Karney and Bradbury 1995).

1.1.2. Intimacy Skills

One form of dyadic coping likely to help protect marriages during the TtP is a type of social support we refer to here as intimacy skills. Consistent with Reis and Shaver (1988) interpersonal process model of intimacy, intimacy skills refer to how effectively spouses disclose emotional distress (e.g., anxiety, sadness, sense of vulnerability) as well as give and receive empathic support when discussing potentially sensitive topics. Self-report and observational studies have linked couples' capabilities to engage in emotionally intimate dialogues to greater marital satisfaction (e.g., Greeff and Malherbe 2001; Meeks et al. 1998; Mirgain and Cordova 2007; Osgarby and Halford 2013; Patrick et al. 2007), and less deterioration in problem solving skills and marital dissolution over time (Sullivan et al. 2010). Emotionally focused intimate dialogues appear to be particularly helpful, yet difficult to enact, when partners are facing significant personal stressors (Bodenmann et al. 2015; Kuhn et al. 2018), such as a physical illness (e.g., Manne and Badr 2010; Porter et al. 2012) or psychological disorder (e.g., Hanley et al. 2013). Couples' educational prevention and clinical interventions programs also posit that partners' ability to effectively share and respond to one another's personal vulnerabilities during emotionally focused dialogues are critical mechanisms to promote marital satisfaction and stability (e.g., Sullivan et al. 2010; Wiebe and Johnson 2016).

The TtP represents a salient stage to observe couples' emotional intimacy skills because it often evokes strong feelings, ranging from joy, anticipation, awe, and love for the new infant to uncomfortable emotions such as anxiety, apprehension, irritation, and insecurity as spouses adjust to fatigue, new roles, and a new lifestyle (Cowan and Cowan 1992; Ryan and Padilla 2019). Furthermore, both spouses are experiencing the same stressful life event rather than only one spouse experiencing a particular difficulty. Indeed, ample opportunities occur for spouses to share and empathize about their respective emotional reactions to the TtP (Pistrang et al. 2001), and greater emotional support from a partner during pregnancy predicts less post-natal depression and anxiety (Pilkington et al. 2015). In addition, greater constructive communication during pregnancy is a fairly consistent predictor of less deterioration in post-birth marital functioning across studies (Cox et al. 1999; Doss et al. 2009; Rholes et al. 2014). Nevertheless, couples with the highest levels of prenatal relationship positives, such as emotional intimacy, tend to exhibit the largest decreases in marital well-being following biological births and adoption (Doss and Rhoades 2017). Thus, prenatal dyadic strengths need to be identified that predict the trajectory of change over time in married couples' intimacy skills. We could not, however, locate such studies in the TtP literature. To address this need, we directly observed married husbands' and wives' emotionally-laden disclosures (i.e., shared feelings of anxiety and vulnerability about becoming a parent) and supportive responses to disclosures (i.e., validating comments and emotionally positive non-verbal reactions) during late pregnancy and when their first biological child was 3, 6 and 12 months old. Ratings also encompassed spouses' warmth and affection (i.e., shared humor, physical affection) that could increase the frequency of emotional disclosures and punishing responses (i.e., invalidating comments and emotionally negative non-verbal reactions) that could decrease emotional disclosures (Kuhn et al. 2018; Mirgain and Cordova 2007). Notably, mixed theory and findings exist on whether gender predicts differences in spouses' emotional skillfulness, with especially scarce studies existing on couples coping the TtP. Available evidence, however, implies that wives would exhibit higher emotional skillfulness than husbands during this stage (Yu et al. 2011; Knoll et al. 2007).

1.2. Spiritual and Religious Marital Resources across the TtP

1.2.1. Global S/R Indices

Spirituality and religiousness (henceforth referred to as S/R) encompass an intriguing yet understudied sphere of life that may facilitate couples' marital functioning as they adapt to parenthood (Mahoney and Boyatzis 2019). Major world religions have long taught that sustaining a stable, well-functioning marriage within which to conceive and raise a child are highly valued goals for women and men (Goodman et al. 2013; Mahoney 2013). Findings based on brief measures of S/R support the notion that spouses who are more involved in organized religion may be more motivated to act in ways that protect and preserve their marriage across the TtP (Mahoney et al. 2008; Mahoney 2010). For example, a four-item measure of private prayer, importance of religion, and individual and joint religious attendance related to greater maternal, but not paternal, marital satisfaction over the transition (Nock et al. 2008). In a study of mothers, frequent attendance at religious services while pregnant predicted less post-partum declines in marital satisfaction compared to infrequent or no attendance (Dew and Wilcox 2011). However, Doss et al. (2009) found that a one-item measure of religious involvement before the birth of a first child did not predict later changes in marital satisfaction. With regard to co-parenting dynamics, which could impinge on the quality of dyadic marital relations, greater general S/R has been tied to wives engaging in greater maternal gatekeeping in childcare (Schoppe-Sullivan et al. 2015) as well as more infant care and domestic labor than husbands (Mahoney and Boyatzis 2019). Finally, more religiously engaged fathers in a low SES setting are more likely to take paternity leave to care for infants and, if more engaged in child care, they are less likely to have conflicts with the mother (Petts 2018).

While valuable and intriguing, available peer-reviewed quantitative studies on the role of S/R in facilitating marital adjustment across the TtP are limited in two key ways (Goodman et al. 2013; Mahoney et al. 2008; Mahoney 2010). First, brief indices of S/R tend to exhibit limited variability which may contribute to mixed or null results. Second, such measures cannot disentangle specific S/R processes that theoretically should motivate partners to support and rely on one another to cope with the strains of the TtP from S/R processes that are likely to undermine marital functioning. Hence, in this study, we examined two conceptually-based and specific S/R factors that have been identified in studies on S/R and marriage that should motivate new parents to engage in supportive intimate dialogues with one another as they adjust to the TtP.

1.2.2. Sanctification of Marriage

Sanctification refers to perceiving an aspect of life, such as one's marriage, as having divine significance and character (Mahoney et al. 2013; Pargament and Mahoney 2005). Community and national surveys have found that most married Americans view their union as having sacred qualities, such as holy, blessed, sacred (i.e., non-theistic sanctification), and as being a manifestation of a Higher Power (i.e., theistic sanctification) to some degree (e.g., Ellison et al. 2011; Mahoney et al. 1999). Greater belief regarding sanctity of one's marriage has been tied to greater subjective marital satisfaction, forgiveness, supportive dyadic coping, and sacrifice (e.g., Ellison et al. 2011; Rusu et al. 2015; Sabey et al. 2014). Studies using structural equation or fixed effects modeling with longitudinal data also show that greater sanctification of marriage predicts better observed problem-solving behavior and more positivity by husbands and wives during videotaped interactions where couples were asked to discuss their core conflicts during the TtP (Kusner et al. 2014; Rauer and Volling 2015). Couples who perceive sexual relations with a spouse as sanctified also report more sexual satisfaction cross-sectionally (Uecker and Willoughby 2018). Likewise, the more newlyweds view marital sexuality as sanctified, the more marital and sexual satisfaction as well as more frequent sex they report longitudinally (Hernandez-Kane and Mahoney 2018).

The above empirical findings imply that perceiving marriage as embodying divine qualities and/or a deity's presence during pregnancy could be a resource that motivates first-time parents to give and receive more emotional support to each other across the TtP. This hypothesis is consistent with theory and research on sanctification across multiple domains of life, including family relationships (Mahoney et al. 2013; Pargament and Mahoney 2005; Pargament et al. 2017). More specifically, (Mahoney et al. 2009, 2013) have proposed that greater perceived sanctification of one's marriage can lead to a greater commitment and investment of time and energy to the union, elicit strong emotions, and function as a powerful personal and social resource that spouses tap into during events that place stress on their bond. Thus, the more that parents experience a marriage during late pregnancy as an embodiment of God's intentions, an expression of ultimate purposes, and the inspiration of profound feelings, such as wonder, reverence, and gratitude, then the more they may prioritize giving and receiving emotional support to each other as a means to guard against parenthood disrupting marriage as a foundation of their family unit which, in turn, is also likely to be viewed as a sacred object that merits protection.

1.2.3. Spiritual Intimacy

Spiritual intimacy between a dyad refers to engaging in spiritual disclosure and providing empathic support to a partner who offers such disclosures (Kusner et al. 2014). Thus, this process represents a particular sub-type of intimacy focused on the sensitive domain of openly sharing opinions or experiences or (dis)beliefs about supernatural phenomenon that cannot be proven as ontologically "true" but tap into profound concerns and ultimate desires. People may hesitate to reveal such information due to fears or experiences of being dismissed, misunderstood, or ridiculed by the listener. Conversely, eliciting such disclosures from another person may especially require responding in an open-minded, empathic, and non-punishing manner (Mirgain and Cordova 2007). Theoretically, greater spiritual intimacy may foster peoples' sense they have found a special loved one with whom they can share their deepest aspirations and hopes as well as faith-based (dis)beliefs, doubts, troubles, or struggles. Disclosing one's spiritual or religious worldview or experiences can leave individuals feeling especially vulnerable to rejection or criticism because disclosures about supernatural powers, existential concerns, and/or S/R communities can be difficult, if not impossible, to verify as ontologically or morally defensible (Brelsford and Mahoney 2008; Mahoney 2013). Like other family dyads (Brelsford and Mahoney 2008; Desrosiers et al. 2011), however, couples' ability to talk about these sensitive topics in a candid and supportive manner may foster a greater sense of trust, attachment, emotional safety, and togetherness or "we-ness." Such conversations before having a child may thus set the stage for couples later being able and willing to engage in emotionally focused dialogues about new parenthood where they share their vulnerabilities, fears, questions, and struggles in parenting an infant, an arena of discussion that can also be highly debatable and challenge deeply held values or preconceptions about marriage and family life.

Empirically, in longitudinal studies, spiritual intimacy has predicted less negativity and more positivity during observed conflict interactions using fixed effects modeling (Kusner et al. 2014). Furthermore, among adult child-parent dyads, spiritual disclosure has been cross-sectionally tied to greater collaboration and less verbal aggression after controlling for disclosure about other sensitive topics (Brelsford and Mahoney 2008), and spiritual disclosure and support has been correlated more parental care and less overprotection by mothers and fathers (Desrosiers et al. 2011). In sum, across the TtP, spiritual intimacy could be expected to predict spouses' observable skills in disclosing highly emotionally laden information and responding to such disclosures in a supportive, non-judgmental manner (Kusner et al. 2014; Mahoney 2013).

1.3. Summary

The primary goal of this study was to examine whether greater sanctification and spiritual intimacy during pregnancy would predict higher levels of observed intimacy by both spouses over the TtP using a multilevel dyadic-discrepancy approach for growth-curve modeling with a linear mixed effects model. Theoretically, both constructs should function as protective factors that propel new parents to invest more effort into sharing and listening to one another's struggles with new parenthood to avoid the high spiritual and psychological costs to themselves and their child if their union deteriorated across this transition. We also examined the unique contribution of each construct in predicting observed emotional support but we did not make predictions about mediational effects due to the paucity of studies examining both processes in concert. Given that our primary analyses involved the trajectory of change over time in married couples' observed intimacy skills across the TtP, we note here that prior research has generally found decreases in marital satisfaction and increases in negative marital interactions across this transition. Thus, we anticipated couples would display a decline in intimacy skills after the first few months of having an infant due to fatigue and restructuring their lives, followed by at least some rebound in marital closeness during the second half of the first year of parenthood. We also expected that wives would likely exhibit greater intimacy skills than husbands, but this hypothesis was tentative and not a primary focus of the study. Finally, we examined whether our primary findings varied as a function of gender and time, but we did not make predictions about interaction effects with either factor due the scarcity of relevant prior studies.

2. Method

2.1. Participants

Participants were 164 married husbands and wives who underwent the transition to parenthood with both spouses' first biological child. The mean ages of husbands and wives, respectively, were

28.7 (SD = 4.4) and 27.2 (SD = 4.0). Self-described ethnicity for wives and husbands, respectively, was 92.0% and 85.0% White; 3.7% and 5.0% Asian American; 3.7% and 5.5% African American; 0% and 3.7% Hispanic/Latino; and 0.62% and 0.62% Other. The highest education for husbands and wives, respectively, was 11% and 6% high school, 28% and 21% partial college or post-high school education, 42% and 46% college degree, and 19% and 27% graduate/professional degree. Household income at pregnancy was broadly distributed as follows: 8% at $0–$25,000, 29% at $25–50,000, 30% at $50–75,000, 19% at $75,000–100,000, and 13% at greater than $100,000. Couples in the sample were married an average of 2.7 years, in a relationship for about 5.9 years and had cohabited for about 3.5 years; 53% had cohabited prior to marriage. The self-reported religious affiliation for wives was 35% non-denominational Christian, 31% Protestant, 27% Catholic, 4% None, 3% Other, and 0.6% Jewish, and for husbands was 30% Protestant, 29% non-denominational Christian, 27% Catholic, 7% None, 6% Other, and 0.6% Jewish; using these categories, 55% of couples reported same religious affiliation. More broadly, 85% of the pairs reported being affiliated with the same general religious tradition (i.e., Christian, Jewish, Muslim, Other, or No affiliation). Couples were no more involved in organized religion than other married U.S. couples with biological offspring based on national norms (National Survey of Family Growth) of wives' religious attendance (Mahoney et al. 2009).

2.2. Procedures

Couples were drawn from a mid-sized, Midwestern city and surrounding suburban and rural communities, and recruited primarily from childbirth classes (64%), with the rest responding to announcements posted in medical offices, retail locations or newspapers (14%), word of mouth referrals (15%) or direct mail (8%). Inclusionary criteria were that spouses: (1) were married, (2) pregnant with each individual's first biological child, and (3) both spoke English.

Data were collected in couples' homes. Each spouse read and completed consent forms for the project, which was approved by the university's Institutional Review Board. The couples participated in a 10 min, videotaped, emotionally focused interaction (details to follow), and each spouse completed questionnaires, with a research assistant present to answer questions and to monitor that spouses independently answered items. Couples were assessed in approximately their 9th month of pregnancy (T1) and re-assessed three more times over the course of the next year: at four (T2), seven (T3), and thirteen months (T4) after the first visit; the infants at these respective time points were thus approximately 3, 6 and 12 months old. Couples were paid $75.00, $100.00, $100.00, and $125.00 for their participation in waves 1–4, respectively. Relatively little participation attrition occurred, with 164 of the 178 couples who participated during pregnancy completing all four waves.

2.3. Participant Reported Measures of Major Variables

2.3.1. Sanctification of Marriage

To assess the sanctification of marriage during pregnancy, we revised the 20-item measure from Mahoney et al. (1999) so that: (a) 10 items used full sentences rather than single adjectives to assess whether the spouse viewed the marriage as having sacred qualities (i.e., non-theistic sanctification) without reference to a deity (e.g., My marriage is ... "sacred to me," "seems like a miracle to me," "part of a larger spiritual plan"), and (b) ten items assessed the extent to which the participants agreed that the marriage was a manifestation of God (i.e., theistic sanctification) with prior items about involvement in religious groups omitted (e.g., "God played a role in how I ended up being married to my spouse," "I sense God's presence in my relationship with my spouse"). Since different people use different terms to refer to "God," instructions asked participants to substitute their own word for God as needed. Each spouse rated items on a 7-point Likert scale ranging from 1 (strongly disagree) to 7 (strongly agree). In this study, each spouse's responses were summed and then averaged for analyses (for husbands, item M = 5.22, SD = 1.34; for wives, item M = 5.45, SD = 1.29) with alpha coefficients of 0.97 for both. This study thus builds on previous research on the original sanctification of marriage scales that found high internal consistency and evidence of convergent and construct validity (Mahoney et al. 1999).

2.3.2. Spiritual Intimacy

To assess spiritual intimacy during pregnancy, we modified four items from a 20-item index of spiritual disclosure previously used with college students (Brelsford and Mahoney 2008) so each spouse answered two items about disclosure by self and two items about the spouse's disclosure. We created four new items so each spouse answered two items about support by self and two items about the spouse's support. Thus, each spouse answered a total of four items about spiritual intimacy skills used by the self: "I feel safe being completely open and honest with my spouse about my faith," "I tend to keep my spiritual side private and separate from my marriage (reverse scored)," "I try not to be judgmental or critical when my spouse shares his/her ideas about spirituality," and "I try to be supportive when my spouse discloses spiritual questions or struggles," and four items about the partner's spiritual intimacy skills: "My spouse doesn't disclose her/his thoughts or feelings about spirituality with me," (reverse scored), "My spouse shares his/her spiritual questions or struggles with me," "My spouse really knows how to listen when I talk about my spiritual needs, thoughts, and feelings," and "My spouse is supportive when I reveal my spiritual questions or struggles to her/him." Items were rated on a Likert-scale from "not at all" (0) to "a great deal" (3). Husbands' and wives' ratings about each spouse were summed and averaged to create joint reports of each spouse's spiritual intimacy skills for analyses (for husbands, item M = 2.25, SD = 0.47; for wives, item M = 2.33, SD = 0.42) with alpha coefficients of 0.73 and 0.67, respectively.

2.4. Spouses' Observed Emotional Intimacy Skills

2.4.1. Eliciting and Videotaping Marital Interactions

Spouses were asked to talk with one another about their respective emotions of vulnerability, anxiety, worry, or insecurity about the pregnancy and becoming a new parent at each time point. To prime the couple for the interaction, research assistants provided each spouse with a list of 18–23 common questions or concerns at each time point about pregnancy or being a new parent that could potentially trigger such emotions. They asked spouses to read the list, mentally reflect on, and jot down notes on the back of the checklist on their own personal feelings of vulnerability or self-doubt for a few minutes to prepare to talk to their spouse about those feelings. Once both partners indicated they were ready to talk to one another, research assistants turned on video equipment and left the couple alone for ten minutes to talk to one another.

2.4.2. Observational Coding

Four separate teams (T1, T2, T3, T4) of three research assistants coded the four waves of videotaped marital interactions using a coding system that incorporated aspects of the System for Coding Interactions in Dyads (SCID) by Neena Malik and Kristin Lindahl (2000, as cited in Malik and Lindahl 2004) as well as the Intimacy Coding System by Marina Dorian and James Cordova (1999, as cited in Dorian and Cordova 2004), and the Emotion Skills Coding System by Shilagh Mirgain and James Cordova (Mirgain and Cordova 2003). Both sets of researchers gave permission for their systems to be modified for the purposes of this study. The original four codes from the Intimacy Coding System were used, but renamed as follows: Self Disclosure, Positive Support toward the Partner, Affection-Warmth-Display of Positive Emotions, and Negativity toward the Partner. The specific codes from the Emotion Skills Coding System and the SCID were used to supplement the content of the coding manual for the first three codes. All three coders on a team rated each spouse on each code on a 7-point scale ranging from 1 to 7 (1 = none to very low; 7 = very high). For analyses, Negativity toward Partner was reverse coded so a higher score meant less negativity. Table 1 displays the means, standard deviations, and ranges of the three coders' averaged ratings on each of the four codes and a total observed emotional intimacy score at each time point for each spouse. Coders' averaged ratings of spouses' behavior fell at the low to moderate end for positivity and low end for negativity of the rating scale. Not displayed are intercorrelations among the four measured marital regressors at each time point, which ranged from Pearson correlations equal to 0.18 to 0.36 for wives and 0.17 to 0.43 for husbands.

Table 1. Descriptive Information for Predictor Variable: Observed Emotional Intimacy.

Variable	Time Point	Time Point		SD		Intraclass Correlation
		Husbands	Wives	Husbands	Wives	Coefficients
Positive Self-Disclosure	T1	4.17	4.81	1.36	1.09	0.85
	T2	2.90	3.57	1.02	1.11	0.85
	T3	3.58	4.35	1.18	1.14	0.89
	T4	3.34	4.15	1.10	1.18	0.93
Positive Support	T1	3.92	4.22	1.08	0.93	0.78
	T2	2.92	3.28	1.05	0.90	0.81
	T3	3.44	3.50	1.22	1.06	0.87
	T4	3.37	3.42	1.13	1.01	0.89
Negativity toward Partner Reverse scored	T1	6.40	6.58	0.91	0.72	0.85
	T2	5.46	5.88	1.29	1.46	0.85
	T3	5.62	5.86	1.31	1.25	0.91
	T4	5.92	6.00	1.23	1.20	0.94
Affection/Warmth	T1	3.97	4.17	1.16	1.05	0.83
	T2	3.13	3.45	1.22	1.70	0.87
	T3	3.77	3.96	1.31	1.23	0.89
	T4	3.84	4.02	1.13	1.05	0.92
Total Emotional Intimacy	T1	18.46	19.78	3.47	2.69	0.91
	T2	14.41	16.18	3.77	3.34	0.86
	T3	16.41	17.67	4.12	3.56	0.91
	T4	16.47	17.59	3.53	3.14	0.94

Table 2 also displays the intraclass correlation coefficients (ICC) that document the inter-rater reliability of coding teams. The ICCs for each code, collapsed across spouses, ranged as follows: positive self-disclosure = 0.85–0.93; positive support = 0.78–0.89; negativity = 0.85–0.94; and affection/warmth = 0.83–0.92. Combined emotional intimacy scores were used for primary analyses and the ICCs for these variables were T1 = 0.91, T2 = 0.86, T3 = 0.91, and T4 = 0.94. Intercorrelations between husbands' and wives' total emotional intimacy skills were $r = 0.58$ ($p < 0.001$) for T1, $r = 0.77$ ($p < 0.001$) for T2, $r = 0.76$ ($p < 0.001$) for T3, and $r = 0.68$ ($p < 0.001$) for T4.

Table 2. Bivariate Correlations between Major Study Variables at Each Time Point.

	Husbands' Observed Emotional Intimacy				Wives' Observed Emotional Intimacy			
	T1	T2	T3	T4	T1	T2	T3	T4
T1 Husbands' Self-Report Sanctification	0.23 **	0.17 *	0.20 **	0.22 **	0.15 †	0.13	0.13	0.20 *
T1 Wives' Self-Report Sanctification	0.08	0.08	0.11	0.13	0.12	0.10	0.08	0.15
T1 Joint-Report Husbands' Spiritual Intimacy	0.31 ***	0.35 ***	0.28 ***	0.27 ***	0.30 ***	0.30 ***	0.26 ***	0.27 ***
T1 Joint-Report Wives' Spiritual Intimacy	0.27 ***	0.35 ***	0.37 ***	0.30 ***	0.32 ***	0.37 ***	0.36 ***	0.37 ***

Note. † approached significance at 0.0524, * $p < 0.05$, ** $p < 0.01$, *** $p < 0.001$. All Pearson product-moment correlations coefficients represent a sample of $N = 164$.

2.5. Data Analytic Plan: Multilevel Dyadic-Discrepancy Approach for Growth Curve Modeling

To examine the major questions of this study, we used the multilevel dyadic-discrepancy approach for growth-curve modeling, using a linear mixed effects model (Fitzmaurice et al. 2004) on a transformed data set of multiple waves of data (Singer and Willett 2003). To facilitate comprehension of results, we next elaborate on this analytic approach. The dyadic-discrepancy aspect of the statistical model uses data from husbands and wives in the same model and thus allows for differences in trajectories between wives and husbands to be directly tested, which is not possible when trajectories are estimated in separate models for husbands and wives (Lyons and Sayer 2005). Specifically, a dummy code is added to the data matrix (−0.5 for husbands, and 0.5 for the wives), which represents a unit difference in the outcome variable between spouses and allows for detecting whether females are higher or lower than males in exhibiting intimacy skills. Furthermore, the dyadic-discrepancy approach allows the mean couple observed intimacy skills to be modeled and, if desired, for both the gender difference and the mean couple response to be modeled as functions of time and other covariates (DeMaris et al. 2011). The linear mixed effects model of the analytic approach is also useful in several ways. It allows some coefficients to be fixed, i.e., invariant, over all respondents. Other coefficients, e.g., the equation intercept and effects of time, are allowed to vary over respondents; they are considered to be random growth parameters. Because the model contains both fixed and random effects, the model is referred to as "mixed" (Fitzmaurice et al. 2004).

Furthermore, multilevel modeling allows for the analyses of two different levels of data. The first level of analysis examines within-individual change to describe each person's individual growth trajectory, and the second level asks about interindividual differences to determine the relationship between predictors and the shape of each person's individual growth trajectory (Singer and Willett 2003). This approach also rigorously addresses the issue of the degree of interdependence of husbands' and wives' behavior by controlling for the correlation among husbands' and wives' responses and adjusts the error variance for the interdependence of husband and wife outcomes within the same couple (Lyons and Sayer 2005). More technically, the level 1 model is an unconditional model containing only the effect of passing time. The very first step is to estimate a model containing only a random intercept. This provides the variance decomposition for the outcome; that is, the total variability in observed emotional intimacy skills between and within couples across couple, gender, measure, and time. Next is added the gender-of-spouse dummy. This model shows the average couple mean of intimacy skills and the average gender discrepancy in intimacy skills. Then the time effect is added and the model shows the initial couple mean of intimacy skills and how it changes with time (i.e., the slope/trajectory). Finally, at level 1, we add the potential interaction of the gender discrepancy with time (DeMaris et al. 2011). At level 2, a model can be created to include explanatory predictors of the dyadic discrepancy in intimacy skills and the trajectory of intimacy skills over time. Separate models can then be created to observe the impact of each S/R variable on the trajectory separately, and a final model can be created with both S/R variables to see if their individual effects persisted. Lastly, the same procedure is used to calculate the overall R-squared and the proportion of within couple variation accounted for by the trajectory over time. In summary, using this type of statistical model allowed us to examine how husbands' and wives' observed emotional intimacy skills changed across time, and whether the two S/R variables predicted the trajectories in spouses' behaviors. More examples of this model and explication of the mathematical equations can be found in Lyons and Sayer (2005) and DeMaris et al. (2011).

The observed data in this study were well suited for the analytic plan by: (1) having three or more waves of data, (2) an outcome whose values changes systematically across time, (3) a sensible metric for clocking time, and (4) the same observational coding system used reliably by independent teams of coders at each time point (considerations for when to use a multi-level model can be found in (Singer and Willett 2003)). In this study, there were a few technical video recording problems resulting in a few observations of the 164 cases not being video recorded or audio being lost at T1 ($N = 4$), at T3 ($N = 1$), and at T4 ($N = 7$). Our analytic model, however, accounted for this fairly low level of attrition because the mixed effects model is flexible in accommodating any degree of imbalance in longitudinal data and accounts for covariance among the repeated measures in a relatively parsimonious way by not requiring each participant to have the same number of observations or that the observations be measured the same number of times (Fitzmaurice et al. 2004).

To run analyses, the data matrix was structured as follows. First, it is routine in dyadic models to use parallel measures of the spouses' responses to survey items, or, in this study, the direct observations of the two partners' behaviors. This creates enough degrees of freedom to accurately estimate the measurement-error term in the first level of the model, while maintaining enough degrees of freedom for modeling the time trajectory in an appropriate manner, and sets up the creations of growth trajectories, as two data points per member of the dyad are needed to create regression lines (DeMaris et al. 2011). Parallel scales are created by observing participant responses (typically to survey items) with similar standard deviations, pairing them together, and then randomly assigning each item in the pair to a different subscale (A or B). The responses by each spouse consisted of observations of behavior by three raters on each team rating the four types of behavior for each spouse (i.e., 12 coded behaviors) at each of four time points rather than spouses' responses to survey items. Thus, parallel scales were created by observing standard deviations among all raters for all observed behaviors at each time point for each spouse, resulting in parallel scales (A or B) of six coded behaviors for husbands and wives separately for all four time points. Although this creates scales with different items at each time for husbands and wives, the parallelism is more important, as all items are assumed to be measuring the same underlying construct.

Additionally, the data had to be transformed into a person-period dataset which contained a separate record for each time period for each partner (Singer and Willett 2003). This study, therefore, had 2 measures, for each of the 2 spouses for each of the 4 time periods for 164 couples, for a total of $2 \times 2 \times 4 \times 164 = 2624$ observations total. Furthermore, all independent variables were grand-mean-centered and a time variable was created (0 for the first wave, and then 4, 7, and 13 representing the number of months since the initial wave of data was collected). Furthermore, a time squared variable was created to test for a quadratic effect of time. Additionally, as explained earlier, a code was created to measure the gender gap; this is similar to dummy coding in that it creates a unit difference that represents the discrepancy between husbands and wives while allowing for interpretation of other variables in terms of average effects across spouses (DeMaris et al. 2011). Once the data set was organized in the manner described above, the means of observed emotional intimacy skills of husbands and wives were plotted to determine the trajectory of the growth curve. The dyadic discrepancy mixed effects analyses were then done in multiple steps, and all analyses were completed using SAS and the PROC MIXED procedure.

3. Results

Preliminary analyses were conducted to observe whether demographic variables (each spouse's highest level of education, duration of marriage, and household income) were correlated with observed spouses' behaviors. Husbands' education was the only variable that was significant ($r = 0.27$ to $r = 0.44$ across the four time points, all at $p < 0.001$) and thus included in analyses. In addition, the magnitude of the bivariate correlations between spouses' self-reported sanctification of marriage and joint reports of spouses' spiritual intimacy at pregnancy was $r = 0.42$ ($p < 0.001$) for husbands and $r = 0.24$ ($p < 0.001$ for wives), indicating the two predictor variables were sufficiently independent to be treated as separate variables in analyses.

3.1. Descriptive Bivariate Correlations between Predictor and Criterion Measures

Table 2 displays the bivariate correlations between the two S/R variables and observed emotional intimacy skills at each time point for wives and husbands. Husbands' self-reports of sanctification at Time 1 were significantly correlated with all four time points of husband's observed skills, while only correlating with wives' observed skills at Time 4. No significant correlations emerged for wives' reports of sanctification of marriage with intimacy skills by either spouse. Joint reports of both spouses' spiritual intimacy were significantly correlated with both spouses observed emotional intimacy skills at all four time points.

3.2. Trajectory of Observed Emotional Intimacy Skills

As displayed in Figure 1, the shape of the trajectory in observed emotionally intimate behaviors was similar for both husbands and wives, and exhibited a pattern where behaviors decreased at Time 2, came back up again at Time 3, and stayed relatively stable from Time 3 to 4. Figure 1 displays the total means for husbands' and wives' parallel scales for each time point. The primary trend is concave, with a minimum emotional intimacy reached at Time 2, a trend that was consistent with theoretical expectation. We elected to capture this trend using a quadratic function of time in our growth-curve model. Although one might argue for a cubic function, the additional interpretational complexity of adding time-cubed to the model did not seem warranted, given that modeling the time trend was not the primary focus of the study. The quadratic function allowed us to adequately model the nonlinearity in time while preserving model parsimony and interpretability.

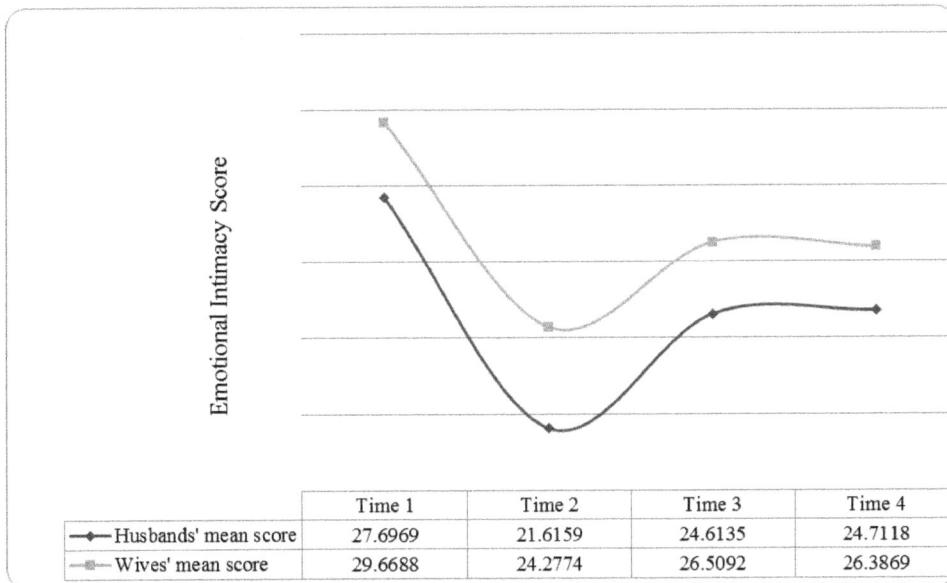

	Time 1	Time 2	Time 3	Time 4
Husbands' mean score	27.6969	21.6159	24.6135	24.7118
Wives' mean score	29.6688	24.2774	26.5092	26.3869

Figure 1. Growth trajectories of husbands' and wives' observed emotional intimacy at all four time points. Means are for parallel measures created for analyses.

3.3. Gender Difference in Emotional Intimacy Skills

Prior to taking the gender difference into account, an unconditional means model was run in order to observe the composition of variance in the model across measure, gender, and time. We found 41.9% of the variability in observed emotional intimacy skills to be between couples, while 58.1% was within couples, but across measure, gender, and time. Also, the variance parameter for the intercept was significant, so that there is significant variability in mean intimacy across couples. The grand mean emotional intimacy score over couples, gender, measure, and time was 25.66.

The next step was to add time and the gender difference in to the model. Significant variability was found in both couple mean observed emotional intimacy skills and the gender difference in observed emotional intimacy across couples. This is the variability that we tried to account for with predictors. The initial average couple mean emotional intimacy was 27.83 ($p < 0.0001$) and, on average, the gender difference at any given time is that wives are 2.05 units higher than husbands ($p < 0.0001$).

The next step was to add an interaction of time and time squared with the gender difference. In this model, the variance parameters were all significant; however, the fixed effects for the interactions were not significant. This indicates that the effect of time did not differ across genders (see Model 1 in Table 3). The interactions of the gender difference with time and time squared were therefore not included in the remaining models.

Table 3. Restricted maximum likelihood coefficient estimates (standard errors) for curvilinear mixed-effects models of emotional intimacy.

Explanatory Variable	Model 1	Model 2	Model 3	Model 4
Level 1 fixed effects				
Intercept	27.829 ***	20.477 ***	21.866 ***	21.683 ***
	(0.323)	(1.663)	(1.604)	(1.606)
Gender Gap	2.115 ***	1.945 ***	1.860 ***	1.820 ***
	(0.341)	(0.248)	(0.253)	(0.252)
Time (months)	−1.144 ***	−1.146 ***	−1.145 ***	−1.145 ***
	(0.100)	(0.100)	(0.100)	(0.100)
Time Squared (months)	0.082 ***	0.082 ***	0.082 ***	0.082 ***
	(0.008)	(0.008)	(0.008)	(0.008)
Gendergap x Time	0.072			
	(0.117)			
Gendergap x Time Squared	−0.009			
	(0.009)			
Level 2 fixed effects				
Husband's Education		1.300 ***	1.054 ***	1.086 ***
		(0.289)	(0.279)	(0.279)
Sanctification of Marriage		0.023 **		0.013
		(0.008)		(0.008)
Spiritual Intimacy			0.288 ***	0.253 ***
			(0.060)	(0.063)
Variance Parameters				
Intercept	13.898 ***	12.490 ***	11.431 ***	11.393 ***
	(1.910)	(1.775)	(1.664)	(1.658)
Gender Gap	6.587 ***	6.451 ***	6.795 ***	6.666 ***
	(1.105)	(1.092)	(1.142)	(1.128)
Time (months)	1.071 ***	1.072 ***	1.074 ***	1.073 ***
	(0.182)	(0.182)	(0.182)	(0.182)
Time Squared (months)	0.006 ***	0.006 ***	0.006 ***	0.006 ***
	(0.001)	(0.001)	(0.001)	(0.001)
Level 1 error	13.282 ***	13.286 ***	13.286 ***	13.285 ***
	(0.428)	(0.428)	(0.428)	(0.428)

Note. ** $p < 0.05$, *** $p < 0.001$.

3.4. Sanctification and Spiritual Intimacy Predicting Observed Emotional Intimacy Skills

After completing unconditional models, the next step was to conduct analyses to determine the relationship between spiritual variables during pregnancy and observed emotional intimacy skills over time. Each spiritual predictor variable was added into its own model prior to creating a final full model. In Model 2, which included sanctification of marriage, all variance parameters and fixed effects were significant. A significant effect emerged for sanctification of marriage, so that sanctification increases average observed emotional intimacy behaviors at any given time (see Model 2 in Table 3).

A similar finding was found in Model 3 when just spiritual intimacy was entered in the model. Again, all variance parameters and fixed effects were significant, so that spiritual intimacy increased average observed emotional intimacy at any given time point. Furthermore, the BIC was the lowest for this model compared to all other models, indicating that it is the best model out of all that were analyzed. Furthermore, interaction effects were tested between the gender gap with spiritual intimacy and with sanctification; these interactions were not significant and therefore not in the final model. Model 4 included sanctification and spiritual intimacy; the significant effect of sanctification disappeared when included in the model alongside spiritual intimacy. Although the two spiritual constructs were not highly correlated (i.e., $r = 0.42$ for husbands and $r = 0.24$ for wives), spiritual intimacy uniquely predicted observed emotional intimacy after controlling for sanctification.

4. Discussion

This longitudinal study investigated whether the sanctification of marriage and spiritual intimacy during pregnancy predicted married heterosexual parents' emotionally intimate dialogues about becoming a first-time parent across the TtP. In general, both spouses displayed a curvilinear trajectory in their observed intimacy skills, with both spouses' disclosures about their emotional vulnerabilities and supportive responses to each other declining between late pregnancy and when the baby was 3 months old, then rising again when the baby was 6 months old, and remaining stable when the infant was 12 months old. Such a trajectory is similar to observational studies of couples' problem-solving interactions across the TtP where parents' communication skills when discussing their conflicts become less positive and more negative after the child is born (e.g., Houts et al. 2008; Trillingsgaard et al. 2014), although here wives consistently exhibited higher observed intimacy skills than their husbands. This gender effect mirrors studies where women report offering more emotional support to their husbands during the TtP (Yu et al. 2011; Knoll et al. 2007). More centrally, as expected, each spouse's self-report of sanctity of marriage and couples' joint reports of each spouses' spiritual intimacy skills during late pregnancy predicted higher observed emotional intimacy skills by each parent across the TtP, with no differences in these findings due to gender.

Our result that wives' and husbands' perceptions of their marriage being imbued with sacred qualities and/or a manifestation of God/higher power during pregnancy predicted their respective observed intimacy skills over the TtP reinforces prior studies suggesting that the sanctification of marriage can function as a resource that facilitates positive marital dynamics. For example, this S/R factor also predicts more observed warmth and collaboration and better problem-solving skills by both spouses when they discuss core marital conflicts using fixed effects modeling (Kusner et al. 2014) and structural equation modeling (Rauer and Volling 2015). Greater sanctity of marriage also buffers married first-time parents from marital distress typically associated with viewing oneself as under or over-benefitting in the union (DeMaris et al. 2010). Furthermore, greater sanctity of marriage has been repeatedly tied to greater subjective marital satisfaction, forgiveness, and sacrifice (e.g., Rusu et al. 2015; Sabey et al. 2014). Thus, the current study's findings echo theory and research on sanctification across multiple domains of life positing that viewing a union as sacred motivates people to invest effort to protect their bond, especially during times of stress (Mahoney 2013; Mahoney et al. 2013; Pargament et al. 2017).

Although fewer prior studies exist on spiritual intimacy, our findings also highlight the potential value of this dyadic S/R construct to facilitate spouses' willingness to share and listen supportively to one another's emotional vulnerabilities across the TtP. Spiritual intimacy involves discussing one's subjective views, needs, thoughts, and feelings about spirituality, which can leave one feeling vulnerable to scrutiny because disclosures about one's views about supernatural powers, existential concerns, and/or S/R communities can be difficult, if not impossible, to verify as ontologically or morally defensible (Brelsford and Mahoney 2008; Mahoney 2013). Like other family dyads (Brelsford and Mahoney 2008; Desrosiers et al. 2011), couples' ability to explore such sensitive topics in an open and supportive manner may foster a greater sense of trust, attachment, emotional safety, and togetherness or "we-ness." Such conversations during pregnancy may foster couples' willingness to engage in intimate dialogues about new parenthood where the optimal course of action in coping with an infant may also often be ambiguous and challenge deeply held values including choices tied to family life. Our results reinforce empirical findings from longitudinal studies where spiritual intimacy predicts better marital communication when first-time parents are observed discussing their core conflicts (Kusner et al. 2014) and less deterioration in marital and sexual satisfaction for newlyweds (Hernandez-Kane and Mahoney 2018).

Taking a step back, given the long-term risks to parents and offspring tied to deterioration in marital satisfaction and stability, researchers have called for the identification of adaptive dyadic coping mechanisms that may help couples better manage normative life stressors and thereby avoid the widespread declines in relational well-being due to the TtP and passage of time for childless couples (Mitnick et al. 2009). Effectively engaging in emotionally-focused intimate dialogues has clearly been identified as one important dyadic resource (Reis and Shaver 1988; Mirgain and Cordova 2007), and relational factors have been uncovered that facilitate such interactions. For example, higher self-reported mindful awareness (Wachs and Cordova 2007), compassionate love (Collins et al. 2014), and romantic competence encompassing psychological insightfulness, mutuality in balancing and maximizing both partners' needs, and emotion regulation (Davila et al. 2017) have been tied to observations of married or romantic partners' skillfulness in listening to and expressing supportive emotions across a variety of social support tasks. This study adds sanctification and spiritual intimacy as two specific S/R resources to the potential menu of potential adaptive dyadic resources that could, with more basic research, be candidates to integrate into educational programs to help couples cope with the TtP.

Delving further into the intricacies of intimacy interactions, being motivated to care about another person's well-being (i.e., empathic concern), not just possessing the ability to comprehend another person's distressing thoughts and feelings (i.e., empathic accuracy) may be critical in promoting interpersonal responsiveness. For instance, Winczewski et al. (2016) found that when a spouse exhibited high empathic concern during marital dialogues, higher empathic accuracy was associated with greater responsiveness to the partner; however, if the listener's empathic concern was low then his or her greater empathic accuracy predicted being less caring and responsive. Such moderator effects of empathic concern on links between empathic accuracy and responsiveness did not differ based on whether the couples engaged in a conflictual or supportive dialogue, nor were explained or moderated by relationship satisfaction. Building upon these findings, sanctification and spiritual intimacy may encompass two dyadic resources that facilitate empathic concern, accuracy, and responsiveness. Although neither S/R process could be deemed sufficient nor necessary for all couples, both factors may motivate many couples to care about their partner's well-being. That is, viewing marriage as a sacred bond or one's spouse as a special individual to share one's vulnerabilities about S/R matters could prompt spouses to be concerned about the other's distress and draw on such empathic insights for the benevolent goals to protect the partner and union from distress. Reciprocally, spouses may be more willing to share their emotional vulnerabilities, recognizing that lowering one's defenses when experiencing stressors offers a means to solicit support and bond with a spouse.

Finally, in this study, we explored the unique effects of sanctification and spiritual intimacy in predicting observed intimacy skills (see Table 3, Model 4). Spiritual intimacy contributed significantly to emotional intimacy after taking into account the sanctification of marriage, whereas the reverse was not true. This implies spiritual intimacy may partly or fully drive sanctification effects. Notably, higher engagement in organized religious groups by spouses in the past or present may help foster sanctification beliefs and pro-social relationship values and behaviors such as generosity and commitment (Wilcox and Dew 2016). Yet those who no longer or rarely attend religious services may benefit from being able and willing to engage in spiritual dialogues which, in turn, may reinforce (dis)beliefs in the sanctity of one's union. Thus, spiritual intimacy may be a construct that mediates sanctification effects, and facilitates relational well-being for couples who are and aren't highly embedded in religious groups. But to verify such speculations, our findings would need to be replicated and extended to couples from diverse backgrounds.

Limitations and Future Research Directions

The strengths of this study included using a longitudinal design to examine causal effects of couples reports of two S/R variables, direct observations of each spouse's emotional intimacy skills to rule out monomethod bias to account for results, and analytic strategies to address the interdependence of spouses' functioning. This study has limitations nonetheless. For practical reasons, we restricted our sample to heterosexual, married, first-time coparents in relatively short-duration and well-adjusted unions. We presume that greater sanctification and spiritual intimacy would likewise benefit unmarried, remarried, same-sex, cohabiting, or non-residential coparents who are generally satisfied with their unions. Notably, while the mean levels of both S/R resources are likely to be the most elevated for "traditional couples" (i.e., married heterosexuals with biological children), sanctification has been linked to greater relationship satisfaction for same-sex (Phillips et al. 2017) and cohabiting or dating couples (Henderson et al. 2018), and more parenting satisfaction for married and unmarried parents (Nelson and Uecker 2018). Nevertheless, this study's findings about both adaptive S/R factors need to be replicated within diverse families. Future work also needs to be done to identify S/R dyadic processes that would likely exacerbate distressed couples' difficulties (Goodman et al. 2013; Mahoney 2013). Like other pathological processes, the baserates of such processes are likely to be low and more prevalent in clinic-referred samples rather than generally satisfied couples. Our study was also limited to couples who married prior to the birth of both spouses' first biological child which represents a declining portion of all childbearing liaisons (Cherlin 2010). Such couples tend to be more affluent, well-educated, and likely to self-describe as Caucasian than unmarried and/or cohabiting coparents (Cherlin 2010). Consistent with US norms of married, heterosexual coparents, our spouses predominantly identified as Christian, but future work should verify the expectation that both constructs would operate similarly among more socioeconomically and religiously diverse samples (Goodman et al. 2013; Mahoney 2010). Finally, future studies could delve into couples' interpretations of items on both S/R measures and whether intimate dialogues about other sensitive and value-laden topics tied to family life (e.g., sexuality, politics) yield similar findings to spiritual intimacy.

Overall, this study adds to emerging research on adaptive S/R dyadic processes that may be helpful to many couples. Specifically, viewing a marital relationship as sacred and engaging in spiritually intimate dialogues appears to function as a resource that encourages first-time parents to sustain their emotional intimacy as they face the stressors of integrating an infant into their family unit. Both constructs longitudinally predicted wives' and husbands' skills in revealing and handling their partner's emotional vulnerabilities with care which, in turn, is likely to help protect and preserve their union as they travel down the challenging road of parenthood.

Author Contributions: The manuscript is based on the first author's dissertation. A.M. and K.I.P. conceived the broader project from data for this project was used. E.P. conceived and designed the study for her dissertation, chaired by A.M. with K.I.P. and A.D. as involved committee members. E.P. and A.D. analyzed the data; E.P., A.M., K.I.P. and A.D. co-authored the paper.

Funding: This research was supported by grants from the John Templeton Foundation (10976, 11604, 11605) and in part by the Center for Family and Demographic Research, Bowling Green State University, whose core funding is from the United States Department of Health and Human Services, National Institutes of Health, Eunice Kennedy Shriver National Institute of Child Health and Human Development (R24HD050959-01). There were no costs to publish this article in open access.

Conflicts of Interest: The authors declare no conflict of interest.

References

Bodenmann, Guy, Nathalie Meuwly, Janine Germann, Fridtjof W. Nussbeck, Markus Heinrichs, and Thomas N. Bradbury. 2015. Effects of Stress on the Social Support Provided by Men and Women in Intimate Relationships. *Psychological Science* 26: 1584–94. [CrossRef] [PubMed]

Bradbury, Thomas N., Frank D. Fincham, and Steven R. H. Beach. 2000. Research on the Nature and Determinants of Marital Satisfaction: A Decade in Review. *Journal of Marriage and the Family* 62: 964–80. [CrossRef]

Brelsford, Gina M., and Annette Mahoney. 2008. Spiritual Disclosure between Older Adolescents and Their Mothers. *Journal of Family Psychology* 22: 62–70. [CrossRef] [PubMed]

Cherlin, Andrew J. 2010. *The Marriage Go-Round: The State of Marriage and the Family in America Today*. New York: Vintage Books.

Collins, Nancy L., Heidi S. Kane, Molly A. Metz, Christena Cleveland, Cynthia Khan, Lauren Winczewski, Jeffrey Bowen, and Thery Prok. 2014. Psychological, Physiological, and Behavioral Responses to a Partner in Need: The Role of Compassionate Love. *Journal of Social and Personal Relationships* 31: 601–29. [CrossRef]

Cowan, Carolyn Pape, and Philip A. Cowan. 1992. *When Partners Become Parents: The Big Life Change for Couples*. New York: Basic Books.

Cox, Martha J., Blair Paley, Margaret Burchinal, and C. Chris Payne. 1999. Marital Perceptions and Interactions across the Transition to Parenthood. *Journal of Marriage and the Family* 61: 611–25. [CrossRef]

Davila, Joanne, Haley Wodarczyk, and Vickie Bhatia. 2017. Positive Emotional Expression among Couples: The Role of Romantic Competence. *Couple and Family Psychology: Research and Practice* 6: 94–105. [CrossRef]

DeMaris, Alfred, Annette Mahoney, and Kenneth I. Pargament. 2010. Sanctification of Marriage and General Religiousness as Buffers of the Effects of Marital Inequity. *Journal of Family Issues* 31: 1255–78. [CrossRef] [PubMed]

DeMaris, Alfred, Annette Mahoney, and Kenneth I. Pargament. 2011. Doing the Scut Work of Infant Care: Does Religiousness Encourage Father Involvement? *Journal of Marriage and Family* 73: 354–68. [CrossRef] [PubMed]

Desrosiers, Alethea, Brien S. Kelley, and Lisa A. Miller. 2011. Parent and peer relationships and relational spirituality in adolescents and young adults. *Psychology of Religion and Spirituality* 3: 39–54. [CrossRef]

Dew, Jeffrey, and W. Bradford Wilcox. 2011. If Momma Ain't Happy: Explaining Declines in Marital Satisfaction among New Mothers. *Journal of Marriage and Family* 73: 1–12. [CrossRef]

Don, Brian P., and Kristin D. Mickelson. 2014. Relationship Satisfaction Trajectories across the Transition to Parenthood among Low-risk Parents. *Journal of Marriage and Family* 76: 677–92. [CrossRef]

Dorian, Marina, and James V. Cordova. 2004. Coding Intimacy in Couples' Interactions. In *Couple Observational Coding Systems*. Edited by Patricia K. Kerig and Donald H. Baucom. Mahwah: Erlbaum, pp. 243–56.

Doss, Brian D., and Galena K. Rhoades. 2017. The Transition to Parenthood: Impact on Couples' Romantic Relationships. *Current Opinion in Psychology* 13: 25–28. [CrossRef] [PubMed]

Doss, Brian D., Galena K. Rhoades, Scott M. Stanley, and Howard J. Markman. 2009. The Effect of the Transition to Parenthood on Relationship Quality: An 8-Year Prospective Study. *Journal of Personality and Social Psychology* 96: 601–19. [CrossRef] [PubMed]

Ellison, Christopher G., Andrea K. Henderson, Norval D. Glenn, and Kristine E. Harkrider. 2011. Sanctification, Stress, and Marital Quality. *Family Relations: An Interdisciplinary Journal of Applied Family Studies* 60: 404–20. [CrossRef]

Falconier, Mariana K., Jeffrey B. Jackson, Peter Hilpert, and Guy Bodenmann. 2015. Dyadic Coping and Relationship Satisfaction: A Meta-Analysis. *Clinical Psychology Review* 42: 28–46. [CrossRef] [PubMed]

Fitzmaurice, Garrett M., Nan M. Laird, and James H. Ware. 2004. *Applied Longitudinal Analysis*. Hoboken: Wiley-Interscience.

Goodman, Michael A., David C. Dollahite, Loren D. Marks, and Emily Layton. 2013. Religious Faith and Transformational Processes in Marriage. *Family Relations: An Interdisciplinary Journal of Applied Family Studies* 62: 808–23. [CrossRef]

Greeff, Abraham P., and Hildegarde L. Malherbe. 2001. Intimacy and Marital Satisfaction in Spouses. *Journal of Sex & Marital Therapy* 27: 247–57. [CrossRef]

Hanley, Kaitlin E., Feea R. Leifker, Alysia Y. Blandon, and Amy D. Marshall. 2013. Gender Differences in the Impact of Posttraumatic Stress Disorder Symptoms on Community Couples' Intimacy Behaviors. *Journal of Family Psychology* 27: 525–30. [CrossRef] [PubMed]

Henderson, Andrea K., Christopher G. Ellison, and Norval D. Glenn. 2018. Religion and Relationship Quality among Cohabiting and Dating Couples. *Journal of Social Issues* 39: 1904–32. [CrossRef]

Hernandez-Kane, Krystal M., and Annette Mahoney. 2018. Sex through a Sacred Lens: Longitudinal Effects of Sanctification of Marital Sexuality. *Journal of Family Psychology* 32: 425–34. [CrossRef] [PubMed]

Holmes, Erin Kramer, Takayuki Sasaki, and Nancy L. Hazen. 2013. Smooth versus Rocky Transitions to Parenthood: Family Systems in Developmental Context. *Family Relations: An Interdisciplinary Journal of Applied Family Studies* 62: 824–37. [CrossRef]

Houts, Renate M., Kortnee C. Barnett-Walker, Blair Paley, and Martha J. Cox. 2008. Patterns of Couple Interaction during the Transition to Parenthood. *Personal Relationships* 15: 103–22. [CrossRef]

Karney, Benjamin R., and Thomas N. Bradbury. 1995. The Longitudinal Course of Marital Quality and Stability: A Review of Theory, Methods, and Research. *Psychological Bulletin* 118: 3–34. [CrossRef] [PubMed]

Kluwer, Esther S., and Matthew D. Johnson. 2007. Conflict Frequency and Relationship Quality across the Transition to Parenthood. *Journal of Marriage and Family* 69: 1089–106. [CrossRef]

Knoll, Nina, Rolf Kienle, Katharina Bauer, Bettina Pfüller, and Aleksandra Luszczynska. 2007. Affect and Enacted Support in Couples Undergoing In-vitro Fertilization: When Providing Is Better than Receiving. *Social Science & Medicine* 64: 1789–801. [CrossRef]

Kuhn, Rebekka, Thomas N. Bradbury, Fridtjof W. Nussbeck, and Guy Bodenmann. 2018. The Power of Listening: Lending an Ear to the Partner during Dyadic Coping Conversations. *Journal of Family Psychology* 32: 762–72. [CrossRef] [PubMed]

Kusner, Katherine G., Annette Mahoney, Kenneth I. Pargament, and Alfred DeMaris. 2014. Sanctification of Marriage and Spiritual Intimacy Predicting Observed Marital Interactions across the Transition to Parenthood. *Journal of Family Psychology* 28: 604–14. [CrossRef] [PubMed]

Lyons, Karen S., and Aline G. Sayer. 2005. Longitudinal Dyad Models in Family Research. *Journal of Marriage and Family* 67: 1048–60. [CrossRef]

Mahoney, Annette. 2010. Religion in Families, 1999–2009: A Relational Spirituality Framework. *Journal of Marriage and Family* 72: 805–27. [CrossRef] [PubMed]

Mahoney, Annette. 2013. The Spirituality of Us: Relational Spirituality in the Context of Family Relationships. In *APA Handbook of Psychology, Religion, and Spirituality: Context, Theory, and Research*. APA Handbooks in Psychology. Edited by Kenneth I. Pargament, Julie J. Exline and James W. Jones. Washington, DC: American Psychological Association, Vol. 1, pp. 365–89. [CrossRef]

Mahoney, Annette, and Chris J. Boyatzis. 2019. Transition to Parenthood. In *Handbook of Parenting*, 5th ed. Edited by Marc H. Bornstein. New York: Routledge.

Mahoney, Annette, Kenneth I. Pargament, Tracey Jewell, Aaron B. Swank, Eric Scott, Erin Emery, and Mark Rye. 1999. Marriage and the Spiritual Realm: The Role of Proximal and Distal Religious Constructs in Marital Functioning. *Journal of Family Psychology* 13: 321–38. [CrossRef]

Mahoney, Annette, Kenneth I. Pargament, Nalini Tarakeshwar, and Aaron B. Swank. 2008. Religion in the Home in the 1980s and 1990s: A Meta-Analytic Review and Conceptual Analysis of Links between Religion, Marriage, and Parenting. *Journal of Family Psychology* 15: 559–96. [CrossRef]

Mahoney, Annette, Kenneth I. Pargament, and Alfred DeMaris. 2009. Couples Viewing Marriage and Pregnancy through the Lens of the Sacred: A Descriptive Study. *Research in the Social Scientific Study of Religion* 20: 1–45. [CrossRef]

Mahoney, Annette, Kenneth I. Pargament, and Krystal M. Hernandez. 2013. Heaven on Earth: Beneficial Effects of Sanctification for Individual and Interpersonal Well-Being. In *The Oxford Handbook of Happiness*. Oxford Library of Psychology. Edited by Susan A. David, Ilona Boniwell and Amanda Conley Ayers. New York: Oxford University Press, pp. 397–410.

Malik, Neena M., and Kristin M. Lindahl. 2004. System for Coding Interactions in Dyads. In *Couple Observational Coding Systems*. Edited by Patricia K. Kerig and Donald H. Baucom. Mahwah: Erlbaum, pp. 173–88.

Manne, Sharon, and Hoda Badr. 2010. Intimacy Processes and Psychological Distress among Couples Coping with Head and Neck or Lung Cancers. *Psycho-Oncology* 19: 941–54. [CrossRef] [PubMed]

Meeks, Brenda S., Susan S. Hendrick, and Clyde Hendrick. 1998. Communication, Love and Relationship Satisfaction. *Journal of Social and Personal Relationships* 15: 755–73. [CrossRef]

Mirgain, Shilagh A., and James V. Cordova. 2003. The development and preliminary validation of the Emotional Skillful ness Coding System. Poster session presented at the Annual Meeting of the Association for the Advancement of Behavioral Therapy, Boston, MA, USA.

Mirgain, Shilagh A., and James V. Cordova. 2007. Emotion Skills and Marital Health: The Association between Observed and Self-Reported Emotion Skills, Intimacy, and Marital Satisfaction. *Journal of Social and Clinical Psychology* 26: 983–1009. [CrossRef]

Mitnick, Danielle M., Richard E. Heyman, and Amy M. Slep. 2009. Changes in Relationship Satisfaction across the Transition to Parenthood: A Meta-analysis. *Journal of Family Psychology* 23: 848–52. [CrossRef] [PubMed]

Nelson, Justin J., and Jeremy E. Uecker. 2018. Are Religious Parents More Satisfied Parents? Individual-and Couple-Level Religious Correlates of Parenting Satisfaction. *Journal of Family Issues* 39: 1770–96. [CrossRef]

Nock, Steven L., Laura A. Sanchez, and James D. Wright. 2008. *Covenant Marriage: The Movement to Reclaim Tradition in Marriage*. Piscataway: Rutgers University Press.

Osgarby, Susan M., and W. Kim Halford. 2013. Couple Relationship Distress and Observed Expression of Intimacy during Reminiscence about Positive Relationship Events. *Behavior Therapy* 44: 686–700. [CrossRef] [PubMed]

Pargament, Kenneth I., and Annette Mahoney. 2005. Sacred Matters: Sanctification as a Vital Topic for the Psychology of Religion. *International Journal for the Psychology of Religion* 15: 179–98. [CrossRef]

Pargament, Kenneth I., Doug Oman, Julie Pomerleau, and Annette Mahoney. 2017. Some Contributions of a Psychological Approach to the Study of the Sacred. *Religion* 47: 718–44. [CrossRef]

Patrick, Shawn, James N. Sells, Fran G. Giordano, and Toni R. Tollerud. 2007. Intimacy, Differentiation, and Personality Variables as Predictors of Marital Satisfaction. *The Family Journal* 15: 359–67. [CrossRef]

Petts, Richard. 2018. Paternity Leave, Father Involvement, and Parental Conflict: The Moderating Role of Religious Participation. *Religions* 9: 289. [CrossRef] [PubMed]

Phillips, Russell E., David Kalp, Michael Lucci, Alex Maccarelli, Sierrah Avant, David Cenkner, and Rachel Herndon. 2017. Initial Validation of Measures of Sanctification in Same-Sex Romantic Relationships and Sexual Behavior. *Journal for the Scientific Study of Religion* 56: 836–51. [CrossRef]

Pilkington, Pamela D., Lisa C. Milne, Kathryn E. Cairns, James Lewis, and Thomas A. Whelan. 2015. Modifiable partner factors associated with perinatal depression and anxiety: A systematic review and meta-analysis. *Journal of Affective Disorders* 178: 165–80. [CrossRef] [PubMed]

Pistrang, Nancy, Anna Picciotto, and Chris Barker. 2001. The communication of empathy in couples during the transition to parenthood. *Journal of Community Psychology* 29: 615–36. [CrossRef]

Porter, Laura S., Donald H. Baucom, Francis J. Keefe, and Emily S. Patterson. 2012. Reactions to a Partner-assisted Emotional Disclosure Intervention: Direct Observation and Self-report of Patient and Partner Communication. *Journal of Marital and Family Therapy* 38: 284–95. [CrossRef]

Rauer, Amy, and Brenda Volling. 2015. The Role of Relational Spirituality in Happily-Married Couples' Observed Problem-Solving. *Psychology of Religion and Spirituality* 7: 239–49. [CrossRef]

Reis, Harry T., and Phillip Shaver. 1988. Intimacy as an Interpersonal Process. In *Handbook of Personal Relationships: Theory, Research and Interventions*. Edited by Steve E. Duck, Dale F. Hay, Stevan E. Hobfoll, William E. Ickles and Barbara M. Montgomery. Oxford: Wiley, pp. 367–89.

Rholes, W. Steven, Jamie L. Kohn, and Jeffry A. Simpson. 2014. A Longitudinal Study of Conflict in New Parents: The Role of Attachment. *Personal Relationships* 21: 1–21. [CrossRef]

Rusu, Petruta P., Peter Hilpert, Steven R. H. Beach, Maria N. Turliuc, and Guy Bodenmann. 2015. Dyadic Coping Mediates the Association of Sanctification with Marital Satisfaction and Well-Being. *Journal of Family Psychology* 29: 843–49. [CrossRef] [PubMed]

Ryan, Rebecca M., and Christina M. Padilla. 2019. Transition to Parenthood. In *Handbook of Parenting*, 3rd ed. Edited by Marc H. Bornstein. New York: Routledge, pp. 513–55.

Sabey, Allen K., Amy J. Rauer, and Jakob F. Jensen. 2014. Compassionate Love as a Mechanism Linking Sacred Qualities of Marriage to Older Couples' Marital Satisfaction. *Journal of Family Psychology* 28: 594–603. [CrossRef] [PubMed]

Schoppe-Sullivan, Sarah J., Lauren E. Altenburger, Meghan A. Lee, Daniel J. Bower, and Claire M. Kamp Dush. 2015. Who Are the Gatekeepers? Predictors of Maternal Gatekeeping. *Parenting: Science and Practice* 15: 166–86. [CrossRef] [PubMed]

Singer, Judith D., and John B. Willett. 2003. *Applied Longitudinal Data Analysis: Modeling Change and Event Occurrence*. New York: Oxford University Press. [CrossRef]

Sullivan, Kieran T., Lauri A. Pasch, Matthew D. Johnson, and Thomas N. Bradbury. 2010. Social Support, Problem Solving, and the Longitudinal Course of Newlywed Marriage. *Journal of Personality and Social Psychology* 98: 631–44. [CrossRef] [PubMed]

Trillingsgaard, Tea, Katherine J. W. Baucom, and Richard E. Heyman. 2014. Predictors of Change in Relationship Satisfaction during the Transition to Parenthood. *Family Relations: An Interdisciplinary Journal of Applied Family Studies* 63: 667–79. [CrossRef]

Uecker, Jeremy E., and Brian J. Willoughby. 2018. Joint Religiosity and Married Couples' Sexual Satisfaction. *Psychology of Religion and Spirituality*. [CrossRef]

Wachs, Karen, and James V. Cordova. 2007. Mindful Relating: Exploring Mindfulness and Emotion Repertoires in Intimate Relationships. *Journal of Marital and Family Therapy* 33: 464–81. [CrossRef] [PubMed]

Wiebe, Stephanie A., and Susan M. Johnson. 2016. A Review of the Research in Emotionally Focused Therapy for Couples. *Family Process* 55: 390–407. [CrossRef] [PubMed]

Wilcox, W. Bradford, and Jeffrey Dew. 2016. The Social and Cultural Predictors of Generosity in Marriage: Gender Egalitarianism, Religiosity, and Familism. *Journal of Family Issues* 37: 97–118. [CrossRef]

Winczewski, Lauren A., Jeffrey D. Bowen, and Nancy L. Collins. 2016. Is Empathic Accuracy Enough to Facilitate Responsive Behavior in Dyadic Interaction? Distinguishing Ability from Motivation. *Psychological Science* 27: 394–404. [CrossRef] [PubMed]

Yu, Mansoon, Jane A. McElory, Linda F. C. Bullock, and Kevin D. Everett. 2011. Unique Perspectives of Women and their Partners using the Prenatal Psychosocial Profile Scale. *Journal of Advanced Nursing* 67: 1767–78. [CrossRef] [PubMed]

religions

MDPI

Article

Religious Activities, Christian Media Consumption and Marital Quality among Protestants

Joe D. Wilmoth * and Muhammad Riaz

School of Human Sciences, Mississippi State University, Starkville, MS 39762, USA; mr2062@msstate.edu
* Correspondence: Joe.Wilmoth@msstate.edu; Tel.: +1-662-325-1799

Received: 14 January 2019; Accepted: 13 February 2019; Published: 18 February 2019

check for
updates

Abstract: Although associations between religiosity and marital quality have been demonstrated in previous research, mechanisms still remain unclear. Three 3-step hierarchical multiple regression analyses were conducted to determine whether 10 individual, dyadic or family religious activities or uses of 7 forms of Christian media predicted positive relationship quality, negative interaction and intimate partner violence in a sample of North American Protestants. Joint spousal and family religious activities predicted higher levels of relationship quality. Individual activities, such as reading the Bible, and parent-child activities, such as praying with children and discussing Christians values with children, predicted lower levels of relationship quality. Listening to Christian talk radio and viewing Christian websites or blogs predicted lower levels of relationship quality. The authors inferred that individuals in low-quality relationships use activities such as reading the Bible, listening to Christian talk radio, and viewing Christian websites and blogs to seek information to improve relationships or promote healthy adaptation. Similarly, the authors speculated that praying with children and discussing spiritual values with them were seen as interventionary measures to protect children when parents were in low-quality relationships.

Keywords: marital quality; religious practices; Christian media consumption; intimate partner violence

1. Introduction

The relationship between religion and marital quality is complex (Atkins and Kessel 2008; Eggebeen and Dew 2009; Vaaler et al. 2009), but generally religious behavior and values have been associated with higher marital quality (Fincham et al. 2011; Mahoney 2010; Mahoney et al. 2001). The couples that practice their religion in every aspect of life tend to improve their relationship not only with God but also their spouse (Chaney et al. 2016). However, findings sometimes are inconsistent, and questions remain concerning the mechanisms that explain this relationship. This study expands the existing research by examining the relationship between religious activities and marital quality among North American Protestants. Distinctive contributions to the literature include the exploration of how the consumption of Christian media is related to marital quality and how religious activities and Christian media consumption are related to Intimate Partner Violence (IPV).

More than two decades ago, Fincham and Linfield (1997) observed that marital quality includes both positive and negative dimensions that are distinct and should be measured separately, and Fincham and colleagues have created validated scales that measure the constructs separately (Rogge et al. 2017). A negative interaction in relationships has been associated with lower satisfaction and higher rates of relationship dissolution (see Gottman and Notarius 2000 for review). Our study explores the association between negative interaction and religious activities, including the use of Christian media.

Religious media have received increased attention (Campbell 2017; Cheong 2017). According to the Christian Bookseller's Association (2017), sales of books, Bibles, music and other products exceed $5 billion. An increased use of social media and the Internet by churches also is reported (Newman and Benchener 2008). However, there is little or no existing research about how the consumption of these media—often even empirically-based content—is related to marital quality. For example, Doss et al. (2009) noted they were not aware of research addressing the effectiveness of relationship-themed self-help books (secular or sectarian) designed to enhance marriages or to help with specific relationship problems. Our study helps to address the gap of the knowledge related to Christian media and marital quality.

Some research is related to this topic incidentally rather than explicitly. A few studies have looked at the effects of various media on relationships, but we could find none that specifically explored the Christian media variables in our study. For example, some studies examine the relationship between television viewing and marital quality. Robinson and Martin (2008) found that happier people report more social activity and more religious involvement and newspaper reading but that more television viewing was associated with lower happiness, controlling for marital status. Various streams of research look at the relationship between listening to music and a variety of well-being measures (e.g., quality of sleep, (Urponen et al. 1988) and anxiety among dementia patients (Sung et al. 2010)), but we could find no studies that examined marital quality and listening to Christian music.

Based on their recent study, DeAngelis et al. (2018) observed that "readers approach scripture with preconceived biases conditioned by life experiences and other social constraints" (p. 12). Thus, people will turn to scripture for a variety of reasons and with varied perspectives based, in part, on their own needs. For example, they found that respondents with poor physical health were more likely to read scripture to find insight into attaining health. Their findings suggest that reading scripture, and perhaps using other Christian media, could be a help-seeking behavior that also could be relevant for individuals in distressed marriages looking for insight on improving marital quality.

As part of a larger longitudinal study, Doss et al. (2009) examined help-seeking behaviors among 213 couples that had been recruited by religious organizations to receive one of two forms of a relationship education program. Although the participants were recruited by religious organizations, the resources they sought out were not necessarily Christian in orientation. The researchers framed their study in terms of where couples sought help when they faced relationship challenges. Among the categories of help-seeking, books (cf., marital therapy and workshops/retreats) were the most commonly used ($n = 49$). The authors found that reading self-help books with relationship themes reflected help-seeking for individuals in distressed marriages. These findings would suggest that the consumption of Christian media, specifically books, is a help-seeking behavior for individuals in low-quality relationships.

There has been increased research regarding the effect of technology use on relationships (e.g., Roberts and Meredith 2016; Shen 2015; Padilla-Walker et al. 2012). Kerkhof et al. (2011) found that compulsive Internet use predicts lower levels of marital quality, though not vice versa. Several studies examine the effectiveness of formal Internet-based relationship education programs. Duncan et al. (2009) compared the effectiveness of web-based marriage and relationship education with traditional face-to-face formats. They found that both approaches produced positive changes compared to the control group and that there was no difference in the amount of change between the intervention approaches. Several studies have examined the effectiveness of a computer-based preventive intervention (ePREP) on IPV (Braithwaite and Fincham 2007; Braithwaite and Fincham 2009; Braithwaite and Fincham 2011; Braithwaite and Fincham 2014). In each case, the authors determined that an online intervention could be an effective means of reducing the incidence or severity of IPV. Although this research associates Internet use with a higher marital quality, the programs in these studies differ from our variables in that they are (1) structured, couple focused and empirically based and (2) not explicitly Christian.

IPV is a serious problem in the United States and internationally, but research regarding IPV in Protestant churches is limited. According to a 2015 data brief from the Centers for Disease Control and Prevention (Smith et al. 2018), more than 30 percent of both women and men have experienced physical violence in the context of intimate relationships. The criteria for IPV are not universal and can include sexual violence, physical violence, stalking and psychological violence. The data for our study are based on responses to this question: "Have there been instances of pushing, grabbing, shoving, hitting and/or slapping within your relationship in the last twelve months?"

There has been little research related to religion and IPV. Ellison et al. (1999) found that regular attendance at religious services was associated with lower rates of IPV, though dissimilarity in religious views and practice were associated with higher rates of IPV. More recently, Ellison et al. (2007) found that church attendance protected against IPV, especially for African-American and Hispanic men. Brinkerhoff et al. (1992) determined that religion had little or no relation to spousal violence. Todhunter and Deaton (2010) explored whether nine religiosity variables from Wave III of the National Longitudinal Study of Adolescent Health (Add Health) influenced male-perpetrated IPV. They found no predictive model for Christian male-perpetrated IPV and questioned the merit of focusing on religious or spiritual values in faith-based interventions aimed at male batterers. Our study examines some of the same variables but also looks at the relationship of Christian media consumption among Protestants.

More than 40 percent of the U.S. population identifies with Protestant churches (Pew Research Center 2015), making research on this population of continued importance. For this particular study, which measures traditional religious practices such as church attendance, Bible reading and prayer, this population is important because of the emphasis on these behaviors among Protestants. For example, compared to Catholics, Protestants are 25 percent more likely to attend services at least weekly and are 153 percent more likely to participate in prayer or scripture study groups (Pew Research Center). The use of Christian media also is more common among Protestants: Compared to Catholics, Protestants are 52 percent more likely to watch religious television, 87 percent more likely to listen to religious talk radio, 145 percent more likely to listen to Christian rock music and 80 percent more likely to share their own faith online (Pew Research Center 2014).

We suggest that the Relational Spirituality Framework (Mahoney 2010) is an appropriate lens through which to view our study. This framework "discriminates three stages of family relationships over time: (a) formation, or the creation and structure of family relationships; (b) maintenance, or processes to conserve family relationships; and (c) transformation, or fundamental changes in the structure or processes of distressed family relationships" (p. 807). Depending on the relationship and individual histories, participant experiences potentially could fall within any of these three states. For example, for engaged or newly married couples, religious behaviors and media consumption could be part of the process of building a solid foundation for a healthy, lasting marriage. For more than a fifth of our participants, those that have been married 10–15 years, these behaviors could be approached as a way to maintain or promote marital satisfaction and stability. An individual experiencing IPV may utilize religious or media resources to leave a distressed marriage or to seek positive transformation from distressed to satisfying. In this vein, the same behavior could be enacted from entirely different motivations by different people in different circumstances. For one participant, discussing the Bible with a spouse could be an eagerly anticipated activity that reinforces marital satisfaction, whereas for someone else the discussion could be an ongoing platform for conflict or even violence. Similarly, one individual could use social media to express fond memories or delightful experiences from a satisfying marriage, while others might seek out advice on Christian websites about how to extricate themselves from a dangerous relationship.

Based on previous research and considering the Relational Spirituality Framework, we anticipate the following general findings from the analysis of our data collected from North American Protestants:

Hypothesis 1. *Higher levels of participation in religious-related activities will predict a higher level of positive marital quality, a lower level of negative interaction and a lower level of IPV.*

Hypothesis 2. *Higher levels of Christian media consumption will predict a lower level of positive marital quality, higher levels of negative interaction and higher levels of IPV.*

2. Materials and Methods

This study utilizes secondary data from the Family Needs Survey administered during 2012 and 2013 by FamilyLife as a service to Protestant churches to assess the health of families in individual congregations (Gritzon 2013). Using this relatively large but nonrandom sample ($N = 6613$), we examine the relationship of individual and dyadic spiritual activities to marital quality. To protect the confidentiality of the local churches, data were provided to the researchers without identifying information. Thus, the location, size and specific denomination of the congregations are not known. FamilyLife reported to the researchers that the data include diversity in denominations, location, geography and size and represent a variety of Protestant denominations from throughout North America. Use of the data was secured through a license with FamilyLife. Since these were existing data, the authors had no input into the formulation of items included in the survey. However, the dataset includes multiple variables of possible interest to scholars of religion and families, including some widely used and psychometrically validated scales. Institutional Review Board approval was granted by the Office for Research Compliance at Mississippi State University (IRB-16-443).

The majority of the participants were female ($n = 4001$; 60.5%), and the modal age category was 50–59 years ($n = 1448$; 21.9%). The number of years married was more widely dispersed, with the most common ranges being 10–19 years ($n = 1213$; 22.2%) and more than 40 years ($n = 1321$; 24.2%). The most common relationship status was in a first marriage ($n = 4274$; 64.6%), with other statuses including engaged ($n = 88$; 1.3%), cohabiting ($n = 51$; 0.8%), widowed ($n = 372$; 5.6%), separated ($n = 32$; 0.5%), divorced ($n = 360$; 5.4%) and remarried ($n = 988$; 14.9%). Some commonly used demographic variables such as ethnicity/race, education and income were not included in the data.

See Tables 1 and 2 for summaries of all the variables. A correlation table including all variables was too cumbersome for inclusion here but is available from the corresponding author.

Table 1. A summary of the interval variables.

Variable	*N*	*M*	*SD*	Range	SEM
Positive marital quality	5407	33.78	5.65	32	0.077
Negative interaction	5359	8.30	2.60	10	0.035
Spiritual development	6465	2.95	0.02	8	0.018
Read the Bible	6408	3.81	1.40	5	0.017
Concentrated prayer	6370	4.56	1.43	5	0.018
Family devotion	6163	2.65	1.30	5	0.016
Pray with your spouse	6086	2.56	1.32	5	0.017
Read or discuss the Bible with spouse	6068	2.78	1.22	5	0.016
Talk about spiritual values with child	5904	3.26	1.45	5	0.019
Pray for children	6158	4.69	1.69	5	0.021
Pray with children	5836	2.98	1.70	5	0.022
Share Christ with others	6191	3.17	1.07	5	0.014
Watch Christian television/video	6164	2.66	1.02	5	0.013
Listen to Christian talk radio	6190	2.80	1.34	5	0.017
Listen to Christian music	6277	3.58	1.50	5	0.019
Read Christian book or magazine	6240	3.11	1.17	5	0.015
Use online social networking tools	6217	3.61	1.88	5	0.024
Listen to sermon/teaching audio/podcast	6190	2.73	1.15	5	0.015
View Christian web sites/blogs	6005	2.49	1.05	5	0.014

Table 2. A summary of the categorical and ordinal variables.

Variable	Categories	*n*	%
Intimate partner violence in last 12 months			
	Never	5337	[a] 95.8
	Once	139	2.5
	Twice	54	1.0
	3–5 times	30	0.5
	6–10 times	4	0.1
	More than 10 times	6	0.1
	Total	5570	100.0
Gender			
	Male	2612	39.5
	Female	4001	60.5
	Total	6613	100.0
Age			
	19 and under	79	1.2
	20–29	500	7.6
	30–39	934	14.1
	40–49	1300	19.7
	50–59	1448	21.9
	60–69	1310	19.8
	70 or over	1042	15.8
	Total	6613	100.0
Years married			
	0–4	378	6.9
	5–9	543	9.9
	10–19	1213	22.2
	20–29	1076	16.3
	30–39	937	17.1
	40+	1321	24.2
	Total	5468	100.0
How long have you been a Christian?			
	I am not a Christian	16	0.2
	0–5 years	82	1.3
	6–10 years	97	1.5
	10+ years	6232	97.0
	Total	6427	100.0
How often do you attend worship services?			
	Less than once a month	254	3.9
	Once a month	182	2.8
	Twice a month	496	7.6
	Three times a month	1318	20.2
	Four or more times a month	4261	65.4
	Total	6511	100.0

[a] The percentages are calculated based on the number of valid responses.

2.1. Criterion Variables

Three criterion (dependent) variables were selected for this study: positive marital quality, negative interaction and IPV. To test the validity of our decision to use negative interaction as a discrete construct separate from positive marital quality, we conducted a principal component analysis entering all 14 items making up the three criterion variables. Three components emerged after six iterations, based on an Eigenvalue greater than 1. The items that loaded on the second component were the five items in our Negative Interaction Scale and the single item measuring IPV, with the IPV item having a visibly smaller loading. The items with the highest loadings on the first and third components were the eight items in our Positive Marital Quality Scale. The analysis was consistent with our use of the Negative Interaction Scale as a separate criterion variable.

2.1.1. Positive Marital Quality Scale

The variable Positive Marital Quality was measured by combining and modifying two existing scales: Marital Satisfaction Scale (Schumm et al. 1985) and Positive Bonding Scale (Allen et al. 2010).

The modified Marital Satisfaction Scale ($\alpha = 0.898$) includes the following questions, each measured using a 5-point Likert-type scale ranging from 1 = very dissatisfied to 5 = very satisfied:

- How satisfied are you with the way you connect with your spouse/fiancé/significant other?
- How satisfied are you with how your relationship functions day-to-day?
- How satisfied are you with your spouse/fiancé/significant other's contributions to your relationship?
- How satisfied are you with your own contributions to your relationship?

The Positive Bonding Scale included the following items, each measured using a 5-point Likert-type scale with possible responses ranging from 1 = strongly disagree to 5 = strongly agree:

- We regularly have great conversations where we just talk as good friends.
- I want this relationship to stay strong no matter what difficult times we may encounter.
- I believe we can handle whatever conflicts that may arise in the future.
- My relationship with my spouse/fiancé/significant other is more important to me than almost anything else in my life.

2.1.2. Negative Interaction Scale

The second criterion variable was adapted from the Danger Signs Scale (Stanley et al. 2002). The scale ($\alpha = 0.832$) includes the five items below, which were measured with a 3-point Likert-type scale which had the following possible responses: 1 = almost never, 2 = once in a while and 3 = frequently.

- Little arguments escalate into ugly fights with accusations, criticisms, name calling and/or bringing up past hurts.
- My partner criticizes or belittles my opinions, feelings or desires.
- My spouse/fiancé/significant other seems to view my words or actions more negatively than I intended for them to be.
- When we have a problem to solve, how often does it feel like we are on opposite teams?
- When we argue, one of us withdraws, that is, doesn't want to talk about it anymore or leaves the scene.

2.1.3. Intimate Partner Violence

The third criterion variable is a single-item measure of IPV taken from the Danger Signs Scale that asks, "Have there been any instances of pushing, grabbing, shoving, hitting and/or slapping within your relationship in the last twelve months?" Possible responses were 1 = never, 2 = once, 3 = twice, 4 = 3–5 times, 5 = 6–10 times and 6 = more than 10 times.

2.2. Predictor Variables

Three categories of predictor (independent) variables were included in the analysis: control variables, religious activities and Christian media consumption.

2.2.1. Control Variables

Based on previous research that associates them with marital quality, the following were included as control variables:

- gender

    o   1 = male
    o   2 = female

- age

  - ○ 1 = 19 and under
  - ○ 2 = 20–29
  - ○ 3 = 30–39
  - ○ 4 = 40–49
  - ○ 5 = 50–59
  - ○ 6 = 60–69
  - ○ 7 = 70 or over

- years married

  - ○ 1 = 0–4 years
  - ○ 2 = 5–9 years
  - ○ 3 = 10–19 years
  - ○ 4 = 20–29 years
  - ○ 5 = 30–39 years
  - ○ 6 = 40+ years

- "How long have you been a Christian?"

  - ○ System missing = Don't know
  - ○ 0 = I'm not a Christian
  - ○ 1 = 0–5 years
  - ○ 2 = 6–10 years
  - ○ 3 = 10+ years

- Spiritual development

  - ○ 0 = No spiritual development
  - ○ 1 = Very low
  - ○ 2 = Low
  - ○ 3 = Low average
  - ○ 4 = Medium
  - ○ 5 = Slightly above average
  - ○ 6 = Above average
  - ○ 7 = High
  - ○ 8 = Very high
  - ○ 9 = Maximum spiritual development

2.2.2. Religious Activities

- Worship attendance

  - ○ 1 = Less than once a month
  - ○ 2 = Once a month
  - ○ 3 = Twice a month
  - ○ 4 = Three times a month
  - ○ 5 = Four or more times a month

The following religious activity variables all are measured with the same potential responses, which are listed after the list of variables:

- Bible reading
- Prayer
- Having a family devotion
- Praying with a spouse
- Reading/discussing the Bible with a spouse
- Talking about spiritual values with the children
- Praying for the children
- Praying with the children
- Sharing Christ with others

  - ○ 1 = does not apply
  - ○ 2 = rarely/never
  - ○ 3 = occasionally
  - ○ 4 = several times a month
  - ○ 5 = several times a week
  - ○ 6 = almost every day

2.2.3. Christian Media Consumption

All Christian media variables used the same possible responses, which are listed following the variables below.

- Watch Christian television/video
- Listen to Christian talk radio
- Listen to Christian music
- Read a Christian book and/or magazine
- Use online social networking tools (i.e., Facebook, Twitter, YouTube, etc.)
- Listen to sermon/teaching audio/podcast
- View Christian websites/blogs

  - ○ 1 = does not apply
  - ○ 2 = rarely/never
  - ○ 3 = occasionally
  - ○ 4 = several times a month
  - ○ 5 = several times a week
  - ○ 6 = almost every day

2.3. Analytical Strategy

Three 3-step hierarchical multiple regression analyses were conducted to determine whether religious activities (including the use of Christian media) demonstrated surplus explanatory power relative to more general types of predictors in relation to positive marital quality, negative interaction and IPV. For all three analyses, the same predictor variables were entered in the same order. Missing cases were excluded listwise.

3. Results

Three 3-step hierarchical multiple regression analyses were conducted to determine whether religious activities predicted positive marital quality, negative interaction and IPV. The significance level was set at 0.05. See Tables 3–5 for the regression summaries.

3.1. Positive Marital Quality

In step 1 of the regression analysis where Positive Marital Quality was the criterion variable, the control variables added were gender, age, years married, length of time as a Christian and spiritual development. Gender ($\beta = -0.049$; $p = 0.002$) and spiritual development ($\beta = 0.182$; $t = 11.158$; $p < 0.001$) were significant predictors of positive marital quality. Step 1 was statistically significant ($\Delta R^2 = 0.04$, $F(5,3899) = 29.69$, $p < 0.001$) and explained 3.5% of the variance. Tests to see if the data met the assumption of collinearity indicated that multicollinearity was not a concern (Gender: Tolerance = 0.97, VIF = 1.03; Age: Tolerance = 0.35, VIF = 2.86; years married: Tolerance = 0.35, VIF = 2.83; years a Christian: Tolerance = 0.98, VIF = 1.03; and spiritual development: Tolerance = 0.93, VIF = 1.08).

In step 2, individual and family-centered religious activities were added to the model. Four of the control variables were significant predictors: gender ($p = 0.038$), age ($p < 0.001$), years married ($p = 0.038$) and spiritual development ($p < 0.001$). Among the variables measuring religious activities, reading the Bible ($\beta = -0.110$; $t = -5.474$; $p < 0.001$), praying with a spouse ($\beta = 0.105$; $t = 5.499$; $p < 0.001$), reading/discussing the Bible with a spouse ($\beta = 0.218$; $t = 10.560$; $p < 0.001$), talking about spiritual values with the children ($\beta = -0.098$; $t = -4.393$; $p < 0.001$), praying for the children ($\beta = 0.076$; $t = 3.713$; $p < 0.001$) and praying with the children ($\beta = -0.162$; $t = -2.166$; $p = 0.030$) were significant predictors. Step 2 was statistically significant ($\Delta R^2 = 0.07$, $F(10,3904) = 30.47$, $p < 0.001$) and explained 6.8% of the variance. Tests to see if the data met the assumption of collinearity indicated that multicollinearity was not a concern (attend worship: Tolerance = 0.79, VIF = 1.26; read the Bible: Tolerance = 0.57, VIF = 1.74; individual prayer: Tolerance = 0.66, VIF = 1.53; family devotion: Tolerance = 0.69, VIF = 1.47; pray with a partner: Tolerance = 0.64, VIF = 1.58; read/discuss the Bible with a partner: Tolerance = 0.54, VIF = 1.86; discuss spiritual values with the children: Tolerance = 0.46, VIF = 2.15; pray for the children: Tolerance = 0.56, VIF = 1.80; pray with the children: Tolerance = 0.45, VIF = 2.24; and share Christ: Tolerance = 0.76, VIF = 1.31).

Media-related religious activities were added in step 3. Among the control variables, age ($p = 0.038$) and spiritual development ($p < 0.001$) were significant predictors of positive marital quality. Among the religious activities, reading the Bible ($p < 0.001$), praying with a spouse ($p < 0.001$), reading/discussing the Bible with a spouse ($p < 0.001$), talking about spiritual values with the children ($p < 0.001$) and praying for the children ($p = 0.001$) were significant predictors. Among the media variables, only listening to Christian talk radio ($\beta = -0.068$; $t = -3.522$; $p < 0.001$) and viewing Christian websites/blogs ($\beta = -0.049$; $t = -2.680$; $p = 0.007$) were significant predictors of positive marital quality. Step 3 was statistically significant ($\Delta R^2 = 0.01$, $F(22,3904) = 23.30$, $p < 0.001$) and explained 1.2% of the variance over and above other variables. The final model explained 11.7% of the variance. Tests to see if the data met the assumption of collinearity indicated that multicollinearity was not a concern (Christian TV: Tolerance = 0.69, VIF = 1.44; Christian talk radio: Tolerance = 0.62, VIF = 1.62; Christian music: Tolerance = 0.55, VIF = 1.80; Christian book or magazine: Tolerance = 0.59, VIF = 1.70; social networking: Tolerance = 0.71, VIF = 1.42; sermon recordings: Tolerance = 0.81, VIF = 1.24; and Christian websites: Tolerance = 0.68, VIF = 1.48).

Consistent with previous research, joint spousal religious activities were positive predictors of positive marital quality, as was praying for the children. However, individual activities (Bible reading) and parent-child dyadic activities (talking about spiritual values and prayer) were associated negatively with marital satisfaction. The only two media-related activities that were significant (Christian talk radio and Christian websites/blogs) also had a negative relationship with positive marital quality.

3.2. Negative Interaction

In step 1 of the regression analysis with negative interaction as the criterion variable, only spiritual development among the control variables was a statistically significant predictor ($\beta = -0.093$; $t = -4.988$; $p < 0.001$). Step 1 was statistically significant ($\Delta R^2 = 0.02$, $F(5,3897) = 16.12$, $p < 0.001$) and explained 2.0% of the variance. Tests to see if the data met the assumption of collinearity indicated that multicollinearity was not a concern (Gender: Tolerance = 0.98, VIF = 1.03; Age: Tolerance = 0.35,

VIF = 2.89; years married: Tolerance = 0.35, VIF = 2.87; years a Christian: Tolerance = 0.98, VIF = 1.03; and spiritual development: Tolerance = 0.93, VIF = 1.08).

In step 2, individual and family-centered religious activities were added to the model. Spiritual development ($p < 0.001$) was the only control variable that was a statistically significant predictor. Among the variables measuring religious activities, reading the Bible ($\beta = 0.072$; $t = 3.514$; $p < 0.001$), having a family devotion ($\beta = -0.050$; $t = -2.642$; $p = 0.008$), praying with a spouse ($\beta = -0.078$; $t = -3.979$; $p < 0.001$), reading/discussing the Bible with a spouse ($\beta = -0.139$; $t = -6.582$; $p < 0.001$), talking about spiritual values with the children ($\beta = 0.048$; $t = 2.099$; $p = 0.036$) and praying with the children ($p = 0.006$) were significant predictors. Step 2 was statistically significant ($\Delta R^2 = 0.04$, $F(15,3887) = 15.217$, $p < 0.001$) and explained 3.5% of the variance. Tests to see if the data met the assumption of collinearity indicated that multicollinearity was not a concern (attend worship; Tolerance = 0.79, VIF = 1.27; read the Bible: Tolerance = 0.57, VIF = 1.74; individual prayer: Tolerance = 0.65, VIF = 1.53; family devotion: Tolerance = 0.68, VIF = 1.47; pray with a partner: Tolerance = 0.64, VIF = 1.57; read/discuss the Bible with a partner: Tolerance = 0.54, VIF = 1.84; discuss spiritual values with the children: Tolerance = 0.47, VIF = 2.14; pray for the children: Tolerance = 0.55, VIF = 1.80; pray with the children: Tolerance = 0.45, VIF = 2.22; and share Christ: Tolerance = 0.77, VIF = 1.31).

Media-related religious activities were added in step 3. Spiritual development ($p < 0.001$) was the only control variable that predicted a negative interaction in this step. Among religious activities, predictors included family devotions ($p = 0.005$), praying with a spouse ($p < 0.001$), reading/discussing the Bible with a spouse ($p < 0.001$) and praying with the children ($p = 0.011$). The only Christian media variables that were statistically significant predictors of negative interaction were listening to Christian talk radio ($\beta = 0.094$; $t = 4.723$; $p < 0.001$) and viewing Christian websites/blogs ($\beta = 0.050$; $t = 2.670$; $p = 0.008$). Step 3 was statistically significant ($\Delta R^2 = 0.01$, $F(7,3880) = 12.41$, $p < 0.001$) and explained 1.0% of the variance over and above other variables. Tests to see if the data met the assumption of collinearity indicated that multicollinearity was not a concern (Christian TV: Tolerance = 0.69, VIF = 1.45; Christian talk radio: Tolerance = 0.61, VIF = 1.63; Christian music: Tolerance = 0.55, VIF = 1.81; Christian book or magazine: Tolerance = 0.59, VIF = 1.70; social networking: Tolerance = 0.70, VIF = 1.43; sermon recordings: Tolerance = 0.80, VIF = 1.24; and Christian websites: Tolerance = 0.68, VIF = 1.48).

Confirming Hypothesis 2, joint spousal or family religious activities were negative predictors of negative interaction. However, disconfirming our hypothesis, praying with the children was a positive predictor of negative interaction, and consistent with our hypothesis, the only two media-related activities that were significant predictors of negative interaction (Christian talk radio and Christian websites/blogs) both had a positive relationship with negative interaction.

3.3. Intimate Partner Violence

In step 1 of the regression analysis where IPV was the criterion variable, years married ($\beta = -0.060$; $t = -2.265$; $p = 0.024$) was the only control variable that predicted IPV. Step 1 was statistically significant ($\Delta R^2 = 0.004$, $F(5,3969) = 3.31$, $p = 0.006$) and explained 0.3% of the variance. Tests to see if the data met the assumption of collinearity indicated that multicollinearity was not a concern (Gender: Tolerance = 0.98, VIF = 1.03; Age: Tolerance = 0.35, VIF = 2.83; years married: Tolerance = 0.36, VIF = 2.81; years a Christian: Tolerance = 0.98, VIF = 1.02; and spiritual development: Tolerance = 0.93, VIF = 1.07).

In step 2, individual and family-centered religious activities were added to the model. Years married ($p = 0.024$) remained the only control variable that predicted IPV, with couples married fewer years more likely to experience violence. Among the religious activity variables, praying with the children ($\beta = 0.053$; $t = 2.250$; $p = 0.009$) was the only significant predictor, with those that prayed with their children being more likely to experience IPV. Step 2 was statistically significant ($\Delta R^2 = 0.004$, $F(10,3959) = 2.03$, $p = 0.011$). Tests to see if the data met the assumption of collinearity indicated that multicollinearity was not a concern (attend worship: Tolerance = 0.79, VIF = 1.26; read the Bible: Tolerance = 0.58, VIF = 1.74; individual prayer: Tolerance = 0.66, VIF = 1.52; family devotion:

Tolerance = 0.69, VIF = 1.48; pray with a partner: Tolerance = 0.64, VIF = 1.56; read/discuss the Bible with a partner: Tolerance = 0.54, VIF = 1.84; discuss spiritual values with the children: Tolerance = 0.47, VIF = 2.14; pray for the children: Tolerance = 0.56, VIF = 1.80; pray with the children: Tolerance = 0.45, VIF = 2.24; share Christ: Tolerance = 0.77, VIF = 1.30).

Christian media-related religious activities were added in step 3. Years married ($p = 0.019$) was the only control variable that predicted IPV. The only statistically significant religious activity variable that predicted the criterion variable was praying with the children ($p = 0.037$). Among the Christian media variables, the only significant predictor of IPV was listening to Christian talk radio ($\beta = 0.062$; $t = 3.110$; $p = 0.002$). Step 3 was statistically significant ($\Delta R^2 = 0.01$, $F(7,3952) = 2.27$, $p < 0.001$) and explained 0.7% of the variance over and above other variables. Tests to see if the data met the assumption of collinearity indicated that multicollinearity was not a concern (Christian TV: Tolerance = 0.69, VIF = 1.44; Christian talk radio: Tolerance = 0.62, VIF = 1.62; Christian music: Tolerance = 0.55, VIF = 1.81; Christian book or magazine: Tolerance = 0.59, VIF = 1.70; social networking: Tolerance = 0.70, VIF = 1.42; sermon recordings: Tolerance = 0.81, VIF = 1.24; and Christian websites: Tolerance = 0.68, VIF = 1.48).

Few of the variables of interest predicted IPV. Consistent with previous research that links IPV to younger ages, those that were married longer tended to be less likely to experience violence in the relationship. However, consistent with the findings of Todhunter and Deaton (2010), none of the religious activity variables appearing in previous research predicted IPV. However, praying with the children was a positive predictor of IPV. Among Christian media, only listening to Christian talk radio was significant, predicting a greater likelihood of IPV.

Table 3. A summary of the hierarchical regression analysis for variables predicting a positive marital quality ($N = 6613$).

Variable	Step 1			Step 2			Step 3		
	B	SEB	β	B	SEB	β	B	SEB	β
Gender	−0.554	0.180	−0.049 **	−0.374	0.180	−0.033 *	−0.321	0.185	−0.028
Age	−0.140	0.109	−0.034	−0.455	0.113	−0.111 ***	−0.478	0.116	−0.117 ***
Years married	0.119	0.099	0.032	0.194	0.097	−0.052 *	0.180	0.096	0.048 *
How long a Christian	−0.301	0.324	−0.015	−0.159	0.314	−0.008	−0.113	0.312	−0.006
Spiritual development	0.719	0.064	0.182 ***	0.523	0.072	0.132 ***	0.526	0.071	0.133 ***
Attend services				−0.113	0.098	−0.020	−0.043	0.099	−0.007
Bible reading				−0.447	0.082	−0.110 ***	−0.311	0.086	−0.076 ***
Prayer				0.085	0.074	0.021	0.102	0.074	0.026
Family devotion				0.120	0.084	0.026	0.133	0.084	0.029
Pray with spouse				0.472	0.086	0.105 ***	0.488	0.085	0.108 ***
Read/discuss Bible with spouse				1.108	0.105	0.218 ***	1.157	0.105	0.228 ***
Talk to children about spiritual values				−0.397	0.090	−0.098 ***	−0.359	0.090	−0.088 **
Pray for children				0.287	0.077	0.076 ***	0.254	0.077	0.067 **
Pray with children				−0.162	0.075	−0.049 **	−0.135	0.074	−0.041
Share Christ							0.101	0.094	0.019
Christian TV/video							−0.027	0.105	−0.005
Christian talk radio							−0.283	0.080	−0.068 ***
Christian music							−0.080	0.075	−0.022
Christian book or magazine							−0.051	0.096	−0.011
Social media							0.061	0.054	0.018
Sermon/teaching audio							−0.089	0.083	−0.018
Christian websites							−0.262	0.098	−0.049 **
R^2_{change}			0.037 ***			0.068 ***			0.012 ***
F		26.691 ***			30.468 ***			23.304 ***	

$* p < 0.05. ** p < 0.01. *** p < 0.001.$

Table 4. A summary of the hierarchical regression analysis for variables predicting a negative interaction ($N = 6613$).

Variable	Step 1			Step 2			Step 3		
	B	SEB	β	B	SEB	β	B	SEB	β
Gender	0.031	0.084	0.006 **	−0.066	0.086	−0.013	−0.077	0.089	−0.015
Age	−0.018	0.051	−0.010	−0.089	0.054	−0.047	0.093	0.056	−0.049 **
Years married	−0.027	0.046	−0.016	−0.052	0.046	−0.030	−0.049	0.046	−0.028
How long a Christian	−0.152	0.152	−0.016	−0.212	0.150	−0.022	−0.220	0.150	−0.023

Table 4. *Cont.*

Variable	Step 1			Step 2			Step 3		
	B	SEB	β	B	SEB	β	B	SEB	β
Spiritual development	−0.240	0.030	−0.131 ***	−0.170	0.034	−0.093 ***	−0.172	0.034	−0.094 ***
Attend services				−0.031	0.047	−0.012	−0.047	0.047	−0.018
Bible reading				0.137	0.039	−0.072 ***	0.079	0.041	−0.041
Prayer				−0.024	0.035	−0.013	−0.031	0.035	−0.017
Family devotion				−0.106	0.040	−0.050	−0.112	0.040	−0.053
Pray with spouse				−0.163	0.041	−0.078 ***	−0.170	0.041	−0.081 **
Read/discuss Bible with spouse				−0.328	0.050	−0.139 ***	−0.336	0.050	−0.143 ***
Talk to children about spiritual values				0.090	0.043	−0.048 ***	0.077	0.043	0.041
Pray for children				−0.046	0.037	−0.026	−0.034	0.037	−0.019 **
Pray with children				0.099	0.036	0.064 **	0.090	0.035	0.069 *
Share Christ				0.023	0.044	0.009	0.003	0.045	0.001
Christian TV/video							−0.032	0.050	−0.012
Christian talk radio							0.181	0.038	0.094 ***
Christian music							−0.033	0.036	−0.019
Christian book or magazine							0.060	0.046	0.026
Social media							−0.021	0.026	−0.015
Sermon/teaching audio							−0.037	0.040	−0.016
Christian websites							0.125	0.047	−0.050 **
R^2_{change}			0.020 ***			0.035 ***			0.010 ***
F		16.115 ***			15.217 ***			12.409 ***	

$* p < 0.05.\ ** p < 0.01.\ *** p < 0.001.$

Table 5. A summary of the hierarchical regression analysis for the variables predicting intimate partner violence (IPV) (*N* = 6613).

Variable	Step 1			Step 2			Step 3		
	B	SEB	β	B	SEB	β	B	SEB	β
Gender	−0.004	0.012	−0.006	−0.008	0.013	−0.011	−0.005	0.013	−0.006
Age	0.004	0.007	−0.016	−0.010	0.008	−0.036	0.008	0.008	0.030
Years married	−0.015	0.007	−0.060 *	−0.015	0.007	−0.061 *	−0.016	0.007	−0.063
How long a Christian	−0.030	0.022	−0.022	−0.031	0.022	−0.023	−0.030	0.022	−0.021
Spiritual development	−0.006	0.004	−0.023	−0.010	0.005	−0.036	−0.009	0.005	−0.032
Attend services				−0.001	0.007	−0.003	−0.002	0.007	−0.005
Bible reading				0.010	0.006	−0.038	0.009	0.006	0.033
Prayer				—	0.005	0.000	0.000	0.005	−0.001
Family devotion				−0.006	0.006	−0.020	−0.006	0.006	−0.021
Pray with spouse				0.001	0.006	0.003	0.000	0.006	0.001
Read/discuss Bible with spouse				−0.010	0.007	−0.029	−0.010	0.007	−0.030
Talk to children about spiritual values				0.000	0.006	−0.002	−0.001	0.006	−0.005
Pray for children				−0.006	0.005	−0.022	−0.005	0.005	−0.020
Pray with children				0.012	0.005	0.053 *	0.011	0.005	0.049 *
Share Christ				0.010	0.006	0.027	0.008	0.007	0.049
Christian TV/video							0.010	0.007	0.025
Christian talk radio							0.018	0.006	0.062 **
Christian music							−0.002	0.005	−0.007
Christian book or magazine							−0.007	0.007	−0.021
Social media							−0.005	0.004	−0.023
Sermon/teaching audio							−0.010	0.006	−0.029
Christian websites							0.005	0.007	0.014
R^2_{change}			0.004 **			0.003 ***			0.005 ***
F		3.305 ***			2.027 ***			2.268 ***	

$* p < 0.05.\ ** p < 0.01.\ *** p < 0.001.$

4. Discussion

This study investigated the relationship between marital quality and seventeen religion-related activities in a sample of Protestant Christians from North America. We hypothesized that higher levels of participation in individual, dyadic and family religious activities would predict higher levels of positive marital quality, lower levels of negative interaction and lower levels of IPV, whereas the consumption of Christian media would predict lower levels of positive marital quality, higher levels of negative interaction and higher levels of IPV.

4.1. Control Variables

Before discussing the findings related to our hypotheses, it would be beneficial to examine briefly the outcomes related to the control variables. Based on previous research, we anticipated that being a male, being a Christian for a longer time and having higher levels of spiritual development would predict higher levels of positive marital quality and lower levels of negative interaction as well as IPV and that greater age and longer marriages would predict lower levels of marital quality. Sometimes, these expectations were confirmed. However, often, there was no relationship between the control variable and the criterion variable, and, sometimes, the relationship was in an unexpected direction. These inconsistencies seem to be related to findings by Wilmoth et al. (2015) that demonstrated the interaction effects of age and negative interaction with religiosity on marital satisfaction.

Although the single-item variable Spiritual Development has not been used widely in prior research, it was included as a control variable in these analyses because of the findings of Wilmoth et al. (2018) that Spiritual Development was a consistently salient predictor of individual well-being. As expected, in these analyses, Spiritual Development was one of the most consistent and powerful predictors of marital quality.

4.2. Hypothesis 1

Although attendance at religious services has a complex relationship with marital quality (Booth et al. 1995; Vaaler et al. 2009), generally, attendance has been found to be associated positively with marital quality in a number of studies (e.g., Lichter and Carmalt 2009; Mahoney et al. 1999; Strawbridge et al. 2001) and, in some studies, has served as a single-item proxy for religiosity (e.g., Lim 2015; Wen 2010; Wilmoth et al. 2014; Young 2011). Generally, it is included in scales that measure religiosity (e.g., Koenig and Büssing 2010). However, in this study, attendance did not emerge as a predictor of marital quality in any of the analyses. At least two possible reasons for this surprising non-finding are (1) the religious homogeneity of this sample: All participants were associated with a Protestant church, whose members typically attend more frequently than some other Christian groups (Pew Research Center 2015); (2) the likely effect of multicollinearity, with the control variables explaining the variance otherwise explained by attendance. For example, although test results for multicollinearity were within acceptable limits, Spiritual Development was correlated with every other predictor variable at a level of $p < 0.001$.

Both prayer and Bible reading/study generally are included in scales measuring religiosity (e.g., Koenig and Büssing 2010), and both have been associated positively with marital quality (Fincham and Beach 2014; Marks 2005; Phillips et al. forthcoming; Robinson 1994). However, individual prayer never emerged as a predictor of marital quality in this study, possibly for the same reasons suggested above for attendance at religious services. In addition to religious homogeneity as a possible explanation, we speculate that a pious individual in a lower-quality relationship is likely to perceive prayer as a means of improving the quality of the relationship. This conjecture is consistent with the findings of Booth et al. (1995) that an increase in marital happiness increases the extent to which religion influences church service attendance as well as the conclusion of Doss et al. (2009) that reading self-help books with relationship themes reflected help-seeking for individuals in distressed marriages.

Although observing religious rituals has been associated with multiple benefits for marriages, having family devotions did not predict positive marital quality in our study. This non-finding is consistent with the expectation that family devotions can be a bonding experience for couples and families but a source of conflict and resentment for other families.

Joint religious activities such as praying together or reading the Bible together have been associated with positive marital quality (Ellison and Wilcox 2010; Lichter and Carmalt 2009). For xample, Lichter and Carmalt found that, for both husbands and wives, high rates of joint participation (e.g., praying together) was positively associated with higher scores in each level of marital quality. Similarly, Mahoney et al. (1999) found that participating in joint religious activities, including praying together and discussing spiritual issues, was related to higher levels of marital adjustment and perceived benefits from marriage. As expected, these variables were positively correlated with positive marital quality in our study.

The communication of parents with their children about values (e.g., sexual, Suleiman et al. 2016) generally is associated with positive results, and discussing faith values with children is considered important for the intergenerational transmission of faith. Longitudinal research has found that transmitting religious values promoted emotional closeness between parents and children (Bengtson et al. 2013). Thus, we anticipated that talking to children about spiritual values would predict a higher couple relationship quality. However, this variable had a significant negative relationship with positive marital quality. We suspect that a religious parent would discuss spiritual values with children to guard against deleterious effects of a negative relationship between parents.

The only Christian media variables that predicted positive marital quality were listening to Christian talk radio and viewing Christian websites or blogs. In both cases, the association was in the expected direction: Individuals with lower levels of positive marital quality were more likely to listen to Christian talk radio or to view Christian websites or blogs. Although we could not find research related specifically to Christian talk radio, Rubin (2000) found that talk radio listeners often perceive a host to be a relational partner and credible source of information. We speculate that individuals in troubled relationships could seek out Christian talk radio programs, particularly those focused on family-centered topics (e.g., *FamilyLife* and *Focus on the Family*) to find solutions to relationship problems. Similarly, an individual in an unhappy relationship could seek out relationship advice on Christian websites or blogs.

4.3. Negative Interaction

Most research investigating the relationship between religious behavior and marital quality does not distinguish between positive marital quality and negative interaction. Thus, most of the discussion in the previous section is relevant for our comments regarding negative interaction. However, there are some specific findings that merit additional comments.

Mahoney's review (Mahoney 2005) noted that greater levels of religiousness have not been associated with an increase in maladaptive communication in marriage. Mahoney et al. (1999) used several measures of marital quality, including the frequency of conflict. Though conflict is not synonymous with a negative interaction, the concepts are closely related. Mahoney et al. found that joint religious activities such as praying together were associated with lower levels of conflict. In contrast, Booth et al. (1995) found that increases in religiosity were not related to decreases in marital conflict.

Although having family devotions did not have a significant relationship with positive marital quality or IPV, it had a negative association with negative interaction in relationships ($p = 0.007$). We suspect this may reflect the finding of Booth et al. (1995) that increases in marital happiness predicted greater religious involvement.

As expected, joint religious activities such as praying together or reading the Bible together negatively predicted negative interaction. This is in line with the findings of Mahoney et al. (1999), who found that praying together and other religious activities predicted lower levels of conflict.

The communication of parents with their children about spiritual values had a positive relationship with negative interaction. As mentioned in the previous section, we suspect that a religious parent would discuss spiritual values with their children when concerned about the potential negative effects of a distressed relationship between parents. Praying with children also had a positive relationship with negative interaction, and we speculate that the same principle would be at work here.

Confirming Hypothesis 2, individuals that listened more frequently to Christian talk radio or that viewed Christian websites more often had higher levels of negative interaction. As discussed earlier, we suspect this behavior is driven by the desire to find answers for unhappy relationships.

4.4. Intimate Partner Violence

Some additional observations about IPV are relevant. The number of years married predicted lower levels of IPV. One explanation for this association is that couples that experienced IPV would be likely to dissolve their relationships earlier. This is consistent with observations that young age may be a risk factor for IPV among adults (Johnson et al. 2014).

The only individual, dyadic or family religious activity that predicted IPV was praying with the children. As discussed earlier, this association likely indicates an attempt by a victim of IPV to find helpful information or spiritual support. The failure of religious activities to predict IPV was consistent with the earlier findings of Todhunter and Deaton (2010) but differed from the findings of Ellison et al. (2007).

Listening to Christian talk radio is the only media-related variable that predicted IPV. This finding is consistent with Hypothesis 2. Although no previous research has examined the relationship between Christian talk radio and IPV—or marital quality in general—this finding is expected in light of the research by Doss et al. (2009) that couples facing relationship challenges sought help by reading books and of the study by DeAngelis et al. (2018) that showed individuals use the reading of scripture as a help-seeking behavior. Listening to talk radio should be an even more likely target of help-seeking in light of the findings by Rubin (2000) that talk radio listeners often consider a host to be not only a relational partner but also a credible source of information.

Although there is no way to know the severity of violence in any of these relationships, the definition of IPV in this study used less violent behaviors than many other measures (cf., Smith et al. 2018). Also, fewer than 5 percent of the respondents reported incidents of IPV, compared to more than 30 percent in the U.S. population (Smith et al. 2018).

5. Conclusions

This research has several limitations, some of which are related to the sample. Because the participants all were associated with Protestant Christian churches, the findings cannot be generalized to other religious groups and, considering the diversity within Protestantism, cannot be generalized to specific Protestant denominations. Although the sample was not selected at random, the expected large percentage of responses within each congregation suggests responses likely are representative of each participating congregation; however, the congregations were not selected randomly and possibly are not representative of Protestant congregations in general. The use of denominational affiliation would have been a useful control variable, but that information was not available to the authors.

Also, there are limitations related to the instrument. For example, the questionnaire did not include traditional demographic variables such as ethnicity, education or income. Also, the questions related to Christian media were exploratory in nature and should be refined to answer further questions more accurately and thoroughly. DeAngelis et al. (2018) suggested that more nuanced measures should be used to study why individuals read scriptures, and the same principle would be relevant for research into why individuals use various Christian media. For example, it would have been helpful to address the motivations for using these media: Were participants seeking help for distressed marriages, or were they utilizing the media for personal enrichment or pleasure? Another limitation of the data is that only individual data were collected, whereas couple data would be helpful in future research. Despite these limitations, we believe our analyses provide new information that is beneficial for both academics and practitioners.

This study was conducted with the expectation that religious activities and Christian media-related activities would predict higher relationship quality while the use of Christian media would predict lower relationship quality. Generally, our expectations were correct, although certain religious activities (e.g., praying with the children) were associated with lower levels of positive marital quality, higher levels of negative interaction and a greater likelihood of IPV. We suspect that any causation in these relationships, particularly between media use and relationship quality, might be bidirectional or flow from the relationship quality to the religious activities or media consumption. Perhaps individuals in poor-quality relationships seek out media (and other religious resources) looking for ways to improve their marriages. In contrast, couples with stable and satisfying marriages would be more likely to read the Bible or to pray together. Further, we suspect that some religious activities are perceived to provide preventive or remedial benefits by spouses in distressed relationships.

It also should be noted that rates of IPV were much lower in this sample than in the general population. Clergy and family practitioners in religious settings can use this information to identify possible problematic relationships, and purveyors of Christian media can use the information to craft content that would address relationship issues.

Author Contributions: J.D.W. conceived and designed the study, conducted the statistical analyses, and wrote most of the paper. M.R. provided substantial assistance in the search of related research literature.

Funding: This research received no external funding, but the data were made available by FamilyLife.

Conflicts of Interest: The authors declare no conflict of interest.

References

Allen, Elizabeth S., Galena K. Rhoades, Scott M. Stanley, and Howard J. Markman. 2010. Hitting home: Relationships between recent deployment, posttraumatic stress symptoms, and marital functioning for Army couples. *Journal of Family Psychology* 24: 280–88. [CrossRef] [PubMed]

Atkins, David C., and Deborah E. Kessel. 2008. Religiousness and infidelity: Attendance, but not faith and prayer, predict marital fidelity. *Journal of Marriage and Family* 70: 407–18. [CrossRef]

Bengtson, Vern L., Norella M. Putney, and Susan Harris. 2013. *Families of Faith*. New York: Oxford University Press. [CrossRef]

Booth, Alan, David R. Johnson, Ann Branaman, and Alan Sica. 1995. Belief and behavior: Does religion matter in today's marriage? *Journal of Marriage and Family* 57: 661–71. [CrossRef]

Braithwaite, Scott R., and Frank D. Fincham. 2007. ePREP: Computer based prevention of relationship dysfunction, depression and anxiety. *Journal of Social and Clinical Psychology* 26: 609–22. [CrossRef]

Braithwaite, Scott R., and Frank D. Fincham. 2009. A randomized clinical trial of a computer based preventive intervention: Replication and extension of ePREP. *Journal of Family Psychology* 23: 32–38. [CrossRef] [PubMed]

Braithwaite, Scott R., and Frank D. Fincham. 2011. Computer-based dissemination: A randomized clinical trial of ePREP using the actor partner interdependence model. *Behaviour Research and Therapy* 49: 126–31. [CrossRef] [PubMed]

Braithwaite, Scott R., and Frank D. Fincham. 2014. Computer-based prevention of intimate partner violence in marriage. *Behaviour Research and Therapy* 54: 12–21. [CrossRef] [PubMed]

Brinkerhoff, Merlin B., Elaine Grandin, and Eugen Lupri. 1992. Religious involvement and spousal violence: The Canadian case. *Journal for the Scientific Study of Religion* 31: 15–31. [CrossRef]

Campbell, Heidi A. 2017. Surveying theoretical approaches within digital religion studies. *New Media & Society* 19: 15–24. [CrossRef]

Chaney, Cassandra, Lucy Shirisia, and Linda Skogrand. 2016. "Whatever God has yoked together, let no man put apart": The effect of religion on black marriages. *Western Journal of Black Studies* 40: 24–41.

Cheong, Pauline H. 2017. The vitality of new media and religion: Communicative perspectives, practices, and changing authority in spiritual organization. *New Media & Society* 19: 25–33.

Christian Bookseller's Association. 2017. UNITE 2017 Fact Sheet. Available online: http://cbaonline.org/unite-2017-fact-sheet/ (accessed on 23 February 2017).

DeAngelis, Reed T., John P. Bartkowski, and Xiaohe Xu. 2018. Scriptural coping: An empirical test of hermeneutic theory. *Journal for the Scientific Study of Religion*. [CrossRef]

Doss, Brian D., Galena K. Rhoades, Scott M. Stanley, and Howard J. Markman. 2009. Marital therapy, retreats, and books: The who, what, when, and why of relationship help-seeking. *Journal of Marital and Family Therapy* 35: 18–29. [CrossRef] [PubMed]

Duncan, Stephen F., April Steed, and Carma Martino Needham. 2009. A comparison evaluation study of web-based and traditional marriage and relationship education. *Journal of Couple & Relationship Therapy* 8: 162–80. [CrossRef]

Eggebeen, David, and Jeffrey J. Dew. 2009. The role of religion in adolescence for family formation in young adulthood. *Journal of Marriage and Family* 71: 108–21. [CrossRef] [PubMed]

Ellison, Christopher G., John P. Bartkowski, and Kristin L. Anderson. 1999. Are there religious variations in domestic violence? *Journal of Family Issues* 20: 87–113. [CrossRef]

Ellison, Christopher G., Jenny A. Trinitapoli, Kristin L. Anderson, and Byron R. Johnson. 2007. Race/ethnicity, religious involvement, and domestic violence. *Violence Against Women* 13: 1094–112. [CrossRef]

Ellison, Christopher G.; Amy M. Burdette, and W. Bradford Wilcox. 2010. The couple that prays together: Race and ethnicity, religion, and relationship quality among working-age adults. *Journal of Marriage and Family* 72: 963–75. [CrossRef]

Fincham, Frank D., and Steven R. H. Beach. 2014. I say a little prayer for you: Praying for partner increases commitment in romantic relationships. *Journal of Family Psychology* 28: 587–93. [CrossRef]

Fincham, Frank D., and Kenneth J. Linfield. 1997. A new look at marital quality: Can spouses feel positive and negative about their marriage? *Journal of Family Psychology* 11: 489–502. [CrossRef]

Fincham, Frank D., Christine Ajayi, and Steven R. H. Beach. 2011. Spirituality and marital satisfaction in African American couples. *Psychology of Religion and Spirituality* 3: 259–68. [CrossRef]

Gottman, John. M., and Clifford I. Notarius. 2000. Decade review: Observing marital interaction. *Journal of Marriage and the Family* 6: 927–47. [CrossRef]

Gritzon, Glenn. 2013. *Super-Composite for 2012–2013 of the Family Needs Survey Findings*. Little Rock: FamilyLife, Available online: www.familylife.com/familyneedssurvey (accessed on 23 January 2014).

Johnson, Wendi L., Peggy C. Giordano, Wendy D. Manning, and Monica A. Longmore. 2014. The age-IPV cure: Changes in the perpetration of intimate partner violence during adolescence and young adulthood. *Journal of Youth and Adolescence* 44: 708–26. [CrossRef] [PubMed]

Kerkhof, Peter, Catrin Finkenauer, and Linda D. Muusses. 2011. Relational consequences of compulsive Internet use: A longitudinal study among newlyweds. *Human Communication Research* 37: 147–73. [CrossRef]

Koenig, Harold G., and Arndt Büssing. 2010. The Duke University Religion Index (DUREL): A Five-item measure for use in epidemiological studies. *Religions* 1: 78–85. [CrossRef]

Lichter, Daniel T., and Julie H. Carmalt. 2009. Religion and marital quality among low-income couples. *Social Science Research* 38: 168–87. [CrossRef]

Lim, Chaeyoon. 2015. Religion and subjective well being across religious traditions: Evidence from 1.3 million Americans. *Journal for the Scientific Study of Religion* 54: 684–701. [CrossRef]

Mahoney, Annette. 2005. Religion and conflict in marital and parent-child relationships. *Journal of Social Issues* 61: 689–706. [CrossRef]

Mahoney, Annette. 2010. Religion in families, 1999–2009: A relational spirituality framework. *Journal of Marriage and Family* 72: 805–27. [CrossRef]

Mahoney, Annette, Kenneth I. Pargament, Tracey Jewell, Aaron B. Swank, Swank Eric Scott, Erin Emery, and Mark Rye. 1999. Marriage and the spiritual realm: The role of proximal and distal constructs in marital functioning. *Journal of Family Psychology* 13: 321–38. [CrossRef]

Mahoney, Annette, Kenneth I. Pargament, Nalini Tarakeshwar, and Aaron B. Swank. 2001. Religion in the home in the 1980s and 1990s: A meta-analytic review and conceptual analysis of links between religion, marriage, and parenting. *Journal of Family Psychology* 15: 559–96. [CrossRef] [PubMed]

Marks, Loren. 2005. How does religion influence marriage? Christian, Jewish, Mormon, and Muslim perspectives. *Marriage & Family Review* 38: 85–111. [CrossRef]

Newman, Cynthia. M., and Paul G. Benchener. 2008. Marketing in America's large protestant churches. *Journal of Business & Economics Research* 6: 1–8. Available online: https://www.cluteinstitute.com/ojs/index.php/JBER/article/view/2384/2431 (accessed on 15 February 2019). [CrossRef]

Padilla-Walker, Laura M., Sarah M. Coyne, Ashley M. Fraser, W. Justin Dyer, and Jeremy B. Yorgason. 2012. Parents and adolescents growing up in the digital age: Latent growth curve analysis of proactive media monitoring. *Journal of Adolescence* 35: 1153–65. [CrossRef] [PubMed]

Pew Research Center. 2014. Religion and Electronic Media: One-in-Five Americans Share Their Faith Online. Available online: http://www.pewforum.org/2014/11/06/religion-and-electronic-media/ (accessed on 15 February 2019).

Pew Research Center. 2015. U.S. Public Becoming Less Religious. Available online: http://assets.pewresearch.org/wp-content/uploads/sites/11/2015/11/201.11.03_RLS_II_full_report.pdf (accessed on 15 February 2019).

Phillips, Tommy M., Loren D. Marks, Alice C. Long, Jennifer R. Smith, Brandan E. Wheeler, Michael A. Goodman, Trevan G. Hatch, and Sterling K. Wall. forthcoming. Family home evening as a model for promoting family health.

Roberts, James A., and David E. Meredith. 2016. My life has become a major distraction from my cell phone: Partner phubbing and relationship satisfaction among romantic partners. *Computers in Human Behavior* 54: 134–41. [CrossRef]

Robinson, Linda C. 1994. Religious orientation in enduring marriage: An exploratory study. *Review of Religious Research* 35: 207–18. [CrossRef]

Robinson, John. P., and Steven Martin. 2008. What do happy people do? *Social Indicators Research* 89: 565–71. [CrossRef]

Rogge, Ronald D., Frank D. Fincham, Dev Crasta, and Michael R. Maniaci. 2017. Positive and negative evaluation of relationships: Development and validation of the Positive-Negative Relationship Quality (PN-RQ) Scale. *Psychological Assessment* 8: 1028–43. [CrossRef] [PubMed]

Rubin, Alan M. 2000. Impact of motivation, attraction, and parasocial interaction on talk radio listening. *Journal of Broadcasting & Electronic Media* 44: 635. [CrossRef]

Schumm, Walter R., Stephen A. Anderson, Jonathan E. Benigas, Mary B. McCutchen, Charles L. Griffin, Janet E. Morris, and Gary S. Race. 1985. Criterion-related validity of the Kansas Marital Satisfaction Scale. *Psychological Reports* 56: 719–22. [CrossRef]

Shen, George C. 2015. How quality of life affects intention to use social networking sites: Moderating role of self-disclosure. *Journal of Electronic Commerce Research* 16: 276–89. Available online: http://search.ebscohost.com/login.aspx?direct=true&AuthType=ip,shib&db=bth&AN=111084810&site=eds-live&custid=magn1307 (accessed on 15 February 2019).

Smith, Sharon G., Xinjian Zhang, Kathleen C. Basile, Melissa T. Merrick, Jing Wang, Marcie-jo Kresnow, and Jieru Chen. 2018. *National Intimate Partner and Sexual Violence Survey (NISVS): 2015 Data Brief (Updated)*; Atlanta: National Center for Injury Prevention and Control, Centers for Disease Control and Prevention. [CrossRef]

Stanley, Scott M., Howard J. Markman, and Sarah W. Whitton. 2002. Communication, conflict, and commitment: Insights on the foundations of relationship success from a national survey. *Family Process* 41: 659–75. [CrossRef] [PubMed]

Strawbridge, William J., Sarah J. Shema, Richard D. Cohen, and George A. Kaplan. 2001. Religious attendance increases survival by improving and maintaining good health behaviors, mental health, and social relationships. *Annals of Behavioral Medicine* 23: 68–74. [CrossRef] [PubMed]

Suleiman, Ahna Ballonoff, Jessica S. Lin, and Norman A. Constantine. 2016. Readability of educational materials to support parent sexual communication with their children and adolescents. *Journal of Health Communication* 21: 534–43. [CrossRef] [PubMed]

Sung, Huei-Chuan, Anne M. Chang, and Wen-Li Lee. 2010. A preferred music listening intervention to reduce anxiety in older adults with dementia in nursing homes. *Journal of Clinical Nursing* 19: 1056–64. [CrossRef] [PubMed]

Todhunter, Robbin G., and John Deaton. 2010. The relationship between religious and spiritual factors and the perpetration of intimate partner violence. *Journal of Family Violence* 25: 745–53. [CrossRef]

Urponen, Helka, Ilkka Vuori, Joel Hasan, and Markku Partinen. 1988. Self-evaluations of factors promoting and disturbing sleep: An epidemiological survey in Finland. *Social Science & Medicine* 26: 443–50. [CrossRef]

Vaaler, Margaret L., Christopher G. Ellison, and Daniel A. Powers. 2009. Religious influences on the risk of marital dissolution. *Journal of Marriage and Family* 71: 917–34. [CrossRef]

Wen, Ya-Hui. 2010. Religiosity and death anxiety. *The Journal of Human Resource and Adult Learning* 6: 31–7.

Wilmoth, Joe. D., Carolyn E. Adams-Price, Joshua J. Turner, Abigail D. Blaney, and Laura Downey. 2014. Examining social connections as a link between religious participation and well-being among older adults. *Journal of Religion, Spirituality, & Aging* 26: 259–78. [CrossRef]

Wilmoth, Joe D., Abigail D. Blaney, and Jennifer R. Smith. 2015. Marital satisfaction, negative interaction, and religiosity: A comparison of three age groups. *Journal of Religion, Spirituality, and Aging* 27: 222–40. [CrossRef]

Wilmoth, Joe D., Loriena Yancura, Melissa A. Barnett, and Brittney Oliver. 2018. The contributions of religious practice, existential certainty, and raising grandchildren to well-being in older adults. *Journal of Religion, Spirituality & Aging* 30: 212–33. [CrossRef]

Young, M. 2011. Religiosity and health behavior—What does research tell us? *American Journal of Health Education* 42: 4–11. [CrossRef]

![religions logo] **religions**

MDPI

Article

Their Fault, Not Mine: Religious Commitment, Theological Conservatism, and Americans' Retrospective Reasons for Divorce

Samuel L. Perry

Department of Sociology, University of Oklahoma, 780 Van Vleet Oval, Kaufman Hall 335A, Norman, OK 73019, USA; samperry@ou.edu

Received: 3 July 2018; Accepted: 3 August 2018; Published: 7 August 2018

check for updates

Abstract: How does religion influence the ways divorcées frame their divorce experience? Building on Mills's "vocabularies of motive" concept, I theorize that Americans who are more religious or affiliated with a conservative Protestant tradition will be more likely to emphasize their former spouse's role in the divorce while minimizing their own. Data are taken from a large, representative sample of divorced Americans in the 2014 Relationships in America survey. Analyses affirm that divorced Americans who attend worship services more frequently are more likely to say that their former spouse wanted the divorce more than they did. Looking at 17 specific reasons for divorce, those who feel religion is more important to them are consistently more likely to select reasons that put blame on their former spouse or circumstances, while frequent attendees are less likely to cite their own behaviors or intentions. Though less consistent, notable patterns also emerged for conservative Protestants. Given the stigma against divorce in many religious communities, I argue that divorcées in such communities likely feel internal pressure to account for their divorce in ways that deflect blame.

Keywords: evangelicals; marriage; divorce; religious attendance; vocabularies of motive

1. Introduction

A vast literature has explored the relationship between religion and marital stability, with studies consistently showing that divorce is less common among Americans who are more religious (Amato and Rogers 1997; Brown et al. 2008; Bulanda and Brown 2007; Call and Heaton 1997; Chi and Houseknecht 1985; Glenn and Supancic 1984; Lehrer and Chiswick 1993; Massoglia et al. 2011) and hold theologically conservative beliefs (Call and Heaton 1997; Vaaler et al. 2009; but see Glass and Levchak 2014). This is often attributed to the stronger collective sanctions that conservative Christian communities have against divorce as well as their general sanctification of the marriage relationship (see reviews in Amato 2010; Lehrer and Son 2017; Mahoney 2010; Mahoney et al. 2001; Weaver et al. 2002). Yet, despite all that we know about the religious correlates of divorce, we still know very little about the role religion plays in shaping the ways divorcées explain their divorce in hindsight. Do the retrospective accounts that devoutly-religious or theologically conservative Americans give for their divorce differ in predictable ways from those who are relatively less religious or conservative?

The answer to this question is not inconsequential. Divorce is a historically stigmatizing experience (Gerstel 1987). This has been especially true within many conservative faith communities where divorcées often report feeling marked socially (Konieczny 2016; Konstam et al. 2016; Sullivan 2012) while also grappling with internal shame (Jenkins 2010, 2014; Simonič and Klobučar 2017). Recognizing the ways religious factors might influence how divorced Americans publicly account for their own divorce in retrospect would help us understand how Americans socially process—or even *re*-interpret—the experience of divorce in light of broader community sanctions.

Drawing on data from a unique, large, and representative sample of divorced Americans, this study examines how religion potentially influences the retrospective reasons divorced men and women highlight as contributing to their divorce. Building on the "vocabularies of motive" concept articulated by C. Wright Mills (1940) and subsequent others (Burke 1969; Perry 2017a), I theorize that, because divorce is often stigmatized among conservative religious communities, divorced respondents who are more religious or affiliated with conservative Protestantism will be more likely to portray their divorce in ways that emphasize their former spouse's faults and initiation of the event and less likely to blame themselves. Before proceeding with the analyses, however, the following section discusses the connection between religion and divorce and introduces the "vocabularies of motive" concept in order to theorize expectations about how religion shapes divorced Americans' retrospective accounts of their divorce.

2. Background

2.1. Religion and Divorce in the United States

Studies on the social correlates of marital stability find that individual religiosity (measured in a variety of ways) tends to be negatively—though often only weakly—associated with experiencing a divorce (Mahoney 2010). Focusing primarily on religious service attendance as an indicator of religious commitment, some studies have found a non-significant relationship between attendance and divorce (Perry and Schleifer 2018; Vaaler et al. 2009), while most others find the two factors to be significantly correlated (Amato and Rogers 1997; Brown et al. 2008; Bulanda and Brown 2007; Clydesdale 1997; Massoglia et al. 2011; Perry 2018; Sweezy and Tiefenthaler 1996; Wilcox 2004; Wilcox and Wolfinger 2016). Importantly, the association could be bi-directional due to the religious stigma that divorced Americans often face in religious contexts. That is, people may simply be less likely to attend church *after* their divorce, just as religious attendance or commitment more generally may discourage divorce (Brown 2015; Konstam et al. 2016; Sullivan 2012). Even so, longitudinal studies of religion and divorce have shown that religious commitment does indeed seem to have a temporal, directional effect on the likelihood of divorce over time (Amato and Rogers 1997; Bulanda and Brown 2007; Perry 2018).

Despite the consistent association between religiosity and divorce, however, the link between theological beliefs or affiliation and divorce is less consistent. Several studies have found that affiliation with conservative Protestantism is either unassociated with divorce after controlling for relevant sociodemographic factors (Barna Group 2001, 2004; Call and Heaton 1997; Glenn and Supancic 1984; Wilcox 2009) or even positively associated with divorce, particularly in the aggregate (Chi and Houseknecht 1985; Glass and Levchak 2014; Mullins et al. 2006). Indeed, some studies suggest that the extreme pro-marriage norms espoused by theologically conservative religious communities actually indirectly *increase* marital dissolution by promoting earlier marriage and lower female education (Glass and Levchak 2014; Lehrer and Son 2017). Other studies, however, find that those in conservative Protestant traditions (Barna Group 2008; Gray 2013; Perry 2018; Sweezy and Tiefenthaler 1996) and those who otherwise hold conservative theological views (Lehrer and Chiswick 1993; Vaaler et al. 2009; but see Heaton and Pratt 1990) are generally less likely to be divorced than the irreligious. A number of studies also find that religious homogamy—marrying someone of similar faith tradition and/or commitment—also tends to be positively associated with married couples staying together (Call and Heaton 1997; Heaton and Pratt 1990; Lehrer and Chiswick 1993; Vaaler et al. 2009).

Explaining the connection between religion and divorce, those who find religiosity lessens the probability of divorce argue that devoutly religious individuals likely internalize their community's standards about the importance of marriage and the seriousness of marital dissolution (Lehrer 2004, p. 709; Mahoney et al. 2001). Others suggest that religious communities likely also place social pressure on individuals to work through problems in marriage, reluctantly permitting divorce only as a "last resort" (Jenkins 2005; Levitt and Ware 2006), often only for situations of abandonment or sexual infidelity (Gilkerson 2015; Van Biema 2007), and within some conservative Protestant camps not even then (Piper 2009)[1]. Both of these factors heighten the possibility that Americans within these religious communities will experience more acute internal and social consequences when divorce actually occurs.

2.2. Religion and the Experiences of Divorcées

Even though devoutly religious, theologically conservative Americans tend to strongly oppose divorce in theory, members of these communities still experience divorce at rates at or just below those of other Americans (Glass and Levchak 2014; Wilcox and Wolfinger 2016). How do these men and women experience their divorce within these communities? Findings from qualitative, small-sample studies of divorcées consistently reveal that men and women often feel like their divorce stigmatizes them in the eyes of other believers. Despite the fact that clergy often report wanting their congregation to care for individuals experiencing family disruption (Edgell 2006; Jenkins 2014), these clergy are paradoxically often very vocal about defending the sanctity of marriage, and criticizing the surrounding "individualistic" American culture for its perceived devaluation of marriage (Jenkins 2005; Konieczny 2016). This can consequently convey the message that churchgoers who get divorced (regardless of circumstances) are selfish, broken, and/or unspiritual. For example, Jenkins' (Jenkins 2010, 2014) ethnographic and interview-based study of divorce within the context of congregations shows that divorced churchgoers often anticipated gossip and judgment from their fellow congregants, forcing them to grapple with social shame. This, in combination with the fact that divorce was rarely talked about in many congregations, heightened the isolation her respondents felt. Importantly, Jenkins also recounts how her interviewees, through religious rituals, engage in emotional self-work, creating a "new self" and re-imagining their lives in light of beliefs they chose to emphasize.

Elsewhere, Konstam et al.'s (2017) interview-based study of women experiencing divorce finds that both religious and irreligious women alike feared how those in certain religious communities would stigmatize them. Indeed, several noted being surprised when their own congregations proved more welcoming toward them then they had expected. Several others, however, felt that conservative anti-divorce beliefs not only inclined their religious communities to stigmatize their divorce, but were largely to blame for Western society's overall negative evaluation of divorcées. And most recently, Simonič and Klobučar's (2016) exploratory, qualitative study of 11 divorced women reveals how personal spiritual practices allowed these women to combat feelings of isolation and shame by reinterpreting their experience, specifically, by seeing God as on their side, loving and strengthening them through their ordeal. These qualitative studies, though with relatively few participants, affirm that those in religious communities do indeed struggle with feelings of shame and perceived stigma, and a consistent theme in their accounts is the need to reinterpret or reimagine their situation in ways that attenuate feelings of dissonance or isolation. In the following section I consider Mills's (1940) "vocabularies of motive" concept in order to frame expectations about the ways religion may influence divorcées' accounts of their experience.

2.3. Vocabularies of Motive, Religion, and Retrospective Reasons for Divorce

"Accounts" or explanations of motive, according to C. Wright Mills (1940; see also Burke 1969; Perry 2017a), serve an important social function in that they situate one's own behavior in a way such that others can not only understand the reasons behind that behavior, but affirm them. Because such explanations serve a primarily *social* function, Mills proposed that sociologists should not think of motives as subjective "springs" from which action flows, but rather as standard vocabularies that

---

1   For example, a well-known Baptist pastor and author, John Piper (2009, p. 159) argues that because marriage is supposed to represent Christ and his church, and because Jesus would never divorce his church, the Bible, therefore, does not permit divorce for Christians under *any* circumstances: " . . . as long as Christ keeps his covenant with the church, and as long as the church, by the omnipotent grace of God, remains the chosen people of Christ, then the very meaning of marriage will include: *What God has joined, only God can separate*" (italics his).

situate action within defined social situations. Social actors give an "account" of their motives for specific reasons, and those reasons are usually because those accounts or vocabularies of motive are those that are socially condoned by a particular audience given the social situation. Different institutional situations call for different vocabularies of motive to account for certain lines of behavior[2]. Indeed, Mills criticized the scholarly quest for "real motives" since he believed that such quests proceed from the faulty premise that real motives are something essential to the individual, which we cannot observe empirically. Rather, he proposed that social scientists are better served by analyzing vocabularies of motive to better understand the social situation in which such vocabularies are learned and expected. He concluded, "Rather than interpreting actions and language as external manifestations of subjective and deeper lying elements in individuals, the research task is the locating of particular types of action within typal frames of normative actions and socially situated clusters of motive" (Mills 1940, p. 913).

In other words, the "accounts" or reasons people give for their behavior in retrospect tell us not only (or even primarily) about their *actual* motivations, but about the broader social milieu which required those specific reasons to justify the action socially. Religious adherents, for example, may tell an interviewer that they give alms to the poor out of genuine charity. Whether that is *really* their motive is not empirically observable. Thus, what is more instructive for social scientists, according to Mills, is the implication that the adherents' social community apparently requires alms-giving to be done with charitable motivations, and thus requires community members to account for that giving with the appropriate vocabularies of motive.

Mills's "vocabularies of motive" concept is useful for interpreting divorcées' retrospective explanations for their divorce. It is impossible to discern whether a divorce happened precisely for the reasons that a divorced man or woman reports, potentially years after the fact. But this is not problematic if we understand retrospective "reasons" for a divorce using Mills's conceptual framework, namely, as "accounts" that social actors are providing to situate their behavior in a way that is consonant with their own self-concept and according to what are deemed to be appropriate reasons for divorce within their particular reference group. Different patterns of reasons for divorce, therefore, will inform our understanding of how different social contexts require different accounts to justify divorce.

Because deeply religious, theologically conservative Americans are more likely to view divorce as sinful and stigmatizing, I expect that their retrospective reasons for their divorce will differ from others' in patterned, predictable ways. Specifically, I expect that divorcées who are more religious or affiliated with conservative Protestantism—the subculture most opposed to divorce (Ellison et al. 2012; Martin and Parashar 2006; Stokes and Ellison 2010)—will be more likely to (1) indicate that their former spouse wanted the divorce more than they did, thus citing their former spouse as the initiator, and (2) frame their divorce in ways that deflect blame from themselves and place the blame on their former spouse's character or behavior. While not the primary focus of this study, I also anticipate these reasons given for divorce to be somewhat gendered, based on typical relationship patterns. For example, I expect that women will be more likely than men to express that they sought a divorce because of their former spouse's physical abuse, obsession with their career, or pornography use, since these are less likely to be a cause for divorce among men.

---

[2] Importantly, Mills did not think of these socially-approved "accounts" as lies necessarily (though he acknowledges some might be lies), because he believed these vocabularies of motive were often internalized by the actor to genuinely shape their future action. For example, he explained, "The long acting out of a role, with its appropriate motives, will often induce a man to become what at first he merely sought to appear. [...] vocabularies of motives for different situations are significant determinants of conduct." (1940, p. 908). And later, he writes, "To term [motives] justification is not to deny their efficacy. Often anticipations of acceptable justifications will control conduct. ('If I did this, what could I say? What would they say?') Decisions may be, wholly or in part, delimited by answers to such queries" (1940, p. 907).

3. Methods

3.1. Data

Data are taken from the 2014 Relationships in America (RIA) survey. The RIA survey was distributed to a national probability sample of 15,738 adults between the ages of 18 and 60 years old in January and February 2014. Data collection was sponsored by the Austin Institute for the Study of Family and Culture and conducted by the research firm GfK. GfK recruited the first online research "panel"[3] that is representative of the US population, called the "KnowledgePanel." Members in the KnowledgePanel are randomly recruited by telephone and mail surveys. Those households are provided with access to the Internet and computer hardware if necessary[4]. The main survey completion rate for the RIA survey instrument was 62 percent. Cases in the RIA sample were assigned a weight based on the sampling design and their probability of being selected, ensuring a sample that was representative of American adults aged 18–60. These sample weights are used in all analyses. For a more comprehensive discussion of sampling and data collection procedures, see Litschi et al. (2014). Because this study focuses on the responses of Americans who had been heterosexually married[5] and divorced, the analyses focused on the 3023 respondents who answered the RIA survey question about which spouse wanted the divorce, and the 2124 respondents who provided specific reasons for why they got a divorce.

3.2. Measures

3.2.1. Retrospective Accounts of the Divorce

The outcomes for this study are measures tapping respondents' retrospective interpretations of their divorce. For the first measure, respondents were asked to "choose the best answer that describes how (their most recent) marriage ended." Respondents were given five options, including (1) "I wanted the marriage to end, but my spouse did not," (2) "I wanted it to end more than my spouse did," (3) "We both wanted it to end," (4) "My spouse wanted it to end more than I did," and (5) "My spouse wanted the marriage to end, but I did not." Higher scores on the question indicate that the divorce—at least in the respondent's view—was initiated and pursued by the former spouse rather than the respondent. Because the measure has five values, I use ordinary least squares (OLS) regression for the analysis.

For respondents who chose options 1, 2, or 3 for the previous question (indicating that either they or both they and their former spouse wanted the divorce for whatever reasons), the RIA survey also asked, "For which of the following reasons did you want a divorce?" The RIA then provided 17 different reasons, to which respondents could indicate yes = 1, or no = 0. Respondents could answer "yes" to as many reasons as appropriate. In order to observe patterns in the ways religious factors were associated with different reasons for divorce, I grouped the reasons into (1) those that clearly placed the blame largely with the respondent's former spouse (e.g., "Spouse's pornography use" or "Spouse's immaturity"); (2) those in which the blame was placed more on the respondent (e.g., "I wanted to pursue a different life" or "My own romantic or sexual relationship with someone else"); and (3) those in which other circumstances are identified and/or the blame is unclear (e.g., "Problems

---

3   Though this is the term used by GfK, the data are cross-sectional and do not represent a "panel" in a longitudinal sense.
4   Unlike other Internet research panels sampling only individuals with Internet access who volunteer for research, this panel was based on a sampling frame which included both listed and unlisted numbers, and those without a landline telephone; it was not limited to current Internet users or computer owners and did not accept self-selected volunteers. An evaluation of the Knowledge Networks' Internet probability sample survey methodology compared favorably to online nonprobability samples as well as random-digit-dial telephone surveys (Chang and Krosnick 2009).
5   While the RIA does not ask respondents about whether their most recent marriage was heterosexual or homosexual, to increase the likelihood that divorced respondents were in heterosexual marriages, I excluded men and women who indicated in the RIA that they had never had sex with someone of the opposite sex. In ancillary analyses, I also excluded respondents who reported any homosexual relationships either at all or in the past 12 months. While these changes lowered the sample size, they did not change the substantive findings for the main analyses.

with spouse's family" or "We married too young"). Because the reasons differ so greatly for male and female respondents (e.g., almost no men reported wanting a divorce because of their former spouse's pornography use), along with models for the full sample, I also estimate separate regression models by gender to predict the likelihood that respondents affirmed a particular reason. Because the outcomes are dichotomous, I use binary logistic regression models to predict each.

Lastly, based on the different categories of "divorce reasons" described in the previous paragraph, I create three additive indexes using the three groups of RIA questions in which respondents primarily blame their former spouse (called "blame ex"), where they blame themselves ("blame self"), or blame circumstances or some other factor ("blame circumstances"). Though each index has a different value range because of the different number of questions falling into each, I standardize each as Z-scores to make coefficients comparable across models. Because each has multiple values, I use OLS regression as my model estimation procedure.

3.2.2. Religion Variables

The key independent variables for the analysis are respondents' religious affiliation, the importance of religion in the respondent's life, and their frequency of religious service attendance. Because my interest is in the differences between conservative Protestants and others in the reasons they affirm for divorce, I created a dummy variable using the following information. Respondents were first asked their general religious affiliation. Those who chose "Protestant" were given options of "fundamentalist," "evangelical," "mainline," "liberal," "Pentecostal," or "none of these."[6] I collapsed respondents who identified as "fundamentalist," "evangelical," or "Pentecostal" into one "conservative Protestant" group coded 1 with other Americans coded 0 (Woodberry and Smith 1998). For importance of religion, respondents were asked, "How important (if at all) is religious faith to you?" Responses ranged from 1 = "not important at all" to 5 = "more important than anything else," and I included this as a continuous measure. Lastly, respondents were asked, "How often, if ever, do you normally attend religious services?" Responses ranged from 1 = "never" to 8 = "more than once a week", and this is also included as a continuous measure.

3.2.3. Controls

The analyses include a number of sociodemographic controls. For the full models, gender is included as a control variable (female = 1, male = 0). For all models, age is measured in years from 18 to 60. Dummy variables are included for marital status (married = 1), parental status (any children = 1), race (white = 1, other race = 0), and region (southern residence = 1, elsewhere = 0). Educational attainment is measured in categories from 1 = less than high school to 4 = bachelor's degree or higher. And household income is measured with 19 values from 1 = less than $5000 to 19 = $175,000 or more. Table 1 presents descriptive information for all variables used in the analyses.

---

[6] "Fundamentalist" and "Evangelical" are labels that explicitly align one with theological (and often cultural) conservatism, while "Pentecostal" refers more to a variety of theology among conservative Protestants. "Mainline" Protestants traditionally include Lutherans, Presbyterians, Methodists, Episcopalians, Anglicans, United Church of Christ, Disciples of Christ, Quakers, and several varieties of American Baptist (not Southern Baptists). Members of these denominations would most often fall into the "liberal" classification as well.

Table 1. Descriptive statistics.

Variables	Range	Full Sample		Men		Women	
		Mean or %	SD	Mean or %	SD	Mean or %	SD
How much of divorce was former spouse's initiation?	1–5	2.7	1.4	3.2	1.3	2.4	1.3
Reasons for Divorce							
Blame More With Former Spouse							
Spouse's immaturity	0–1	30%		26%		32%	
Abandonment	0–1	7%		6%		8%	
Spouse's pornography use	0–1	5%		1%		8%	
Spouse's romantic/sexual infidelity	0–1	29%		31%		28%	
Physical abuse	0–1	15%		7%		20%	
Spouse's career came before family	0–1	5%		5%		5%	
Emotional abuse	0–1	28%		13%		37%	
Spouse unresponsive to my needs	0–1	33%		30%		35%	
Alcohol or drug use	0–1	24%		14%		29%	
Revelations from spouse's past	0–1	5%		4%		5%	
Blame More With Respondent							
My own romantic/sexual infidelity	0–1	12%		11%		12%	
Grew tired of making a poor match work	0–1	31%		33%		30%	
I wanted to pursue different life	0–1	17%		16%		17%	
Circumstances at Fault/Blame Unclear							
Problems with spouse's family	0–1	15%		15%		15%	
Insurmountable cultural/religious differences	0–1	5%		6%		4%	
We married too young	0–1	21%		24%		19%	
Different financial priorities/spending patterns	0–1	25%		25%		25%	
Independent Variables							
Conservative Protestant	0–1	15%		16%		14%	
Importance of religion	1–5	3.3	1.2	3	1.3	3.4	1.1
Religious service attendance	1–8	3.3	2.5	3.1	2.5	3.4	2.5
Female	0–1	64%					
Age	18–60	48	8.8	48	8.5	48	8.9
Married	0–1	51%		57%		48%	
Any children	0–1	78%		75%		80%	
Educational attainment	1–4	2.7	0.9	2.7	0.9	2.7	0.9
Household income	1–19	11.8	4.4	12.2	4.4	11.4	4.3
White	0–1	70%		65%		73%	
Southern residence	0–1	44%		44%		44%	0.50

Source: 2014 Relationships in America Survey.

3.3. Plan of Analysis

The analysis proceeds as follows. First, Table 2 presents OLS regression models predicting how much respondents attribute their most recent divorce to their former spouse's initiation as opposed to their own. I include a full-sample model and separate models for both men and women. Models present unstandardized regression coefficients and standard errors.

Table 2. Ordinary least squares regression predicting how much a respondent attributes their most recent divorce to their former spouse's initiation.

Predictors	Full Sample	Men Only	Women Only
Conservative Protestant	0.06	0.02	0.11
	(0.07)	(0.10)	(0.10)
Importance of religion	0.04	0.03	0.05
	(0.03)	(0.04)	(0.04)
Religious service attendance	0.04 ***	0.03 +	0.05 **
	(0.01)	(0.02)	(0.02)
Female	−0.83 ***		
	(0.05)		
Age	0.01	0.02 ***	−0.01
	(0.00)	(0.00)	(0.00)
Married	−0.17 ***	−0.14 +	−0.20 **
	(0.05)	(0.08)	(0.07)
Any children	0.06	0.10	−0.02
	(0.06)	(0.09)	(0.08)
Educational attainment	−0.01	−0.03	−0.01
	(0.03)	(0.04)	(0.04)
Household income	−0.01	−0.01	−0.01
	(0.01)	(0.01)	(0.01)
White	0.21 ***	0.27 ***	0.16 *
	(0.05)	(0.08)	(0.08)
Southern residence	−0.03	−0.05	−0.02
	(0.05)	(0.07)	(0.07)
Constant	2.68 ***	2.14 ***	2.22 ***
	(0.18)	(0.26)	(0.24)
Adjusted R	0.10	0.02	0.02
N	3023	1337	1686

Source: 2014 Relationships in America Survey. **Note:** Odds ratios with standard errors in parentheses. + $p < 0.10$; * $p < 0.05$; ** $p < 0.01$; *** $p < 0.001$ (two-tailed test).

Tables 3 and 4 present binary logistic regression models predicting affirmative answers for each of the 17 listed reasons for getting a divorce in the RIA survey. In order to conserve space, the 17 outcomes variables are listed along the far-left row and only key predictor variables (conservative Protestant affiliation, religious importance, religious service attendance, and gender) are listed across the top column. All models, however, include the full array of controls. Table 3 presents logistic regression models for the full sample. Table 4 presents outcomes with the sample split by gender due to drastically different response patterns for men and women.

Table 3. Binary logistic regression models predicting retrospective reasons for divorce (full sample).

Outcome: Reasons for Divorce	Key Predictors			
	Cons. Prot.	Importance	Attendance	Female
Blame More with Former Spouse				
Spouse's immaturity	0.81	1.01	0.98	1.32 **
	(0.15)	(0.05)	(0.03)	(0.11)
Abandonment	0.46 *	1.18 +	1.00	1.04
	(0.32)	(0.10)	(0.04)	(0.19)
Spouse's pornography use	1.75 *	1.05	1.03	9.31 ***
	(0.28)	(0.11)	(0.05)	(0.41)
Spouse's romantic/sexual infidelity	1.26 +	1.12 *	1.00	0.85
	(0.14)	(0.05)	(0.02)	(0.10)
Physical abuse	0.81	1.31 ***	0.99	3.02 ***
	(0.19)	(0.07)	(0.03)	(0.16)
Spouse's career came before family	0.36 *	0.95	1.05	1.18
	(0.42)	(0.11)	(0.05)	(0.22)
Emotional abuse	1.01	1.23 ***	1.00	3.56 ***
	(0.15)	(0.06)	(0.03)	(0.13)
Spouse unresponsive to my needs	0.71 *	0.97	1.00	1.24 *
	(0.15)	(0.05)	(0.02)	(0.10)
Alcohol or drug use	1.00	1.09	0.97	2.36 ***
	(0.16)	(0.06)	(0.03)	(0.12)
Revelations from spouse's past	0.86	1.08	0.94	0.99
	(0.35)	(0.11)	(0.06)	(0.22)
Blame More with Respondent				
My own romantic/sexual infidelity	0.86	1.09	0.92 *	1.11
	(0.23)	(0.07)	(0.04)	(0.15)
Grew tired of making a poor match work	0.89	0.96	0.93 **	0.89
	(0.15)	(0.05)	(0.03)	(0.10)
I wanted to pursue different life	0.96	0.95	0.89 ***	1.13
	(0.20)	(0.06)	(0.03)	(0.13)
Circumstances at Fault/Blame Unclear				
Problems with spouse's family	0.80	1.21 **	0.92 *	0.95
	(0.20)	(0.07)	(0.03)	(0.13)
Insurmountable cultural/religious differences	1.01	1.02	1.02	0.63 *
	(0.31)	(0.11)	(0.05)	(0.21)
We married too young	0.96	1.08	0.95 +	0.71 **
	(0.17)	(0.06)	(0.03)	(0.11)
Different financial priorities/spending patterns	0.81	1.03	0.95 +	1.00
	(0.16)	(0.06)	(0.03)	(0.11)

Source: 2014 Relationships in America Survey (*N* for all models = 2124). **Note:** Odds ratios with standard errors in parentheses. All models include variables for age, gender, marital status, parental status, educational attainment, household income, race, southern residence, evangelical affiliation, importance of religion, and religious service attendance. + $p < 0.10$; * $p < 0.05$; ** $p < 0.01$; *** $p < 0.001$ (two-tailed test).

Table 4. Binary logistic regression models predicting retrospective reasons for divorce.

	Men Only (N = 769)			Women Only (N = 1355)		
Outcome: Reasons for Divorce	Cons. Prot.	Importance	Attendance	Cons. Prot.	Importance	Attendance
Blame More with Former Spouse						
Spouse's immaturity	0.67	1.01	0.96	0.92	1.01	0.99
	(0.27)	(0.08)	(0.04)	(0.19)	(0.07)	(0.03)
Abandonment	0.41	1.37 *	0.93	0.47 *	1.12	1.04
	(0.58)	(0.16)	(0.08)	(0.38)	(0.12)	(0.05)
Spouse's pornography use	NA	1.27	1.02	1.97 *	1.02	1.03
	NA	(0.44)	(0.23)	(0.29)	(0.12)	(0.05)
Spouse's romantic/sexual infidelity	1.86 **	1.21 *	0.90 *	0.97	1.08	1.05
	(0.24)	(0.08)	(0.04)	(0.19)	(0.07)	(0.03)
Physical abuse	0.37 +	1.20	1.04	0.93	1.36 ***	0.97
	(0.53)	(0.15)	(0.07)	(0.21)	(0.08)	(0.03)
Spouse's career came before family	0.33 +	0.80	1.28 **	0.33 +	1.09	0.92
	(0.66)	(0.17)	(0.09)	(0.57)	(0.14)	(0.07)
Emotional abuse	1.01	1.13	1.03	1.01	1.28 ***	0.99
	(0.32)	(0.12)	(0.06)	(0.18)	(0.07)	(0.03)
Spouse unresponsive to my needs	1.10	1.09	0.92 *	0.53 **	0.89 +	1.05
	(0.24)	(0.08)	(0.04)	(0.20)	(0.07)	(0.03)
Alcohol or drug use	1.72 +	1.10	0.82 ***	0.83	1.09	1.01
	(0.31)	(0.11)	(0.06)	(0.19)	(0.07)	(0.03)
Revelations from spouse's past	0.79	1.19	0.97	0.89	1.02	0.93
	(0.56)	(0.18)	(0.09)	(0.46)	(0.14)	(0.07)
Blame More with Respondent						
My own romantic/sexual infidelity	1.29	1.16	0.97	0.57 +	1.02	0.91 *
	(0.32)	(0.12)	(0.06)	(0.34)	(0.10)	(0.05)
Grew tired of making a poor match work	1.05	0.96	0.94	0.79	0.95	0.92 *
	(0.24)	(0.08)	(0.04)	(0.20)	(0.07)	(0.03)
I wanted to pursue different life	0.85	1.11	0.92	0.95	0.86 +	0.88 **
	(0.31)	(0.10)	(0.05)	(0.27)	(0.08)	(0.04)
Circumstances at Fault/Blame Unclear						
Problems with spouse's family	1.35	1.22 +	0.89 *	0.51 *	1.18 +	0.93 +
	(0.29)	(0.11)	(0.06)	(0.30)	(0.09)	(0.04)
Insurmountable cultural/religious differences	1.96 +	1.16	0.98	0.42	0.83	1.08
	(0.40)	(0.17)	(0.08)	(0.59)	(0.16)	(0.07)
We married too young	1.46	1.40 ***	0.85 ***	0.61 *	0.85 *	1.06
	(0.25)	(0.09)	(0.05)	(0.24)	(0.08)	(0.04)
Different financial priorities/spending patterns	1.05	1.10	0.88 +	0.68 +	0.96	1.00
	(0.26)	(0.09)	(0.05)	(0.21)	(0.07)	(0.03)

Source: 2014 Relationships in America Survey. **Note**: Odds ratios with standard errors in parentheses. All models include variables for age, marital status, parental status, educational attainment, Household income, race, southern residence, evangelical affiliation, importance of religion, and religious service attendance. $+ p < 0.10$; $* p < 0.05$; $** p < 0.01$; $*** p < 0.001$ (two-tailed test).

Lastly, in order to provide a summary analysis for the trends observed in Tables 3 and 4, I estimate religion's effect on each of the three additive indexes I constructed using the three groups of RIA questions: *blame ex*, *blame self*, and *blame circumstances*. I estimate OLS regression models for the full sample and men and women separately to examine the effects of religion measures on each of these outcomes with relevant controls in place.

4. Results

Table 2 presents OLS regression models predicting how much of the divorce respondents attribute to the initiation of their former spouse versus their own. While those who are affiliated with conservative Protestantism or believe their religion is more important to them are no different from other Americans in this regard, those who attend religious services more frequently are significantly more likely to report that their former spouse was the one who initiated the divorce, not them. Splitting the sample by gender shows that the coefficient for religious attendance points in the same direction for both men and women, though it is only marginally significant for men. Tests for interaction effects (available upon request), however, found no significant interaction between gender and worship attendance, and thus, it is likely that the marginal significance for men is due to reduced sample size. Religious attendance, in other words, is similarly predictive of attributing the initiation of the divorce to one's former spouse for both men and women.

How does religion predict specific reasons that respondents give for their divorce? Table 3 presents odds ratios from binary logistic regression models predicting each of the 17 reasons the RIA provided for why divorced respondents sought a divorce (those reported not seeking the divorce at all were not asked this question). Clearly, religiosity and conservative Protestant affiliation are simply not significantly associated with many of the provided reasons with controls in place. Some of the significant associations show inconsistent patterns, while others show discernable trends. Those affiliated with conservative Protestantism, for example, are less likely than other Americans to cite that they divorced their former spouse because of their former spouse's abandonment, obsession over career, or their being unresponsive to the respondent's needs. But conservative Protestant affiliates are more likely to report divorcing their former spouse because of their pornography use or sexual/romantic infidelity (marginal), which suggests that sexual "cheating" may provide social justification for conservative Protestants to pursue divorce.

The other two religion variables show more consistent associations with divorce accounts. Among the significant associations between various divorce reasons and religious importance, Americans who feel that religion is more important to them are *always* more likely than other Americans to choose responses that blame their former spouse's mistakes or faults, never less likely. Specifically, Americans who report that religion is more important to them are more likely to affirm that they got a divorce because of their former spouse's abandonment (marginal), sexual/romantic infidelity, physical abuse, or emotional abuse. They are also more likely to affirm that they got a divorce because of problems with their former spouse's family.

Religious service attendance shows a similar trend, but is significant for a different set of outcomes. Those who attend worship services more frequently are not significantly more likely to choose divorce reasons that blame their former spouse, but they are significantly *less* likely than other Americans to affirm any of the reasons that blame themselves for the divorce. People who attend worship services more frequently are less likely to say that they got a divorce because of their own sexual/romantic infidelity, because they were tired of making a bad match work, or because they wanted to pursue a different life path. They also appear to be less likely than other Americans to select divorce reasons that either blame circumstances or leave blame unclear.

The last column shows the association between being female and choosing various divorce reasons, suggesting significant contrasts between how women and men account for their split in retrospect. Women are more likely than men to cite their former spouse's immaturity, pornography use, physical and emotional abuse, unresponsiveness to their needs, and substance abuse. Conversely, women are less likely than men to say the got a divorce because they married too young or they had insurmountable cultural or religious differences.

Given these stark contrasts between the ways women and men select reasons for their divorce, how might the associations between religious factors and divorce reasons differ by gender? Results from Table 4 show that much of the core trends remain the same, namely, men and women who believe religion is more important to them are more likely to select divorce reasons that blame the former spouse for the divorce, while women who attend religious services more frequently are significantly less likely to select reasons that blame themselves.

Interesting gender differences turn up for conservative Protestants, however. Conservative Protestant men, for example, are more likely than others to say they divorced their former spouse because of her romantic/sexual infidelity, while conservative Protestant women are more likely to say they divorced their former spouse because of his pornography use. Again, this likely suggests a central role that sexual fidelity plays in the conservative Protestant subculture not only within relationships, but in justifying divorces.

The regression analyses in Table 5 allow me to summarize the trends observed in Tables 3 and 4 by predicting affirmative responses for each group of divorce reasons, namely, those that: blame the former spouse, blame the respondent, or blame circumstances. While conservative Protestants, either in the full sample or for men and women separately, are not consistently associated with patterns of responses, there are again clear patterns of associations for religious importance and religious service attendance. Specifically, men and women who believe that religion is more important to them are more likely to affirm divorce reasons that place the blame with the former spouse. Men with higher religious importance are also more likely than other men to blame their circumstances. In contrast, men and women who attend religious services more often are less likely than others to affirm divorce reasons that blame themselves, and frequent male attendees are also less likely to blame their circumstances.

Table 5. Ordinary least squares regression predicting whether respondents are more likely to affirm reasons that mostly blame their former spouse, themselves, or other circumstances for their divorce.

Predictors	Full Sample			Men Only			Women Only		
	Blame Ex	Blame Self	Blame Circ.	Blame Ex	Blame Self	Blame Circ.	Blame Ex	Blame Self	Blame Circ.
Conservative Protestant	-0.09	-0.05	-0.09	-0.01	0.02	0.20 +	-0.14	-0.11	-0.27 ***
	(06)	(0.07)	(0.07)	(0.09)	(0.11)	(0.11)	(0.09)	(0.08)	(0.08)
Importance of religion	0.07 **	-0.01	0.05 *	0.07 *	0.03	0.13 ***	0.07 *	-0.05	-0.02
	(0.02)	(0.02)	(0.03)	(0.03)	(0.04)	(0.04)	(0.03)	(0.03)	(0.03)
Religious service attendance	-0.01	-0.05 ***	-0.03 **	-0.03 *	-0.04 *	-0.08 ***	0.01	-0.05 ***	0.00
	(0.01)	(0.01)	(0.01)	(0.02)	(0.02)	(0.02)	(0.01)	(0.01)	(0.01)
Female	0.37 ***	0.00	-0.10 *						
	(0.05)	(0.05)	(0.05)						
Age	-0.01 ***	-0.01 *	-0.01 ***	-0.01 *	-0.00	-0.00	-0.02 ***	-0.01 +	-0.02 ***
	(0.00)	(0.00)	(0.00)	(0.00)	(0.00)	(0.01)	(0.00)	(0.00)	(0.03)
Married	-0.11 *	-0.04	0.08 +	-0.01	-0.12	0.15 +	-0.15 *	0.00	0.05
	(0.05)	(0.05)	(0.05)	(0.07)	(0.08)	(0.08)	(0.06)	(0.06)	(0.06)
Any children	0.06	-0.09	0.09 +	-0.05	0.01	0.17 +	0.12 +	-0.13 +	0.07
	(0.05)	(0.05)	(0.05)	(0.07)	(0.08)	(0.09)	(0.07)	(0.07)	(0.07)
Educational attainment	0.03	0.06 *	0.04	0.03	0.00	-0.01	0.02	0.08 *	0.07 *
	(0.03)	(0.03)	(0.03)	(0.04)	(0.04)	(0.05)	(0.04)	(0.03)	(0.03)
Household income	-0.01	0.02 ***	0.00	-0.01	0.03 **	0.01	-0.01	0.02 **	0.00
	(0.01)	(0.01)	(0.01)	(0.01)	(0.01)	(0.01)	(0.01)	(0.01)	(0.01)
White	0.18 ***	-0.03	0.03	0.26 ***	0.05	-0.01	0.12 +	-0.08	0.07
	(0.05)	(0.05)	(0.05)	(0.07)	(0.08)	(0.08)	(0.07)	(0.06)	(0.06)
Southern residence	-0.01	-0.04	-0.03	0.01	-0.07	0.01	-0.04	-0.01	-0.04
	(0.04)	(0.04)	(0.04)	(0.06)	(0.07)	(0.08)	(0.06)	(0.06)	(0.05)
Constant	0.15	0.17	0.43 **	-0.11	-0.08	-0.16	0.72 ***	0.34	0.68 ***
	(0.15)	(0.16)	(0.16)	(0.20)	(0.24)	(0.26)	(0.22)	(0.21)	(0.20)
Adjusted R	0.07	0.04	0.02	0.02	0.01	0.03	0.03	0.05	0.04
N	2,124			769			1355		

Source: 2014 Relationships in America Survey. **Note:** Odds ratios with standard errors in parentheses. + $p < 0.10$; * $p < 0.05$; ** $p < 0.01$; *** $p < 0.001$ (two-tailed test).

5. Discussion and Conclusions

This article sought to test whether religion predicted the ways divorced Americans account for their divorce retrospectively. Building on Mills's (1940) "vocabularies of motive" concept, I reasoned that actors tend to give "accounts" that situate their past behaviors or experiences in ways that will be socially appropriate for their reference groups. Because Americans who are more deeply imbedded within theologically conservative communities would be more likely to face social stigma or internalized shame for a divorce (Jenkins 2010, 2014; Konstam et al. 2016), I hypothesized that religious commitment and theological conservatism would be associated with Americans seeking to frame their divorce in ways that place the blame on their former spouse, and, correspondingly, deflect blame from themselves. Drawing on a unique, large, and representative sample of divorced Americans, and examining a variety of potential reasons that people give for seeking a divorce, the analyses have generally affirmed these expectations. Specifically, men and women who attend religious services more frequently are more likely to say that their former spouse initiated the divorce rather than them and, even among those who affirm that they sought the divorce, those who attend worship services more often are *always* less likely to affirm reasons for divorce that blame themselves. Conversely, men and women for whom religion is more important are consistently more likely to affirm divorce reasons that lay the blame on their former spouse's flaws or mistakes, and never their own.

The findings from this study contribute to our understanding of religion and divorce in several important ways. While there has been a tremendous amount of research on the religious correlates of divorce, the current study has extended this literature by examining how religion influences the ways divorcées think about—or at least report—their divorce in hindsight.

Importantly, previous research on religion in the lives of divorcées emphasized the importance of religious practice and belief in re-imagining or re-creating a new self in light of one's religious identity (Jenkins 2010, 2014; Simonič and Klobučar 2017). Findings from this study suggest that this may extend to the ways religious individuals process their divorce socially. While some divorced Americans report backing away from religious community after the divorce for fear of judgment or stigma (Brown 2015; Konstam et al. 2016; Sullivan 2012), the fact that religiously committed Americans in my study were more likely to portray their former spouse as the initiator of the divorce and blame their former spouse's faults, while also being less likely to cite their own contribution to the divorce, suggests that some divorcées may deal with potential stigma or shame by re-articulating their divorce in ways that deflect blame or guilt. This would be completely consistent with the "vocabularies of motive" idea since religious actors would naturally want to explain their experience in a way that is consistent with the moral evaluations of their religious community and their own self-concept.

The findings also showed that these trends tend to hold across gender. While there were certainly some gendered patterns in the reasons divorcées cited for their divorce (e.g., women were far more likely to cite physical or emotional abuse as a reason for divorce, and men almost never affirmed divorcing their former spouse because of her pornography use), religious commitment seemed to predict similar patterns in the divorce reasons that respondents affirmed. For men and women alike, religious attendance predicted a greater likelihood of reporting that a respondent's former spouse wanted the divorce more than they did; religious importance was positively associated with citing divorce reasons that blamed the former spouse; and worship attendance was negatively associated with affirming reasons that blamed the respondent. Thus, religion's influence on the retrospective divorce accounts of respondents seems to transcend gender, despite the fact that those reasons are themselves highly gendered.

Interestingly, while religious importance and religious service attendance were both consistently associated with divorce reasons, the association between conservative Protestantism and divorce reasons was less consistent. Sometimes conservative Protestant men and women were more likely to blame the divorce on certain faults or flaws in the former spouse, while other times they were less likely to do so. Among the consistent findings for conservative Protestants—in line with my earlier expectations—was that they were never more likely than other Americans to cite reasons that blamed themselves for their divorce. While this study did not explore trends among Catholics due to the extremely small sample size of traditional Catholics who had been divorced, it is likely that traditional Catholics would exhibit similar trends to conservative Protestants in being less likely to cite reasons for divorce that blame themselves. In addition to community opinions, traditional Catholics are also influenced by official Catholic teaching, which condemns divorce except in extreme circumstances and even forbids remarried divorcées from taking communion. While conservative Protestants might worry about community stigma, traditional Catholics might need to deflect blame for the divorce for the sake of avoiding explicit exclusion from their faith community.

Another interesting finding for conservative Protestantism was the gendered patterns of citing reasons for divorce that blamed the former spouse's pornography use (for women) or sexual/relational infidelity (for men). This is likely because sexual infidelity is often thought of as one of the only "biblical" grounds for divorce within conservative Protestant communities. Jesus cited marital unfaithfulness as the only exception clause to the rule that his followers should not divorce and remarry (Matthew 5:32, 19:9). And because Jesus could be interpreted as considering lustful gazes and thoughts as analogous (or even equal to) physical adultery (Matthew 5:28), some conservative Protestants have argued that habitual pornography use is also grounds for divorce (Gilkerson 2015). Consequently, even though married conservative Protestants by and large are statistically less likely than other Americans to commit adultery (Burdette et al. 2007) or view pornography (Perry 2016, 2017b; but see Perry 2017c), conservative Protestants may be more inclined to emphasize these reasons for divorce since they are the ones that are most legitimate within that religious tradition.

Before concluding, several data limitations should also be acknowledged to chart a path for future research. First, given these data, this article can make no claim that the reasons respondents cite for their divorce were the actual contributing factors to that divorce. The "vocabularies of motive" framework allows me to sidestep that problem theoretically by focusing on the accounts themselves rather than the actual divorce. However, to the extent that the reasons cited by respondents reflect the *actual* situation as it happened, the connection between religion and the divorce could be different. That is, persons who are more deeply religious might *actually* be less likely to initiate the divorce, and perhaps, even when they are involved in initiating the divorce, could be less likely to contribute to the failure of the marriage than their former spouse. The data unfortunately do not allow me to confirm whether this is in fact the case. A possible solution to this problem for future studies would be to use dyadic data, where both former spouses are interviewed about their divorce experience, and researchers could check to confirm whether the associations between religion and respondents' retrospective reasons for divorce correspond to those given by their former spouse. Another potential limitation is the limited number of religion measures. While religious importance, religious attendance, and religious affiliation are indeed core measures often used by religion scholars, other useful measures not included in the RIA would be a measure of biblical literalism, which is often found to powerfully predict attitudes toward divorce (Ellison et al. 2012; Martin and Parashar 2006; Stokes and Ellison 2010). Another helpful measure would be a more direct question regarding how one's religious community actually feels about divorce in general or their divorce specifically.

It is worth speculating briefly about whether the observed associations in this study may change over time. Despite increasing acceptance of divorce in the United States (Stokes and Ellison 2010), it still remains a stigmatizing situation, particularly for those within religious communities (Jenkins 2010, 2014; Konieczny 2016; Konstam et al. 2016; Simonič and Klobučar 2017; Sullivan 2012). Focusing on the explanations divorcées cite for their divorce suggests that religious individuals may mitigate some of that social stigma or shame by deflecting blame from themselves and toward their former spouse. To the extent that being within a "pro-marriage" community means also being in an "anti-divorce" community, the observed association between religion and reasons for divorce may remain consistent. This is, of course, assuming that divorced persons choose to stay in faith communities where they feel their divorce is socially frowned upon. Research has shown that some divorcées opt to leave church, fearing they will be judged unfairly (Brown 2015; Konstam et al. 2016; Sullivan 2012). To the extent that divorce also results in disengaging from religious participation, congregations and clergy have good reason to address the stigma and shame divorcées often feel. Consistent with this, Konieczny (2016) points out that an increasing number of conservative Christian congregations are seeking to introduce new ministries targeting disrupted families and seeking to erase the shame divorced adherents may feel. This may point to a gradual decoupling of the "pro-marriage" stance from the perception of being more hostile to divorce (and divorcées) in more faith communities.

Funding: This research received no external funding.

Conflicts of Interest: There author declares no conflict of interest.

References

Amato, Paul R. 2010. Research on Divorce: Continuing Trends and New Developments. *Journal of Marriage and Family* 72: 650–66. [CrossRef]

Amato, Paul R., and Stacy J. Rogers. 1997. A Longitudinal Study of Marital Problems and Subsequent Divorce. *Journal of Marriage and Family* 59: 612–24. [CrossRef]

Barna Group. 2001. Born Again Adults Less Likely to Co-Habit, Just as Likely to Divorce. Available online: https://www.barna.com/research/born-again-adults-less-likely-to-co-habit-just-as-likely-to-divorce/ (accessed on 15 March 2018).

Barna Group. 2004. Born Again Christians as Likely to Divorce as Are Non-Christians. Available online: https://www.barna.com/research/born-again-christians-just-as-likely-to-divorce-as-are-non-christians/ (accessed on 15 March 2018).

Barna Group. 2008. New Marriage and Divorce Statistics Released. Available online: https://www.barna.org/barna-update/family-kids/42-new-marriage-and-divorce-statistics-released#.Vplht_krKUm (accessed on 15 March 2018).

Brown, Matthew. 2015. 20 Percent of Church-Goers No Longer Attend Church after a Divorce. *Deseret News.* Available online: https://www.deseretnews.com/article/865640436/20-percent-of-churchgoers-no-longer-attend-church-after-a-divorce-2-and-the-loss-among-children-is.html (accessed on 15 March 2018).

Brown, Edna, Terri L. Orbuch, and Jose A. Bauermeister. 2008. Religiosity and Marital Stability among Black American and White American Couples. *Family Relations* 57: 187–97. [CrossRef]

Bulanda, Jennifer Roebuck, and Susan L. Brown. 2007. Race-ethnic Differences in Marital Quality and Divorce. *Social Science Research* 36: 945–67. [CrossRef]

Burdette, Amy C., Christopher G. Ellison, Darren E. Sherkat, and Kurt A. Gore. 2007. Are There Religious Variations in Marital Infidelity? *Journal of Family Issues* 28: 1553–81. [CrossRef]

Burke, Kenneth. 1969. *A Grammar of Motives.* Berkeley: University of California Press.

Call, Vaughn R. A., and Tim B. Heaton. 1997. Religious Influence on Marital Stability. *Journal for the Scientific Study of Religion* 36: 382–92. [CrossRef]

Chang, Linchiat, and Jon A. Krosnick. 2009. National Surveys Via Rdd Telephone Interviewing Versus the Internet: Comparing Sample Representativeness and Response Quality. *Public Opinion Quarterly* 73: 641–78. [CrossRef]

Chi, S. Kenneth, and Sharon K. Houseknecht. 1985. Protestant Fundamentalism and Marital Success: A Comparative Approach. *Sociology and Social Research* 69: 351–74.

Clydesdale, Timothy T. 1997. Family Behaviors among Early U.S. Baby Boomers: Exploring the Effects of Religion and Income Change, 1965–1982. *Social Forces* 7: 605–35. [CrossRef]

Edgell, Penny. 2006. *Religion and Family in a Changing Society.* Princeton: Princeton University Press.

Ellison, Christopher G., Nicholas H. Wolfinger, and Aida I. Ramos-Wada. 2012. Attitudes toward Marriage, Divorce, Cohabitation, and Casual Sex Among Working-Age Latinos: Does Religion Matter? *Journal of Family Issues* 34: 295–322. [CrossRef]

Gerstel, Naomi. 1987. Divorce and Stigma. *Social Problems* 34: 172–86. [CrossRef]

Gilkerson, Luke. 2015. Porn Use as Grounds for Divorce: How My Opinion Changed. Available online: http://www.covenanteyes.com/2015/10/08/porn-use-as-grounds-for-divorce-how-my-opinion-changed/ (accessed on 15 March 2018).

Glass, Jennifer, and Philip Levchak. 2014. Red States, Blue States, and Divorce: Understanding the Impact of Conservative Protestantism on Regional Variation in Divorce Rates. *American Journal of Sociology* 119: 1002–46. [CrossRef]

Glenn, Noval D., and Michael Supancic. 1984. The Social and Demographic Correlates of Divorce and Separation in the United States: An Update and Reconsideration. *Journal of Marriage and Family* 46: 563–75. [CrossRef]

Gray, Mark M. 2013. Divorce Still Less Likely among Catholics. Available online: http://nineteensixty-four. blogspot.ca/2013/09/divorce-still-less-likely-among.html (accessed on 15 March 2018).

Heaton, Tim B., and Edith L. Pratt. 1990. The Effects of Religious Homogamy on Marital Satisfaction and Stability. *Journal of Family Issues* 11: 191–207. [CrossRef]

Jenkins, Kathleen E. 2005. *Awesome Families: The Promise of Healing Relationships in the International Churches of Christ.* New Brunswick: Rutgers University Press.

Jenkins, Kathleen E. 2010. In Concert and Alone: Divorce and Congregational Experience. *Journal for the Scientific Study of Religion* 49: 278–92. [CrossRef]

Jenkins, Kathleen E. 2014. *Sacred Divorce: Religion, Therapeutic Culture, and Ending Life Partnerships.* New Brunswick: Rutgers University Press.

Konieczny, Mary Ellen. 2016. Individualized Marriage and Family Disruption Ministries in Congregations: How Culture Matters. *Sociology of Religion* 77: 144–70. [CrossRef]

Konstam, Varda, Samantha Karwin, Teyana Curran, Meaghan Lyons, and Selda Celen-Demirtas. 2016. Stigma and Divorce: A Relevant Lens for Emerging and Young Adults. *Journal of Divorce & Remarriage* 57: 173–94.

Lehrer, Evelyn L. 2004. Religion as a Determinant of Economic and Demographic Behavior in the United States. *Population and Development Review* 30: 707–26. [CrossRef]

Lehrer, Evelyn L., and Carmel U. Chiswick. 1993. Religion as a Determinant of Marital Stability. *Demography* 30: 385–404. [CrossRef] [PubMed]

Lehrer, Evelyn L., and Yeon Son. 2017. Marital Instability in the United States: Trends, Driving Forces, and Implications for Children. IZA Institute for Labor Economics. Available online: https://papers.ssrn.com/ sol3/papers.cfm?abstract_id=2903125 (accessed on 15 March 2018).

Levitt, Heidi M., and Kimberly N. Ware. 2006. Religious Leaders' Perspectives on Marriage, Divorce, and Intimate Partner Violence. *Psychology of Women Quarterly* 30: 212–22. [CrossRef]

Litschi, Andrew, David Gordon, Austin Porter, Mark Regnerus, Jane Ryngaert, and Larissa Sarangaya. 2014. Relationships in American Survey. The Austin Institute for the Study of Family and Culture. Available online: http://relationshipsinamerica.com/ (accessed on 15 March 2018).

Mahoney, Annette. 2010. Religion in Families, 1999–2009: A Relational Spirituality Framework. *Journal of Marriage and Family* 72: 805–27. [CrossRef] [PubMed]

Mahoney, Annette, Kenneth I. Pargament, Nalina Tarakeshwar, and Aaron B. Swank. 2001. Religion in the Home in the 1980s and 1990s: A Meta-Analytic Review and Conceptual Analysis of Links between Religion, Marriage, and Parenting. *Journal of Family Psychology* 15: 559–96. [CrossRef] [PubMed]

Martin, Steven P., and Sangeeta Parashar. 2006. Women's Changing Attitudes toward Divorce, 1974–2002: Evidence for an Educational Crossover. *Journal of Marriage and Family* 68: 29–40. [CrossRef]

Massoglia, Michael, Brianna Remster, and Ryan D. King. 2011. Understanding the Incarceration-Divorce Relationship. *Social Forces* 90: 133–55. [CrossRef]

Mills, C. Wright. 1940. Situated Actions and Vocabularies of Motive. *American Sociological Review* 5: 904–13. [CrossRef]

Mullins, Larry C., Kimberly P. Brackett, Donald W. Bogie, and Daniel Pruett. 2006. The Impact of Concentrations of Religious Denominational Affiliations on the Rate of Currently Divorced in Counties in the United States. *Journal of Family Issues* 27: 976–1000. [CrossRef]

Perry, Samuel L. 2016. From Bad to Worse? Pornography Consumption, Spousal Religiosity, Gender, and Marital Quality. *Sociological Forum* 31: 441–64. [CrossRef]

Perry, Samuel L. 2017a. *Growing God's Family: The Global Orphan Care Movement and the Limits of Evangelical Activism.* New York: NYU Press.

Perry, Samuel L. 2017b. Spousal Religiosity, Religious Bonding, and Pornography Consumption. *Archives of Sexual Behavior* 46: 561–74. [CrossRef] [PubMed]

Perry, Samuel L. 2017c. Not Practicing What You Preach: Religion and Incongruence between Pornography Beliefs and Usage. *Journal of Sex Research* 55: 369–80. [CrossRef] [PubMed]

Perry, Samuel L. 2018. Pornography Use and Marital Separation: Evidence from Two-Wave Panel Data. *Archives of Sexual Behavior* 47: 1869–80. [CrossRef] [PubMed]

Perry, Samuel L., and Cyrus Schleifer. 2018. Till Porn Do Us Part? A Longitudinal Examination of Pornography Use and Divorce. *Journal of Sex Research* 55: 284–96. [CrossRef] [PubMed]

Piper, John. 2009. *This Momentary Marriage: A Parable of Permanence*. Wheaton: Crossway.

Simonič, Barbara, and Nataša Rijavec Klobučar. 2017. Experiencing Positive Religious Coping in the Process of Divorce: A Qualitative Study. *Journal of Religion and Health* 56: 1644–54. [CrossRef] [PubMed]

Stokes, Charles, and Christopher G. Ellison. 2010. Religion and Attitudes toward Divorce Laws among U.S. Adults. *Journal of Family Issues* 31: 1279–304. [CrossRef]

Sullivan, Susan Crawford. 2012. *Living Faith: Everyday Religion and Mothers in Poverty*. Chicago: University of Chicago Press.

Sweezy, Kate, and Jill Tiefenthaler. 1996. Do State-Level Variables Affect Divorce Rates? *Review of Social Economy* 1: 46–65.

Vaaler, Margaret, Christopher G. Ellison, and Daniel A. Powers. 2009. Religious Influences on the Risk of Marital Dissolution. *Journal of Marriage and Family* 71: 917–34. [CrossRef]

Van Biema, David. 2007. An Evangelical Rethink on Divorce? *Time Magazine*. November 7. Available online: http://content.time.com/time/printout/0,8816,1680709,00.html (accessed on 15 March 2018).

Weaver, Andrew J., Judith A. Samford, Virginia J. Morgan, David B. Larson, Harold G. Koenig, and Kevin J. Flannely. 2002. A Systematic Review of Research on Religion in Six Primary Marriage and Family Journals: 1995–1999. *American Journal of Family Therapy* 30: 293–309. [CrossRef]

Wilcox, W. Bradford. 2004. *Soft Patriarchs, New Men. How Christianity Shapes Fathers and Husbands*. Chicago: University of Chicago Press.

Wilcox, W. Bradford. 2009. How Focused on the Family? Evangelical Protestants, the Family, and Sexuality. In *Evangelicals and Democracy in America*. Edited by Steve Brint and Jean R. Schroedel. New York: Russell Sage, vol. 1, pp. 251–75.

Wilcox, W. Bradford, and Nicholas H. Wolfinger. 2016. *Soul Mates: Religion, Sex, Love, and Marriage among African Americans and Latinos*. New York: Oxford University Press.

Woodberry, Robert D., and Christian Smith. 1998. Fundamentalism et al: Conservative Protestants in America. *Annual Review of Sociology* 24: 25–56. [CrossRef]

![religions logo] **MDPI**

Article

A Qualitative Study of Ramadan: A Month of Fasting, Family, and Faith

Zahra Alghafli [1], Trevan G. Hatch [2], Andrew H. Rose [3], Mona M. Abo-Zena [4], Loren D. Marks [2,*] and David C. Dollahite [2]

[1] Rwabi Al-Khaleej Counseling Center, Dammam 31482, Saudi Arabia; zalgha1@hotmail.com
[2] School of Family Life, Brigham Young University, Provo, UT 84602, USA; trevan_hatch@byu.edu (T.G.H.); david_dollahite@byu.edu (D.C.D.)
[3] Department of Sociology, Anthropology, & Social Work, Texas Tech University, Box 41012, Lubbock, TX 79409-1012, USA; andrew.rose@ttu.edu
[4] College of Education and Human Development, University of Massachusetts Boston, MA 02125, USA; Mona.abozena@umb.edu
* Correspondence: loren_marks@byu.edu

Received: 21 January 2019; Accepted: 31 January 2019; Published: 19 February 2019

[check for updates]

Abstract: Islam is a major world religion and the Muslim population is one of the fastest growing religious populations in the Western world, including in the United States. However, few research studies have examined the lived religious experience of U.S. Muslim families. Much of the attention on Islam among researchers and the media tends to be on controversial aspects of the religion. The purpose of this paper is to examine the unique religious practice of the month-long fast of Ramadan, especially its perceived role on marital and familial relationships from an insider's perspective. Content analysis of in-depth, qualitative interviews of twenty diverse Shia and Sunni Muslim families living in the United States (N = 47 individuals) yielded several emergent themes. This study presents and explores data on the focal theme: "fasting brings us closer together." These data suggest that Ramadan serves a sacred, unifying, and integrating purpose for many of the 47 practicing Muslim mothers, fathers, and youth in this study. Meanings and processes involved in Ramadan and family relationships are explored and explained. Implications and applications of the research findings are discussed and some potential directions for future research are outlined.

Keywords: Ramadan; Muslim families; religion; fasting; Islam; qualitative

---

1. Introduction

Islam is one of the world's fastest growing religions and observing Ramadan marks one of the five pillars of the faith, yet there is little scholarly focus on the Ramadan experience in psychology or family studies journals (Alghafli et al. 2014a). In this article, based on in-depth, face-to-face interviews with Muslim families living in the United States, we provide a focused look at the utility, meaning, and power of the month-long fast of Ramadan for wives, husbands, and children based on their own firsthand reports. The article appears to be one of the first to closely examine this unique religious practice through the application of qualitative research methods to families.

The month of Ramadan refers to the ninth month of the Islamic calendar when "accountable" (i.e., post-puberty) Muslims fast during daylight hours. Per Islamic law, those who are ill, elderly, pregnant, breastfeeding, menstruating, or traveling are not obligated to completely abstain from food, drink, and sexual activity while fasting, but all other Muslims are exhorted to engage in the Ramadan fast (Alghafli et al. 2014b).

O you who believe! Fasting is prescribed for you as it was prescribed for those before you, that you may become Al-Muttaqun (the pious). (Fasting) for a fixed number of days, but if any of you is ill or on a journey, the same number (should be made up) from other days. And as for those who can fast with difficulty, (i.e., an old man, etc.), they have (a choice either to fast or) to feed a poor person (for every day). But whoever does good of his own accord, it is better for him. And that you fast, it is better for you if only you know. (Quran 2:183–84; Khan 1971)

Indeed, fasting during the month of Ramadan is prescribed and exhorted as one of the Five Pillars of Islam—a foundation of the Muslim faith (Alghafli et al. 2014a). Ramadan, for many practicing Muslims, is the most sacred time of the year, a time that is devoted to enriching spirituality in several ways, including reading the Quran, saying additional prayers (*salat*), and reciting supplications (Ziaee et al. 2006, pp. 409, 411). Islamic teachings are primarily derived from the Quran, and the compilations of the sayings (*hadith*) of Prophet Muhammad PBUH.

Abu Hurayrah reported that the Messenger of Allah (peace and blessings be upon him) said: Every action a son of Adam does shall be multiplied—a good action by ten times its value, up to 700 times. Allah says: With the exception of fasting, which belongs to Me, and I reward it accordingly. For, one abandons his desire and food for My sake.

There are two occasions of joy for a fasting person: one when he breaks his fast, and the other when he meets his Lord, and the (bad) breath (of a fasting person) is better in the sight of Allah than the fragrance of musk. (Malik n.d., 18:58)

Ideally, Ramadan serves as a religious catalyst for individuals to refine their behaviors and improve their relationships with both Allah and those with whom they interact most closely, including and especially, family.

We will briefly overview three bodies of literature: (a) social science research on religion and family life, (b) social science research on religious practice among Muslims and Muslim Families, and (c) a contextualizing overview of Ramadan. The first body of literature includes hundreds of studies, while research on the latter two topics is meager at best.

2. Social Science Research on Religion and Family Life

Some emergent findings regarding the religion–health connection at the individual level are relatively striking (e.g., 7.6 year longevity increases among those who attend worship services more than weekly (Hummer et al. 1999, pp. 277–78)); cancer rates at half the prevalence of the general population for some actively religious groups, including members of The Church of Jesus Christ of Latter-day Saints who—like Muslims—integrate significant fasting into their lives (Enstrom 1998).

Empirical findings relating to what Darwin Thomas has called "the religion and family connection" tend to be less dramatic in scope and magnitude than those identified between religious involvement and physical health, but several modest connections have been identified (Marks and Dollahite 2017, p. 1). For example, in a prominent study of eight aspects of father involvement in relation to religion, sociologist Valerie King (2003) found that: "influence of religiousness on father involvement is generally modest and should not be overstated. . . . Nevertheless, certain aspects of father involvement are more frequent among the more religious, including better quality relationships . . . and stronger feelings of obligation for contact with children" (p. 392).

King's findings related to the potential influences of "religiousness" on the father involvement are similar to those in scores of other social science studies examining different aspects of religion and family relationships (see Bengtson et al. (2013), for a discussion of mother and father influence across time). Correlations between religious involvement and salutary outcomes in family relationships are generally positive and generally small to moderate in magnitude—as observed by numerous scholars who have reviewed the religion and family literature across the past 25+ years (Burr et al. 2012; Koenig et al. 2001; Koenig et al. 2012; Mahoney 2010; Mahoney et al. 2001; Marks 2006; Marks et al. 2011; Thomas and Cornwall 1990). Even so, recurring findings over the past two to three decades include: (1) significantly lower divorce rates among same-faith married couples (Bahr 1981; Call and Heaton 1997; Lehrer and Chiswick 1993; Lehrer 2009); (2) relatively high reported marital satisfaction and/or fidelity rates (particularly among same-faith marriages), as noted in both quantitative-focused studies and reviews (Bahr and Chadwick 1985, pp. 411–13; Dollahite et al. 2004; Marks et al. 2011; Thomas and Cornwall 1990), as well as qualitative-based reports (Lambert and Dollahite 2006; Lu et al. 2013; Kaslow and Robison 1996; Robinson 1994; Robinson and Blanton 1993); and (3) the typically positive influence of rituals and sacred practices (including prayer, scripture study, etc.) on both marital and parent–child relationships (Dudley and Kosinski 1990; Fiese et al. 1993, 2002; Fiese and Tomcho 2001; Mahoney et al. 2001, pp. 583–87; Marks 2004; Marks and Dollahite 2012; Spagnola and Fiese 2007; for exceptions related to compulsory family worship, see Burr et al. 2012, pp. 118–19; Lee et al. 1997). This latter finding related to sacred family practices as an opportunity to promote positive family cohesion is of relevance in connection with the present article's focus on Ramadan. As scholars have observed, however, the samples in most extant studies are predominantly, even overwhelmingly, Christian and racially White, while relatively little is known about religious and racial/ethnic minority families, including Muslims (Alghafli et al. 2014a, pp. 814–15; Marks and Dollahite 2011).[1]

Additionally, in spite of the growing body of empirical research on the religion and family connection, social scientists still know relatively little about the deeper whys, hows, and processes at work behind the "sacred matters" (Burr et al. 2012; Marks and Dollahite 2011; Pargament and Mahoney 2005). One leading family scholar, Bill Doherty, has theorized that three dimensions—*inclusion, control* and *intimacy*—lie at the heart or "core" of healthy family interactions (Doherty et al. 1991, p. 227). Marks, Dollahite, and Hatch (Marks et al. 2017) have noted each of these dimensions at work in the sacred family practice of Shabbat among Jewish families, opening the door to questions regarding possible parallels in other faiths, including Islam.

Unfortunately, empirical research and/or scholarly evidence that conveys deeper insight and awareness regarding connections between religious practices and family relationships for Muslim families is scarce (Alghafli 2015). More specifically, there is a dearth of empirical social science literature that sheds light on practicing Muslim families living in the United States, though some work is emerging (see Alghafli et al. 2014b, 2017; Britto and Amer 2007; Franceschelli and O'Brien 2014; Hatch et al. 2017). First, however, we offer a brief overview of the extant research on Muslims and Muslim families, most of which is based on non-U.S. samples.

2.1. Social Science Research on Muslims and Muslim Families

A considerable portion (about 23%) of the earth's population reportedly ascribes to the religion of Islam (Pew 2017b). Islam has been a major force in human history for nearly one-and-a-half millennia, particularly in the Eastern hemisphere (Alghafli et al. 2014b, p. 815). In recent years, Islam is becoming more prominent in several parts of the Western hemisphere as well (Abdullah 2007, p. 43; Pew 2017a). Indeed, a recent Pew (2017a) study projected that within the next three decades the global Muslim population will increase by 73% (compared to 35% of the world's population) and will go from 1.6 billion in 2010 (23% of global population) to 2.8 billion in 2050 (29.7% of the world's population), nearly matching the Christian population. The primary reason for this growth is higher fertility rates than in the general population in every region of the world where Muslims reside (Pew 2017a).

Estimates of the number of Muslims in America range from two to seven million, with perhaps the most rigorous data indicating 2.3 million (Pew 2007). According to Pew, about 63% of U.S. Muslims are first-generation immigrants (Pew 2011). Based on this data of Muslim growth worldwide, including

---

[1] For notable book-length exceptions of research focused on racial minorities and religion, see (Taylor et al. 2004; Wilcox and Wolfinger 2016).

in North America, the U.S. Muslim population cannot be ignored or marginalized as people who are distant and less relevant.

Despite the various countries of origin and ethnic backgrounds of many actively religious Muslim immigrants in the United States, they tend to hold similar religious beliefs and worldviews based on the Quran and the Prophet Mohammed's (Peace Be Upon Him (PBUH))[2] traditions.[3] For many (and perhaps most) practicing Muslims, their religiously prescribed daily life is organized around their shared and sacred religious beliefs, practices, values, and rituals (Ghaffari and Çiftçi 2010). The larger question, however, remains: Does this pattern of involvement in Islamic belief and practice seem to make a measurable difference in the lives of individual persons?

Over the past decade, Abdel-Khalek, a professor of psychology at Kuwait University, has conducted a study examining the relationship between religiosity and subjective well-being, happiness, self-esteem, quality of life, and life satisfaction among Muslim populations. Since 2006, Abdel-Khalek's total sample size in ten related studies exceeds 17,000 participants from nations including Saudi Arabia, Qatar, Kuwait, Egypt, Palestine, Lebanon, and Algeria, as well as the United States. Abdel-Khalek's cross-national samples have included children, adolescents, and adults and have repeatedly found, across diverse samples, moderate correlations between higher levels of religiosity and more favorable subjective reports of happiness and well-being as well as better mental health (i.e., lower neuroticism, lower depression) and better physical health. In a separate study, Tiliouine, Cummins, and Davern (Tiliouine et al. 2009) explored the relationship between Muslim religiosity and a diverse range of life and health domains in a sample of 2909 Algerian males and females. Findings corroborated a positive relationship between religiosity and subjective well-being, as do at least three other studies (i.e., Hassouneh-Phillips 2001, 2003; Manganaro and Alozie 2011).

On a different note, multiple studies have found recurring and significant differences relating to gender, indicating better health for men versus women[4] on both physical and mental health measures (Abdel-Khalek 2009, 2012; Abdel-Khalek and Eid 2011). While Abdel-Khalek's psychological studies are of significance and value, they address *individual*-level religiosity and well-being. Very few research studies have examined how Muslim practices influence *familial* and relational aspects of life. In summary, a dearth of empirical research on religious Muslim families remains—including families living in the United States (Alghafli 2015).

2.2. Ramadan: A Brief Overview and Contextualization

As previously mentioned, Ramadan, the ninth month of the Islamic calendar, is a time of fasting, which is one of the Five Pillars of Islam (the other Pillars include the creed or declaration of faith, prayer [*salat*], charity [*zakat*], and pilgrimage [*haj*] to Mecca at least once) (Alghafli et al. 2014b, p. 818). The month of fasting begins with the sighting of the new moon. During Ramadan, practicing Muslims do not eat or drink during daylight hours. While Ramadan usually calls to mind physical fasting from food, the fast is also to involve careful restraint from various temptations and also includes "fasting" or refraining from vain talk, expressing anger, and other behaviors that reflect lapses in moral composure. Abu Hurayrah reported that the Prophet (PBUH) said, "Fasting is a shield; so when one of

---

[2] Consistent with usage among many Muslim scholars, and out of respect to our Muslim participants, when we refer to the founding prophet of Islam we include "PBUH" (Peace Be Upon Him).

[3] Following Muhammad's (PBUH) death in 632 CE, the Umma (Muslim nation) split into two major factions: Shia Muslims and Sunni Muslims. Both agree on the main Islamic pillars involving the reality and nature of Allah (God) and Mohammad's prophetic calling and mission. Both branches pray five times a day (*salat*), fast during the daylight hours for one month every year (*Ramadan*), give money to the poor (*zakat*), and follow the same sacred book (The Quran). The two branches of Islam differ primarily in their views regarding the appropriate successor of Mohammed (for a more detailed discussion, see Alghafli et al. 2014b).

[4] Another body of studies examines gender-role attitudes among Muslim women (Bartkowski and Read 2003; Piela 2010; Read 2003) and women's roles in society (Read 2002, 2004).

you is fasting he should neither indulge in obscene language nor should he raise his voice in anger. If someone attacks him or insults him, let him say: 'I am fasting!'" (Muslim 1151, 13:212)

In fasting from food and drink following the sunset, it is customary for Muslims to eat a meal (*suhoor*) after the evening prayer (*maghrib*) (Glasse 1989, pp. 329–30). Those exempted from fasting include young children, menstruating women, the elderly, and the sick. Generally, children are introduced to fasting by incremental steps; they may start with a half day and then gradually increase to multiple days. Since the Islamic calendar is lunar, Ramadan is not tied to any particular season of the year, but shifts by approximately 11 days on the Gregorian calendar each year. Thus, fasting (including abstaining from fluids) during summer months where the days are longer and hotter presents different challenges than fasting during the winter months (Lewis and Churchill 2009).

Ramadan also requires abstaining from sexual activity during the (daytime) fast. When a person breaks their fast at sundown, they may engage in sexual activities with their spouse. Finally, in addition to the physical forms of discipline outlined, during Ramadan practicing Muslims tend to increase their religious observances like offering many supplementary prayers and engaging in intensive reading sessions of the Quran (Glasse 1989, pp. 329–30).

3. Method

The American Families of Faith research project, co-directed by the fifth and sixth authors of this article, is a national, qualitative study of 200 racially, religiously, and economically diverse families from all eight major geographic regions of the United States. In this project, we employ a strengths-based approach, studying "exemplar" (i.e., clergy-referred) families to garner information regarding healthy processes (Marks and Dollahite 2011). The present article is based on in-depth qualitative interviews with the Muslim subsample of the American Families of Faith project.[5] In this method section, we will address issues including: (a) sample, (b) interview procedures, (c) data analysis, and (d) reflexivity, respectively.

3.1. Sample

We attended Muslim religious services and celebrations at various sites, and met with Muslim imams and leaders. We explained The American Families of Faith research project and requested help from leaders in these Muslim communities in obtaining interview referrals (and entrée) with families who were highly involved in the faith community and also seemed to have strong and happy marriages. In doing so, we engaged in purposive or prototypical sampling (Daly 2007, p. 175), striving to learn from families who had apparently high levels of success in combining their religious faith and family relationships.

The total sample for this article was 20 families (N = 47 individuals; 20 wives/mothers, 20 husbands/fathers, 7 adolescent offspring[6]. More specifically, there were 14 Sunni families and six Shia families. The combined sample was diverse in terms of: (a) adult age (early 30s to early 60s); (b) race/ethnicity (including African American, Arab (from Iraq, Jordan, and Palestine), Western European, Eastern European, Indian (India), Malaysian, and Iranian participants); and (c) socioeconomic status (education levels ranged from some high school to Ph.D./M.D. degrees). The Muslim families resided in five regions, including New England (MA); Mid-Atlantic (PA); Pacific (CA); Mid-West (OH), and Gulf Coast (LA) regions.

The seven adolescent offspring who participated in the interviews ranged from 10 to 20 (mean age = 16 years). Adult participants had been married for a mean of about 19 years and were the parents of

---

[5] See https://americanfamiliesoffaith.byu.edu.
[6] Families averaged about four children each, but only seven adolescent children were interviewed due to limitations related to Internal Review Board (IRB) approval.

at least one child between 2 and 18 years of age (Mean = 4 children). This latter feature allowed us to examine parent–child relationships, in addition to marital relationships.

3.2. Interview Procedures

Interviews based on a semistructured questionnaire were conducted with each couple with both spouses present. No questions on the semistructured questionnaire directly addressed fasting. However, in response to questions asking about sacred practices that held special meaning for them, Muslim families frequently (and often passionately) discussed the importance of Ramadan, thereby making the present study possible.

The length of the interview varied from couple to couple, with an average time of about 90–120 min. With each question, both the wife and husband were given an opportunity to respond—and opportunity to respond first typically alternated with each question.

Life experiences and narratives were sought to add depth, richness, and color to the combined interview data. During the joint interviews, wives and husbands would often encourage each other, adding details, making corrections, and offering their alternative perspective. We do not believe that joint interviewing is the best approach to all (or even most) topics. Often it is desirable to interview family members independently for reasons including, but not limited to: fear of disclosure, power differential, moderating desirability effect, and fear of repercussion (Seymour et al. 1995). Indeed, some of our recent (but unrelated) work has sought to employ interviews with: (a) the wife individually, (b) the husband individually, *and* (c) the couple together (Plauche et al. 2016).[7] With these important caveats noted, however, our overall experience was that for the focal topics at hand (family religious practices, strong marriage/family relationships), the approach of joint interviewing worked well, consistent with the experience and recommendation of previous researchers who have found that this approach can shed light on the different kinds of knowledge held by each spouse (Arksey 1996; Edgell 1980; Seymour et al. 1995). Conjoint interviewing can also produce clearer and more complete pictures as interviewees fill in each other's gaps and memory lapses (Seymour et al. 1995). In addition, joint interviewing offers (to the observant interviewer) insights into the nature of the relationship and connections between couples through observation of nonverbal communication (Arksey 1996).

3.3. Qualitative Data Analysis

Interviews were recorded and then transcribed verbatim. Files were then saved as Microsoft Word documents by researchers from the American Families of Faith project. The first author performed grounded theory-based open coding and axial coding independently (Strauss and Corbin 1998, pp. 101–42). She also compiled Numeric Content Analyses (NCA) of the predominant coded themes, noting how many total occurrences were documented within and across interviews (Marks 2015, pp. 496, 501). As a check for inter-rater reliability, two additional co-authors reviewed the coded interviews and the supporting thematic files composed of qualitative interview excerpts (that were documented by interview and page number). Seven major, emergent themes were identified by the first author and confirmed by the second and fifth authors. These efforts are consistent with the construction of a data audit trail exhorted by many qualitative researchers (Denzin and Lincoln 2000; Handel 1996; Marks 2015). A few of the central themes were presented in a recent article (Alghafli et al. 2014b). Another theme (meanings behind the *Hijab* or practice of veiling/covering in Islam) is discussed in another recent manuscript (Alghafli et al. 2017). In this article, we focus on a single theme but do so in depth: "Fasting brings us closer to each other." We now turn to the issue of reflexivity in qualitative research.

---

[7] For more detailed discussion of this issue, see (Marks et al. 2008; Marks and Dollahite 2011).

3.4. Reflexivity

Reflexivity refers to self-observation and skepticism in the process and results of the research (Anastas 1999, p. 7). In other words, it is "practicing bias regulation through bias recognition, rather than through the denial of bias" (Pieper 1989, p. 18). We agree with the practice of revealing biases and experiences that relate to the data being considered, and in the spirit of transparency and authenticity, we share relevant information next.

All five authors, like the adult participants in our study: (a) are in long-term marriages, (b) are parents, and (c) are religiously active and involved in both home and faith community settings. More specifically, the first author is a Muslim, a wife and mother. The fourth author is also a Muslim, a wife and mother. The second, third, fifth, and sixth authors are all members of The Church of Jesus Christ of Latter-day Saints, husbands and fathers. As a result, the authors combine to create a team with both insider and outsider perspectives, as recommended in recent work on qualitative methodology (Marks 2015, p. 498).

4. Findings

The salience of the Ramadan fast was raised frequently by both Sunni and Shia participants. In an effort to convey an authentic "insider perspective" via the participants' own voices, about 30 illustrative examples from the primary data are shared in connection with the focal theme of this article. That overarching theme, drawn from the participants' own words, is: "Fasting brings us closer to each other." Although this concept will serve as our focus in our Findings section, we address this overarching theme from three different vantage points. These are provided by Doherty and colleagues' (Doherty et al. 1991) "three core dimensions" involved in family rituals of inclusion, control, and intimacy. As adapted for the present study, the dimensions include: (a) Inclusion and Involvement of All Family Members in Ramadan, (b) Control, Discipline, and the Sacred Context of Ramadan, and (c) Intimacy, Unity, and Togetherness during Ramadan. These dimensions will be discussed respectively.

4.1. Dimension 1: Inclusion and Involvement of All Family Members in Ramadan

Muhammad, a Shia husband, mentioned that Ramadan is a pinnacle family event for him. When asked about the reasons why, he stated that during Ramadan, "We have more family discussion." For example, Muhammad mentioned that when breaking their fast, his family all talk with each other: "'How is your day? How are you doing?' and this and that, and then you sit and eat. We all break the fast together." Muhammed's wife, Alya, continued:

> We all have to sit and eat. It is not like [one person says], 'I will eat now' [and another says], 'I will grab something later.' [No], we all sit down and eat [together].

Alya's emphasis on "sit[ting] down and eat[ing]" together is a concept to which we will return near the end of this article.

One Shia husband talked about Ramadan as a family time that *everyone* looks forward to, parents and children. He stated, "[Our] boys are looking towards Ramadan all year. We look forward to it as a family, *we all fast together* as a family."

A Sunni Muslim father named Ismail, like other participants, specifically discussed the Ramadan fast not as a practice or ritual but as an "experience" ... something a family *all goes through "together every day."*

> ***Ismail** (Sunni husband):* [W]e get up early, very early in the morning [to] have a meal together, like a breakfast. We have a meal together, and then after the meal, we read Quran, our scripture. And after we do that, it's time for prayer. We pray together ... [Then], in the evening (after sunset), which is the time of breaking [our] fast, again, the same thing happens as during the morning. We all come together as a family, and we eat together and we thank

God together, we pray together. After [that] we break the fast. And then we do more prayers. So the whole month of Ramadan is a very unique experience. We do a lot less of the worldly things and a lot more of godly things than we normally do. . . . When you do those kinds of things together every day . . . it . . . bring[s] people together and it strengthens our beliefs and [our] family.

Ismail's description of the fast is permeated by words of unity—with "we," "together," and "family" occurring a composite of nearly 20 times. Indeed, the fact that Muslim families fast (and break their fast) at specific times and in unison seems to enrich family members' interactions and bonds.

Reports from Muhammad, Alya, and Ismail repeatedly underscore the importance of *Dimension 1: Inclusion and Involvement of All Family Members in Ramadan.* We now turn to Dimension 2.

4.2. Dimension 2: Control, Discipline, and the Sacred Context of Ramadan

Outsiders to Islam often marvel at the discipline required for a month-long fast. The Muslim participants in our study, however, more frequently emphasized the spiritual and/or relational discipline inherent in the sacred context of Ramadan. Many reported an emphasis on other (nondietary) behaviors that need extra attention and control during the sacred month.

Restricting the understanding of fasting in Islam to the literal definition, without accounting for the spirit of the practice, however, is an apparent oversimplification from the perspective of many of our participants. Muslim texts referencing the Prophet Mohammed (PBUH) state, "Whoever does not give up forged speech and evil actions, Allah is not in need of his leaving his food and drink (i.e., Allah will not accept his fasting)" (Al-Bukhari 1903, 30:13).

Some participants mentioned Ramadan as a sacred, spiritual journey that the whole family experiences together. One father shared his family's experience by explaining:

[Ramadan] is a very, very good experience for us. I think what fasting does is [that] it makes everything else so insignificant. Seeing the family, the marriage, human life—[these are] really the most important things in the world, because everything else means nothing, really. [During the year] we do get carried away with worldly things, the houses, the cars, and all of that, I think—[but Ramadan] really brings you right to the ground and [gets you] grounded with God.

For this father, fasting is foundational and "brings you right to the ground." Another father explained, "Ramadan has been prescribed to us where every Muslim is supposed to [fast]. It's one of the five pillars of Islam."

Noreen (a *Sunni* wife), while generally discussing the role of Islam in her marriage, mentioned fasting as an exemplary religious arrangement between herself and her husband that demands that they refrain from arguing. Noreen, like others, invoked "we" and "together" repeatedly in connection with Ramadan, but her language referred to the marital "we" of Noreen and her husband. She stated:

I think that religion affects our married life because in this point we can agree, and we spend some time without arguing. For example, when we both fast, we do our activities together. We break the fast together [and] we wake up midnight and eat before fasting. So we do these types of things together. . . . At this point we again agree and that's how religion is making our life, going together and growing together.

In the above excerpt by Noreen, she began by mentioning "arguing" between herself and her husband, and then she alternatively referenced harmonious times she and her husband spend together during Ramadan—with an emphasis on the religious activities they participate in together. In these few lines, Noreen uses the word "agree" twice and "together" five times when talking about her marriage in connection with fasting. We note that Noreen begins her response by using the first person singular 'I,' but then shifts to the plural and marital 'we,' which she uses at least eight times in four lines. In other words, Noreen is not only emphasizing the importance of control and discipline in her marital conversations during Ramadan, she is also emphasizing unity and togetherness in marital and family relations. Having addressed *Dimension 2: Control, Discipline, and the Sacred Context of Ramadan*, we next turn to the latter phenomenon of interest raised by Noreen, unity. Indeed, *Intimacy, Unity, and Togetherness* are the foci of our third and final dimension, discussed next.

4.3. Dimension 3: Intimacy, Unity, and Togetherness during Ramadan

In almost every interview in which Ramadan[8] was mentioned, both the wife and husband, often with animation and excitement, talked about the fast as a time when family members get *closer* to each other than perhaps at any other time.

> ***Gulam***[9] *(Sunni husband):* The thing that we really enjoy and cherish is the month of Ramadan because we do so many things together as a family. We wake up in the middle of the night. We sit together, we eat together, and we pray together. [We] go to [mosque] and bring food. And we get together as a family.

In five brief sentences, Gulam uses the word "family" twice, "together" five times, and the family-referencing pronoun "we" eight times—a total of 15 allusions to family unity.

Noreen emphasized the marital harmony she associates with Ramadan. Alya focused on the familial unity that is promoted. Alya's husband Muhammad agreed with his wife about the salience of Ramadan, explaining that for him:

> It is really the first day [of Ramadan] that gets me the most, for some reason. I do not know [why]. The first day of Ramadan [to me, means] more than ... any other day of the year. The first day of Ramadan is important to me. ... The first month that my daughter had to fast and at the end of the day, we were sitting next to each other, that was the best. I was proud of her.

Muhammed's reflections identify additional benefits of the Ramadan fast; the literal physical and emotional closeness of parent and child, father and daughter, and a resulting sense of paternal pride. Muhammad presents Ramadan in a way that seems to strengthen the familial circle.

Each of the narratives presented reflect the participants' lived experiences and their perceived associations between the shared Ramadan fast and heightened levels of unity, closeness, and warmth in the participants' family lives and relationships. Indeed, participants report that Ramadan binds family members emotionally and draws them closer to each other, physically and spiritually.

In addition to the consideration of Ramadan as a sacred month where Muslims are encouraged to improve their religious beliefs and practices, the sacred month of fasting seems to literally and figuratively set the table for more pure, more peaceful, and more meaningful family interactions.

Even though fasting is a physical and mental challenge and a sacrifice, the reported individual and family-level benefits and the long-term rewards of this shared and sacred family practice appear to be worth the challenges and costs in the lives of most of the Muslim participants we interviewed. As sociologists of religion Stark and Finke (2000) note: "[P]eople will only accept high religious costs if these result in such high levels of religious benefits that the [overall] result is a favorable exchange ratio. [In sum], people attend not only to cost, but to value in making their decisions (p. 51). Indeed, for many of the Muslim families we interviewed, the Ramadan fast seems to embody the essence of a 'high-cost but high-value' sacred family practice" (Marks et al. 2009, p. 15).

As discussed previously, in an influential article 25 years ago, Doherty, Colangelo, and Hovander (Doherty et al. 1991) posited that "three core dimensions of family interaction—*inclusion, control* and *intimacy*—constitute an optimal priority sequence for managing ... stressful experiences" (p. 227,

---

8   Muslim participants frequently used the words Ramadan and fasting interchangeably.
9   All names are pseudonyms to protect anonymity.

emphasis added). As in our American Families of Faith work with family-level religious practices with other groups (Marks et al. 2017; Marks et al. 2008), Doherty's "three core dimensions" repeatedly arose in our Muslim participants' reflections regarding their Ramadan celebrations, which involved: (a) the *inclusion* of all family members, (b) the structured *control* and predictability of consistent rituals that add stability and reduce chaos, and (c) the resulting closeness, unity, "we-ness," and *intimacy* between spouses, as well as between parents and children. As we conclude the Findings section, we present a final narrative excerpt with all three core dimensions in mind:

> **Maryam** (*Shia* wife): I think my children, my husband, and I *[inclusion: "we" = wife, husband, children]*—altogether at the same time—we are trying to control ourselves and avoid doing some things. It is like we are playing a game together and when you are playing a game with other friends, you have fun with them. . . . We are breaking our fast together *[control/structure: a set time, a set place, a set table]* and we think, "Oh, all of us are playing a game, ahhh!" [The breaking of the fast] gets us closer to each other *[intimacy: "fast together," relational closeness]*.

Maryam, like others earlier, injects several (p. 10) collectivist terms (e.g., "altogether," "we," "together," and "us") into a few brief lines, emphasizing the reportedly pervasive unity inspired by Ramadan. For Maryam and her family, it seems that Ramadan is a sacred practice that integrates inclusion and a sense of control/structure that promotes intimacy in ways that reflect the optimal pattern of family interaction promoted by Doherty and colleagues.

In the broader American Families of Faith project, we have found similar patterns in other religious families (e.g., *Shabbat* in observant Jewish families (Marks et al. 2017), but based on the participants' reports, Ramadan serves a sacred, unifying, integrating purpose for many of the 47 practicing Muslim mothers, fathers, and children in this study.

5. Discussion

This study, first and foremost, aims to add the voices and perspectives of practicing, highly religious U.S. Muslims so that prevalent, media-based images are supplemented by systematic, empirically grounded research. More specifically, beyond examining the importance of religion in the lives of these families, this study attempts to explore and explain why and how fasting, as a lived religious practice, matters to the participants.

There are important lessons to be learned from strong, healthy families from minority religions because they, of necessity, have built family strength without the support of the cultural mainstream—perhaps even overcoming antipathy in order to thrive. Unfortunately, rather than examine these families as potential models of strength, the experience of antipathy of lived religion has too often carried into various settings. This study extends the invitation to learn from strengths and to avoid antipathy.

For Muslim individuals and families, although Ramadan is a time of meaning, unity, and shared faith, the month-long fast is full of challenges and hardships (Alghafli 2015). Not eating and drinking for 10 h or more per day is difficult and requires restraint and discipline, particularly for Muslims who live in non-Muslim countries and are surrounded by people who eat and drink in shared work and school environments throughout the 30 days of the fast.

Even so, the participants indicated their perceptions that fasting as a religious practice tends to connect and unite family members. This connection seems to assist participants during crisis and hardships, as they feel protected, cared for, and surrounded by "mercy" and "blessings." This finding seems to be consistent with other research literature addressing sacred rituals and practices that are home-based and/or which involve the whole family (Doherty 2002; Marks and Dollahite 2012) and is in line with the Hadith, Narrated by Abu Huraira: Allah's Messenger (PBUH) said, "When the month of Ramadan starts, the gates of the heaven are opened and the gates of Hell are closed and the devils are chained." (Al-Bukhari 1903, 30:13)

5.1. Limitations and Directions for Future Research

The focus of the present study on Ramadan has been almost exclusively on family relationships. There are likely profound, individual-level effects, challenges, and influences associated with Ramadan—personal meaning making—that lie outside of this study's family-focused purview. However, individual-level and psychological influences associated with Ramadan warrant close attention as well. Additionally, the present piece does not address the important sociological element of faith community and the collectivistic and sacred role of the *masjid* (mosque) during Ramadan. The present study's failure to convey the richness of faith community context should not be interpreted as a signal that the *masjid* was unimportant to these families. In other words, this article's focus on family was intended to convey, with specificity and depth, a portion of the broader constellation of Islam; a constellation that includes family but also involves: (1) personal, introspective, and psychological elements of Ramadan; and (2) sociological, communal, and *masjid*-based elements of Ramadan. We recommend that future research address both the intrapersonal and the sociological, offering value-added perspectives to familial and relational foci of this article.

5.2. Implications and Applications

Being aware of the influence these practices have in the lives of Muslim families can provide great benefit for educators, counselors, and therapists who are seeking to better understand and to effectively assist practicing Muslim couples and families. Furthermore, the current study can enrich religious leaders within the Muslim community with more information about family life, marriage, and parent–child relationships, as these leaders often serve as counselors, and as a main source of information and advice in Muslim religious communities (Abdullah 2007, p. 44). While the present sample was purposive and not generalizable, the likelihood is high that Islam as a lived religion and, specifically, Ramadan as a shared and sacred family practice are similarly influential and vital in the lives and families of many other U.S. Muslims.

Additionally, while the family foundation is certainly important, many Muslims are also highly connected with the ways fasting has connected Muslims over generations, currently across time and space (when/where practicing Muslims start and stop at the same relative time of the day, irrespective of location). Further, in addition to the self-discipline and sacrifice for Allah made by this private act of worship and resulting connection, fasting also reportedly promotes empathy with the poor. Indeed, the Ramadan fast concludes with the practice of *zakat*[10] (the pillar of alms-giving and charity) that exhorts able Muslims to give one fortieth or 2.5% of their non-essential wealth (Marks et al. 2009).

Quantitative survey and poll-based research data indicate that the Muslim population in the United States continues to grow, both in raw numerical strength and in percentage of the overall population (Pew 2017a). Further, nearly two-thirds (63%) of all U.S. Muslims are first-generation immigrants who are only commencing their family stories and family expansion on Western ground and in Western culture (Pew 2011). Zaid bin Khalid Al-Juhani narrated that: The Messenger of Allah said: "Whoever provides the food for a fasting person to break his fast with, then for him is the same reward as his (the fasting person's), without anything being diminished from the reward of the fasting person." (At-Tirmidhi 807) For a variety of reasons, including this multiplicative one, how Muslim individuals and families interact with others and bring together people at the table continues to expand. At the front end of this time of transition and change, it becomes increasingly important to have a deeper and, ideally, a quantitatively *and qualitatively* enhanced awareness of what lies at or near the center of meaning and function for many of these individuals and families.

---

10 There is a different (lesser) zakat that is made before *Eid ul Fitr* prayer. This is *Zakt ul fitr* and is usually the equivalent of the price of one meal in the area where the giver is living (religious leaders set the price in each region) or about $10 per each member of the household (including babies and elderly or people who aren't obligated to fast). This is then distributed to the poor so that all may enjoy the breaking of the fast with a meal.

Author Contributions: Conceptualization, Z.A., T.G.H., and L.D.M.; methodology, Z.A., T.G.H., D.C.D., and L.D.M.; software, T.G.H.; validation, T.G.H., M.M.A.-Z., and L.D.M.; formal analysis, Z.A., T.G.H., and L.D.M.; investigation, Z.A., T.G.H., D.C.D., and L.D.M.; resources, Z.A., T.G.H., A.H.R., M.M.A.-Z., D.C.D., and L.D.M.; data curation, Z.A., T.G.H., D.C.D., and L.D.M.; writing—original draft preparation, Z.A., T.G.H., and L.D.M.; writing—review and editing, A.H.R., M.M.A.-Z., and D.C.D.; project administration, D.C.D., and L.D.M.; funding acquisition, D.C.D., and L.D.M.

Funding: Loren D. Marks and David C. Dollahite express thanks to the Eliza R. Snow Fellowship at BYU for generous support of the American Families of Faith research project. The present article is based on the Strong Muslim Families branch of that project.

Conflicts of Interest: The authors declare no conflicts of interest.

References

Abdel-Khalek, Ahmed. 2009. Religiosity, Subjective Well-Being, and Depression in Saudi Children and Adolescents. *Mental Health, Religion & Culture* 12: 803–15.

Abdel-Khalek, Ahmed. 2012. Associations between Religiosity, Mental Health, and Subjective Well-Being among Arabic Samples from Egypt and Kuwait. *Mental Health, Religion & Culture* 15: 741–58.

Abdel-Khalek, Ahmed M., and Ghada K. Eid. 2011. Religiosity and Its Association with Subjective Well-Being and Depression among Kuwaiti and Palestinian Muslim Children and Adolescents. *Mental Health, Religion & Culture* 14: 117–27.

Abdullah, Somaya. 2007. Islam and Counseling: Models of Practice in Muslim Communal Life. *Journal of Pastoral Counseling* 42: 42–55.

Al-Bukhari, Sahih. 1903. Book 30, Hadith 13. Available online: https://sunnah.com/bukhari/30/13 (accessed on 12 February 2019).

Alghafli, Zahra. 2015. Familial Relationships among Muslim Couples and Parents in the U.S.: A Qualitative Study. Ph.D. dissertation, Louisiana State University, Baton Rouge, LA, USA.

Alghafli, Zahra, Trevan G. Hatch, and Loren D. Marks. 2014a. Islam. In *The Social History of the American Family*. Edited by Marilyn J. Coleman and Lawrence H. Ganong. Thousand Oaks: Sage, pp. 769–72.

Alghafli, Zahra, Trevan G. Hatch, and Loren D. Marks. 2014b. Religion and Relationships in Muslim Families: A Qualitative Examination of Devout Married Muslim Couples. *Religions* 5: 814–33. [CrossRef]

Alghafli, Zahra, Loren D. Marks, Trevan G. Hatch, and Andrew H. Rose. 2017. Veiling in Fear or in Faith? Meanings of the Hijab to Practicing Muslim Wives and Husbands in USA. *Marriage & Family Review* 53: 696–716.

Anastas, Jeane W. 1999. *Research Design for Social Work and the Human Sciences*, 2nd ed. New York: Columbia University Press.

Arksey, Hilary. 1996. Collecting Data through Joint Interviews. *Social Research Update* 15: 1–4.

At-Tirmidhi, Jami. 807. Book 8, Hadith 126. Available online: https://sunnah.com/tirmidhi/8/126 (accessed on 12 February 2019).

Bahr, Howard M. 1981. Religious Intermarriage and Divorce in Utah and the Mountain States. *Journal for the Scientific Study of Religion* 20: 251–61. [CrossRef]

Bahr, Howard M., and Bruce A. Chadwick. 1985. Religion and Family in Middletown, USA. *Journal of Marriage & Family* 47: 407–14.

Bartkowski, John P., and Jennan G. Read. 2003. Veiled Submission: Gender, Power, and Identity among Evangelical and Muslim Women in the United States. *Qualitative Sociology* 26: 71–92. [CrossRef]

Bengtson, Vern L., Norella M. Putney, and Susan Harris. 2013. *Families and Faith: How Religion is Passed Down Across Generations*. New York: Oxford.

Britto, Pia Rebello, and Mona M. Amer. 2007. An Exploration of Cultural Identity Patterns and the Family Context among Arab Muslim Young Adults in America. *Applied Developmental Science* 11: 137–50. [CrossRef]

Burr, Wesley R., Loren D. Marks, and Randal D. Day. 2012. *Sacred Matters: Religion and Spirituality in Families*. New York: Routledge/Taylor & Francis Group.

Call, Vaughn R. A., and Tim B. Heaton. 1997. Religious Influence on Marital Stability. *Journal for the Scientific Study of Religion* 36: 382–92. [CrossRef]

Daly, Kerry J. 2007. *Qualitative Methods for Family Studies and Human Development*. Thousand Oaks: Sage.

Denzin, Norman K., and Yvonna S. Lincoln, eds. 2000. *Handbook of Qualitative Research*, 2nd ed. Sage: Thousand Oaks.

Doherty, William J. 2002. *The Intentional Family: Simple Rituals to Strengthen Family Ties*. New York: Quill.

Doherty, William J., Nicholas Colangelo, and Deborah Hovander. 1991. Priority Setting in Family Change and Clinical Practice: The Family FIRO Model. *Family Process* 30: 227–40. [CrossRef]

Dollahite, David C., Loren D. Marks, and Michael A. Goodman. 2004. Religiosity and Families: Relational and Spiritual Linkages in a Diverse and Dynamic Cultural Context. In *The Handbook of Contemporary Families: Considering the Past, Contemplating the Future*. Edited by Marilyn J. Coleman and Lawrence H. Ganong. Thousand Oaks: Sage, pp. 411–31.

Dudley, Margaret G., and Frederick A. Kosinski Jr. 1990. Religiosity and Marital Satisfaction: A Research Note. *Review of Religious Research* 32: 78–86. [CrossRef]

Edgell, Stephen. 1980. *Middle-Class Couples*. London: George Allen and Unwin.

Enstrom, James E. 1998. Health Practices and Cancer Mortality Rates among Active California Mormons. In *Latter-Day Saint Social Life: Social Research on the LDS Church and its Members*. Edited by James T. Duke. Salt Lake City: Bookcraft, pp. 441–60.

Fiese, Barbara H., and Thomas J. Tomcho. 2001. Finding Meaning in Religious Practices: The Relation between Religious Holiday Rituals and Marital Satisfaction. *Journal of Family Psychology, Families and Religion* 15: 597–609. [CrossRef]

Fiese, Barbara H., Karen A. Hooker, Lisa Kotary, and Janet Schwagler. 1993. Family Rituals in the Early Stages of Parenthood. *Journal of Marriage and the Family* 55: 633–42. [CrossRef]

Fiese, Barbara H., Thomas J. Tomcho, Michael Douglas, Kimberly Josephs, Scott Poltrock, and Tim Baker. 2002. A Review of 50 Years of Research on Naturally Occurring Family Routines and Rituals: Cause for Celebration? *Journal of Family Psychology, Family Routines and Rituals* 16: 381–90. [CrossRef]

Franceschelli, Michela, and Margaret O'Brien. 2014. 'Islamic Capital' and Family Life: The Role of Islam in Parenting. *Sociology* 48: 1190–206. [CrossRef]

Ghaffari, Azadeh, and Ayşe Çiftçi. 2010. Religiosity and Self-Esteem of Muslim Immigrants to the United States: The Moderating Role of Perceived Discrimination. *International Journal for the Psychology of Religion* 20: 14–25. [CrossRef]

Glasse, Cyril. 1989. Ramadan. In *The Concise Encyclopedia of Islam*. London: Stacey International, pp. 329–30.

Handel, Gerald. 1996. Family Worlds and Qualitative Family Research: Emergence and Prospects of Whole-Family Methodology. *Marriage & Family Review* 24: 335–48.

Hassouneh-Phillips, Dena. 2001. Polygamy and Wife Abuse: A Qualitative Study of Muslim Women in America. *Health Care for Women International* 22: 735–48. [CrossRef]

Hassouneh-Phillips, Dena. 2003. Strength and Vulnerability: Spirituality in Abused American Muslim Women's Lives. *Issues in Mental Health Nursing* 24: 681–94. [CrossRef] [PubMed]

Hatch, Trevan, Zahra Alghafli, Loren Marks, Andrew Rose, Jennifer Rose, Benjamin Hardy, and Nathaniel Lambert. 2017. Prayer in Muslim Families: A Qualitative Exploration. *Journal of Religion & Spirituality in Social Work: Social Thought* 36: 73–95.

Hummer, Robert A., Richard G. Rogers, and Charles B. Nam. 1999. Religious Involvement and U.S. Adult Mortality. *Demography* 36: 273–85. [CrossRef] [PubMed]

Kaslow, Florence, and James A. Robison. 1996. Long-Term Satisfying Marriages: Perceptions of Contributing Factors. *American Journal of Family Therapy* 24: 153–70. [CrossRef]

Khan, Muhammad M. 1971. *Sahih Bukhari: Translation of the Meaning of the Quran*. Saudi Arabia: Almadina Islamic University.

Koenig, Harold G., Michael E. McColleugh, and David B. Larson, eds. 2001. *Handbook of Religion and Health*, 1st ed. New York: Oxford University Press.

Koenig, Harold G., Dana E. King, and Verna Benner Carson, eds. 2012. *Handbook of Religion and Health*, 2nd ed. New York: Oxford University Press.

King, Valarie. 2003. The Influence of Religion on Fathers' Relationships with Their Children. *Journal of Marriage and Family* 65: 382–95. [CrossRef]

Lambert, Nathaniel M., and David C. Dollahite. 2006. How Religiosity Helps Couples Prevent, Resolve, and Overcome Marital Conflict. *Family Relations: An Interdisciplinary Journal of Applied Family Studies* 55: 439–49. [CrossRef]

Lee, Jerry W., Gail T. Rice, and V. Bailey Gillespie. 1997. Family Worship Patterns and Their Correlation with Adolescent Behavior and Beliefs. *Journal for the Scientific Study of Religion* 36: 372–81. [CrossRef]

Lehrer, Evelyn. L. 2009. *Religion, Economics, and Demography*. New York: Routledge.

Lehrer, Evelyn L., and Carmel U. Chiswick. 1993. Religion as a Determinant of Marital Stability. *Demography* 30: 385–404. [CrossRef] [PubMed]

Lewis, Bernard E., and Buntzie E. Churchill. 2009. *Islam: The Religion and the People*. Upper Saddle River: Wharton School Publishing.

Lu, Yaxin, Loren D. Marks, Olena Nesteruk, Michael Goodman, and Loredana Apavaloaie. 2013. Faith, Conversion, and Challenge: A Qualitative Study of Chinese Immigrant Christian Marriage (in the USA). *Journal of Comparative Family Studies* 44: 227–47. [CrossRef]

Mahoney, Annette. 2010. Religion in Families, 1999–2009: A Relational Spirituality Framework. *Journal of Marriage and Family* 72: 805–27. [CrossRef]

Mahoney, Annette, Kenneth I. Pargament, Nalini Tarakeshwar, and Aaron B. Swank. 2001. Religion in the Home in the 1980s and 1990s: A Meta-Analytic Review and Conceptual Analysis of Links between Religion, Marriage, and Parenting. *Journal of Family Psychology, Families and Religion* 15: 559–96. [CrossRef]

Malik, Muwatta. n.d. Book 18, Hadith 58. Available online: https://sunnah.com/urn/406940 (accessed on 12 February 2019).

Manganaro, Lynne L., and Nicholas O. Alozie. 2011. Gender Role Attitudes: Who Supports Expanded Rights for Women in Afghanistan? *Sex Roles: A Journal of Research* 64: 516–29. [CrossRef]

Marks, Loren. 2004. Sacred Practices in Highly Religious Families: Christian, Jewish, Mormon, and Muslim Perspectives. *Family Process* 43: 217–31. [CrossRef] [PubMed]

Marks, Loren. 2006. Religion and Family Relational Health: An Overview and Conceptual Model. *Journal of Religion and Health* 45: 603–18. [CrossRef]

Marks, Loren. 2015. A Pragmatic, Step-by-Step Guide for Qualitative Methods: Capturing the Disaster and Long-Term Recovery Stories of Katrina and Rita. *Current Psychology: A Journal for Diverse Perspectives on Diverse Psychological Issues* 34: 494–505. [CrossRef]

Marks, Loren D., and David C. Dollahite. 2011. Mining the Meanings and Pulling out the Processes from Psychology of Religion's Correlation Mountain. *Psychology of Religion and Spirituality* 3: 181–93. [CrossRef]

Marks, Loren D., and David C. Dollahite. 2012. "Don't Forget Home": The Importance of Sacred Ritual in Families. In *Understanding Religious Rituals*. Edited by John P. Hoffman. New York: Routledge, pp. 186–203.

Marks, Loren D., and David C. Dollahite. 2017. *Religion and Families*. New York: Routledge.

Marks, Loren D., Katrina Hopkins, Cassandra Chaney, Pamela A. Monroe, Olena Nesteruk, and Diane D. Sasser. 2008. 'Together, We Are Strong': A Qualitative Study of Happy, Enduring African American Marriages. *Family Relations: An Interdisciplinary Journal of Applied Family Studies* 57: 172–85. [CrossRef]

Marks, Loren D., David C. Dollahite, and Jeffrey P. Dew. 2009. Enhancing Cultural Competence in Financial Counseling and Planning: Understanding Why Families Make Religious Contributions. *Journal of Financial Counseling and Planning* 20: 14–26.

Marks, Loren. D., David C. Dollahite, and Joanna Jacob Freeman. 2011. Faith in Family Life. In *Successful Marriages and Families: Proclamation Principles and Research Perspectives*. Edited by Alan J. Hawkins, David C. Dollahite and Thomas W. Draper. Provo: BYU Studies, pp. 185–95.

Marks, Loren D., Trevan G. Hatch, and David C. Dollahite. 2017. Sacred Practices and Family Processes in a Jewish Context: Shabbat as the Weekly Family Ritual Par Excellence. *Family Process* 57: 448–61. [CrossRef]

Muslim, Sahih. 1151. Book 13, Hadith 212. Available online: https://sunnah.com/muslim/13/212 (accessed on 12 February 2019).

Pargament, Kenneth I., and Annette Mahoney. 2005. Sacred Matters: Sanctification as a Vital Topic for the Psychology of Religion. *International Journal for the Psychology of Religion* 15: 179–98. [CrossRef]

Pew. 2007. *Muslim Americans: Middle Class and Mostly Mainstream*; Washington, DC: Pew Research Center, May. Available online: www.pewresearch.org/2007/05/22/muslim-americans-middle-class-and-mostly-mainstream/ (accessed on 12 February 2019).

Pew. 2011. *Muslim Americans: No Signs of Growth in Alienation or Support for Extremism*; Washington, DC: Pew Research Center, August. Available online: www.people-press.org/2011/08/30/muslim-americans-no-signs-of-growth-in-alienation-or-support-for-extremism/ (accessed on 12 February 2019).

Pew. 2017a. *Why Muslims Are the World's Fastest-Growing Religious Group*; Washington, DC: Pew Research Center, April. Available online: www.pewresearch.org/fact-tank/2015/04/23/why-muslims-are-the-worlds-fastest-growing-religious-group/ (accessed on 12 February 2019).

Pew. 2017b. *World's Muslim Population More Widespread than You Might Think*; Washington, DC: Pew Research Center, January. Available online: www.pewresearch.org/fact-tank/2013/06/07/worlds-muslim-population-more-widespread-than-you-might-think/ (accessed on 12 February 2019).

Piela, Anna. 2010. Muslim Women's Online Discussions of Gender Relations in Islam. *Journal of Muslim Minority Affairs* 30: 425–35. [CrossRef]

Pieper, Martha H. 1989. The Heuristic Paradigm. *Smith College Studies in Social Work* 60: 8–34. [CrossRef]

Plauche, Hannah Pearce, Loren D. Marks, and Alan J. Hawkins. 2016. Why We Chose to Stay Together: Qualitative Interviews with Separated Couples Who Chose to Reconcile. *Journal of Divorce & Remarriage* 57: 317–37.

Read, Jen'nan Ghazal. 2002. Challenging Myths of Muslim Women: The Influence of Islam on Arab-American Women's Labor Force Activity. *Muslim World* 92: 19. [CrossRef]

Read, Jen'nan Ghazal. 2003. The Sources of Gender Role Attitudes among Christian and Muslim Arab-American Women. *Sociology of Religion* 64: 207–22. [CrossRef]

Read, Jen'nan Ghazal. 2004. Family, Religion, and Work among Arab American Women. *Journal of Marriage and Family* 66: 1042–50. [CrossRef]

Robinson, Linda C. 1994. Religious Orientation in Enduring Marriage: An Exploratory Study. *Review of Religious Research* 35: 207–18. [CrossRef]

Robinson, Linda C., and Priscilla W. Blanton. 1993. Marital Strengths in Enduring Marriages. *Family Relations: An Interdisciplinary Journal of Applied Family Studies* 42: 38–45. [CrossRef]

Seymour, Julie, Gill Dix, and Tony Eardley. 1995. *Joint Accounts: Methodology and Practice in Research Interviews with Couples*. New York: Social Research Policy Unit.

Spagnola, Mary, and Barbara H. Fiese. 2007. Family Routines and Rituals: A Context for Development in the Lives of Young Children. *Infants & Young Children* 20: 284–99.

Stark, Rodney, and Roger Finke. 2000. *Acts of Faith*. Berkeley: University of California.

Strauss, Anselm, and Juliet Corbin. 1998. *Basics of Qualitative Research*. Thousand Oaks: Sage.

Taylor, Robert J., Linda M. Chatters, and Jeff Levin. 2004. *Religion in the Lives of African Americans: Social, Psychological, and Health Perspectives*. Thousand Oaks: Sage.

Thomas, Darwin L., and Marie Cornwall. 1990. Religion and Family in the 1980s: Discovery and Development. *Journal of Marriage & Family* 52: 983–92.

Tiliouine, Habib, Robert A. Cummins, and Melanie Davern. 2009. Islamic Religiosity, Subjective Well-Being, and Health. *Mental Health, Religion & Culture* 12: 55–74.

Wilcox, W. Bradford, and Nicholas H. Wolfinger. 2016. *Soul Mates: Religion, Sex, Love, and Marriage among African Americans and Latinos*. New York: Oxford.

Ziaee, Vahid, M. Razaei, Zahra Ahmadinejad, Hidayatullah Shaikh, R. Yousefi, Lotfollah Yarmohammadi, F. Bozorgi, and M. Javad Behjati. 2006. The Changes of Metabolic Profile and Weight during Ramadan Fasting. *Singapore Medical Journal* 47: 409–14. [PubMed]

MDPI
St. Alban-Anlage 66
4052 Basel
Switzerland
Tel. +41 61 683 77 34
Fax +41 61 302 89 18
www.mdpi.com

Religions Editorial Office
E-mail: religions@mdpi.com
www.mdpi.com/journal/religions

www.ingramcontent.com/pod-product-compliance
Lightning Source LLC
Chambersburg PA
CBHW051313020426

42333CB00028B/3319